the Unofficial Guide® to Bed & Breakfasts in the Southeast

1st Edition

Hal Gieseking

Every effort has been made to ensure the accuracy of information throughout this book. Bear in mind, however, that prices, schedules, etc., are constantly changing. Readers should always verify information before making final plans.

IDG Books Worldwide, Inc.
An International Data Group Company
909 Third Avenue
New York, New York 10022

Produced by Menasha Ridge Press

ISBN 0-7645-6222-3

ISSN ISSN pending

Manufactured in the United States of America

10 9 8 7 6 5 4 3 2 1

First edition

Contents

List of Maps

About the Author and Illustrator

Hal Gieseking is the author of 14 books on business and travel. He is a past president of the Society of American Travel Writers. His former posts include serving as consumer editor of *Travel Holiday* magazine (then a *Reader's Digest* publication) and travel correspondent for *CBS Morning News.* He is currently an official photographer for Famous & Historic Trees (a division of the American Forests) and a freelance writer/consultant based in Williamsburg, Virginia, and freely sharing his opinions with his wife Margaret and his West Highland Terrier Jonathan.

Born and raised in New York City, *Giselle Simons* received her Bachelor of Fine Arts degree from Cornell University. She currently lives on Manhattan's Upper West Side, where she works as an illustrator, architectural design drafter, and graphic designer. She is caretaker to a dog, two cats, an increasing number of fish, and her husband, Jeff.

Acknowledgments

Thank you! This book, covering nine states and almost 300 bed-and-breakfasts, could not have been researched and written without a lot of help from editors, advisors, and helpers. My sincere thanks goes to all of these wonderful people: Rebecca Adkins, Molly Merkle, Holly Cross, Laura Didyk, Melissa Chiou, John and Beth Engler, Chuck and Helen Fischer, Archie and Jean Fripp, Bob and Charlotte Gaut, Jerry and Ruth Cannan, Marge Gieseking, Herb Hiller, Lorry Heverly, Richard and Helen Janssen, Vicki Juul, Melissa Mills, Rebecca Moore, Amanda Ryan, Jenny Stacy, Ed Stone, Carol Timblin, Paul and Diane Waller, and Nichole Williamson.

My thanks also to all of the bed-and-breakfast owners and hosts who answered our questions and accepted our criticisms as well as our praises in good humor.

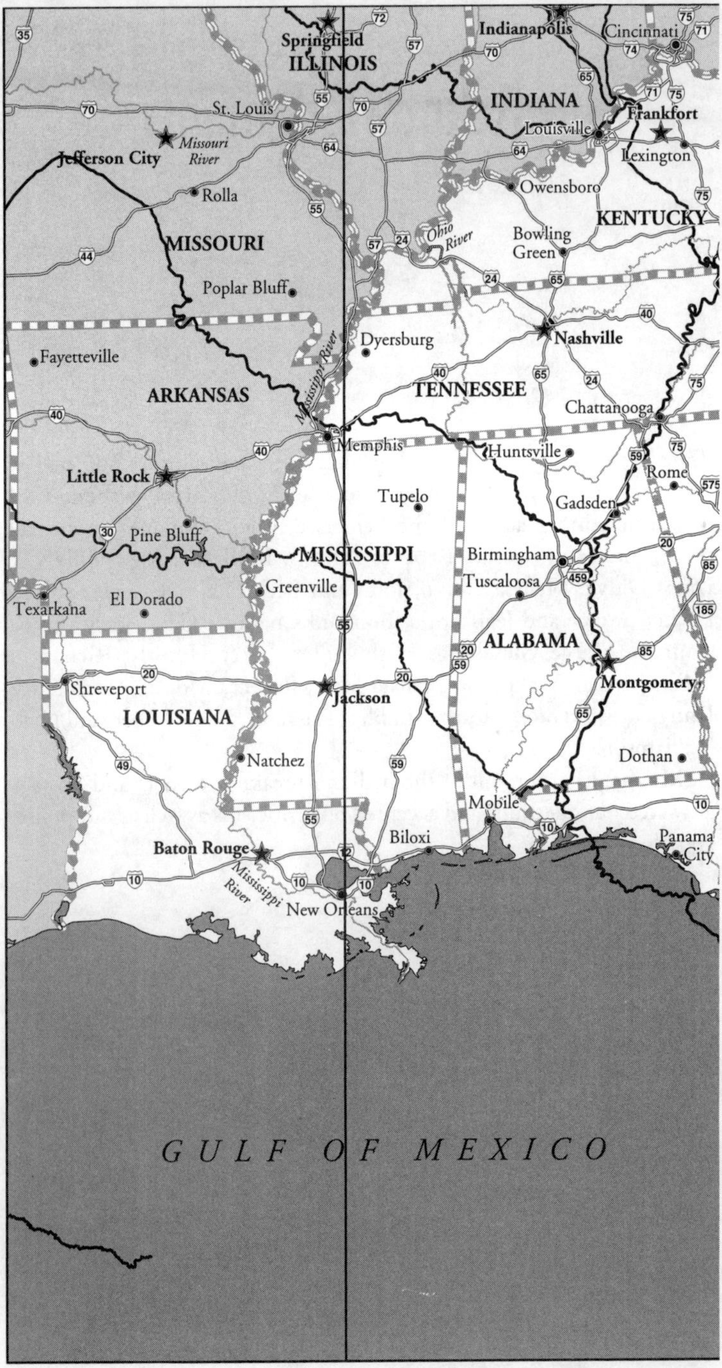
Springfield
ILLINOIS
Indianapolis
Cincinnati
INDIANA
St. Louis
Frankfort
Louisville
Lexington
Missouri River
Jefferson City
Owensboro
Rolla
KENTUCKY
MISSOURI
Ohio River
Bowling Green
Poplar Bluff
Nashville
Dyersburg
Fayetteville
Mississippi River
TENNESSEE
ARKANSAS
Chattanooga
Memphis
Huntsville
Little Rock
Rome
Tupelo
Gadsden
Pine Bluff
MISSISSIPPI
Birmingham
Greenville
Tuscaloosa
Texarkana
El Dorado
ALABAMA
Montgomery
Shreveport
Jackson
LOUISIANA
Natchez
Dothan
Mobile
Biloxi
Panama City
Baton Rouge
Mississippi River
New Orleans
GULF OF MEXICO

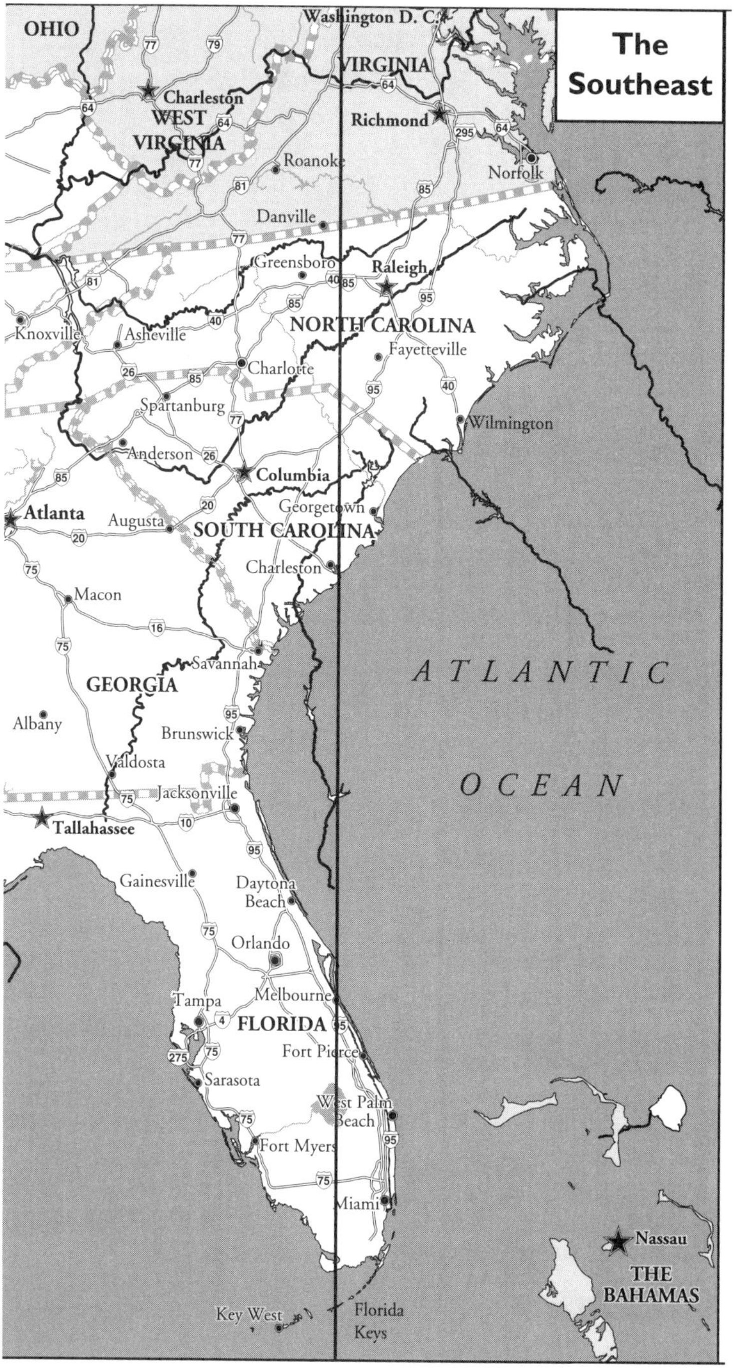
The Southeast
OHIO
Washington D. C.
VIRGINIA
Charleston
WEST VIRGINIA
Richmond
Roanoke
Norfolk
Danville
Greensboro
Raleigh
Knoxville
Asheville
NORTH CAROLINA
Fayetteville
Charlotte
Spartanburg
Wilmington
Anderson
Columbia
Atlanta
Augusta
Georgetown
SOUTH CAROLINA
Charleston
Macon
Savannah
GEORGIA
ATLANTIC OCEAN
Albany
Brunswick
Valdosta
Jacksonville
Tallahassee
Gainesville
Daytona Beach
Orlando
Tampa
Melbourne
FLORIDA
Fort Pierce
Sarasota
West Palm Beach
Fort Myers
Miami
Nassau
THE BAHAMAS
Key West
Florida Keys

Introduction

How Come "Unofficial"?

The book in your hands is part of a unique travel and lifestyle guidebook series begun in 1985 with *The Unofficial Guide to Walt Disney World.* That guide, a comprehensive, behind-the-scenes, hands-on prescription for getting the most out of a complex amusement park facility, spawned a series of like titles: *The Unofficial Guide to Chicago, The Unofficial Guide to New Orleans,* and so on. Today, dozens of *Unofficial Guides* help millions of savvy readers navigate some of the world's more complex destinations and situations.

The *Unofficial Guides to Bed & Breakfasts* continue the tradition of insightful, incisive, cut-to-the-chase information, presented in an accessible, easy-to-use format. Unlike in some popular books, no property can pay to be included—those reviewed are solely our choice. And we don't simply rehash the promotional language of these establishments. We visit the good, the bad, and the quirky. We finger the linens, chat with the guests, and sample the scones. We screen hundreds of lodgings, affirming or debunking the acclaimed, discovering or rejecting the new and the obscure. In the end, we present detailed profiles of the lodgings we feel represent the best of the best, select lodgings representing a broad range of prices and styles within each geographic region.

We also include introductions for each state and zone to give you an idea of the nearby general attractions. Area maps with the properties listed by city help you pinpoint your general destination. And detailed mini indexes help you look up properties by categories and lead you to places that best fit your needs.

With *The Unofficial Guides to Bed & Breakfasts,* we strive to help you find the perfect lodging for every trip. This guide is unofficial because we answer to no one but you.

Letters, Comments, and Questions from Readers

We expect to learn from our mistakes, as well as from the input of our readers, and to improve with each book and edition. Many of those who use the *Unofficial Guides* write to us to ask questions, make comments, or share their own discoveries and lessons learned. We appreciate all such input, both positive and critical, and encourage our readers to continue writing. Readers' comments and observations will contribute immeasurably to the improvement of revised editions of the *Unofficial Guides.*

How to Write the Author

Hal Gieseking
The Unofficial Guide to Bed & Breakfasts in the Southeast
P.O. Box 43673
Birmingham, AL 35243

When you write, be sure to put your return address on your letter as well as on the envelope—they may get separated. And remember, our work takes us out of the office for long periods of research, so forgive us if our response is delayed.

What Makes It a Bed-and-Breakfast?

Comparing the stale, sterile atmosphere of most hotels and motels to the typical bed-and-breakfast experience—cozy guest room, intimate parlor, friendly hosts, fresh-baked cookies, not to mention a delicious breakfast—why stay anywhere *other than* a bed-and-breakfast? But this isn't a promotional piece for the bed-and-breakfast life. Bed-and-breakfasts are not hotels. Here are some of the differences:

A bed-and-breakfast or small inn, as we define it, is a small property (about 3 to 25 guest rooms, with a few exceptions) with hosts around, a distinct personality, individually decorated rooms, and breakfast included in the price (again, with a few exceptions). Many of these smaller properties have owners living right there; at others, the owners are nearby, a phone call away.

Recently, the bed-and-breakfast and small inn trade has taken off—with mixed results. This growth has taken place on both fronts: the low and high ends. As bed-and-breakfasts gain popularity, anyone with a spare bedroom can pop an ad in the Yellow Pages for "Billy's Bedroom B&B." These enterprises generally lack professionalism, don't keep regular hours or days of operation, are often unlicensed, and were avoided in this guide.

On the other end of the spectrum are luxury premises with more amenities than the finest hotels. Whether historic homes or lodgings built to be bed-and-breakfasts or inns, interiors are posh, baths are private and en suite, and breakfasts are gourmet affairs. In-room whirlpool tubs and fireplaces are *de rigueur,* and extras range from in-room refrigerators (perhaps stocked with champagne) to complimentary high tea to free use of state-of-the-art recreational equipment to . . . the list goes on! (One longtime innkeeper, whose historic home was tidily and humbly maintained by hours of elbow grease and common sense, dubbed this new state of affairs "the amenities war.")

The result is an industry in which a simple homestay bed-and-breakfast with a shared bath and common rooms can be a budget experience, whereas a new, upscale bed-and-breakfast can be the luxury venue of a lifetime.

Who Stays at Bed-and-Breakfasts?

American travelers are finally catching on to what Europeans have known for a long time. Maybe it's a backlash against a cookie-cutter, strip-mall landscape, or a longing for a past that maybe never was, and for an idealized, short-term interaction with others. Maybe it's a need for simple pleasures in a world over the top with theme parks and high-tech wonders. Who can say for sure?

The bed-and-breakfast trade has grown so large that it includes niches catering to virtually every need: some bed-and-breakfasts and small inns are equipped to help travelers conduct business, others provide turn-down service and fresh flowers by the honeymooners' canopied bed, and still others offer amenities for reunions or conferences. Whatever your needs, there is a bed-and-breakfast or small inn tailored to your expectations. The challenge, one this guide was designed to help you meet, is sifting through the choices until you find the perfect place.

Romantics

More and more, properties are establishing at least one room or suite with fireplace, whirlpool, canopied king, and the trappings of romance. Theme rooms can also be especially fun for fantasizing. Always check out the privacy factor. Sometimes a property that caters to families has a carriage house in the back or a top-floor room away from the others. If an inn allows children under age 16, don't be surprised if it's noisy; look for ones that are for older children or adults only.

Families

Face it, moms and dads: rumpled surroundings will sometimes have to be accepted where children are welcome. You may have to give up pristine decor and breakfast tea served in bone china for the relaxed, informal mood, but on the upside, you won't have to worry as much about Caitlin or Michael knocking over the Wedgwood collection on the sideboard.

When an establishment says kids are "welcome," that usually means a really kid-friendly place. Check the age restrictions. If your children are underaged but well behaved, let the host know; often they will make exceptions. (But be sure it's true—other guests are counting on it.) On the flip side, honeymooners or other folks who might prefer common areas free of crayons, and breakfasts without sugar-frosted confetti, may want to look elsewhere.

Generally, bed-and-breakfasts are not ideal for high-action kids. But if your children enjoy games, puzzles, books, a chance for quiet pleasures, and meeting others; if they don't need TVs; and if they can be counted on to be thoughtful and follow instructions ("whisper before 9 a.m.," "don't put your feet on the table"), you and your kids can have a wonderful experience together—and so can the rest of the guests.

Business Travelers

For individual business travelers, bed-and-breakfasts and small inns are becoming much more savvy at anticipating your needs, but in differing degrees. Although phone lines and data ports are fairly common, they vary from one bed-and-breakfast to another. Some say they offer data ports when in fact they have two phone jacks in every room but only one phone line servicing the entire property. This can be fine for a three-room inn in the off-season, but if you're trying to conduct business, look for properties with private lines and/or dedicated data ports. If in doubt, ask. Rooms are often available with desks, but these also vary, particularly in surface area and quality of lighting. If this is an important feature, ask for specifics and make sure you secure a room with a desk when you reserve.

Some establishments even offer couriers, secretarial support, and laundry/dry cleaning. And for business travelers who don't have time to take advantage of a leisurely and sumptuous breakfast, hosts often provide an early-morning alternative, sometimes continental, sometimes full.

Finally, there are intangibles to consider. After the sterile atmosphere of the trade show, meeting hall, or boardroom, a small inn with a host and a plate of cookies and a personal dinner recommendation can be nice to come home to.

The atmosphere is also a plus for business meetings or seminars: The relaxed surroundings are quite conducive to easygoing give and take. During the week when guest rooms are often available, some bed-and-breakfasts and small inns are usually eager to host business groups. Discounts are often included and special services, such as catering and equipment, are offered if you rent the entire property. But forget weekends; these properties are still tourist oriented.

Independents

If you are on your own, small lodgings are ideal. Look for a place with single rates, and even if a special rate isn't listed, you can often negotiate a small discount. If you want some interaction, just sit in the parlor, lounge, or common rooms and talk to people before meals. Most of the time if you're friendly and interested, you'll get an invite to join someone at a table. You could talk to the innkeepers about this even before you arrive, and they might fix you up with friendly folks. (And if you are traveling with others, invite a single to join you.) As for breakfast, communal tables are perfect for singles. Note our profiles to choose properties with that in mind.

Groups

Whether you are part of a wedding, reunion, or just a group of people who want to travel together, an inn or bed-and-breakfast is a delightful place to stay. The atmosphere is special, your needs are taken care of in a personal way, the grounds are most often spacious and lovely, and in the evening you can all retire in close proximity. It's especially fun when you take over the whole place—so you may want to choose an especially small property if that's your goal.

Those with Special Needs

Look in our profiles for mention of disabled facilities or access. Then call for details to determine just how extensive the accessibility is. Remember also that some of these houses are quite old, and owners of a small bed-and-breakfast will not have a team of accessibility experts on retainer, so be specific with your questions. If doorways must be a certain width to accommodate a wheelchair or walker, know how many inches before you call; if stairs are difficult for Great Aunt Agnes, don't neglect to find out how many are present outside, as well as inside. And if a property that seems otherwise special doesn't seem to have facilities, perhaps you can patch things together, such as a room on the first floor. Realistically, though, some historic properties were built with many stairs and are situated on hilltops or in rural terrain, so you will have to choose very carefully.

If you suffer from allergies or aversions, talk this over when you book. A good innkeeper will make every attempt to accommodate you. As for food, if you request a special meal and give enough notice, you can often get what you like. That's one of the joys of a small, personalized property.

You and Your Hosts

Hosts are the heart of your small inn or bed-and-breakfast experience and color all aspects of the stay. They can make or break a property, and sometimes an unassuming place will be the most memorable of all because of the care and warmth of the hosts. Typically, they are well versed in navigating the area and can be a wealth of "insider information" on restaurants, sight-seeing, and the like.

Though many—most, in these guides—hosts live on the premises, they often have designed or remodeled their building so that their living quarters are separate. Guests often have their own living room, den, parlor, and sitting room; you may be sharing with other guests, but not so much with your hosts. The degree of interaction between host families and guests varies greatly; we try to give a feel for the extremes in the introduction to each profile. In most cases, hosts are accessible but not intrusive; they will swing through the common areas and chat a bit, but are sensitive to guests' need for privacy. Sometimes hosts are in another building altogether; in the other extreme, you intimately share living space with your hosts. This intimate, old-style bed-and-breakfast arrangement is called a "homestay." We try to note this.

In short, most bed-and-breakfast hosts are quite gracious in accommodating travelers' needs, and many are underpinning their unique small lodging with policies and amenities from hotel-style lodgings. But bed-and-breakfasts and small inns are not the Sheraton, and being cognizant of the differences can make your experience more pleasant.

Planning Your Visit

When You Choose

If you're not sure where you want to travel, browse through our listings. Maybe something in an introduction or a description of a property will spark your interest.

If you know you are going to a certain location, note the properties in that zone, and then read the entries. You can also call for brochures or take a further look at Web sites, especially to see rooms or to book directly. We've provided a listing of some useful Web sites.

When You Book

Small properties usually require booking on your own. Some travel agents will help, but they may charge a fee, because many small properties don't give travel agents commissions. The fastest, easiest ways to book are through the Internet or a reservation service, but if you have special needs or questions, we suggest contacting properties directly to get exactly what you want.

Ask about any special needs or requirements, and make sure your requests are clear. Most of these properties are not designed for people in wheelchairs, so be sure to ask ahead of time if you need that accessibility.

Helpful Web Sites	
www.virtualcities.com	*innsnorthamerica.com*
bbchannel.com	*johansens.com*
bbonline.com	*relaischateaux.fr/[name of inn]*
bnbcity.com	*travel.com/accom/bb/usa*
bnbinns.com	*travelguide.com*
epicurious.com	*trip.com*
getawayguides.com	*triple1.com*
innbook.com	*virtualcities.com*
inns.com	

Specify what's important to you—privacy, king-size bed, fireplace, tub versus shower, view, first-floor access. A host won't necessarily know what you want, so make sure you decide what is important—writing it down will help you remember. Note the room you want by name, or ask for the "best" room if you're not sure. Remember to ask about parking conditions—does the property have off-street parking or will you have to find a place on the street? And if air-conditioning is a must for you, always inquire—some bed-and-breakfasts do not have it.

Verify prices, conditions, and any factors or amenities that are important to you. The best time to call is in the early afternoon, before new guests arrive for the day and when hosts have the most free time. Book as soon as possible; for weekends and holidays, preferred properties could be filled a year or more in advance.

A Word about Negotiating Rates

Negotiating a good rate can be more straightforward at a bed-and-breakfast than at a hotel. For starters, the person on the other end of the line will probably be the owner and will have the authority to offer you a discount. Second, the bed-and-breakfast owner has a smaller number of rooms and guests to keep track of than a hotel manager and won't have to do a lot of checking to know whether something is available. Also, because the number of rooms is small, each room is more important. In a bed-and-breakfast with four rooms, the rental of each room increases the occupancy rate by 25 percent.

To get the best rate, just ask. If the owner expects a full house, you'll probably get a direct and honest "no deal." On the other hand, if there are rooms and you are sensitive about price, chances are you'll get a break. In either event, be polite and don't make unreasonable requests. If you are overbearing or contentious on the phone, the proprietor may suddenly discover no rooms available.

Some Considerations

Like snowflakes, no two bed-and-breakfasts are alike. Some are housed in historic homes or other buildings (churches, fraternal halls, barns, castles . . . !). Some are humble and cozy, some are grand and opulent. Some are all in one building, while others are scattered among individual, free-standing units. Some offer a breakfast over which you'll want to linger for hours, others . . . well, others make a darn good muffin. Bed-and-breakfasts are less predictable than hotels and motels but can be much more interesting. A few bed-and-breakfast aficionados have discovered that "interesting" sometimes comes at a price. This guide takes the "scary" out of "interesting" and presents only places that meet a certain standard of cleanliness, predictability, and amenities. However, there are certain questions and issues common to bed-and-breakfasts and small inns that first-time visitors should consider:

Choosing Your Room

Check out your room before lugging your luggage (not having elevators is usually part of the charm). This is standard procedure at small properties and saves time and trouble should you prefer another room. When a guest room has an open door, it usually means the proud innkeeper wants you to peek. You may just find a room that you like better than the one you are assigned, and it may be available, so ask.

Bathrooms

Americans are picky about their potties. The traditional (sometimes referred to as "European-style") bed-and-breakfast set-up involved several bedrooms sharing a bath, but this is becoming less common. Even venerable Victorians are being remodeled to include private baths. In fact, many bed-and-breakfasts offer ultra-luxurious bath facilities, including jetted tubs, dual vanities, and so forth. Our advice is not to reject shared bath facilities out of hand, as these can be excellent values. Do check the bedroom-to-bath ratio, however. Two rooms sharing a bath can be excellent; three or more can be problematic with a full house.

Security

Many bed-and-breakfasts have property locks and room locks as sophisticated as hotels and motels. Others do not. For the most part, inns with 3½ stars or more have quality locks throughout the premises. (Many with lower rankings do as well.) Beyond locks, most bed-and-breakfasts provide an additional measure of security in that they are small properties, generally in a residential district, and typically with live-in hosts on the premises. Single female travelers might take comfort in coming "home" to a facility like this as opposed to a 150-room hotel with a cardlock system but God-knows-what lurking in the elevator.

Privacy

At a hotel, you can take your key and hole up in solitude for the duration of your stay. It's a little harder at a bed-and-breakfast, especially if you take part in a family-style breakfast (although many inns offer the option of an early continental breakfast if you're pressed for time or feeling antisocial, and some offer en-suite breakfast service—these options are noted in the profiles). Most bed-and-breakfast hosts we've met are very sensitive to guests' needs for privacy and seem to have a knack for being as helpful or as unobtrusive as you wish. If privacy is hard to achieve at a given property, we've noted that in the profile.

Autonomy

Most bed-and-breakfasts provide a key to the front door and/or an unlocked front door certain hours of the day. While you might be staying in a family-style atmosphere, you are seldom subject to rules such as a curfew. (A few properties request that guests be in by a specific time; these policies are noted and rare.) Some places have "quiet hours," usually from about 10 or 11 p.m. until about 7 a.m. Such policies tend to be in place when properties lack sufficient sound insulation and are noted in the profile. Generally, higher ratings tend to correspond with better sound insulation.

What the Ratings Mean

We have organized this book so that you can get a quick idea of each property by checking out the ratings, reading the information at the beginning of each entry and then, if you're interested, reading the more detailed overview of each property. Obviously ratings are subjective, and people of good faith (and good taste) can and do differ. But you'll get a good, relative idea, and the ability to quickly compare properties.

Overall Rating The overall ratings are represented by stars, which range in number from one to five and represent our opinion of the quality of the property as a whole. It corresponds something like this:

★★★★★	The Best
★★★★½	Excellent
★★★★	Very Good
★★★½	Good
★★★	Good Enough
★★½	Fair
★★	Not So Good
★½	Barely Acceptable
★	Unacceptable

The overall rating for the bed-and-breakfast or small inn experience takes into account all factors of the property, including guest rooms and public rooms, food, facilities, grounds, maintenance, hosts, and something we'll call "specialness," for lack of a better phrase. Many times it involves the personalities and pesonal touches of the hosts.

Some properties have fairly equal star levels for all of these things, but most have some qualities that are better than others. Also, large, ambitious properties that serve dinner would tend to have a slightly higher star rating for the same level of qualities than a smaller property (the difference, say, between a great novel and a great short story; the larger it is the harder it is to pull off, hence the greater the appreciation). Yet a small property can earn five stars with a huge dose of "specialness."

Overall ratings and room quality ratings do not always correspond. Although guest rooms may be spectacular, the rest of the inn may be average, or vice versa. Generally, though, we've found through the years that a property is usually consistently good or bad throughout.

Room Quality Rating The quality ratings, stated in the form of a letter grade, represent our opinion of the quality of the guest rooms and bathrooms only. For the room quality ratings we factored in view, size, closet space, bedding, seating, desks, lighting, soundproofing, comfort, style, privacy, decor, "taste," and other intangibles. A really great private bathroom with a claw-foot tub and antique table might bring up the rating of an otherwise average room. Conversely, poor maintenance or lack of good lighting will lower the rating of a spacious, well-decorated room. Sometimes a few rooms are really special while others are standard, and we have averaged these where possible. It's difficult to codify this, but all factors are weighed, and the grades seem to come up easily.

It corresponds something like this:

A = Excellent B = Very Good C = Good D = Acceptable

Although we rated room quality for every bed-and-breakfast inspected, it was not always possible to see all of the rooms. Often that was because rooms were occupied by guests and the innkeeper did not want to intrude on their privacy (even if they were away). This is commendable but tough on critics. In such cases we checked those rooms that we stayed in or that were empty or talked with fellow guests about their rooms. This means you could get an uninspected room that you felt was of a higher or lower quality than our room rating. If so, let us know.

Value Rating The value ratings—A to D—are a combination of the overall and room quality ratings, divided by the cost of an average guest room. They are an indication rather than a scientific formulation—a general idea of value for money. If getting a good deal means the most to you, choose a property by looking at the value rating. Otherwise, the overall and room quality ratings are better indicators of a satisfying experience. An A value, A room quality, five-star inn or bed-and-breakfast would be ideal, but most often, you'll find a C value, and you are getting your money's worth. If a wonderful property is fairly priced, it may only get a C value rating, but you still might prefer the experience to an average property that gets an A value rating.

Price Our price range is the lowest-priced room to the highest-priced room in high season. The range does not usually include specially priced times such as holidays and low season. The room rate is based on double occupancy and assumes breakfast is included. It does not assume that other meals are included in the rate. However, be sure to check the inn's Food & Drink category. Lodgings where MAP, which stands for the hotel industry's standard Modified American Plan, is applicable offer breakfast and dinner in the room rate. Unless specifically noted, prices quoted in the profiles do not include gratuities or state and local taxes, which can be fairly steep. Gratuities are optional; use your own discretion. Prices change constantly, so check before booking.

The Profiles Clarified

The bulk of information about properties is straightforward, but much of it is in abbreviated style, so the following clarifications may help. They are arranged in the order they appear in the profile format.

Many of the properties in this book have similar names or even the same name; for example, there's the Governor's House Inn in Charleston, South Carolina, and the Governors House B&B in Talladega, Alabama. Town names, too, can be strikingly similar. Make sure you don't confuse properties or town names when selecting an inn.

Location

First, check the map for location. Our directions are designed to give you a general idea of the property's location. For more complete directions, call the property or check its Web site.

Building

This category denotes the design and architecture of the building. Many of the properties in the *Unofficial Guides* are historically and architecturally interesting. Here are a few architectural terms you may want to brush up on, in no particular order: Hip-roof, Colonial, Craftsman, Queen Anne, Blued Pine, Cape Cod, Northwest Contemporary, Foursquare, Bird's Eye Maple, Art Deco, Rumford fireplace, Georgian, Victorian, Arts and Crafts, Seattle Box, Eastlake, Greek Revival,

Edwardian, claw-foot tub, and many more. The more you know the jargon, the better you can select the property you want.

Food & Drink

For food and drink, we offer a taste of the inn or bed-and-breakfast, so to speak. Most properties go all out to fill you up at breakfast, so that you could easily skip lunch (factor that into the value). In some areas, however, the tourist board regulates that properties can only serve a continental breakfast without a hot dish. Note whether we state "full breakfast," if that experience is paramount. In most cases, a bed-and-breakfast breakfast—even a continental—tends to include more homemade items, greater selection, and greater care in presentation.

In this category, what we call "specialties" are really typical dishes, which may not always be served, but should give you a good idea of the cuisine. And a very few bed-and-breakfasts and inns do not include the breakfast in the price. However, it is almost always offered as an option.

Many inns and bed-and-breakfasts offer afternoon tea, snacks, sherry, or predinner wine and cheese. Note that if an inn offers meals to the public as well as guests, the atmosphere becomes less personal. Also, if MAP is noted in this category, it means the inn offers meals other than breakfast as part of the room rate.

Some inns provide alcoholic beverages to guests, some forbid consumption of alcohol—either extreme is noted in the inn's profile. The norm is that alcohol consumption is a private matter, and guests may bring and consume their own, if they do so respectfully. Glassware is generally provided. Bed-and-breakfasts are not well suited to drunkenness and partying.

A diet and a bed-and-breakfast or small inn go together about as well as a haystack and a lighted match. Come prepared to eat. Some bed-and-breakfasts will serve dinner on request, and we included that info when it was available.

Most bed-and-breakfasts are sensitive to dietary needs and preferences but need to be warned of this in advance. When you make your reservation, be sure to explain if you are diabetic, wheat- or dairy-intolerant, vegetarian/vegan, or otherwise restricted. Many proprietors pride themselves on accommodating difficult diets.

Recreation

We do not usually spell out whether the activities noted in the format are on-site. With some exceptions, assume that golf, tennis, fishing, canoeing, downhill skiing, and the like are not on-site (since these are small properties, not resorts). Assume that games and smaller recreational activities are on the property. But there are some exceptions, so ask.

Amenities & Services

These blend a bit. Generally, amenities include extras, such as swimming pools and games, and services cover perks, such as business support and turning down beds in the evening. Business travelers should note if any services are mentioned and if there are public rooms, group discounts, and so forth to back them up. Almost all bed-and-breakfasts and inns can provide advice regarding touring, restaurants, and local activities; many keep maps and brochures on hand.

Deposit

Unless otherwise noted, "refund" usually means "minus a service charge," which varies from $10 or so to 50 percent or more. The more popular the property, usually the more deposit you'll have to put down, and the further ahead. When canceling after the site's noted policy, most will still refund, less a fee, if the room is rerented. Check back on this.

Discounts

Discounts may extend to singles, long-stay guests, kids, seniors, packages, and groups. Even though discounts may not be listed in the text, it doesn't hurt to ask, as these sorts of things can be flexible in small establishments, midweek, off-season, last-minute, and when innkeepers may want to fill their rooms. This category also includes a dollar figure for additional persons sharing a room (beyond the two included in the basic rate).

Credit Cards

For those properties that do accept credit cards (we note those that do not), we've listed credit cards accepted with the following codes:

V	VISA	MC	MasterCard
AE	American Express	D	Discover
DC	Diners Club International	CB	Carte Blanche

Check-in/Out

As small operators, most bed-and-breakfast hosts need to know approximately when you'll be arriving. Many have check-in periods (specified in the profiles) during which the hosts or staff will be available to greet you. Most can accommodate arrival beyond their stated check-in period but need to be advised so they can arrange to be home or get a key to you. Think about it—they have to buy groceries and go to the kids' soccer games and get to doctors' appointments just like you. And they have to sleep sometime. Don't show up at 11:30 p.m. and expect a smiling bellhop—the same person who lets you in is probably going to be up at 5 or 6 a.m. slicing mushrooms for your omelet!

Check-in times are often flexible, but, as with any commercial lodging, check-out times can be critical, as the innkeeper must clean and prepare your room for incoming guests. If you need to stay longer, ask and you'll often get an extension. Sometimes a host will let you leave your bags and enjoy the common areas after check-out, as long as you vacate your room.

Please take cancellation policies seriously. A "no-show" is not a cancellation! If an establishment has a seven-day, or 72-hour, or whatever, cancellation policy, you are expected to call and cancel your reservation prior to that time, or you could be liable for up to the full amount of your reserved stay. After all, a four-unit bed-and-breakfast has lost 25 percent of its revenue if you arbitrarily decide not to show up.

Smoking

We've indicated in the inn's profile if smoking is banned outright or if there are designated rooms where it's allowed. Usually it's fine to smoke outside, what with the excellent ventilation, but ask your hosts before you light up. Be mindful, too, of how you dispose of the butts—when you flick them into a nearby shrub, it's likely that your hosts, not some sanitation team, will be plucking them out next week.

Pets

We have not mentioned most of the inn-house pets in the profiles, as this situation changes even more frequently than most items. Many properties have pets on the premises. Don't assume that because an establishment does not allow guests to bring pets that pets aren't around. Dogs and cats and birds (and monkeys, pigs, goats, llamas, etc.) are often around. If you foresee a problem with this, be sure to clarify "how around," before booking. If properties allow pets, we have noted this, but most do not. And if you can't bear to leave your own beloved Fido or Miss Kitty for long periods, and want to stay in an inn that does not allow them, good innkeepers often know of reputable boarding facilities nearby.

Open

Properties often claim they are open all year, but they can close at any time—at the last minute for personal reasons or if business is slow. Similarly, properties that close during parts of the year may open specially for groups. If you can get a bunch of family or friends together, it's a great way to stay at popular inns and bed-and-breakfasts that would be otherwise hard to book. And remember, in low-season things slow down, dinners may not be served, and even when some properties are "open," they may be half-closed.

An Important Note

Facts and situations change constantly in the small-lodging business. Innkeepers get divorced, prices go up, puppies arrive, chefs quit in the middle of a stew, and rooms get redecorated, upgraded, and incorporated. So use this format as a means to get a good overall idea of the property, and then inquire when you book about the specific details that matter most. Changes will definitely occur, so check to be sure.

Making the Most of Your Stay

Once you're settled in, it's a good idea to scope out the entire place, or you may not realize until too late that your favorite book was on the shelf, or that an old-fashioned swing would have swung you into the moonlight on a warm evening. If you are alone in the inn, it can feel like the property is yours (and that, in fact, is a good reason to go midweek or off-season).

Take advantage of the special charms of these lodgings: the fireplace, the piano, other guests, the gardens. What makes an inn or bed-and-breakfast experience an integral part of a trip are small moments that can become cherished memories.

Did you love it? You can perhaps duplicate in your daily life some of the touches that made the experience special, whether it was warm towels, an early weekend breakfast by candlelight, or a special recipe for stuffed French toast. Hosts usually enjoy sharing ideas and recipes.

A small inn or bed-and-breakfast, perhaps set in a village or town where at least a few blocks retain a look of history and often grace, encourages you to relax, lie back, unwind, open up, read, talk, get romantic, dream, slow down, look up at the stars and down at the grass, smell the coffee—and of course, the roses climbing on the pergola or lining the walkway. These small lodgings are stress-busters, far away from sitcoms and fast food and the media mania du jour. They are cozy places to settle into and curl up with a book, or a honey, or a dream. Or, if you must, a laptop and a cell phone.

Southeastern Bed-and-Breakfasts

A physician friend who was scheduled to attend a seminar in a Southern city that included a three-night stay at a luxury hotel said, "I'm just not going. I can't stand another night in one of those look-alike, standardized hotel rooms." But he brightened considerably at the thought of staying in a bed-and-breakfast that could be full of pleasant surprises.

While the bed-and-breakfast movement has multiplied and improved all over the nation, few regions have added such distinctive touches as the Southeast, giving new meaning to Southern hospitality.

This guide explores the many different types of bed-and-breakfasts and inns that stretch around the coast from North Carolina to Louisiana and up through Tennessee and Kentucky. They range from houses with an inexpensive spare room on the second floor that offer toast and coffee in the morning to Tara-like mansions from *Gone with the Wind* that serve mushroom quiches and cinnamon French toast swirled with cream cheese as breakfast fare.

More and more travelers are choosing bed-and-breakfast establishments in the Southeast because of the sometimes quirky, often beautiful surprises that reflect the personalities of the hosts. In North Carolina you can stay in a bed-and-breakfast managed by former top executives of the state who provide a glass of sherry in the evening and fascinating "insider" conversations about politics. Or you might be intrigued by a Florida bed-and-breakfast in the Gulf of Mexico that is reached by water taxi and boasts CIA spy stories on display in a little museum behind the inn. Or visit a Tennessee bed-and-breakfast where you can enjoy views of the Great Smoky Mountains and buy paintings of the local scenery right off your bedroom wall. Want to pet an ostrich named Rhett, bathe in a whirlpool tub for two by the light of a fireplace, or play a round of golf with your host? You're not likely to find such treats in super-slick hotels. But you will find all these surprises and more in the Southeastern bed-and-breakfasts in this guide.

A cautionary note: Prices, along with quality, are definitely on the rise in Southeastern bed-and-breakfasts. We were shocked by the rates charged by bed-and-breakfasts in Savannah and Charleston, but we have to admit they are beautiful places—and Bill Gates types are obviously paying these rates since it can often be difficult to book a room. Our advice: Use the Internet or toll-free calls to price shop. And there are many bed-and-breakfasts a little off the beaten path throughout the Southeast that may not have canopied beds and Swedish showers but do offer something we all enjoy—a good bargain. Then you can save your money for the occasional splurge and say hello to the Bill Gates type in the suite next door. "Say, Bill. Do you think now is a good time to buy E-com. stocks?"

About Zones

We feel the divisions of states by tourist regions often border on *Alice in Wonderland* fantasy. Regions or states often give highly appealing promotional names to their areas that are less than helpful to travelers looking for the regions, especially as the lines dividing these areas are invisible county lines. "Say, Mildred, didn't we just pass over from Plantation Land into Waterfall Country?"

We believe we've devised a simpler system, using major interstate highways as dividing lines between zones. For example, if you're traveling down I-95 in Florida and take an exit that leads to the left, you're in the coastal zone; one that leads to the right puts you in the central zone. In some instances interstates neatly divide major cities, such as Atlanta. In those cases we have arbitrarily assigned the city to one zone or the other.

Facilities for Smokers Are Going Up in Smoke

Bad news for addicted smokers: The overwhelming majority of homes visited are nonsmoking facilities. Some hosts even charge a clearing fee of $75 or more to people who smoke in the rooms. Actually, the nonsmoking rule is also a safety factor. Some zoning regulations (true to old standards but nonetheless stupid) prevent owners of many Victorian homes from installing sprinklers. Smoking in these older homes doubles the hazards of fire.

Cholesterol-Filled Breakfasts

In our experience the cholesterol count of the bed-and-breakfast breakfasts increases with every mile you travel farther into the South. The quiche Lorraine, eggs Benedict, and sausage-and-egg casserole syndrome on a regular basis could make your doctor sick on your next visit. A number of bed-and-breakfasts will now honor requests for more healthy cereals, fruit, and other lighter fare, especially if you make the request in advance. But you don't have to skip their bountiful treats completely. Just use moderation, as your good doctor would probably say. The amount of grits served also seems to increase with the cholesterol count; they are the signature dish of many Southern breakfasts. True confession: We regard grits with the same affection we reserve for Hawaiian poi. Yuucch! But some people really seem to enjoy them. So you can have our share that we usually left behind.

Pack a Sense of Humor

Many bed-and-breakfast owners are not professional innkeepers. Some were schoolteachers, plumbers, house painters, government officials, or airline pilots before they bought a house. Then, to supplement their Social Security or to combat loneliness or just for the fun of it, they decided to operate a bed-and-breakfast. That means they will make mistakes or have moods—just like all of us. Don't expect perfection. Be aware that the hosts will usually do everything they can to make your stay pleasant because they want your recommendations and repeat visits. So ask when you have special needs or tell them when a room or a breakfast is too cold or too hot.

But when things *really* go wrong, all you can do is laugh and move on. For example, here are some experiences at bed-and-breakfasts *not* listed in this book. At one establishment some guests were unable to sleep because of a noisy party that seemed to go on and on. Finally they went downstairs and told the *bed-and-breakfast owner* to quiet down! At another, a fully dressed manikin was sitting in the living room, so lifelike that we said "excuse me" when we accidentally bumped into her. Unfortunately she also looked exactly like Norman Bates's mother of *Psycho* fame. Any guest taking a shower in that home would probably lock the bathroom door.

Gathering Information

This is a lodging guidebook. While each zone has a brief introduction, and each profile lists a few nearby attractions, this book in no way purports to be a guidebook to the Southeast.

In addition to consulting one or more of the many useful guidebooks to the Southeast on the market, we suggest turning to the Internet and to your prospective bed-and-breakfast hosts as sources of information. Don't abuse your hosts, but they can (a) steer you to some good phone numbers and other resources, and (b) perhaps mail you a flyer or two about local sites and happenings with your reservation confirmation.

Some of the bed-and-breakfasts profiled in this guide have links from their Web pages to Web pages of interest in their region.

Bed-and-Breakfasts on the Internet

The World Wide Web is full of home pages for bed-and-breakfasts and small inns. It's full of booking services and tourism information sites that link you to home pages and listings for bed-and-breakfasts and small inns. Whenever possible, you—or your computer-savvy kid—should check out the Internet sites of bed-and-breakfasts you want to visit. The vast majority of bed-and-breakfasts we visited now have Internet sites of their own or through bed-and-breakfast roundup sites, like www.bbonline.com. Once you link up to one of the thousands of bed-and-breakfast or small inn sites within the Southeast, you can revel in detailed descriptions and click your way through colored photographs until your head spins (believe us, we know). If you see something you like, you can, in some cases, submit a reservation request online or e-mail the hosts directly for a little cyberchat about your specific needs. And some bed-and-breakfasts make special offers, including reduced rates that are only available to people who book through the Internet.

There's no denying that the Internet is a great resource for travelers in general, and for bed-and-breakfast/small inn seekers in particular. The problem comes in sorting the wheat from the chaff and in remembering that a great Web site does not necessarily equal a great lodging experience. (Think about it: do you want your bed-and-breakfast host spending his time whipping up omelets and cruising the local farmer's market or sitting in front of a computer til 3 a.m. in his underwear scanning photos of his backyard gazebo?) Out-of-date information is another serious problem with Internet listings.

And remember, bed-and-breakfast URLs seem to change frequently. If you can't find the bed-and-breakfast through the URL listed in this guide, type the bed-and-breakfast name and its city in a universal search engine such as www.dogpile.com. It's a terrible name but an efficient way to search a number of different search engines simultaneously.

Mini Indexes

Top 30 Overall

Five Stars

White Doe
Cypress Glen
Maple Grove Inn
Whitestone Country Inn
Ballastone
Kendall Manor Inn
Litchfield Plantation
Blackridge Hall Bed & Breakfast
Inn at Wintersun
1842 Inn
Innisfree Victorian Inn and Garden House
Magnolia Place Inn
Monmouth Plantation
Rhett House Inn
Richmond Hill Inn
Rutledge House Inn
Villa
Collier Inn
Mansion House

Four-and-a-Half Stars

William Thomas House
Gastonian
Grace Hall Bed & Breakfast
Henderson Village
Hippensteal's Mountain View Inn
Magnolia's Bed & Breakfast
Melrose Mansion
Peacock Hill Country Inn
Windsong
Bienvenue House Bed & Breakfast
Two Meeting Street Inn

Top Value

Whitestone Country Inn
Blackridge Hall Bed & Breakfast
Kendall Manor Inn
Grace Hall Bed & Breakfast
Peacock Hill Country Inn
Simply Southern
Claremont House Bed & Breakfast
Statesboro Inn & Restaurant
Amos Shinkle Bed & Breakfast Townhouse
Beautiful Dreamer
Berkeley Manor
Highland Place Bed & Breakfast
Page House Bed & Breakfast
Shellmont Bed & Breakfast Lodge
Caragen House
Lightbourn Inn
Towle House
Cedar Grove Mansion Inn
Coquina Inn Bed & Breakfast
Cottage at Shadowbright
Ashford Manor Bed & Breakfast

Trust Bed & Breakfast
Augustus T. Zeverly Inn
Key West Bed & Breakfast
Wade-Beckham House Bed & Breakfast
Gordon-Lee Mansion
Hibiscus House Bed & Breakfast
Miss Betty's Bed & Breakfast
Ferncourt Bed & Breakfast
Mountain Laurel Inn

Budget

Alabama
Mountain Laurel Inn

Florida
Azalea House Bed & Breakfast
Cottage at Shadowbright
Heritage Country Inn
Key West B&B
Verona House B&B

Georgia
1810 West Inn
Four Chimneys
Hotel Warm Springs B&B
Open Gates B&B
Steadman House

Kentucky
Canaan Land Farm B&B
Inn at Woodhaven

North Carolina
Little Warren B&B

South Carolina
Jefferson House
Serendipity
Southwood Manor

Family Oriented

Alabama
Church Street Inn
Mountain Laurel Inn
Secret Bed & Breakfast Lodge

Florida
A Highland House B&B Inn
Azalea House Bed & Breakfast
Captiva Island Inn
Collier Inn
Cottage at Shadowbright
Cypress Glen
Emerald Hill Inn
Herlong Mansion B&B
Hibiscus House
Higgins House
House on Cherry Street
Key West B&B
PerriHouse B&B Inn
Plantation Manor Inn
Song of the Sea
Thurston House
Villa Nina Island Inn

Georgia
Lodge on Little St. Simons Island
Magnolia Place Inn
Veranda

Kentucky
Amos Shinkle Bed & Breakfast
Inn at Woodhaven
Silver Springs Farm

Louisiana
Bienvenue House
Bulter Greenwood Plantation
Chretien Point Plantation
Country Oaks Cajun Cottages
Degas House
House on Bayou Road B&B
Lake Rosemound Inn
LeRosier Country Inn
Levy-East House
Madewood Plantation House
Oak Alley Plantation
Rip Van Winkle Gardens B&B
Shadetree Inn

Farm or Rural Setting

Sassafrass Inn
Shadowlawn B&B

North Carolina
Cataloochee Ranch
Eseeola Lodge
Hemlock Inn
Inn at the Taylor House
Inn at Winterson
Lovill House B&B
Millstone Inn
Pilot Knob
Pine Crest Inn
Swag Country Inn
Tanglewood Inn

South Carolina
Laurel Hill Plantation B&B Inn
Mansfield Plantation
Schell Haus B&B and Conference Center
Southwood Manor
TwoSuns Inn B&B
Wade-Beckham House B&B

Tennessee
Academy Place
Blue Mountain Mist Country Inn and Cottages
Calico Inn
Eight Gables Inn
Fall Creek Falls B&B Inn
Iron Mountain Inn
Maple Grove Inn
Sweetwater Inn
White Elephant
Whitestone Country Inn

Groups or Weddings

Alabama
Capps Cove
Grace Hall
Ivy Creek Inn
Kendall Manor
Mountain Laurel Inn
Towle House

Florida
Addison House B&B
Clauser's B&B
Herlong Mansion B&B
Highland House B&B Inn
Meadow Marsh B&B
PerriHouse B&B Inn

Georgia
1842 Inn
Bluff View Inn
Captain's Quarters
Eliza Thompson House
Glen-Ella Springs Inn & Conference Center
Gordon-Lee Mansion
Henderson Village
Lily Creek Lodge
Mountain Top Lodge
Nicholson House Inn
President's Quarters
Steadman House
Woodruff House

Kentucky
Inn at Woodhaven
Old Louisville Inn

Louisiana
Ahhh! T'Frere's B&B
Bienvenue House
Chretien Point Plantation
Grand Victorian B&B
Hemingbrough
House on Bayou Road B&B
Lake Rosemound Inn
Madewood Plantation House
Mandevilla B&B
Melrose Mansion
Myrtles Plantation

Historic

North Carolina
Cedars
Harmony House
Hillsborough House Inn
Manor House

South Carolina
Breeden Inn and Carriage House
Chestnut Cottage
Lord Camden Inn
Sandhurst
Wade-Beckham House B&B

Island Setting

Florida
Addison House Bed & Breakfast
Captiva Island Inn
Collier Inn
Key West B&B
Lightbourn Inn
Song of the Sea
Villa Nina Island Inn

Georgia
Lodge on Little St. Simons Island

Louisiana
Rip Van Winkle Gardens B&B

North Carolina
Theodesia's B&B Inn
Tranquil House Inn
White Doe

South Carolina
Litchfield Plantation

Mountain Setting

Alabama
Capps Cove
Ivy Creek Inn
Mountain Laurel Inn

Georgia
Glen-Ella Springs Inn & Conference Center
Gordon-Lee Mansion
Mountain Top Lodge

North Carolina
Cedar Crest Victorian Inn
Eseeola Lodge
Grandview Lodge
Hemlock Inn
Inn at the Taylor House
Inn at Wintersun
Lovill House B&B
Olde Towne Inn
Panes
Pilot Knob
Sourwood Inn
William Thomas House

South Carolina
Bell Tower Inn
Schell Haus B&B and Conference Center

Tennessee
Blue Mountain Mist Country Inn and Cottages
Buckhorn Inn
Fall Creek Falls B&B Inn
Hilton's Bluff B&B Inn
Hippensteal's Mountain View Inn
Iron Mountain Inn
Whitestone Country Inn

No Credit Cards

Georgia
Twin Oaks B&B Cottages

Kentucky
Canaan Land Farm B&B

Louisiana
Country Oaks Cajun Cottages

North Carolina
Panes

South Carolina
Mansfield Plantation
Two Meeting Street Inn

Tennessee
Academy Place
Rose Garden
White Elephant

Romantic

Alabama
Grace Hall
Kendall Manor
Towle House

Florida
Addison House B&B
Azalea House B&B
Cherry Laurel Inn
Clauser's B&B
Collier Inn
Coquina Inn
Cypress ... A Bed & Breakfast Inn
Cypress Glen
Herlong Mansion B&B
Hibiscus House
Higgins House
Key West B&B
Meadow Marsh B&B
Plantation Manor Inn
Thurston House
Villa Nina Island Inn

Georgia
Ballastone
Bluff View Inn
Captain's Quarters
Cottage Inn B&B
Four Chimneys
Gastonian
Gordon-Lee Mansion
Lodge on Little St. Simons Island
Magnolia Place Inn
Nicholson House Inn
Shellmont B&B Lodge
Twin Oaks B&B Cottages

Kentucky
1823 Historic Rose Hill Inn
Amos Shinkle Bed & Breakfast
Inn at Woodhaven
Old Louisville Inn

Louisiana
B&W Courtyards B&B
Bittersweet Plantation
Bois des Chenes B&B
Country French B&B
Grand Victorian B&B
Hemingbrough
House on Bayou Road B&B
Levy-East House
Madewood Plantation House
Maison Des Amis
Melrose Mansion
Old Centenary Inn
Rip Van Winkle Gardens B&B
Shadetree Inn
Victoria Inn

Mississippi
Bay Town Inn
Caragen House
Cedar Grove Mansion Inn
Father Ryan House Inn
Mockingbird Inn

North Carolina
Cedar Crest Victorian Inn
Cumberland Falls
Harborlight Guest House B&B
Henry Shaffner House
Hillsborough House Inn
Inn at the Taylor House
Inn at Wintersun
Inn on Main Street
Lion and the Rose
Millstone Inn
Panes
Pilot Knob
Richmond Hill Inn
Sourwood Inn
Tanglewood Inn
Waverly Inn
White Doe
William Thomas House

South Carolina
1790 House B&B
Abingdon Manor
Alexandra's Inn
Bell Tower Inn
Belvedere B&B
Cannonboro Inn
Cypress Inn
Fantasia B&B
Laurel Hill Plantation B&B Inn
Litchfield Plantation
Magnolia House
Mansfield Plantation
Rhett House Inn
Schell Haus B&B and Conference Center
Southwood Manor
Twenty-Seven State Street B&B
Two Meeting Street Inn

Tennessee
Adams Edgeworth Inn
Blue Mountain Mist Country Inn and Cottages
Calico Inn
Eight Gables Inn
Hippensteal's Mountain View Inn
Linden Manor
Maple Grove Inn
Masters Manor Inn
New Hope B&B
Rose Garden
Sweetwater Inn
Whitestone Country Inn

Rustic

Alabama
Mountain Laurel Inn
Secret B&B Lodge

Florida
Thurston House

Georgia
Glen-Ella Springs Inn & Conference Center
Lodge on Little St. Simons Island
Mountain Top Lodge
Sylvan Falls Mill

Kentucky
1823 Historic Rose Hill Inn
Jailer's Inn

Louisiana
Country Oaks Cajun Cottages
Green Springs B&B

Mississippi
Sassafrass Inn

North Carolina
Cataloochee Ranch
Colonel Ludlow Inn
Eseeola Lodge
Pilot Knob

South Carolina
Laurel Hill Plantation B&B Inn
Mansfield Plantation

Tennessee
Calico Inn
Hilton's Bluff B&B Inn

Smoking OK

Florida
Hotel Leon
Song of the Sea

Kentucky
Swann's Nest at Cygnet Farm

Louisiana
Bulter Greenwood Plantation

North Carolina
Brookstown Inn
Colonel Ludlow Inn
Manor Hous Bed & Breakfast
Pine Crest Inn
Roanoke Island Inn
Tranquil House Inn

South Carolina
Claussen's Inn

Solo Oriented

Alabama
Bay Breeze
Capps Cove
Grace Hall
Ivy Creek Inn
Mountain Laurel Inn
Secret B&B Lodge
Towle House

Florida
Addison House B&B
Cherry Laurel Inn
Herlong Mansion B&B
St. Francis Inn

Georgia
1842 Inn
Captain's Quarters
Dunlap House
Eliza Thompson House
Four Chimneys
Lily Creek Lodge
Mountain Top Lodge
Nicholson House Inn
President's Quarters
Sylvan Falls Mill
Twin Oaks B&B Cottages

Kentucky
Jailer's Inn
Old Louisville Inn

Louisiana
Ahhh! T'Frere's B&B
Country Oaks Cajun Cottages
Grand Victorian B&B
La Maison de Repos
La Maison du Teche
Mandevilla B&B
Myrtles Plantation

Mississippi
Cedar Grove Mansion Inn
Harbour Oaks
Trust B&B

North Carolina
Colonel Ludlow Inn
Greenwood B&B
Hemlock Inn
Miss Betty's B&B
Panes

South Carolina
Calhoun Street B&B
Chestnut Cottage
Claussen's Inn at Five Points
Governor's House Inn
John Rutledge House
Magnolia House
Richland Street B&B
Schell Haus B&B and Conference Center
Serendipity
Shaw House

Tennessee
Calico Inn
Eight Gables Inn
English Manor
Hilton's Bluff B&B Inn
Iron Mountain Inn
Linden Manor
Masters Manor Inn
New Hope B&B
Rose Garden
Sweetwater Inn

Swimming Pool

Alabama
Secret Bed & Breakfast Lodge

Florida
Cherry Laurel Inn
Collier Inn
Cypress Glen
Hibiscus House
Lightbourn Inn
Little Inn by the Sea
PerriHouse B&B Inn
Plantation Manor Inn
St. Francis Inn
Villa Nina Island Inn

Georgia
Cottage Inn Bed and Breakfast
Glen-Ella Springs Inn & Conference Center

Kentucky
Canaan Land Farm B&B

Louisiana
Bulter Greenwood Plantation
Chretien Point Plantation
House on Bayou Road B&B
Melrose Mansion
St. Francisville Inn

Mississippi
Bonne Terre Country Inn
Cedar Grove Mansion Inn
Cedar Grove Plantation
Father Ryan House Inn
Sassafrass Inn

North Carolina
Eseeola Lodge
Greenwood B&B
Hillsborough House Inn
Pilot Knob
William Thomas House

South Carolina
Alexandra's Inn
Breeden Inn and Carriage House
Litchfield Plantation
Lord Camden Inn
Schell Haus B&B and Conference Center
Serendipity
Southwood Manor

Tennessee
Maple Grove Inn

Three Rooms or Fewer

Alabama
Church Street Inn

Florida
Azalea House Bed & Breakfast

Louisiana
Bittersweet Plantation
Chez Des Amis
Country French B&B
La Caboose B&B
La Maison de Repos
La Maison du Teche
Rip Van Winkle Gardens B&B
Shadetree Inn

Mississippi
Magnolia's Bed & Breakfast

North Carolina
Homeplace
Panes
Pearson Place

South Carolina
Bell Tower Inn
Belvedere B&B
Shaw House
Wade-Beckham House B&B

Tennessee
Calico Inn
Hilltop House
Linden Manor
Rose Garden
White Elephant

Twenty Rooms or More

Florida
Song of the Sea

Georgia
1842 Inn
Eliza Thompson House

Mississippi
Cedar Grove Mansion Inn
Old Capitol Inn

North Carolina
Eseeola Lodge
Hemlock Inn
Richmond Hill Inn
Tanglewood Inn
Tranquil House Inn

South Carolina
Claussen's Inn at Five Points
Litchfield Plantation

Tennessee
Whitestone Country Inn

Waterside

Alabama
Bay Breeze Guest House
Original Romar House

Florida
1735 House
Collier Inn
Cypress ... A Bed & Breakfast Inn
Emerald Hill Inn
Highland House Bed & Breakfast
House on Cherry St.
Little Inn by the Sea

Mississippi
Bay Town Inn
Shadowlawn B&B

North Carolina
Harborlight Guest House B&B
Roanoke Island Inn

South Carolina
Litchfield Plantation

North Carolina

Many centuries before the first Europeans arrived, the Algonquin, Sioux, and Iroquoi Indians hunted in the 53,821-square-mile territory that is now North Carolina. They roamed amid the blue mists that shrouded the western ranges, now named the Great Smoky Mountains and the Appalachian Mountains. They fished in the string of barrier islands in the Atlantic Ocean that would one day become a thriving vacation odyssey for thousands of travelers visiting the Outer Banks.

Sir Walter Raleigh led the first English settlement that disturbed the Indians' peace, establishing two colonies. The first colony, the lucky ones, returned to England. The second stayed behind and disappeared off the face of the earth, becoming the famous "Lost Colony."

This vast Native American work- and playground has become a haven today for tourists seeking the coolness of the mountains or the almost limitless beaches along the coast.

No other state we researched has embraced the bed-and-breakfast movement with so much gusto and variety as North Carolina. It gives bed-and-breakfast seekers a choice of super-luxury resort inns in Asheville, a wide array of economical mom-and-pop homes scattered across the plains, and romantic getaways along the coast and Outer Banks, where they ignite fireplaces with a wall switch and allow you to slip into something comfortable like a two-person whirlpool lit by stained glass windows.

The best way to choose the bed-and-breakfast that is right for you is to first decide where you want to go and what you want to see in North Carolina. Here are just a few of the possibilities in the Tar Heel state.

If you want to live the beach life, head for Cape Hatteras and Cape Lookout National Seashores. If you are a history buff, choose from the 66 American Revolutionary War battle sites or follow the trail of General Joseph Johnson, who commanded the last Confederate Army to surrender (in Durham). If you're a fan of TV programs such as *Biography*, go see the homes of Carl Sandburg, Thomas Wolfe, and other famous past and present citizens of the state. Walk through the terrain made famous in the Pulitzer Prize–winning novel *Cold Mountain.*

And stop to talk with some of the interesting bed-and-breakfast hosts, such as a New York real estate agent who decided to invite guests and ostriches to her new bed-and-breakfast, and a top aide to the former governor of North Carolina who opened an extraordinarily opulent home for travelers in downtown Raleigh. All along the way you will meet funny, interesting people, like those the late Charles Kuralt used to interview on his long-running TV vignettes, *On the Road.* Maybe he even got the idea for the series here—North Carolina was his home state.

Travelers through the state should be aware of various legal quirks. It's unlawful to let a dog or cat stay overnight in a hotel, motel, or bed-and-breakfast. Some counties are "dry," with laws that bar all types of liquor. Some hosts avoid this problem by "giving" you free complimentary bourbon and sodas and wine. Others arrange for you to become members of private clubs that serve drinks.

In most guidebooks about North Carolina you almost never see the "H" word—hurricanes. But these savage storms, said by the experts to be increasing in frequency and strength, are regular unwelcome guests in North Carolina. Many, like the devastating Floyd of 1999, hug the southeast coast and then frequently move inland, including many areas of North Carolina in its rampage. A number of bed-and-breakfast homes were affected by wind damage or the subsequent flooding that caused diseases and sanitary problems over thousands of acres.

Our advice: If you're in a coastal area or the Outer Banks of North Carolina and hear the first TV warnings that a hurricane may be on its way, get out! Every available car clogs every available foot of limited road and bridge, creating unwieldy traffic jams. North Carolina's usually reliable ferry system may stop running completely, and may not even start up service again for weeks after a storm because of the debris that gets left in harbors. If you have a bed-and-breakfast reservation for a home in the path of a coming storm, cancel immediately.

But when the sun comes out, North Carolina remains, as always, a dazzling state.

For More Information

North Carolina Travel and Tourism Division
(800) VISITNC
www.visitnc.com

North Carolina Bed and Breakfast Inns and Homes
www.bbonline.com/nc/ncbbi

Map Legend

Apex
B&B's Country Garden Inn, p. 58
Blue Heaven Ostrich Ranch and B&B, p. 59
Pearson Place Bed & Breakfast, p. 60

Asheville
Cedar Crest Victorian Inn, p. 78
Cumberland Falls, p. 79
Inn on Montford, p. 80
Lion and The Rose Bed & Breakfast, p. 81
Richmond Hill Inn, p. 82
Sourwood Inn, p. 83
Wright Inn and Carriage House, p. 84

Beaufort
Cedars, p. 37
Pecan Tree Inn, p. 38

Blowing Rock
Hound Ears Club, p. 85

Boone
Lovill House Inn Bed & Breakfast, p. 86

Bryson City
Hemlock Inn, p. 87

Burnsville
Panes, p. 88

Cape Carteret
Harborlight Guest House Bed & Breakfast, p. 39

Cashiers
Millstone Inn, p. 89

Charlotte
Morehead Inn, p. 61

Clemmons
Manor House Bed & Breakfast Inn, p. 62

Clyde
Windsong, p. 90

Dillsboro
Olde Town Inn, p. 91

Durham
Arrowhead Inn, p. 63

Edenton
Albemarle House Bed & Breakfast, p. 40
Captain's Quarters Inn, p. 41

Fairview
Inn at Wintersun, p. 92

Glenville
Innisfree Victorian Inn and Garden House, p. 64

Greensboro
Greenwood Bed & Breakfast, p. 66

Harbour Village
Theodosia's Bed and Breakfast Inn, p. 42

Hatteras Village
Seaside Inn, p. 43

Hendersonville
Claddagh Inn, p. 93
Waverly Inn, p. 95

Hillsborough
Hillsborough House Inn, p. 67

Linville
Eseeola Lodge, p. 96

Maggie Valley
Cataloochee Ranch, p. 97

Manteo
Roanoke Island Inn, p. 44
Tranquil House Inn, p. 45
White Doe, p. 46

Nags Head
First Colony Inn, p. 47

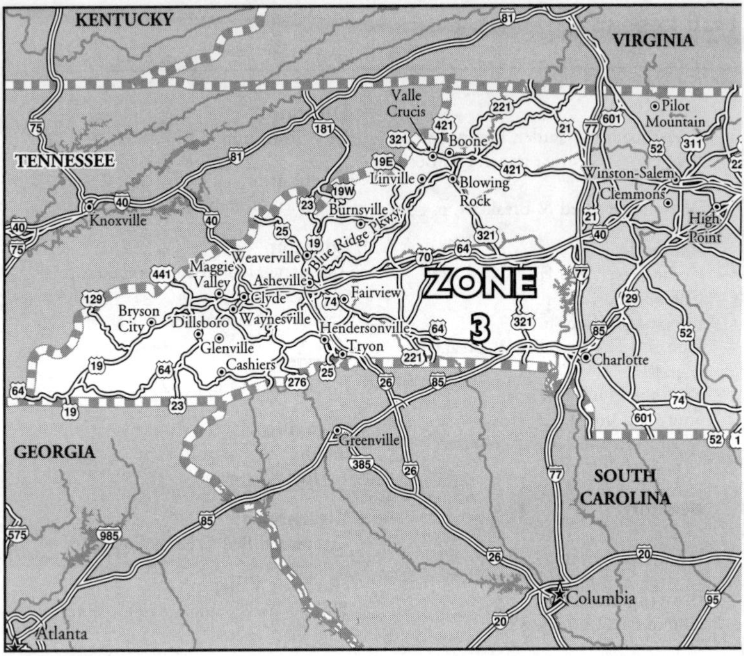

New Bern
Aerie, p. 48
Harmony House Inn, p. 49
New Bern House, p. 50

Ocracoke
Berkeley Manor, p. 51
Castle on Silver Lake, p. 52

Pilot Mountain
Pilot Knob, p. 68

Raleigh
Oakwood Inn Bed & Breakfast, p. 69
William Thomas House, p. 70

Tarboro
Little Warren Bed and Breakfast, p. 53

Tryon
Pine Crest Inn, p. 98

Valle Crucis
Inn at the Taylor House, p. 99

Waynesville
Grandview Lodge, p. 100
Swag Country Inn, p. 101

Weaverville
Dry Ridge Inn, p. 102
Inn on Main Street, p. 103

Wilmington
Catherine's Inn, p. 54

Wilson
Miss Betty's Bed & Breakfast, p. 55

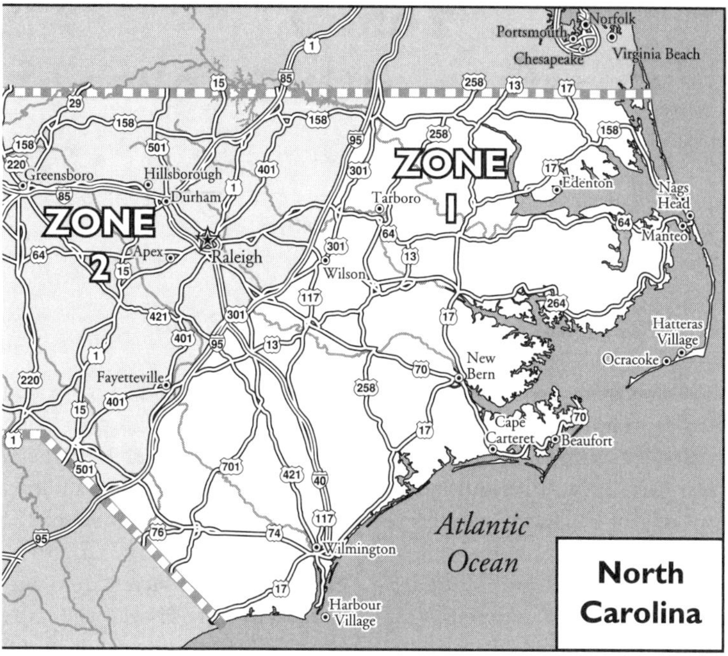

Winston-Salem
Augustus T. Zeverly Inn, p. 71
Brookstown Inn, p. 72
Colonel Ludlow Inn, p. 73
Henry Shaffner House, p. 74
Lady Anne's, p. 75

Tarboro
Little Warren Bed and Breakfast, p. 53

Tryon
Pine Crest Inn, p. 98

Valle Crucis
Inn at the Taylor House, p. 99

Waynesville
Grandview Lodge, p. 100
Swag Country Inn, p. 101

Weaverville
Dry Ridge Inn, p. 102
Inn on Main Street, p. 103

Wilmington
Catherine's Inn, p. 54

Wilson
Miss Betty's Bed & Breakfast, p. 55

Winston-Salem
Augustus T. Zeverly Inn, p. 71
Brookstown Inn, p. 72
Colonel Ludlow Inn, p. 73
Henry Shaffner House, p. 74
Lady Anne's, p. 75

Zone I
Coastal North Carolina

The Outer Banks are a work of art in progress, with the land, beaches, and inlets constantly being reshaped by wind and waves. This 125-mile string of islands has become the vacation home of thousands of Easterners, either part- or full-time. Ad agency and designer types snap up multilevel mansions on Duck, while others surf and swim some of the more isolated stretches of beaches in the U.S. along the National Seashore. Countless families play miniature golf under the eyes of an ugly, concrete dinosaur; run along the path outlined by stone markers at Kitty Hawk, where the Wright Brothers made the world's first powered airplane flights; or attend performances of the "Lost Colony," an outdoor drama that retells the tale of the first English settlers in America who disappeared. In other words, a mixture of Coney Island, culture, noise, and fun, all bordered by endless beaches on the ocean and sound sides of the islands.

Inland cities offer their own attractions, if more quietly. Some travelers come to Wilmington, a seaport town that has finally started to spruce up with new shops and entertainment at the Water Street Market. Smaller towns, such as Edenton on the tip of the Albemarle Sound, New Bern, and Tarboro, offer glimpses of life early in another century.

There are a number of bed-and-breakfast choices in this zone, ranging from one of the great romantic getaways at the White Doe Inn on Roanoke Island to a bed-and-breakfast in New Bern where a ghostly maid reportedly delivers fresh linen in the morning.

For More Information

Outer Banks Chamber of Commerce
(225) 441-8144

Cape Fear Coast Convention and Visitors Bureau
(910) 341-4030

CEDARS, Beaufort

Overall: ★★★★ Room Quality: B Value: C Price: $105–$165

A front stand of cedars gives this proud old inn its name. It has the look of the sea, which may be natural because the original portion was built in 1768 by the son of a New England shipwright. Cedars is perfectly situated right on the waterfront with a view of the many docked ships and within a short walk of a number of good seafood restaurants and shops. The rooms are attractive and comfortable, but we did notice one problem common to many older houses. In the room at the top of the stairs (on the left), there was a step going down into the bathroom from the bedroom—a potential hazard to a sleepy person hurriedly navigating the route at night. The host, Sam Dark, is an extremely friendly man and jack-of-all-trades. He works on painting and refurbishing an adjoining house long into the night, helps put out the breakfast in the morning, and gives advice about the North Carolina ferry service to the Outer Banks. Be sure to ask him—a missed ferry could cost you hours of time. He's helpful in other ways, too. When a guest's car wouldn't start, Sam immediately turned mechanic and trotted out with a battery starter.

Setting & Facilities

Location: Cross drawbridge into Beaufort on Hwy. 70, turn right on Orange St., and go 3 blocks to Front St.
Near: National Seashore, Cape Lookout Lighthouse, NC Maritime Museum
Building: 1768
Grounds: Landscaped yard w/ rose garden
Public Space: Den, large sun deck, porches
Food & Drink: Full Southern breakfast may include fruit, ham, sausage, French toast or pancakes, eggs, muffins
Recreation: Swimming, bird-watching, sailing, kayaking, deep-sea fishing
Amenities & Services: Full local information package in each room, arrangements for lunches, sight-seeing

Accommodations

Units: 11 guest rooms
All Rooms: Cable TV, antiques
Some Rooms: Water view, fireplace
Bed & Bath: Beds vary; private baths
Favorites: Bristol Room w/ king bed, large LR, & fireplace
Comfort & Decor: Pleasant antiques but not fussy

Rates, Reservations, & Restrictions

Deposit: 1st night
Discounts: Midweek corporate rates, long stays
Credit Cards: AE,V, MC
Check-in/Out: 3 p.m./11 a.m.
Smoking: Outside only
Pets: No
Kids: 10 & over
Minimum Stay: None
Open: All year; closed Thanksgiving & Christmas through New Year
Hosts: Sam & Linda Dark
305 Front St.
Beaufort, NC 28516
(252) 728-7036
Fax: (252) 728-1685

PECAN TREE INN, Beaufort

Overall: ★★★½ Room Quality: B Value: C Price: $75–$140

Two women were sitting on the porch, chatting with each other. "She's almost over her addiction." This sounded serious, but they were talking about a friend inside who was doing without Dan Rather and *Jeopardy* in this TV-free home. Guests can walk about a half block to the waterfront and a collection of restaurants and shops. (Prices of souvenirs seem high, geared to tourist landlubbers.) Or just walk through the bed-and-breakfast's attractive 5,500-square-foot herb and flower gardens. Your host, Joe, loves to talk about the historic Beaufort area. But he also sprinkles in some practical tips. "If you're taking the noon ferry to Hatteras, take along a picnic lunch. There's no food served at that boat, and it's a long ride."

Setting & Facilities

Location: Take Rt. 70 east to Beaufort, turn right on Turner St, go 3 blocks, turn left on Front St., then left on Queen St.
Near: North Carolina Maritime Museum, Fort Macon State Park, Rachel Carson National Estuarine Sanctuary, Cape Lookout National Seashore
Building: Victorian
Grounds: Grassy yard w/ trees & gardens
Public Space: 3 large porches, LR, DR, patio, gardens
Food & Drink: Extended cont'l breakfast w/ muffins, cakes, bread, juices, coffee
Recreation: Walking, biking, birding, swimming, surfing
Amenities & Services: Newspapers, local restaurant menus, reservations for dinner & harbor cruises, beach chairs & towels

Accomodations

Units: 7 guest rooms
All Rooms: Antiques
Some Rooms: View of grassy yards, Jacuzzi
Bed & Bath: Canopied, king, queen; private baths
Favorites: Bridal Suite w/ king four-poster canopied bed & 2-person whirlpool tub
Comfort & Decor: Antiques, paintings, and prints throughout

Rates, Reservations, & Restrictions

Deposit: 1 night; 10-day cancellation
Discounts: $10 single; stay 4, 5th day free
Credit Cards: AE, V, MC, D, personal checks
Check-in/Out: 2–8 p.m./11 a.m.
Smoking: No
Pets: No
Kids: 13 & older
Minimum Stay: None
Open: All year
Hosts: Joe & Susan Johnson
116 Queen St.
Beaufort, NC 28516
(252) 728-6733
pecantreeinn@coastalnet.com
www.pecantree.com

HARBORLIGHT GUEST HOUSE BED & BREAKFAST, Cape Carteret

Overall: ★★★ Room Quality: B Value: C Price: $140–$250

This bed-and-breakfast has terrific water views on all sides. But if you haven't visited lately, you should know there have been some major changes. In 1999 Hurricane Floyd wiped out all of the guest rooms on the first floor. Now the owners have moved these guest rooms to the second floor and turned everything into luxury suites, at a higher price. Fortunately, there are still some outstanding amenities as before, such as robes and slippers. Having the option of breakfast in your suite is pure pleasure. One thing Floyd couldn't change was those extraordinary water views from the windows, the deck, and all along the beach. Your hosts can help arrange a trip to one of the barrier islands for shelling and sunning on secluded beaches. The suites offer disabled access.

Setting & Facilities

Location: Hwy. 24 to Bayshore Dr., left on Edgewater Court, right on Live Oak Dr.
Near: Beach, deep-sea fishing charter boats, five major golf courses
Building: Seashore inn w/ New England feel
Grounds: 530-foot shoreline on Bogue Sound
Public Space: None
Food & Drink: Full breakfast: baked pineapple, rum runners French toast, spinach-mushroom quiche
Recreation: Shelling on beach, fishing, sailing, golfing
Amenities & Services: breakfast served en suite in luxury suites

ACCOMMODATIONS

Units: 7 luxury suites
All Rooms: Wonderful water views, white wicker or wrought iron furnishings, cable TV, coffeemaker, private entrance
Some Rooms: Fireplace, fridge
Bed & Bath: Private baths
Favorites: None
Comfort & Decor: The bright, cheerful environment is enhanced by comforting sounds of the sea.

RATES, RESERVATIONS, & RESTRICTIONS

Deposit: Credit card or 1 night; 48-hour cancellation
Discounts: None
Credit Cards: AE, MC, V
Check-in/Out: 3 p.m./11 a.m.
Smoking: Outdoors only
Pets: No
Kids: 16 or older
Minimum Stay: 2 night weekends
Open: All year
Hosts: Bobby & Anita Gill
332 Live Oak Dr.
Cape Carteret, NC 28584
(252) 393-6868 or (800) 624-VIEW
Fax: (252) 393-6868

ALBEMARLE HOUSE BED & BREAKFAST, Edenton

Overall: ★★★ Room Quality: C Value: B Price: $65–$80

Hosts and owners Reuel and Marijane are very personally involved with running this bed-and-breakfast. They will give guests a complete orientation about historic Edenton and recommend places worth seeing. They are artists, and their house is full of stenciling, paintings, and other collections. The bathrooms are modern although not very large. Sailing excursions can be arranged on request. Though this bed-and-breakfast does get some singles who usually travel together, we feel it is mostly a couples-oriented place.

SETTING & FACILITIES

Location: Business 17 to Edenton, 1 block to West Queen St.
Near: Albemarle Sound, Visitors Center
Building: 1900 house
Grounds: None
Public Space: Porch, LR
Food & Drink: Full breakfast; specialties: blueberry pancakes, raspberry-stuffed French toast, apple cinnamon omelets; evening snacks & beverages avail.; special diets accommodated
Recreation: Sight-seeing, golf, boating
Amenities & Services: Reduced rates at local country club w/ swimming, tennis, golf; bikes

ACCOMMODATIONS

Units: 1 2-room suite, 2 guest rooms
All Rooms: Cable TV, AC
Bed & Bath: 2 queens; private baths
Favorites: None
Comfort & Decor: Nautical theme

Rates, Reservations, & Restrictions

Deposit: 1st night
Discounts: Corp.
Credit Cards: V, MC; personal checks preferred
Check-in/Out: 3 p.m./11 a.m.
Smoking: No
Pets: No; kennel reservations made on request
Kids: 11 & older
Minimum Stay: None
Open: All year
Hosts: Reuel & Marijane Schappel
204 W. Queen St.
Edenton, NC 27932
(252) 482-8204
albemarlehouse@inteliport.com
www.bbonline.com/ne/albemarle

CAPTAIN'S QUARTERS INN, Edenton

Overall: ★★★★ Room Quality: B Value: B Price: $55–$95

If the Captain's Quarters were a boat, Bill Pepper would probably be sailing it every night on Albemarle Sound. In fact, from November through April, he offers special sail packages that include a two-night stay at the inn, welcoming hors d'oeuvres or beer, breakfast, walking tour, gourmet dinner with wine, and a three-hour sail on Albemarle Sound. Landlubbers can substitute 18 holes of golf with cart for the sailing part of this package. The cost is $289 per couple for the weekend (or about $145 a day—which makes it a pretty good bargain). Most of the rooms are large, and some have huge modern bathrooms. "A very nice experience," summed up one guest during our exit interview.

Setting & Facilities

Location: Downtown Edenton
Near: Albemarle Sound, Visitors Center
Building: 1907 Colonial Revival
Grounds: None
Public Space: Parlor
Food & Drink: Full 3-course breakfast w/ omelets, strawberry shortcake pancakes, raspberry-stuffed French toast
Recreation: Boating, sight-seeing
Amenities & Services: Ask about special weekends, including "Mystery Weekend" and "Golf and Snooze"

Accommodations

Units: 8 guest rooms
All Rooms: Large w/ ceiling fan, phone, cable TV, sitting area
Bed & Bath: Beds vary; private baths
Favorites: None
Comfort & Decor: Nautical theme throughout

Rates, Reservations, & Restrictions

Deposit: Credit card or check
Discounts: None
Credit Cards: V, MC
Check-in/Out: 4–10 p.m./11 a.m.
Smoking: No
Pets: No
Kids: 8 & older

Minimum Stay: 2 nights some holiday weekends
Open: All year
Hosts: Bill & Phillis Pepper
202 West Queen St.
Edenton, NC 27932
(919) 482-8945 or (800) 482-8945
www.bbchannel.com/bbc/p216930.asp

THEODOSIA'S BED & BREAKFAST INN, Harbour Village

Overall: ★★★½ Room Quality: B Value: D Price: $165–$250

Getting here can be a little complicated. There is a ferry from Southport. People flying into Wilmington or Myrtle Beach can arrange for transfers to the ferry by calling Southern Hospitality at (800) 406-4949. Donna and Garret Albertson have owned this bed-and-breakfast since 1999 and have extensively redecorated the rooms with collections of Delft and other china; a good thing, because the previous owners' tastes were a little too "eclectic." The biggest draws are the beautiful water views and hikes along the beach on a car-less island. Guests have the use of complimentary golf carts during their stay to drive around. Garret says that crime is virtually nonexistent and that nobody locks their doors. Even the dumbest crooks have learned it's tough to make a decent getaway in a golf cart.

SETTING & FACILITIES

Location: 45 mi. SE of Wilmington; reached by ferry
Near: Ocean beach, "Old Baldy" lighthouse, Turtle Conservancy
Building: 1994 Victorian
Grounds: Landscaped seaside setting
Public Space: 2 DRs, 3 sitting rooms, porches
Food & Drink: Full breakfast; specialties: croissant French toast, egg soufflé; dinner by advance reservation; complimentary snacks & beverages
Recreation: Beach activities, birding, canoeing, fishing, golf, tennis
Amenities & Services: Club membership w/ discount on golf, tennis, & dining privileges

Accommodations

Units: 13 guest rooms
All Rooms: Water view, TV w/ premium channels
Some Rooms: Antiques, VCR
Bed & Bath: Queen, king, or double; private baths
Favorites: "Beauty Berry" Room w/ Victorian king bed & dramatic water views
Comfort & Decor: Mixture of classic and antique furnishings

Rates, Reservations, & Restrictions

Deposit: Credit card, check, or cash; 7-day cancellation
Discounts: None
Credit Cards: MC, V, D
Check-in/Out: 3 p.m./11 a.m.
Smoking: No
Pets: No
Kids: Welcome
No-Nos: Serious about not smoking; $250 cleaning fee when guests smoke in room!
Minimum Stay: None
Open: All year
Hosts: Donna & Garret Albertson
P.O. Box 3130
Harbour Village
Bald Head Island, NC 28461
(336) 457-6563 or (800) 656-1812
Fax: (336) 457-6055
www.theodosias.com

SEASIDE INN, Hatteras Village

Overall: ★★ Room Quality: D Value: C Price: $85–$125

"Nothing fancy!" host and owner Sharon Kennedy tells guests. And she is being honest. This is the oldest hotel in Dare County, and it's starting to show its age. Some of the rooms and hallways are dark. But the rooms are clean and "family-friendly"; some rooms have adjoining sleeping areas for children of all ages. A comfortable place to come, sleep, and then head for the beach that is a short ten-minute stroll away—all at a reasonable price. Ask Sharon when she is going to serve her favorite breakfast dessert: peach crêpes with Godiva Chocolate Liqueur on the side.

Setting & Facilities

Location: Take ferry from south or Hwy. 12 from north
Near: Ocean, old shipwreck
Building: Casual seashore style
Grounds: Semiwooded, bare lawn; short hiking trail to beach from B&B in works
Public Space: Two wide porches, indoor reading/writing areas
Food & Drink: Full American breakfast; specialty is mixed eggs & potatoes dish, crêpes for dessert; no meat served
Recreation: Great long beach about a 10-minute hike away; kayaking, bicycling
Amenities & Services: Local newspaper, menus of nearby restaurants

Accommodations

Units: 10 guest rooms
All Rooms: A little dowdy but comfortable
Bed & Bath: King or queen
Favorites: Room #6 is nicest
Comfort & Decor: Original oils, nautical antiques, 1908 baby grand piano

Rates, Reservations, & Restrictions

Deposit: 50%; refund w/ 2 weeks' notice
Discounts: None
Credit Cards: MC, V, D
Check-in/Out: 3 p.m./noon
Smoking: Outdoors only
Pets: No
Kids: All ages welcome
Minimum Stay: None
Open: All year
Hosts: Sharon Kennedy & family
P.O. Box 688
Hatteras, NC 27943
(252) 986-2700
Fax: (252) 986-2923
seasideBB@aol.com
www.hometown.aol.com/seasidebb/website/seasidin.html

ROANOKE ISLAND INN, Manteo

Overall: ★★★★ Room Quality: B Value: B Price: $98–$148

Our favorite place to sit is in green rocking chairs on the second-story front porch looking out over Roanoke Sound toward Nag's Head. This inn is ideal for business travelers. It can also be quite romantic for couples who want to stroll the boardwalk across the street and watch the distant lights on the water or stop for a good dinner at Clara's Sea Food Grill or the Full Moon Cafe (a two-minute walk away). The serve-yourself breakfasts available in the lobby are a disappointment. Some frosted flakes, juices, coffee, and muffins so small you could use them as checkers. The nautical decor of much of this inn will probably appeal more to men, but for women there's always those moonlit boardwalks.

Setting & Facilities

Location: Hwy. 64 from west or Hwy. 158 to Outer Banks; follow "Roanoke Island Festival Park" signs to Manteo & inn
Near: Cape Hatteras National Seashore, Roanoke Island Festival Park, The Lost Colony
Building: Island vernacular
Grounds: Gardens & great view of harbor
Public Space: Lobby w/ magazines, newspapers (open 24 hours w/ guest's key)
Food & Drink: Cont'l breakfast; fridge w/ snacks & soda
Recreation: Biking on 6-mi. path, boat rentals
Amenities & Services: Bikes & safety helmets, maps

Accommodations

Units: 8 guest rooms
All Rooms: Water or garden view, outside entrance, TV, phone
Some Rooms: Hardwood floors, antiques
Bed & Bath: King, twins; private baths
Favorites: None
Comfort & Decor: Nautical and island decor with prints of Lost Colony. Each room has clean, crisp lines, unusual graphics, and sometimes unique handmade furnishings.

Rates, Reservations, & Restrictions

Deposit: None
Discounts: None
Credit Cards: AE, MC, V
Check-in/Out: 3 p.m./11 a.m.
Smoking: Yes
Pets: Sometimes
Kids: Yes, in family units, separate wing
Minimum Stay: 2 days on weekends
Open: Seasonal; "from spring until we're tired"
Host: Ada Hadley
305 Fernando St.
Manteo, NC 27954
(252) 473-5511 or (877) 473-5511
Fax: (252) 473-1019
www.roanokeislandinn.com

TRANQUIL HOUSE INN, Manteo

Overall: ★★★½ Room Quality: B Value: C Price: $89–$189

The location could not be better for people who want to experience the quieter pleasures offered by Roanoake Island, away from some of the commercialism and heavy traffic of Tt. 12, the jangling road spine of the Outer Banks. The rooms are uniformly bright and cheerful at the Tranquil House Inn. The water sounds at night can lull you to sleep. Or walk the boardwalk for some beautiful views of Roanoke Sound. Cross a footbridge to Ice Plant Island and you can board a re-creation of a gaudy but fun sixteenth-century sailing vessel, the *Elizabeth II*. Even though check-in time is 3 p.m., try to avoid the streets of Manteo between 3 and 3:30 p.m. School buses and other early traffic can create delays.

Setting & Facilities

Location: Waterfront in downtown Manteo
Near: Elizabethan Gardens, "The Lost Colony" Outdoor Drama, North Carolina Aquarium
Building: Typical nineteenth-century island inn w/ cypress woodwork
Grounds: On waterfront w/ long boardwalk
Public Space: Deck, restaurant
Food & Drink: Cont'l breakfast (bagels, croissants, fruit); 1587 Restaurant on premises
Recreation: Sight-seeing, fishing, sailing, kayaking
Amenities & Services: Evening wine reception w/ other guests

Accommodations

Units: 25 guest rooms
All Rooms: Hardwood floors, individually decorated, designer wallpaper, dried flower arrangements
Some Rooms: Oriental rugs
Bed & Bath: Four-poster, canopy, queen, king; private hand-tiled baths
Favorites: Room 23—corner room w/ view of Roanoke Sound, Room 32—extra large
Comfort & Decor: Interesting mix of canopied beds, Oriental rugs, and bright colors

Rates, Reservations, & Restrictions

Deposit: Credit card—1 night
Discounts: 10% AAA, AARP
Credit Cards: AE, V, MC, D
Check-in/Out: 3 p.m./11 a.m.
Smoking: Yes, in designated smoking rooms
Pets: No
Kids: Welcome
Minimum Stay: 2 nights on weekends
Open: All year (closed 3 days at Christmas)
Hosts: Don & Lauri Just
405 Queen Elizabeth Ave.
Manteo, NC 27954
(252) 473-1404 or (800) 458-7069
Fax: (252) 473-1526
Djust1587@aol.com
www.TranquilInn.com

WHITE DOE, Manteo

Overall: ★★★★★ Room Quality: A Value: B Price: $145–$225

At first sight, the White Doe Inn looks like a NASA tracking satellite with a huge telephone tower looming behind it. But the moment you step into this beautiful Victorian-style building, all the signals you receive are romantic. In fact, this is one of the most romantic bed-and-breakfasts we visited. We believe single travelers might feel a little forlorn here, but for couples celebrating a wedding, anniversary, or birthday, it's a white frame piece of heaven on earth. Imagine stepping into the Garden Bedchamber, starting the gas fireplace with a flick of a switch, putting on your choice of romantic CDs (neatly stacked next to the player), and later bathing in a two-person whirlpool lit by a stained glass window. Guests in this room can also have their dinner with wine delivered en suite, prepared to order by the bed-and-breakfast's own chef. The Victorian Oriental room in the attic is a deep red color with a two-way fireplace that opens into the bedroom and bathroom. For an extra charge of $35, the chef will prepare a picnic basket for two guests who'd like to dine on the beach or one of the nearby parks. This bed-and-breakfast is wonderful!

SETTING & FACILITIES

Location: In Manteo on Roanoke Island; take Sir Walter Raleigh St. off US 64/264, turn left on Uppowac St.
Near: Wright Brothers National Memorial, Roanoke Island Festival Park, "Lost Colony" Outdoor Drama, Cape Hatteras National Seashore (5-min. drive)
Building: 1898 Queen Victorian style
Grounds: None
Public Space: LR, DR, library, porch
Food & Drink: Full breakfast; specialties: French toast w/ cream cheese & melba sauce or berries, pancakes, crêpes; afternoon tea w/ desserts; evening sherry & cordials
Recreation: Sight-seeing, swimming, surfing, shelling; don't miss world-famous "Lost Colony" performance
Amenities & Services: Bicycles, disabled access (first floor)

ACCOMMODATIONS

Units: 8 guest rooms
All Rooms: Robes, phone, hair dryer, antique decor
Bed & Bath: Queens; private baths
Favorites: Garden Bedchamber w/ fireplace, garden views, en suite dinner service
Comfort & Decor: Wonderfully bright and cheerful with antique decor

RATES, RESERVATIONS, & RESTRICTIONS

Deposit: Credit card; 50% of total reservation
Discounts: None
Credit Cards: AE, V, MC
Check-in/Out: 3–6 p.m./11 a.m.
Smoking: No
Pets: No
Kids: 12 & older
Minimum Stay: 2 nights weekends, 3 nights holidays
Open: All year
Hosts: Bebe & Bob Woody
P.O. Box 1029
319 Sir Walter Raleigh St.
Manteo, NC 27954
(252) 473-9851 or (800) 473-6091
(call 8 a.m.–10 p.m. EST)
Fax: (252) 473-4708
whitedoe@interpath.com
www.whitedoeinn.com

FIRST COLONY INN, Nag's Head

Overall: ★★★★ Room Quality: B Value: C Price: $75–$240

This is an inn built for families. The insulated walls block out sounds between rooms and eliminate most road noises. Most rooms have front and back doors, and all are completely equipped with everything mom or dad would need to heat, cool, fix, and serve lunch or dinner. There are two beaches to choose from, on the Atlantic out back or on the Sound out front (but you have to cross a busy highway to get to this one). Bring the kids here. As one of the eleven hosts said, "We love all children. Even babies."

Setting & Facilities

Location: Mile Post 16 on Virginia Dare Trail
Near: Wright Brothers Memorial, Elizabethan Gardens, National Seashore, lighthouses, "Lost Colony" outdoor drama
Building: 2-story coastal vernacular
Grounds: 5 landscaped acres
Public Space: Library, verandas, sun deck, breakfast room
Food & Drink: Cont'l breakfast
Recreation: Swimming, hiking, sightseeing
Amenities & Services: Newspapers, menus from local restaurants, library with extensive history & field guide collections

Accommodations

Units: 26 guest rooms
All Rooms: Remote heat/air control, TV, phone, microwave, fridge, current magazines
Some Rooms: Large whirlpool, four-poster beds
Bed & Bath: Beds vary; private baths
Favorites: None
Comfort & Decor: All rooms are light and airy and decorated with everything from antique prints to eclectic and interesting furniture styles.

Rates, Reservations, & Restrictions

Deposit: Credit card, first 2 nights; 7-day cancellation
Discounts: Thur. free for guests staying Sun.–Thur.
Credit Cards: AE, MC, V, D
Check-in/Out: 3 p.m./11 a.m.
Smoking: Outdoors only
Pets: No
Kids: Welcome
Minimum Stay: 3 nights holidays; 2 nights weekends
Open: All year
Hosts: The Lawson family
6720 S. Virginia Dare Trail
Nags Head, NC 27959
(254) 441-2343 or (800) 368-9390
Fax: (252) 441-9234
innkeeper@firstcolonyinn.com
www.firstcolonyinn.com

AERIE, New Bern

Overall: ★★★ | Room Quality: C | Value: B | Price: $89–$99

One guest arrived complaining of a bad back. Donna Bennet offered a possible herbal remedy. She has been studying alternative medicine and its beneficial effects for many years and even gives classes on herbal medicines right in this bed-and-breakfast. Even if you do not fully subscribe to holistic healing, it is hard to knock her hot breakfasts, which can include Italian herbed egg with basil and oregano (freshly picked from her garden) and topped with Parmesan cheese and chives.

Setting & Facilities

Location: Follow signs for Rt. 70 or 17 to Tryon Palace; 1 block east of Palace
Near: Tryon Palace, New Bern Academy, Fireman's Museum, Civil War attractions
Building: 1882 Victorian w/ cross-gabled roof
Grounds: Herbal & flower gardens in back
Public Space: Parlor, library, upstairs porches
Food & Drink: Refreshments (tea, lemonade, wine, etc.); hot full breakfast w/ fruit (e.g., baked peaches, broiled grapefruit) & choice of hot entrees (Italian herbed eggs, French toast, Belgian waffles)
Recreation: Walking newly renovated paths in historic district, golfing
Amenities & Services: Newspapers, local restaurant menus

Accommodations

Units: 7 guest rooms
All Rooms: Color cable TV, phone
Some Rooms: Pencil post bed, antique settee w/ matching Victorian chair
Bed & Bath: Twin, queen, or king; private baths; 6 w/ tub shower, 1 w/ walk-in shower
Favorites: "Hidden Room" w/ private entrance, Belmont Room
Comfort & Decor: Antiques, period reproductions

Rates, Reservations, & Restrictions

Deposit: Credit card; 48-hour cancellation
Discounts: AAA, AARP, Mobil Travel members, 10%; corp. rates
Credit Cards: AE, V, MC, D
Check-in/Out: 3–9 p.m./11 a.m.
Smoking: No
Pets: No
Kids: Welcome ("if well behaved")
Minimum Stay: None
Open: All year
Hosts: Doug & Donna Bennetts
509 Pollock St.
New Bern, NC 28562
(252) 636-5553 or (800) 849-5553
Fax: (252) 514-2157
aeriebb@coastalnet.com
www.insiders.com/crystalcoast/wwwads/aerie/index.html

HARMONY HOUSE INN, New Bern

Overall: ★★★★	Room Quality: B	Value: B	Price: $70–$140

"A house divided against itself cannot stand." Well, that's certainly not true of the Harmony House Inn, which is standing quite nicely and is our favorite bed-and-breakfast in New Bern. In 1900 this house was literally sawed in half, with one-half moved nine feet away and a stairway and wall inserted. The original house has seen a lot of history, being occupied during the Civil War by Company K of the 45th Massachusetts regiment. Check out their Web site. Sign the "guestbook" on-line and you could win a free night at the inn.

Setting & Facilities

Location: Historic downtown New Bern
Near: Tryon Palace (former capitol of Colony of North Carolina), eighteenth- & nineteenth-century houses, Fireman's Museum, New Bern Historical Society (Attmore-Oliver House)
Building: 1850 Greek Revival
Grounds: None
Public Space: Parlor, DR, gift shop
Food & Drink: Full breakfast; specialties: orange French toast, stuffed pancakes, egg & bacon casserole; evening social hour in parlor w/ wine, soft drinks, juice; port & sherry at bedtime
Recreation: Sight-seeing, golf, sailing
Amenities & Services: Free local calls

Accommodations

Units: 8 guest rooms, 2 suites
All Rooms: AC, ceiling fan, historic memorabilia, cable TV
Bed & Bath: Queen canopy or four-posters; private baths, including whirlpool tub for 2
Favorites: Benjamin Ellis Suite w/ 2 fireplaces
Comfort & Decor: Spacious guest rooms are nicely decorated with soft colors and feature antiques and reproductions mixed with the host's handmade craft items.

Rates, Reservations, & Restrictions

Deposit: Credit card; 72-hour cancellation
Discounts: Corp., winter rates Jan. & Feb.
Credit Cards: AE, V, MC, D, DC
Check-in/Out: 3–9 p.m./11 a.m.
Smoking: No
Pets: No, but can arrange for kennel
Kids: Welcome
Minimum Stay: None
Open: All year
Hosts: Ed & Sookie Kirkpatrick
215 Pollock St.
New Bern, NC 28560
(252) 636-3810 or (800) 636-3113
harmony@cconect.net
www.harmonyhouseinn.com

NEW BERN HOUSE, New Bern

Overall: ★★ Room Quality: C Value: C Price: $68–$88

If guests should awaken about 6 a.m. to find a maid dressed in black bringing fresh towels, not to worry. It is probably a ghost. This maid has appeared to guests in Room #2, which seems to be a local hangout for a few spirits—including a white-gowned granny who likes to stare out the window. All of this makes for lively storytelling at the New Bern House, which stages "Mystery Weekends." Room #4 has also had some ghostly sightings. We just wish they had a ghost painter who would touch up the hallways, which are getting a little dingy, or a ghost carpenter to plane down the low bridge on the stairs where *guests* can go bump in the night. But the rooms are comfy, the rates are modest, and we'll take fresh towels any way we can get them.

Setting & Facilities

Location: Rt. 17 in downtown New Bern
Near: 1 block from Tryon Palace
Building: 1923 Brick Colonial Revial
Grounds: None
Public Space: Library, parlor
Food & Drink: Full breakfast; early coffee
Recreation: Golf, tennis
Amenities & Services: Newspapers, local restaurant menus, fresh flowers

Accommodations

Units: 7 guest rooms
All Rooms: Phone, clock radio
Bed & Bath: King, queen, or twin; private baths
Favorites: None
Comfort & Decor: Antiques and collectibles

Rates, Reservations, & Restrictions

Deposit: Credit card; 48-hour cancellation
Discounts: Off-season, other discounts; ask
Credit Cards: MC,V
Check-in/Out: 2–9 p.m./11 a.m.
Smoking: No
Pets: No
Kids: 13 & older
Minimum Stay: None
Open: All year
Hosts: Howard Bronson & Marcia Drum
709 Broad St.
New Bern, NC 28560
(252) 636-2250

BERKLEY MANOR, Ocracoke

Overall: ★★★★½ Room Quality: B Value: A Price: $90–$175

Imagine you have just checked into a handsome but laid-back Caribbean plantation house or a Key West home. That's the feeling you get at Berkley Manor. Everywhere you look are soft, pastel colors and redwood, cypress, and red cedar paneling. Our favorite spot is the fourth-floor observation lounge, with views of tiny Ocracoke. The original, apparently eccentric owner once rode his horse up these stairs. But the horse wouldn't go back down until a special ramp was built. Host Robert Attaway will tell you these and many other stories about the inn's origin. These hosts are strictly against smoking—no smoking even on the outside grounds! But if you'd like a tropical experience as close as North Carolina, you just found it. A beautiful place, and the best you'll find on the most southern of the Outer Bank islands. *Note:* In case of a hurricane alert, clear out of Ocracoke! The only way in or out of the island is by ferry, which can stop running before the storm actually arrives. And the ferry may not start up for days after a major storm because of debris in the harbor.

Setting & Facilities

Location: Accessible by ferry only (call (800) BY-FERRY)
Near: National Seashore, Ocracoke Lighthouse
Building: New England
Grounds: 3 wooded acres
Public Space: Twin lobby lounges, 4th-floor observation deck
Food & Drink: Full breakfast; specialties: stuffed French toast, crabcake biscuits
Recreation: 16 miles of beaches, deep-sea charter fishing, kayaking, bird-watching
Amenities & Services: Bicycles, morning newspaper, local menus

Accommodations

Units: 12 guest rooms
All Rooms: Individual climate control
Bed & Bath: Queen or king; private baths
Favorites: Antigua w/ 2-person whirlpool, king bed, private patio
Comfort & Decor: Caribbean plantation style with comfortable furniture and live plants everywhere

Rates, Reservations, & Restrictions

Deposit: Credit card; 2 nights
Discounts: $15 discount single occupancy
Credit Cards: AE, V, MC, D
Check-in/Out: 3–6 p.m./11 a.m.
Smoking: No
Pets: No
Kids: 15 & older
No-Nos: No smoking anywhere
Minimum Stay: None
Open: All year
Hosts: Robert & Amy Attaway
P.O. Box 220
Ocracoke, NC 27960
(800) 832-1223
berkley@beachlink.com
www.berkleymanor.com

CASTLE ON SILVER LAKE, Ocracoke

Overall: ★★½ | Room Quality: C | Value: C | Price: $89–$229

The Castle has the feeling of a gabled New England seaside inn transplanted to the Mid-Atlantic. The inside reminded us of the kind of large, sprawling barnlike structures where you went for ski parties as a kid, hung out in oversized sweatshirts, and talked portentously of Proust and Veblen in front of a roaring fire. Today guests can shoot a game of pool or head for the great 14-mile beach. There are some nice harbor views from the rooms, but watch your head for a "low bridge" when you go up the stairs in the Main House.

Setting & Facilities

Location: At the harbor, right off Hwy. 12
Near: Beautiful beach, fishing fleet
Building: Restored 1994, sprawling wooden structure
Grounds: None
Public Space: Large common area w/ big-screen TV, large decks

Food & Drink: Full breakfast w/ hot entree plus cereals, fruit, juices; afternoon snacks
Recreation: Walking, swimming, bird-watching, boat tours, kayaking
Amenities & Services: Swimming pool & spa, free loaner bikes

Accommodations

Units: 10 guest rooms in Castle, 8 in condos
All Rooms: Phone, fridge, antiques or reproductions
Bed & Bath: Beds vary; private baths
Favorites: None
Comfort & Decor: Rustic ambiance

Rates, Reservations, & Restrictions

Deposit: Credit card; 3-day cancellation
Discounts: None
Credit Cards: V, MC, D
Check-in/Out: 3–4 p.m./11 a.m.
Smoking: Outside only
Pets: No
Kids: 12 & older in main house; all ages welcome in condos
Minimum Stay: 2 days in main house; varies in condos
Open: All year
Hosts: Steve Wright, owner; Pat Van Landingham, innkeeper
P.O. Box 908
Ocracoke, NC 27960
(252) 928-3505 or (800) 471-8848
Fax: (252) 928-3501
Innkeeper@thecastlebb.com
www.thecastlebb.com

LITTLE WARREN BED AND BREAKFAST, Tarboro

Overall: ★★ Room Quality: D Value: C Price: $58–$65

We liked the pleasant, homelike feeling of this bed-and-breakfast, and Tom Miller certainly makes guests feel like family. There is a veritable museum of antique kitchen ware displayed on the walls and a clerk's desk from the turn of the century with Tom's grandfather's store journal. Its first entry was: "Sept. 16, 1901 F.L. Nicholas bought pair shoes, $1.10." However, we were seriously concerned about this bed-and-breakfast when Tarboro hit the national news several weeks running when much of the town was flooded by several hurricane-spawned floods in 1999. Tom advised us that the river fortunately never rose to his house, but some rooms did sustain water stains from the heavy rains. These should be repaired by the time you read this, and his friendly haven is already open for guests. One minor caveat: Though all rooms have private baths, the room at the top of the stairs has a bath downstairs, a little unhandy for sleepy guests in the night. We suggest asking for one of the other two rooms.

Setting & Facilities

Location: Off I-95 take Rocky Mount Exit 138 to 64 East to Tarboro exit; turn left at foot of ramp, right on Wilson, left on Saint Patrick St., then right on Park Ave.
Near: Town common (second oldest in nation after Boston)
Building: 1913 neo-colonial
Grounds: Small lawn
Public Space: LR, DR, den, porch
Food & Drink: Complimentary beverages on arrival (including cocktails); full English or Southern American breakfast
Recreation: Tennis, walking
Amenities & Services: Local restaurant menus, newspapers

Accommodations

Units: 3 guest rooms
All Rooms: Antiques, "early-wedding pieces"
Bed & Bath: Private baths
Favorites: None
Comfort & Decor: Homey with family heirlooms

Rates, Reservations, & Restrictions

Deposit: Credit card; 48-hour cancellation
Discounts: None
Credit Cards: AE, MC, V, D
Check-in/Out: 4–10 p.m./10 a.m.
Smoking: 1st floor, porch
Pets: No
Kids: 6 & older
No-Nos: No kitchen privileges
Minimum Stay: None
Open: All year
Hosts: Patsy & Tom Miller
304 E. Park Ave.
Tarboro, NC 27886
(252) 823-1314 or (800) 309-1314
www.bbonline.com/nc/littlewarren

CATHERINE'S INN, Wilmington

Overall: ★★★½ Room Quality: B Value: B Price: $80–$120

This is an attractively furnished home but could not be called elegant. It is a place where you can feel right at home, sit in one of the two parlors, watch TV, and read or listen to the stereo. Some of the "at home" feeling is fostered by an early morning coffee pot bubbling in the hallway right outside all the guests' doors. One guest comments: "The innkeeper, Catherine, is really dedicated to her guests." The bed-and-breakfast's location is ideal for visiting Wilmington's restaurants and shops or heading for the beach. Catherine advises getting an early start for the beach to avoid heavy surfboard-wielding traffic in the summer months. Wilmington has been hit several times with hurricanes in recent years. If you have made a reservation deposit when a hurricane evacuation order has been issued, you would not be charged. Catherine says that if it is only a "Hurricane Alert" and no storm hits, you could lose your one-night's deposit if you do not come. Frankly, Catherine, we'd stay at home if anybody mentions the "h" word.

SETTING & FACILITIES

Location: Exit right off Cape Fear Memorial Bridge through historic downtown Wilmington; go to Front Street North & turn left
Near: Downtown Wilmington, beaches (20 min.)
Building: 1883 Italianate clapboard house
Grounds: Large lawn, sunken garden, 300-foot riverfront (Cape Fear River)
Public Space: 2 parlors, long front & back porches
Food & Drink: Full breakfast; specialty: apple-stuffed French toast
Recreation: Golf, deep-sea fishing, beach
Amenities & Services: Maps, local restaurant menus, help w/ reservations

ACCOMMODATIONS

Units: 5 guest rooms
All Rooms: On 2nd floor, phone, robes, radio, sitting area
Bed & Bath: King & queen; private baths
Favorites: Queen Room in back w/ good view of Cape Fear River
Comfort & Decor: Homey, not too formal

RATES, RESERVATIONS, & RESTRICTIONS

Deposit: 1 night; credit card
Discounts: Corp.
Credit Cards: V, MC
Check-in/Out: 4–6 p.m./11 a.m.
Smoking: No
Pets: No; boarding facilities recommended
Kids: Welcome; under age 12 by prior arrangement
Minimum Stay: None
Open: All year
Hosts: Walter & Catherine Ackiss
410 S. Front St.
Wilmington, NC 28401
(910) 251-0863 or (800) 476-0723
www.catherinesinn.com

MISS BETTY'S BED & BREAKFAST, Wilson

Overall: ★★★½ Room Quality: C Value: A Price: $50–$80

The late Charles Kuralt, the laid-back sojourner on TV, used to say, "Never eat in a diner called 'Mom's'." We were tempted to say never stay in a bed-and-breakfast named "Miss Betty's" because of the cutesy name. But we would be totally wrong because this Miss Betty's turns out to be a great bargain; you get a lot for as little as $60. *National Geographic* called her street one of the 20 most beautiful in America. The inn is comprised of four separate homes; the fourth is made up of executive suites usually occupied by long-term business travelers. Nice touch: there's a bowl of Hershey kisses in every room. The inn has won awards and many kudos from the press, so Miss Betty can call her place whatever she likes.

Setting & Facilities

Location: Take Exit 121 off I-95, go east to US 264, turn left on College Drive, then right on Nash St.
Near: Antiques shops—Wilson is the "antiques capital of North Carolina"; 4 golf courses
Building: Victorian
Grounds: 1 landscaped acre
Public Space: 4 parlors
Food & Drink: Full breakfast
Recreation: Golf, tennis, antiques shopping
Amenities & Services: None

Accommodations

Units: 10 guest rooms, 4 executive suites in 4 historic homes
All Rooms: Cable TV, AC, private phone w/ data port, disabled access
Bed & Bath: Beds vary; private baths
Favorites: #10, the largest
Comfort & Decor: Filled with American Victorian furniture

Rates, Reservations, & Restrictions

Deposit: Credit card
Discounts: None
Credit Cards: AE, V, MC, & other major cards
Check-in/Out: 3 p.m./11 a.m.
Smoking: Outdoors only
Pets: No
Kids: No
Minimum Stay: None
Open: All year
Hosts: Betty & Fred Spitz
600 W. Nash St.
Wilson, NC 27893-3045
(252) 243-4447 or (800) 258-2058
Fax: (252) 243-4447

Zone 2
Central North Carolina

The central portion of the state is an unusual mixture of farmland and high-tech industry. The Research Triangle area, formed by Raleigh, Durham, and Chapel Hill, has attracted scientists and industry from all over the world. The region doesn't have the vacation enticements of the other two regional zones, but it does serve up surprises. Here are a few examples.

The museums of Raleigh are fabulous. These include the North Carolina Museum of Art, Museum of History, and State Museum of Natural Sciences—and they are all free. In Charlotte you can watch great sports teams play, including championship basketball games by men's and women's teams. At Morehead Planetarium in Chapel Hill you can study the stars, just as the original Apollo astronauts did years before.

A number of adventures are waiting in this central region's bed-and-breakfasts. In Raleigh you can talk politics with a husband and wife who were former top aides to a former North Carolina governor and his wife. At an Apex home you can get a gummy (toothless) handshake from an ostrich named Rhett. Or immortalize a great night of love by writing poetry on the wall of another bed-and-breakfast—don't worry, the poetic expressions are encouraged by the owner. In Winston-Salem you can stay in a home at Tanglewood Park and get lost in a maze constructed of corn.

For More Information

Greater Raleigh Convention and Visitors Bureau
(800) 849-8499

B&B'S COUNTRY GARDEN INN, Apex

Overall: ★★½ Room Quality: C Value: D Price: $90–$130

The writing is on the wall at this bed-and-breakfast. "Our long awaited romantic evening finally came true in the Blue Bonnet Room," wrote one couple, apparently between hugs and kisses. Rather than take away their markers, the host encourages guests to write their feelings on the wall in the Violet Suite. Many honeymooners and anniversary celebrants do just that, warm tributes to the power of love. There's even a Violet Suite option, with a separate sitting room and bed for children. On a less romantic note, the drive up to this country bed-and-breakfast is a little annoying as cars are pinged by the gravel roadway. But the B&B's Country Garden Inn is in a rewarding setting at the top of the hill, right next to a pond with swans. The "just family" atmosphere is pleasant, and if you feel like storing some wine in the family fridge or cooking some luncheon soup in the kitchen, well, go right ahead.

SETTING & FACILITIES

Location: Take Hwy. 64 west 1 mi. past exit Hwy 55 and turn right on Kelly Rd.
Near: Research Triangle Park, businesses & attractions of Raleigh & Durham, Alltel Pavilion at Walnut Creek
Building: 3-story white country frame
Grounds: Ponds & garden
Public Space: LR, kitchen, family room w/ TV
Food & Drink: Full breakfast; specialties: spatato (eggs scrambled w/ potatoes), fried bananas
Recreation: Hiking, sight-seeing nearby towns & cities, fishing in pond
Amenities & Services: Kitchen privileges, fishing gear

ACCOMMODATIONS

Units: 3 guest rooms
All Rooms: Standard furniture; pleasant but not memorable
Bed & Bath: Private baths
Favorites: None
Comfort & Decor: This homey place may remind you of your aunt's well-kept home

RATES, RESERVATIONS, & RESTRICTIONS

Deposit: Credit card
Discounts: 10% AAA, AARP
Credit Cards: AE, V, MC
Check-in/Out: 3 p.m./noon
Smoking: No
Pets: No
Kids: Welcome
Minimum Stay: None
Open: All year
Hosts: Beth & Bud McKinney
1041 Kelly Rd.
Apex, NC 27502
(919) 303-8003 or (800) 251-3171
Fax: (919) 851-3494
budnbeth@aol.com
www.b-and-bcountry-inn.com

BLUE HEAVEN OSTRICH RANCH AND B&B, Apex

Overall: ★★★★ Room Quality: B Value: B Price: $90–$110

"Be kind to ostriches and you'll have a friend for life. And they live up to 80 years." Advice from your host, Madeline, a transplanted New Yorker who raises ten breeding pairs of ostriches near this modern bed-and-breakfast. Rooms are comfortable and spacious and the beds are super-soft. But the unique benefit is the chance to meet Rhett Butler, Scarlet, and the other ostriches, who may gum your hand politely (they have no teeth). Then you can go fishing at the pond at the bottom of the hill. The suite with a complete kitchen and washer/dryer makes you a self-sufficient traveler. Here's a trivia question for your kids: What do you think Madeline does with ostrich feathers? She sells them to automobile manufacturers for use in the final car cleaning on the assembly line, because ostrich feathers are oil-less.

SETTING & FACILITIES

Location: Off Rt. 55 at Apex; near Hwy 64/55 intersection
Near: 15 minutes to downtown Raleigh, convention center
Building: 1-story contemporary
Grounds: 16 acres w/ gardens, trees, & 3-acre pond
Public Space: Great room, sunroom, DR, large deck
Food & Drink: Full breakfast changes daily; served w/ sterling silver & antique glassware
Recreation: Pond fishing from dock or boat; unique tour of ostrich farm
Amenities & Services: Menus & guides for local Raleigh restaurants

ACCOMMODATIONS

Units: 2 guest rooms
All Rooms: Pond view
Some Rooms: 1 suite has full kitchen & washer/dryer
Bed & Bath: Feather beds; private baths
Favorites: Both rooms equally nice
Comfort & Decor: Comfortable furniture, fireplace, and large-screen TV in great room; contemporary interior

RATES, RESERVATIONS, & RESTRICTIONS

Deposit: 1st night
Discounts: $80 midweek
Credit Cards: None
Check-in/Out: 3 p.m./noon
Smoking: Only on smoking porch
Pets: No
Kids: No accommodations unless they sleep in guest's bed; $7 extra for breakfast
No-Nos: Don't visit ostriches without host
Minimum Stay: None
Open: All year
Host: Madeline Calder
2613 Olive Chapel Rd.
Apex, NC 27503
(919) 362-9773
Fax: (919) 362-9773

PEARSON PLACE BED & BREAKFAST, Apex

Overall: ★★ Room Quality: D Value: B Price: $65–$85

Apex is hard to find. It is not listed on many maps or even in the AAA TourBook. But it can be a convenient choice if you have business in and around Raleigh, Durham, and the University of North Carolina at Chapel Hill. The Pearson House is not the most glamorous of the bed-and-breakfasts we reviewed in the area. We would not recommend it for a romantic weekend, perhaps because it is almost too much like home. But there is a comfortable feeling about the place, and Jeanne Floyd is the soul of accommodation. Not feeling well? How about breakfast in bed? Need computer, fax, or e-mail facilities for your business? They're available. The rates are reasonable, even more so if you are a senior traveler. Always remember to ask for this discount. Jeanne would be too polite to ask if you were a senior.

Setting & Facilities

Location: Exit Davis Dr. (from I-40) & go south 13 mi. (name changes to N. Salem St.)
Near: Raleigh, Durham, Chapel Hill, Research Triangle Park, NC State Fairgrounds
Building: 1920 English Cottage
Grounds: 2 acres w/ goldfish pond
Public Space: Sitting room w/ TV & VCR, LR w/ piano & fireplace
Food & Drink: Full breakfast; cookies & tea on arrival
Recreation: Sight-seeing, visiting nearby cities, walking, boating in nearby public lake
Amenities & Services: Newspapers, local restaurant menus; computer, fax, copier, Internet, & e-mail services

Accommodations

Units: 2 guest rooms
All Rooms: Hardwood floors, phone, cable TV, antiques
Bed & Bath: Private baths
Favorites: Blue Room w/ antique Victorian bed & fireplace
Comfort & Decor: Late Victorian style with period antiques, pictures, and four working fireplaces

Rates, Reservations, & Restrictions

Deposit: Credit card
Discounts: Seniors, gov't., weekly
Credit Cards: AE, MC, V, D
Check-in/Out: 3 p.m./11 a.m.
Smoking: No
Pets: Small pets; $25 fee per stay
Kids: Welcome
Minimum Stay: None
Open: All year; closed Christmas Day & sometimes Fourth of July; ask
Host: Jeanne Floyd
1009 North Salem St.
Apex, NC 27502
(919) 362-4290 or (800) 810-8585
Fax: (919) 362-4293
pearsonpl@ipass.net

MOREHEAD INN, Charlotte

Overall: ★★★★ Room Quality: B Value: B Price: $120–$190

In 1907 Charles Coddington was the first man to putt-putt in an automobile across the Mason Dixon line. His second unusual distinction was to build a 14,000-square-foot house "for entertainment." The architect complied, but in the process created a home that was so stylish it later became the headquarters for the local chapter of the American Society of Interior Designers. Since 1984 it has become a well-regarded country inn and site of many weddings and corporate functions. That may be a small problem for individual travelers who could feel a little lost in the crowd during all these special doings. But the inn itself really is charming. The best rooms are the suites (the extra-large Hawthorne, Solarium, and Mt. Vernon suites). You're in the historic Dilworth neighborhood, which is ideal for strolling and jogging. Generally speaking, the northern and southern areas of Charlotte are the most free of crime. Do not even think of smoking in a room. Historic landmark homes are not allowed to install sprinklers. Though these properties take every other possible precaution to prevent fires, it is essential in older buildings that all guests cooperate fully with nonsmoking rules.

SETTING & FACILITIES

Location: On Morehead St. between South & Kenilworth Aves.
Near: Discovery Place, Fourth Ward ("Old City"), Uptown Charlotte, Mint Museum of Art, Wing Haven Garden, Ericsson Stadium (home of the NFL Panthers) 1 mi. away
Building: 1912 mansion
Grounds: Less than an acre of landscaped area
Public Space: Tea room, great room, library, reading parlor
Food & Drink: Cont'l breakfast
Recreation: Sight-seeing, shopping
Amenities & Services: Bikes, complimentary shoe shine

ACCOMMODATIONS

Units: 12 guest rooms
All Rooms: Period antiques
Some Rooms: Fireplace, private balcony
Bed & Bath: Queen or king, including four-poster rice and sleigh beds; private baths
Favorites: Solarium w/ private entrance
Comfort & Decor: Extraordinary antiques

RATES, RESERVATIONS, & RESTRICTIONS

Deposit: Credit card; 48-hour cancellation
Discounts: 10% AAA, AARP, corp. (Sun.–Thur.), frequent guest
Credit Cards: All major credit cards
Check-in/Out: 3 p.m./noon

Deposit: Credit card; 48-hour cancellation
Discounts: 10% AAA, AARP, corp. (Sun.–Thur.), frequent guest
Credit Cards: All major credit cards
Check-in/Out: 3 p.m./noon
Smoking: No; 3 rooms have balcony or garden area for smoking
Pets: No
Kids: Welcome
Minimum Stay: None
Open: All year
Host: Billy Maddalon
1122 E. Morehead St.
Charlotte, NC 28204
(704) 376-3357 or (888) MOREHEAD
Fax: (704) 335-1110
morehead@charlotte.infi.net
www.moreheadinn.com

MANOR HOUSE BED & BREAKFAST, Clemmons

Overall: ★★★½ Room Quality: B Value: C Price: $66–$107

The Manor House is part of a large park, Tanglewood. The history of this park dates back to the days of Queen Elizabeth I. In 1584 Sir Walter Raleigh claimed this land for her. Other historic moments came when a fort was built here to help protect the settlers during the French and Indian War. In 1859 the Manor House was built, and much later (1921) sold to William Reynolds, brother of R.J. Reynolds, who made a fortune with tobacco. Today the entire Reynolds estate has become a large public recreational park offering the manor as a bed-and-breakfast with several other facilities available for overnight stays (a lodge and cabins). We are going on and on about history because we were probably not as impressed by the Manor House as Mr. Reynolds would have liked. The rooms are large and understated. Nice but not extraordinary. They don't have the cozy atmosphere of many other North Carolina bed-and-breakfasts we inspected, such as Lady Anne's in Winston-Salem (see review). We definitely did not like the fact that smoking is permitted in all the rooms. In this era when so many people have stopped smoking and don't like the smell of smoke that sometimes lingers in rooms, we believe it is a mistake for any bed-and-breakfast this large not to have at least some nonsmoking rooms. The outside is beginning to show its age, especially the rusty roof. The surrounding park, however, is magnificent, offering virtually every activity a visitor could want, even including a unique maze constructed of corn.

SETTING & FACILITIES

Location: 9 mi. SW of Winston-Salem on Yadkin River
Near: Greensboro & Charlotte, Reynolda House, Old Salem
Building: 1859 Colonial
Grounds: 1,200 acres of rolling hills w/ a rose garden, arboretum, & fragrance garden
Public Space: Gardens

Food & Drink: Full breakfast w/ blueberry muffins, Danish, fresh fruit, "Chef Georgia's famous French toast"
Recreation: Trail rides, swimming, paddleboats, fishing, golf, tennis
Amenities & Services: Newspapers, list of local restaurants

Accommodations

Units: 5 guest rooms, 5 suites
All Rooms: Park view, decorative fireplace
Bed & Bath: Beds vary; private baths
Favorites: None
Comfort & Decor: Numerous art prints and antiques throughout house

Rates, Reservations, & Restrictions

Deposit: Credit card; 72-hour cancellation
Discounts: 10% for age 60 & older
Credit Cards: AE, V, MC
Check-in/Out: 2 p.m./noon
Smoking: In all rooms
Pets: No
Kids: Welcome
Minimum Stay: None
Open: All year
Host: Linda Pask
4061 Clemmons Rd.
Clemmons, NC 27012
(336) 778-6370
Fax: (336) 778-6379

ARROWHEAD INN, Durham

Overall: ★★★★ Room Quality: B Value: C Price: $98–$215

Located in the suburbs of Durham, this inn offers a surprisingly large area to roam. Guests can discover a butterfly garden, a pear tree that attracts a couple of deer, and a two-foot-tall resident woodchuck. The house was built about 1775—"just a bit older than the U.S."—proclaims the inn's brochure. On the grounds is a touching reminder of the early days—the tombstone of the wife of the original owner. The owners sleep in a separate building, so guests have a great sense of privacy in the well-appointed, beautifully decorated rooms.

Setting & Facilities

Location: In Durham, take Duke St. to Mason Rd.
Near: Duke University, University of North Carolina (Chapel Hill), Research Triangle Park, NC Museum of Life & Science
Building: 1775 Plantation-style manor & carriage house
Grounds: 4 acres w/ 150-year-old magnolia trees
Public Space: "Keeping Room" (large room where breakfast is served), parlor
Food & Drink: Full breakfast w/ baked grapefruit, scones, apple bread, oat pancakes, bacon; refreshments on arrival; special dietary requests honored
Recreation: Sight-seeing
Amenities & Services: Guest fridge, health club guest passes, video library, fax & photocopy machines avail.

Accommodations

Units: 6 guest rooms in manor house, 3 in out buildings
All Rooms: AC, phone
Some Rooms: TV, VCR, robes, data port, fireplace
Bed & Bath: King, queen, & one unusual "king twin"; private baths
Favorites: Carolina Log Cabin w/ king bed in loft overlooking wood-burning fireplace & dbl. whirlpool tub
Comfort & Decor: Each room is individually decorated with very tasteful colors. However, sometimes decor outweighs practical considerations. The Duke Suite, impeccable in eighteenth-century finery, has one tiny closet accessible only by moving a chair.

Rates, Reservations, & Restrictions

Deposit: Credit card; 1 night; 72-hour cancellation
Discounts: Single, corp., ext. stays
Credit Cards: AE, V, MC, & other major cards
Check-in/Out: 3–9 p.m./11 a.m.
Smoking: No
Pets: No, but can help board nearby
Kids: Welcome
Minimum Stay: None
Open: All year
Hosts: Phil & Gloria Teber
106 Mason Rd.
Durham, NC 27712
(919) 477-8430 or (800) 528-2207
Fax: (919) 471-9538
info@arrowheadinn.com
www.arrowheadinn.com

INNISFREE VICTORIAN & GARDEN HOUSE, Glenville

Overall: ★★★★★ Room Quality: A Value: B Price: $109–$235

"I will arise and go now, and go to Innisfree," wrote William Butler Yeats in his poem, "The Lake Isle of Innisfree"—a sentiment widely followed by hundreds of travelers who have made their way to this sprawling Victorian resort. One of the extraordinary rooms is the formal octagonal dining room with a 25-foot ceiling where guests in the main house gather. Breakfast is brought to all the guests in the Garden House suites where they dine in their own breakfast nooks. Bathing is almost an art form with 110-gallon garden tubs that guests can sink into up to their necks while looking out over the mountains and gardens. One guest complained, while walking through all the antiques and lace-canopied beds, "Too frilly! Too much!" But others have been enchanted. We fall in the latter category and will follow Yeats's poetic advice and "go to Innisfree." Tip: Also go to nearby Cashiers for some unique experiences, where toy bears climb trees, a pianist plays Gershwin amid the groceries (Market Basket), and the nearby waterfalls almost outnumber the population.

Setting & Facilities

Location: Hwy. 107 North; across a small road from Lake Glenville
Near: Cashiers, numerous waterfalls, antiques shops
Building: Victorian w/ long porches, 6 cottages
Grounds: 16 acres overlooking lake w/ private beach
Public Space: Parlor, porches, observatory
Food & Drink: Full breakfast served on fine china
Recreation: Golf, horseback riding, swimming, hiking, tennis
Amenities & Services: None

Accommodations

Units: 3 guest rooms & 2 suites in main house, 5 suites in Garden House, 6 housekeeping cottages (ideal for families)
All Rooms: Antiques
Some Rooms: Fireplace, garden & mountain views, garden tub for 2, satellite TV, wet bar, breakfast nook
Bed & Bath: Queens, four-poster; private baths; some w/ whirlpool or shower w/ built-in seat
Favorites: Barrett Suite is very romantic w/ French lace canopy bed, garden tub for 2, private veranda
Comfort & Decor: Elegant antiques everywhere

Rates, Reservations, & Restrictions

Deposit: Credit card; 14-day cancellation
Discounts: For people celebrating a birthday, anniversary, or honeymoon
Credit Cards: AE, V, MC, D
Check-in/Out: 2:30–3:30 p.m./11 a.m.
Smoking: No
Pets: No
Kids: Not in main house or Garden House but welcome in cottages
No-Nos: Pipe & cigarette smoking permitted outside, but no cigars anywhere
Minimum Stay: 2 nights weekends, 3 nights special holidays
Open: All year
Host: Teri Federico
P.O. Box 469
Glenville, NC 28736
(828) 743-2946
www.innisfreeinn.com

GREENWOOD BED & BREAKFAST, Greensboro

Overall: ★★★½ Room Quality: B Value: C Price: $95–$175

What happens when a former New Orleans chef marries a custom decorator? The result could be a handsome bed-and-breakfast just like Greenwood. Bob was the chef, and takes special pride in his breakfasts, so much so that guests are even encouraged to invite others to breakfast! If you call about 15 minutes before arrival, the hosts will light candles in your room for a romantic arrival. And talk about personal service—your hosts may play board or card games with guests, particularly bridge. And Bob has been known to join guests in a round of golf on one of the 12 great golf courses within a short drive (no pun intended).

SETTING & FACILITIES

Location: Exit 125 off I-85 to Market St., then right on Elm to Park Dr.
Near: Oldest minor league baseball park in U.S., championship public golf courses, Rev. War battlefield, furniture market
Building: 1905 Chalet style
Grounds: None
Public Space: 3 parlors, game room, TV lounge, decks, porches
Food & Drink: Full breakfast; specialties: shrimp Creole & crawfish omelets, crêpes suzettes
Recreation: Golf, tennis, horseback riding, swimming
Amenities & Services: Restaurant & golf tee time reservations

ACCOMMODATIONS

Units: 5 guest rooms
All Rooms: Individually decorated, park view, current magazines
Some Rooms: Ceiling fan, window seat
Bed & Bath: King, queen, or twins; full private baths
Favorites: Blue Bell w/ fireplace, brass bed
Comfort & Decor: Original paintings and antiques

Rates, Reservations, & Restrictions

Deposit: Credit card, check, or cash
Discounts: None
Credit Cards: AE, V, MC
Check-in/Out: 4 p.m./11 a.m.
Smoking: No
Pets: No
Kids: 16 & older
Minimum Stay: None
Open: All year
Hosts: Bob & Dolly Guertin
205 N. Park Dr.
Greensboro, NC 27401
(336) 274-6350 or (877) 374-7067
Fax: (336) 274-9943
bob&dolly@greenwoodbb.com
www.greenwoodbb.com

HILLSBOROUGH HOUSE INN, Hillsborough

Overall: ★★★½ Room Quality: B Value: B Price: $95–$200

Although the Hillsborough House Inn is just about in the center of town, it still has a country feel to it. Probably because it sits on a whole country block of seven acres with very extensive gardens. Strolling through the garden takes you to a world of hidden nooks, including loveseats, a hammock built for two, and a gazebo. The only minor annoyance in the main building is in Joe's Room, where the toilet flushes itself occasionally. But why quibble about a setting so romantic and a house that is a veritable art gallery?

Setting & Facilities

Location: Take I-40 Exit 261 to Historic District signs & turn right on East Tryon
Near: Italianate circa 1790 w/ original brick kitchen outbuilding
Building: University of North Carolina at Chapel Hill, Duke University, Research Triangle Park, High Point Furniture Market
Grounds: Yard, garden, ponds, woods w/ trails
Public Space: Front porch, library, morning room, art gallery, DR
Food & Drink: Hot cont'l breakfast; specialties: fruit waffles, egg soufflés; early coffee
Recreation: Antiques shopping, university events, hiking nature trails
Amenities & Services: Newspapers, local restaurant menus w/ reservation service, free maps

Accommodations

Units: 5 guest rooms, suite in separate building
All Rooms: Flowers, ceiling fan, electric blanket, clock radio
Some Rooms: Porch, private kitchenette w/ wet bar, fireplace
Bed & Bath: King or queen; private baths
Favorites: None
Comfort & Decor: Early Victorian decor with mix of antiques and contemporary art; hand-painted bathroom floors. Separate kitchen house suite features three fireplaces and a handmade queen bed in a bower of white branches.

Rates, Reservations, & Restrictions

Deposit: 1 night; 7-day cancellation refund minus $15 fee
Discounts: 4- & 7-day stays
Credit Cards: AE, V, MC
Check-in/Out: 3–6 p.m./11 a.m.
Smoking: No
Pets: No; local boarding avail.
Kids: 10 & older
Minimum Stay: None
Open: All year
Hosts: Lauri & Kirk Michel
209 E. Tryon St.
Hillsborough, NC 27278
(919) 644-1600 or (800) 616-1600
Fax: (919) 644-1308
inn.keeper@rtmx.net
hillsboroughinn.citysearch.com

PILOT KNOB, Pilot Mountain

Overall: ★★★½ Room Quality: B Value: B Price: $115–$135

Many people think of log cabins as aging, spidery relics of eras gone by. But then they probably haven't seen the log cabins at Pilot Knob, which are rustic elegance at its best. The individual cabins afford maximum privacy to families or lovers, with a private parking area by each. "Clean, quiet, and away from everything," said one guest who had just stayed there. And it's convenient. The Blue Ridge Parkway is your highway back to some spectacular nature scenes. You can drive to Doughton State Park, Yadkin Island State Park, and Hanging Rock State Park. Note to fishing enthusiasts: bring your poles. There's a good fishing lake (bass and sunfish) at this bed-and-breakfast, and no fishing license is required on private property.

Setting & Facilities

Location: From Hwy. 52 take a left to Pilot Mt. State Park exit; go right on New Pilot Knob Ln.
Near: Blue Ridge Parkway, Home Creek Historic Farm, Reynolda House (R.J. Reynolds Estate)
Building: Log cabins
Grounds: 50 mountain acres w/ thick forests & a 6-acre lake
Public Space: Large barn now DR, library
Food & Drink: Full breakfast w/ waffles, sausages, coffee cake
Recreation: Hiking, swimming, birdwatching, golf, fishing, hot-air ballooning
Amenities & Services: Heated swimming pool, sauna

Accommodations

Units: 6 cabins
All Rooms: AC, TV, stone fireplace, LR & bath downstairs, BR upstairs, phone, radio, clock, fridge
Some Rooms: Porch
Bed & Bath: Whirlpool tubs for 2
Favorites: None
Comfort & Decor: Rustic elegance

Rates, Reservations, & Restrictions

Deposit: Credit card; 1 night
Discounts: 1 night full rate, succeeding nights 10% off
Credit Cards: MC, V
Check-in/Out: 3 p.m./11 a.m.
Smoking: Yes in cabins; no in DR
Pets: No
Kids: No
Minimum Stay: None
Open: All year
Host: Jim Rouse
P.O. Box 1280
Pilot Mountain, NC 27041
(336) 325-2502
jrouse850@aol.com

OAKWOOD INN BED & BREAKFAST, Raleigh

Overall: ★★★	Room Quality: C	Value: B	Price: $85–$135

Oakwood Inn is like an attractive Victorian lady who can't really decide whether she wants to go into business or become a woman of leisure. Many of the amenities are terrific for business travelers—phones with private lines and data ports for laptop computers in every room, with fax and copy machines available. In the morning they can walk to major downtown business and government offices. But there are also many romantic and friendly touches for leisure travelers—fireplaces that click on with a wall switch, soft Victorian couches, and a chance to mingle with fellow travelers. Who says you can't mix business with pleasure? Tip: Your business card will get you a 10 percent corporate discount.

Setting & Facilities

Location: In downtown Raleigh, historic Oakwood District
Near: State Capitol, Governor's Museums, major museums & galleries
Building: 2-story 1871 Victorian
Grounds: Victorian rose garden with manicured landscape
Public Space: Garden, veranda w/ swings, parlor, DR
Food & Drink: Homemade breakfasts; entree sample: cinnamon swirl French toast stuffed w/ light cream cheese & served w/ hot maple syrup; afternoon refreshments
Recreation: Walking tour of historic Oakwood District (map provided), City Market with funky, fun restaurants & shops, free history & science museums
Amenities & Services: Morning paper delivered to guests' doors, menus of local restaurants; can often make reservations (even on crowded nights) at popular restaurants such as Moe's Diner

ACCOMMODATIONS

Units: 6 guest rooms
All Rooms: Period antiques, remote-operated fireplaces, private phone
Some Rooms: Private veranda w/ swing
Bed & Bath: Beds vary; full private baths
Favorites: Polk Room—most secluded w/ private veranda, antique claw-foot tub, very romantic
Comfort & Decor: Period Victorian furnishings

RATES, RESERVATIONS, & RESTRICTIONS

Deposit: Credit card
Discounts: Corp., AAA, AARP (10%)
Credit Cards: All major credit cards
Check-in/Out: 3–6 p.m./11:30 a.m.
Smoking: Outdoors only
Pets: No
Kids: Welcome
Minimum Stay: None
Open: All year
Hosts: Bill & Charlene Smith alternate w/ Christian & Diane Collinet
411 N. Bloodworth St.
Raleigh, NC 27604
(919) 832-9712 or (800) 267-9712
Fax: (919) 836-9263
oakwoodBB@aol.com
members.aol.com/oakwoodbb/

WILLIAM THOMAS HOUSE, Raleigh

Overall: ★★★★½ Room Quality: A Value: B Price: $103–$140

At first glance the William Thomas House looks like another one of those aging downtown Victorian bed-and-breakfasts where the furniture and hosts are covered with a layer of dust—reason to step on the accelerator. But what a mistake that would have been in this case. Just inside the wide door of this bed-and-breakfast is an oasis of culture, fascinating conversations with hosts who seem to have met everyone in the political arena, and beautifully decorated rooms that are also amazingly comfortable. Host Sarah proclaims, "I've been a Republican since I was 12 years old." And true to her party, she served as executive assistant to the former North Carolina governor's wife. Her husband, Jim, was chief of staff for the same governor. The hallways are lined with political figures and celebrities who have come calling, including Ronald Reagan, Barbara Bush, and Steven Spielberg. Everything in the guest rooms seems designed to help you relax, from the snacks and soft drinks in the refrigerator to the VCR that lets you play favorite movies borrowed from a large collection in the library. You will talk about politics and many other subjects with the hosts, who are genuinely interested in each of their guests. This is an ideal downtown location for business travelers doing business with the state and a romantic getaway for couples who want to museum hop and dine or shop in the City Market area. Raleigh has wonderful museums and restaurants in the downtown area. One warning: Although this neighborhood is generally safe, some locals have advised us against walking several blocks north at night. So be careful as you would in any downtown area of any major city and enjoy this splendid place. The William Thomas House has our vote.

Setting & Facilities

Location: Between Peace College on Peace St. & Governor's Mansion on North Blount St.
Near: Governor's Mansion, State Capitol, History Museum, Natural Science Museum, Mordecai Historic Park
Building: Victorian
Grounds: Deck & porches, perennial garden
Public Space: Parlor, library, 2 porches, DR
Food & Drink: Full breakfast; specialties: baked bananas, Belgian waffles, cheese grits; early coffee
Recreation: Walking tours of nearby museums & state buildings
Amenities & Services: Local restaurant menus, cable TV & VCR w/ videos in library, newspapers

Accommodations

Units: 4 guest rooms
All Rooms: High ceilings, Oriental rugs
Bed & Bath: Beds vary; private baths
Favorites: The Clarinda—the largest
Comfort & Decor: Family antiques, an 1863 Steinway grand piano, and comfortable seating

Rates, Reservations, & Restrictions

Deposit: Credit card
Discounts: Sun.–Thurs.: AAA, seniors, corp., military
Credit Cards: AE, V, MC, CB, D
Check-in/Out: 3 p.m./11 a.m.
Smoking: No
Pets: No
Kids: Welcome
Minimum Stay: None
Open: All year
Hosts: Sarah & Jim Lofton
530 N. Blount St.
Raleigh, NC 27604
(919) 755-9400 or (800) 653-3466
Fax: (919) 755-3966
lofton@williamthomashouse.com
www.williamthomashouse.com

AUGUSTUS T. ZEVELY INN, Winston-Salem

Overall: ★★★★ Room Quality: B Value: A Price: $80–$205

This inn has a great location right in the heart of Old Salem. Walk to historic sites. We believe it's an outstanding bargain for all the services provided at the modest price. Be sure to arrive in time for the wine and cheese reception in late afternoon, and don't forget to check the buffet in the entry hall for yummy chocolate chip cookies at bedtime.

Setting & Facilities

Location: I-40 & Rt. 52 to Winston-Salem & Old Salem
Near: Museum of Early Southern Decorative Arts, Wake Forest University, Historic Village of Reynolds
Building: 1844 brick residence
Grounds: Largest elm tree in Old Salem

Public Space: Library/parlor, DR, breakfast room, porch
Food & Drink: Cont'l plus on weekdays; full breakfast on weekends w/ apple-stuffed French toast, eggs Benedict, hash browns; complimentary evening wine & cheese; free sodas & coffee during day
Recreation: Horse-drawn tours of Old Salem, walking trails, tennis
Amenities & Services: Free local calls, local restaurant guides, disabled access

Accommodations

Units: 12 guest rooms
All Rooms: Views of Old Salem, phone w/ data port, cable TV, writing desk, clock radio
Some Rooms: Steam bath, whirlpool tub, fireplace, microwave, fridge, separate entrance
Bed & Bath: Beds vary; private baths
Favorites: Room 1 w/ original summer cooking fireplace & tile floor reconstructed from original brick pattern
Comfort & Decor: Museum-quality reproductions of furniture

Rates, Reservations, & Restrictions

Deposit: 1st night; 48-hour cancellation
Discounts: AAA 10%, corp. 10% (w/ prior arrangement)
Credit Cards: AE, V, MC
Check-in/Out: 3 p.m./noon
Smoking: 2 smoking guest rooms, not in public rooms
Pets: Small, ground-floor rooms
Kids: Welcome ("if well behaved")
Minimum Stay: None
Open: All year
Host: Lori Long
803 S. Main St.
Winston-Salem, NC 27101
(336) 748-9299 or (800) 928-9299
Fax: (336) 721-2211
ctheall@dddcompany.com
www.winston-salem-inn.com

BROOKSTOWN INN, Winston-Salem

Overall: ★★★★ Room Quality: B Value: C Price: $100–$175

The Brookstown Inn is larger than most of the other bed-and-breakfasts in this book. But how could we not include a bed-and-breakfast that has won so many awards and offers travelers so many visual and visceral treats? The Brookstown building began as the Salem Cotton Manufacturing Company in 1835, and although it has been completely refurbished and modernized, you will still find many decorative trappings of its early days in its exposed beams and old brick interiors. During the week the inn is a favorite of business travelers, who use the conference facilities, exercise equipment, and in-room modem ports. That's why you may find some of the best rates and discounts on weekends when rooms become available. And how can you not love an inn that greets you with wine and cheese on arrival, cookies and milk at night, and puts handmade quilts on every bed? Don't miss the ten-minute walk along a pedestrian path to Old Salem, the area's premier attraction.

SETTING & FACILITIES

Location: Take I-40 to Bus. 40, exit at Cherry St., turn left on Marshall, then left into Brookstown Inn
Near: 2 blocks from Old Salem (restored 1776 Moravian village), downtown area
Building: Restored 1830s cotton mill
Grounds: Attractive courtyard
Public Space: Parlor
Food & Drink: European-style breakfast includes waffles, French toast, fresh fruit
Recreation: Sight-seeing
Amenities & Services: Turn-down w/ handmade chocolate & tomorrow's weather report, free newspapers, local restaurant menu book, exercise facil.

ACCOMMODATIONS

Units: 40 guest rooms, 31 bilevel suites
All Rooms: Indiv. climate control, cable TV, phone w/ voice mail
Some Rooms: Garden tub, decorative fireplace, microwave, fridge
Bed & Bath: Private baths
Favorites: #401 w/ glassed graffiti wall written by nineteenth century female millworkers
Comfort & Decor: Handsome interior brick walls and exposed structural beams. No two rooms have the same look. Each is decorated with early American and English antiques.

RATES, RESERVATIONS, & RESTRICTIONS

Deposit: 1 night; 24-hour cancellation
Discounts: 10% AAA, AARP, corp., groups of 10 or more
Credit Cards: AE, V, MC, DC
Check-in/Out: 2 p.m./noon
Smoking: Nonsmoking rooms avail.
Pets: No
Kids: Welcome; under age 11 stay free
Minimum Stay: None
Open: All year
Hosts: None
200 Brookstown Ave.
Winston-Salem, NC 27101
(336) 725-1120 or (800) 845-4262
Fax: (336) 773-0147
BROJ@aol.com

COLONEL LUDLOW INN, Winston-Salem

Overall: ★★ | Room Quality: C | Value: C | Price: $109–$209

A man traveling on business would probably love the Colonel Ludlow Inn with its billiards table, exercise room with extensive Nautilus equipment, and a golf driving and putting practice area in the backyard. But couples also enjoy some of the extra special services the host provides, such as the microwave ovens and TV/VCRs in all the rooms and the luxury of ordering dinner from a local restaurant and having the host deliver the food to your room. This inn is actually two buildings, both of which are on the National Register of Historic Places.

Setting & Facilities

Location: Business I-40 exit 58, turn right on Broad St., then left on West 5th St. to Summit St.
Near: Old Salem, historic residential neighborhood, Wake Forest University, Reynolds House
Building: 1887 Queen Anne home & 1895 neo-Romanesque home
Grounds: Acre w/ gardens
Public Space: Billiards room, exercise room, parlor, DR, porches
Food & Drink: Juice, fruit cup w/ yogurt, French toast, quiche, muffin; served on fine china in guest's room, DR, or, in warm weather, on the porch
Recreation: Walks, antiques shopping
Amenities & Services: Room service for beer, wine, champagne, & dessert; more than 300 movies & CDs; local restaurant menus

Accommodations

Units: 10 guest rooms
All Rooms: Victorian antiques, candles, stereo system, TV/VCR, stocked small fridge, robes
Some Rooms: Working fireplace
Bed & Bath: Kings; private baths
Favorites: None
Comfort & Decor: Sophisticated Victorian eclectic

Rates, Reservations, & Restrictions

Deposit: None
Discounts: None
Credit Cards: AE, MC, V, D
Check-in/Out: 3–10 p.m./11:30 a.m.
Smoking: Nonsmoking rooms avail.
Pets: No
Kids: 12 & older
Minimum Stay: None
Open: All year
Host: Constance Creasman
434 Summit St.
Winston-Salem, NC 27101
(336) 777-1887 or (800) 301-1887
Fax: (336) 777-0518
innkeeper@bbinn.com
www.bbinn.com

HENRY SHAFFNER HOUSE, Winston-Salem

Overall: ★★½ Room Quality: C Value: C Price: $99–$239

Here's our plus and minus scorecard for this bed-and-breakfast. On the plus side of the ledger: wonderful historic rooms that reflect the life of Winston-Salem in the early years of the last century—as you might expect if it were lived in by the famous and wealthy. Henry Fries Shaffner, with his uncle, founded the giant Wachovia Bank, and built this house with some of his earnings. The Piedmont Room, which was once a large attic, has now been converted into a plush guest room with a double whirlpool tub, wet bar, and sitting area. The Twin City Suite resembles an English country courtyard. The mantle in the dining room was made of wood rescued from a log cabin built in 1776. On the minus side: This inn is hard to reach because of all the one-way streets around it. If you miss the parking lot (you probably will the first time around; it's not well marked), it may take several minutes to get back around to it. During the night, there is a lot of traffic noise from the nearby interstate. The roof is badly stained, which takes away from the stately appearance of the exterior. To sum up: If you finally make it into the parking lot and bring some ear plugs for the traffic sounds, you will enjoy the elegant interiors.

Setting & Facilities

Location: Corner of High & Marshall Sts.
Near: Old Salem, Museum of Early Southern Decorative Arts, Reynolda House Museum
Building: 1907 Tudor-style Queen Anne mansion
Grounds: None
Public Space: Parlor, wraparound porch
Food & Drink: Cont'l plus on weekdays, full breakfast w/ hot entrees (e.g., waffles w/ fresh fruit) on weekends; restaurant on premises
Recreation: Sight-seeing
Amenities & Services: Passes to gym

Accommodations

Units: 6 guest rooms, 3 suites
All Rooms: Carpet, phone, TV
Some Rooms: Nonworking fireplace
Bed & Bath: Queen & king (some interesting types: sleigh, brass, twin shutter beds); private baths
Favorites: Piedmont Room
Comfort & Decor: Antiques and reproductions enhance the elegant Victorian ambiance.

Rates, Reservations, & Restrictions

Deposit: 1 night; 72-hour cancellation
Discounts: Corp.
Credit Cards: AE, V, MC
Check-in/Out: 3–9 p.m./11 a.m.
Smoking: No
Pets: No
Kids: Welcome
Minimum Stay: None
Open: All year
Host: Shirley Ackeret
150 S. Marshall St.
Winston-Salem, NC 27101
(336) 777-0052 or (800) 952-2256
Fax: (336) 777-1188
www.bbonline.com/nc/henry

LADY ANNE'S, Winston-Salem

Overall: ★★★ Room Quality: C Value: A Price: $60–$180

Lady Anne's bills itself as a "Victorian Bed & Breakfast home" and lives up to that phrase in decor. The guest parlor has an old pump organ. Check out the inn's Web site for some good views of their rooms. Best of all, rates during the week start at $60 and represent a real bargain for rooms of this quality with all of their amenities.

Setting & Facilities

Location: From I-40 take the Broad St. exit, turn left on 6th St., then right on Summit
Near: High Point Furniture Center, Benton Convention Center, Historic Old Salem, Wake Forest University, Coliseum
Building: 1890 Victorian
Grounds: None
Public Space: DR, porches, patio, guest parlor
Food & Drink: Full breakfast; specialties: stuffed baked apples, spiced hot pears; evening dessert in room
Recreation: Sight-seeing
Amenities & Services: Free local calls, YMCA guest privileges

Accommodations

Units: 2 guest rooms, 2 suites
All Rooms: Cable TV w/ HBO, robes, phone w/ data port
Some Rooms: Private entrance, fridge, microwave, dbl. whirlpool tub
Bed & Bath: Beds vary; private baths
Favorites: None
Comfort & Decor: Frilly, feminine bedrooms. The Magnolia Room and Summit Suite are very pleasant. The Magnolia is light and airy with a canopy bed and private balcony. The Summit has a two-person whirlpool overlooking the garden area.

Rates, Reservations, & Restrictions

Deposit: None
Discounts: Lower rates for long stays
Credit Cards: All major cards
Check-in/Out: 4:30 p.m./11:30 a.m.
Smoking: No
Pets: No
Kids: No young children (ask)
Minimum Stay: None
Open: All year
Host: Shelley Kirley
612 Summit St.
Winston-Salem, NC 27101
(336) 724-1074
www.bbonline.com/nc/ladyannes

Zone 3
Western North Carolina

If you read the Pulitzer Prize–winning novel *Cold Mountain*, you have a sense of the isolation, majesty, and beauty of the mountains that tower above the western corner of North Carolina. Two mountain ranges, the Great Smoky Mountains and the Blue Ridge Mountains, dominate the area and provide glens for picnics, waterfalls for photographs, rapid rivers for white-water rafting, and many other pleasurable pursuits, ranging from rock climbing and rock collecting to skiing in winter and attending plays and concerts in summer.

Over 100 species of trees are found in the Great Smokies. You can walk the streets of Asheville, where Thomas Wolfe spent his early days. The Biltmore Estate, built by the grandson of one of the world's richest men, Cornelius Vanderbilt, shows you what a person can do with an unlimited bank account and 8,000 acres. The most famous inn in the area is the Grove Park Inn, really a huge resort that by no stretch of the imagination could we call a bed-and-breakfast. But within a 30-mile radius you will find some of the most luxurious bed-and-breakfasts in North Carolina, such as the dazzling Richmond Hill Inn.

The Blue Ridge Parkway is a 469-mile scenic highway that cuts through the center of the region, hugging the crest of the Blue Ridge Mountains and soaring to a 6,410-feet majestic view.

For More Information

Asheville Area Chamber of Commerce
(800) 257-1300

CEDAR CREST VICTORIAN INN, Asheville

Overall: ★★★★ Room Quality: B Value: C Price: $135–$225

One Christmas weekend a young man proposed to his sweetheart at the Biltmore Estate. Then they went right next door to honeymoon at the Cedar Crest Victorian Inn, a suitably romantic place the owners call "a passage to 1890." The classic carved woodwork and Victorian furnishings certainly live up to that advance billing, with fluted columns and beveled mirrors. There are no TVs in the room (good for the "I-only-have-eyes-for-you" honeymooners), but one in the parlor (in case the honeymooners have had their first argument). Breakfast is served buffet style. On warm days most guests choose to sit outside on the wraparound porch.

SETTING & FACILITIES

Location: 1.5 mi. from downtown Asheville (just 0.25 mi. from the north Biltmore Estate entrance)
Near: Biltmore Estate, Chimney Rock Park, Blue Ridge Parkway, NC Arboretum
Building: 1891 Victorian Mansion plus cottage (1915 bungalow)
Grounds: 4 acres overlooking Biltmore Village w/ English flower gardens
Public Space: Parlor, study, grand foyer, multilevel verandas
Food & Drink: Full breakfast w/ hot entree, fruit compotes, croissants; afternoon refreshments geared to season (iced tea & lemonade in summer, hot wassail in winter)
Recreation: Sight-seeing, hiking, fishing, clogging, golf, white-water rafting
Amenities & Services: Croquet & badminton courts (equipment avail. at inn)

ACCOMMODATIONS

Units: 10 guest rooms in mansion plus cottage w/ 2-BR suite & 1-BR suite
All Rooms: Phone, AC
Some Rooms: Fireplace, Victorian lace
Bed & Bath: Queen, featherbed, & canopy; private baths; some w/ claw-foot tub & shower or whirlpool
Favorites: Celebration Suite w/ canopy bed & private sitting room w/ TV & VCR
Comfort & Decor: The ornate fireplace, huge oak staircase, and period antiques give this place a classic feel.

RATES, RESERVATIONS, & RESTRICTIONS

Deposit: 1 night or 50% of entire balance, whichever greater
Discounts: None
Credit Cards: Most credit cards
Check-in/Out: 3–10 p.m./11 a.m.
Smoking: No
Pets: No
Kids: 10 & older
Minimum Stay: 2 nights weekends, 3 nights holidays
Open: All year
Hosts: Jack & Barbara McEwan
647 Biltmore Ave.
Asheville, NC 28803
(828) 252-1389 or (800) 252-0310
www.cedarcrestvictorianinn.com

CUMBERLAND FALLS, Asheville

Overall: ★★★½ Room Quality: B Value: C Price: $105–$210

The breakfast cup of bed-and-breakfasts runneth over in the historic Montford area of Asheville, so you have many choices. Many of the inns cling to the Victorian style, but Cumberland Falls manages to combine the past and present in a casual but comfortable way. Most of the rooms have a bright, airy, modern decor that is more fitting to a European spa. They have a masseuse who will provide massages for $60 an hour. The new innkeepers pride themselves on providing full concierge services, making any possible reservations guests could want—from restaurants to tours of the Biltmore Estate to horseback riding. Fluffy pillows, whirlpool tubs, and a four-course breakfast round out some of the pleasures. Special packages are available that combine stays at the inn with hot-air ballooning and white-water rafting. Check the inn's Internet site for special package offers. When this book went to press, these offers included a "50 percent off special" and a "free night" offer.

Setting & Facilities

Location: Historic Montford District, close to downtown Asheville
Near: Blue Ridge Parkway, Biltmore Estate, Thomas Wolfe Memorial
Building: Turn-of-the-century house
Grounds: Gardens w/ small waterfalls & ponds
Public Space: Small casual LR w/ fireplace, gardens, porch
Food & Drink: Full breakfast w/ eggs Benedict, Belgian waffles w/ whipped cream & strawberry sauce; served bedside or garden-side
Recreation: Sight-seeing
Amenities & Services: Concierge-style services, saltwater aquarium, massage avail.

Accommodations

Units: 5 guest rooms
All Rooms: TV/VCR/CD player
Some Rooms: Garden & waterfall views
Bed & Bath: 100-year-old Victorian bed; dbl. whirlpool tub, claw-foot tub
Favorites: Garden Vista w/ Oriental-style garden & pond view
Comfort & Decor: It's casual and homelike, with an unusual mixture of European modern and comfortable Victorian antiques.

Rates, Reservations, & Restrictions

Deposit: 50%, credit card; 14-day cancellation (longer for fall foliage season & holidays)
Discounts: Midweek & seasonal
Credit Cards: V, MC
Check-in/Out: 3–6 p.m./11 a.m.
Smoking: No
Pets: No
Kids: 10 & older

Minimum Stay: 2 nights on weekends
Open: All year
Hosts: Gary & Patti Wiles
254 Cumberland Ave.
Asheville, NC 28801
(828) 253-4085 or (888) 743-2557
Fax: (828) 253-5566
www.cumberlandfalls.com

INN ON MONTFORD, Asheville

Overall: ★★½ | Room Quality: C | Value: D | Price: $145–$195

This inn has a unique distinction among the several in the historic Montford area of Asheville. It was designed by the same architect who supervised the building of the incredible Biltmore Estate nearby. The place is meticulously clean and well managed but—in our eyes—somewhat ordinary and a little overpriced. The saving grace is the hosts' sense of humor, as evidenced in their descriptions of their special weekends, such as the baking parties where guests help create pastries. Their brochure announcement reads, "You all know what a challenge this is going to be, with (our host's) reputation for mis-measuring."

SETTING & FACILITIES

Location: Exit 4C off I-240 (Montford Ave.)
Near: Biltmore Estate, Thomas Wolfe House, Folk Art Center, Chimney Rock
Building: 1900 English country cottage style
Grounds: Landscaped front & back yards
Public Space: Library, LR, DR, foyer, sunroom
Food & Drink: Full breakfast; specialties: eggs in a nest, almond puff; early coffee/tea delivered to room
Recreation: Hiking, tennis, whitewater rafting, mountain biking
Amenities & Services: Local restaurant reviews, fresh-cut flowers, walking tour guides

ACCOMMODATIONS

Units: 4 guest rooms
All Rooms: Fireplace, phone, AC
Some Rooms: Whirlpool tub, four-poster bed, Persian carpets
Bed & Bath: Queens; private baths
Favorites: Fitzgerald Room w/ 1860 English half tester bed, gas fireplace, partners desk
Comfort & Decor: Antique furnishings (1670–1890 periods)

RATES, RESERVATIONS, & RESTRICTIONS

Deposit: Credit card; 14-day cancellation
Discounts: Midweek, extended stays
Credit Cards: AE, MC, V, D
Check-in/Out: 3–9 p.m./11 a.m.
Smoking: No
Pets: No

Kids: 12 & older
Minimum Stay: 2 nights weekends, 3 nights some holidays
Open: All year
Hosts: Lynn & Ron Carlson
296 Montford Ave.
Asheville, NC 28801
(828) 254-9569 or (800) 254-9569
Fax: (828) 254-9518
info@innonmontford.com
www.innonmontford.com

LION AND THE ROSE BED & BREAKFAST, Asheville

Overall: ★★★½ Room Quality: B Value: C Price: $135–$225

This is the prettiest bed-and-breakfast in the historic Montford area. The rooms are picture postcards of the Victorian era; most extraordinary are the many walls hand-painted by a local artist. Guests can play the antique Steinway piano in one of the two parlors. One footnote for literary buffs: In Thomas Wolfe's *Look Homeward Angel*, the character of Tommy French was based on a former resident of this house—Charles French Toms. Charles was a friend of Thomas Wolfe.

SETTING & FACILITIES

Location: Exit 4C off I-240 (Montford Ave.), corner of Waneta & Montford
Near: Downtown Asheville, 8 min. from Biltmore Estate
Building: 1895 Georgian neo-classical
Grounds: Manicured gardens, century-old trees
Public Space: Parlor, front veranda, side gardens
Food & Drink: Full breakfast; specialty: fresh herb soufflé; afternoon tea
Recreation: Hiking in the Blue Ridge Mountains, white-water rafting
Amenities & Services: Dinner reservations, complimentary fitness center passes on request

Accommodations

Units: 5 guest rooms
All Rooms: Period antiques, robes
Some Rooms: Fireplace, balcony, whirlpool tub
Bed & Bath: Queens; private baths
Favorites: Marion Hall Room w/ 100-year-old antique oak bed & hand-painted walls
Comfort & Decor: Pleasant bedrooms with local touches

Rates, Reservations, & Restrictions

Deposit: 50% of total cost; 14-day cancellation
Discounts: Corp., AAA
Credit Cards: AE, V, MC, D
Check-in/Out: 3–8 p.m./11 a.m.
Smoking: No
Pets: No
Kids: 12 & older
Minimum Stay: 2 nights on weekends
Open: All year
Hosts: Rice & Lisa Yordy
276 Montford Ave.
Asheville, NC 28801
(828) 255-ROSE or (800) 546-6988
Fax: (828) 285-9810
info@lion-rose.com
www.lion-rose.com

RICHMOND HILL INN, Asheville

Overall: ★★★★★ Room Quality: A Value: C Price: $145–$450

It's easy to run out of adjectives in describing the Richmond Hill Inn. Beautiful grounds that include gardens with a brook and waterfall (great spot for wedding photos). Award-winning—four diamond awards from AAA for the inn and for Gabrielle's, the restaurant on the premises. This restaurant is really something (we've run out of adjectives). Entrees include lobster-crusted trout with brown basmati rice and avocado puree and pan-seared rockfish with red bliss potatoes and a tomatillo-banana salsa. To start your dinner conversation, ask the waiter for a definition of "tomatillo," new to us. The inn is listed on the National Register of Historic Places. Richmond Hill Inn is on the expensive side, but certainly worth it for special occasions in your life.

Setting & Facilities

Location: In mountains 3 mi. NW of downtown Asheville, near Hwy. 19/23
Near: Biltmore Estate, Blue Ridge Parkway, galleries, antiques shops
Building: Queen Anne Victorian buildings—historic mansion, Croquet Cottages, Garden Pavilion
Grounds: 6 garden acres w/ croquet court & waterfalls
Public Space: Oak Hall, library, parlor, front porch of mansion
Food & Drink: Full breakfast in garden; Gabrielle's restaurant on site open for dinner
Recreation: Walking trail, croquet
Amenities & Services: Newspaper, croquet court

Accommodations

Units: 36 guest rooms
All Rooms: Phone, TV
Some Rooms: Fireplace, whirlpool tub, private porch
Bed & Bath: Mostly queen, few king; private baths
Favorites: Thomas Pearson Suite w/ private balcony (garden & waterfall views) & whirlpool tub
Comfort & Decor: Mansion rooms feature antiques; cottages are Shaker style; and the Garden Pavilion has antique reproductions.

Rates, Reservations, & Restrictions

Deposit: 1 night; 7-day cancellation
Discounts: Midweek
Credit Cards: AE, V, MC
Check-in/Out: 3 p.m./noon
Smoking: No
Pets: No
Kids: Welcome
Minimum Stay: 2 nights on weekends
Open: All year except midweek Jan. & Feb.
Host: Susan Michel
87 Richmond Hill Dr.
Asheville, NC 28806
(828) 252-7313 or (888) 742-4536
Fax: (828) 252-8726
info@richmondhillinn.com
www.richmondhillinn.com

SOURWOOD INN, Asheville

Overall: ★★★★½ Room Quality: B Value: B Price: $130–$175

Just about ten miles from downtown Asheville you will find a small country inn that pulls off a difficult feat: combining many of the features of a resort with a cozy, homey feeling. You can wander around on cool evenings and return to a wood-burning fireplace, or step out on your own balcony to listen to the summer sounds of the woods, or shoot some billiards with fellow guests in the game room. And there's something else really unusual: whirlpool tubs with mountain views. Jeff, one of your hosts, is very knowledgeable about birds and can offer good tips on bird-watching. Sourwood Inn is a great country escape. Go enjoy!

Setting & Facilities

Location: From Asheville, take Blue Ridge Parkway north to mile marker 135.5 (Bull Gap); turn left after 0.2 mi. on Elk Mt. Scenic Hwy.; B&B sign is on right after 1.7 mi.
Near: Biltmore Estate, downtown Asheville, 2 mi. to Blue Ridge Parkway, fly-fishing streams
Building: Cedar & stone modern country retreat
Grounds: 100 acres of mountain property w/ 2-mi. walking trails
Public Space: Lobby, library, game room, deck w/ rocking chairs, DR, terrace
Food & Drink: Full breakfast w/ hot entrees (e.g., French toast, egg strada, blueberry pancakes)
Recreation: Hiking, bird-watching, fly-fishing, white-water rafting, antiques shopping
Amenities & Services: Local restaurant menus, disabled-access, newspapers, pool table, Ping-Pong

Accommodations

Units: 12 guest rooms & cabin
All Rooms: Wood-burning fireplace, mountain view, balcony
Some Rooms: Hardwood floors, carpet, antiques
Bed & Bath: King or queen; queen & sleeper sofa in cabin; private baths
Favorites: Number10 w/ king bed & sitting room
Comfort & Decor: Comfortable antiques; original and art prints

Rates, Reservations, & Restrictions

Deposit: Credit card
Discounts: None
Credit Cards: AE, V, MC, D
Check-in/Out: 3–9 p.m./noon
Smoking: No
Pets: No
Kids: 12 & older
Minimum Stay: 2 nights on weekends
Open: Weekends in Feb., Mar., until week before Christmas
Hosts: Anne & Nat Burkhardt, Susan & Jeff Curtis
810 Elk Mountain Scenic Hwy.
Asheville, NC 28804
(828) 255-0690
Fax: (828) 255-0480
www.sourwoodinn.com

WRIGHT INN AND CARRIAGE HOUSE, Asheville

Overall: ★★★½ Room Quality: B Value: C Price: $110–$235

The place is practically a role model for a Victorian Home. Steven Spielberg would want to film it if he ever does a Halloween film. It's perfect for people who want the look and feel of a truly Southern bed-and-breakfast. Locals once called it "Faded Glory." But no more! It has been restored with period antiques and handsome woodwork. One unusual pleasure for guests: the loan of a Sony Walkman with a history walk tape for downtown Asheville. Our only concern with this inn is the stairway leading to the third floor of the main house. It is narrow and winding. If you're less than agile, we suggest taking a room on a lower floor.

Setting & Facilities

Location: Exit 4C off I-240 in Asheville
Near: Biltmore Estate, Smoky Mountain National Park
Building: 1898 Queen Anne Victorian
Grounds: Attractive gardens
Public Space: Parlor, drawing room, porch
Food & Drink: Full breakfast; specialties: Bermuda pancakes w/ blueberry syrup, stuffed French toast, sausage, bacon, or ham; afternoon tea; sodas & bottled water avail. all day
Recreation: Hiking, bird-watching, shopping for antiques & crafts
Amenities & Services: Complimentary use of bicycles & helmets, newspapers, lists of local restaurants

Accommodations

Units: 9 guest rooms, 2 suites
All Rooms: AC, TV, phone, fresh flowers, hardwood floors
Some Rooms: Fireplace, balcony; suites have fireplaces and Jacuzzis
Bed & Bath: New mattresses on all beds; private baths
Favorites: None
Comfort & Decor: Victorian antiques & original woodwork

Rates, Reservations, & Restrictions

Deposit: Credit card, 1st night
Discounts: 5th night stay reduced 50%, or 6th night free; 10% corp. rate
Credit Cards: V, MC, D
Check-in/Out: 3–7 p.m./11 a.m.
Smoking: Outdoors only
Pets: No
Kids: 12 & older
Minimum Stay: 2 nights on weekends
Open: All year except first 3 weeks in Jan. & Dec. 24–26
Hosts: Judi & Bill Ayers
235 Pearson Dr.
Asheville, NC 28801
(828) 251-0789 or (800) 552-5724
Fax: (828) 251-0929
info@wrightinn.com
www.wrightinn.com

HOUND EARS CLUB, Blowing Rock

Overall: ★★★★ Room Quality: B Value: D Price: $115–$230

The Hound Ears Club is a 35-year-old private club in the Smoky Mountains of North Carolina. More a lodge than a bed-and-breakfast, this four-star facility caters to the golf enthusiast. All rooms have balconies and many overlook the golf course and beautifully landscaped grounds. Although obviously an older facility, the rooms are large. A masseuse ($50 an hour), dance floor, and a small swimming pool in a grotto help complete the vacation package. A tea house beside the golf course serves light meals in summer. There is a private guard at the gate and nightly patrols. This bed-and-breakfast offers a great mountain escape and some great golf, but it is also a little pricey and a little stuffy (jackets required for gentlemen at dinner, jacket and tie Saturday nights). People who show up in the dining room or lounge at any time wearing blue jeans will probably be banished to the nearest Red Roof Inn.

Setting & Facilities

Location: 6 mi. from Boone; take Hwy. 105 South
Near: Appalachian Cultural Museum, Blowing Rock, Grandfather Mountain, Linville Caverns, Linville Falls, Mystery Hill, Tweetsie Railroad
Building: Chalet-style clubhouse, lodge
Grounds: Large resort area w/ golf course

Public Space: DR, lounge
Food & Drink: Cont'l breakfast; dinner avail. in summer under Modified American Plan (breakfast & dinner)
Recreation: Golf, tennis, sight-seeing
Amenities & Services: Swimming pool (heated to 85°), tennis courts, golf course

Accommodations

Units: 29 guest rooms
All Rooms: Private balcony
Some Rooms: Sitting area
Bed & Bath: King or double; private baths
Favorites: Honeymoon Suite (most spacious w/ king bed)
Comfort & Decor: Modern lodge style

Rates, Reservations, & Restrictions

Deposit: Credit card
Discounts: None
Credit Cards: AE, V, MC
Check-in/Out: 1:30 p.m./11 a.m.
Smoking: Yes ("but policy may change")
Pets: No
Kids: Welcome
No-Nos: DR closed Nov.–Mar.
Minimum Stay: None
Open: All year
Hosts: Mr. & Mrs. Ed Claughton
P.O. Box 188
Blowing Rock, NC 28605
(828) 963-4321
Fax: (828) 963-8030
houndears@boone.net
www.houndears.com

LOVILL HOUSE INN BED & BREAKFAST, Boone

Overall: ★★★ Room Quality: C Value: D Price: $105–$170

There are two things to remember when you come to this bed-and-breakfast. In the summer try to drive through Boone before late afternoon. Rush hour traffic (4–6 p.m.) in this small town can rival big city tie-ups. And don't miss the first meal of the day here. "Breakfasts are outstanding," cooed one overstuffed guest. "Belgian waffles, garden vegetable strada, omelets, eggs Benedict." She added for good measure, "Later, check out Lori's homemade chocolate chip cookies." The Lovill won the AAA "Four Diamond Award" again in 1999, and the hosts clearly deserve it. They are excellent mixers and encourage conversations among the guests. Now, if their rates were just a little lower.

Setting & Facilities

Location: Close to downtown Boone
Near: Blue Ridge Parkway, Grandfather Mountain, ski resorts
Building: 1875 farmhouse
Grounds: 11 heavily wooded acres
Public Space: None
Food & Drink: Full breakfast
Recreation: Skiing, hiking, white-water rafting
Amenities & Services: None

Accommodations

Units: 6 guest rooms
All Rooms: Cable TV, double-insulated walls, phone
Bed & Bath: Beds vary; private baths
Favorites: None
Comfort & Decor: It's homelike with heart-of-pine plank floors and three fireplaces.

Rates, Reservations, & Restrictions

Deposit: Credit card
Discounts: AAA, repeat guests
Credit Cards: MC,V
Check-in/Out: 3–6 p.m./11 a.m.
Smoking: No
Pets: No
Kids: No
Minimum Stay: 2 nights weekends, 3 nights some holidays
Open: Apr.–Feb.
Hosts: Tim & Lori Shahen
404 Old Bristol Rd.
Boone, NC 28607
(828) 264-4204 or (800) 849-9466
innkeeper@lovillhouseinn.com
www.lovillhouseinn.com

HEMLOCK INN, Bryson City

Overall: ★★★	Room Quality: B	Value: B	Price: $137–$186

Hemlock Inn is a relaxed place with the major attraction being the great outdoors, particularly hiking and exploring the Smoky Mountains and riding the Great Smoky Mountain Railway. Meals are served on the Modified American Plan (breakfast and dinner) at the sound of a genuine dinner bell. Mealtime begins with everyone standing up to say blessings. Although this pleases many of the visitors, others of different religious faiths or beliefs could be disturbed by it. Breakfast is served promptly at 8:30 a.m., dinner promptly at 6 p.m. This schedule could be bothersome for people who want to sleep a little late or come back late from a hike. The cottages are convenient for families; three of the four have kitchen facilities.

Setting & Facilities

Location: Take Hwy. 74 to Exit 69, turn right on Hyatt Creek, turn left on Hwy. 19, & follow inn signs
Near: Great Smoky Mountain Nat'l Park
Building: 1952 country casual building plus 4 cottages
Grounds: 50 acres of forestland
Public Space: Porch, breakfast room
Food & Drink: Full breakfast served family style from lazy susans; dinner also served
Recreation: Hiking, tubing on Deep Creek, horseback riding
Amenities & Services: None

Accommodations

Units: 22 guest rooms
All Rooms: Antiques, mountain craft items
Bed & Bath: Beds vary; private baths
Favorites: None
Comfort & Decor: Rustic ambiance with comfortable seating

Rates, Reservations, & Restrictions

Deposit: Credit card
Discounts: None
Credit Cards: V, MC, D
Check-in/Out: Ask
Smoking: No
Pets: No
Kids: Welcome
Minimum Stay: None
Open: Mid-Apr.–Oct.
Hosts: Mort & Lainey White
Galbraith Creek Rd.
Bryson City, NC 28712
(828) 488-2885
Fax: (828) 488-8985
hemlock@dnet.net
www.innbook.com/hemlock.html

PANES, Burnsville

Overall: ★★★ Room Quality: C Value: B Price: $125–$325

The Panes is a pleasant surprise here in the mountains at an elevation of 3,200 feet—a treatment as well as a treat. It offers not only lodging but complete spa treatments from one of your hosts, Nena, who has years of experience as a massage and skin-care technician. You can stay in a large suite in the main house or in a log cabin. Sign up for the "Royal Treatment," which includes overnight accommodations, breakfast and dinner, and one spa treatment that begins shortly after your arrival. The "Panes" name comes from the use of stained glass windows, collected by Nena over the years, throughout the lodge and cabin. You can certainly stay in more glamorous lodgings in this part of North Carolina, but few that will cleanse your facial pores and vibrate your feet.

Setting & Facilities

Location: 15 min. east of Burnsville
Near: Biltmore Estate, Penland School of Arts, Blue Ridge Parkway
Building: Modern 3-story mountain lodge, 150-year-old log cabin
Grounds: 17 acres
Public Space: Hot tub, DR
Food & Drink: Full breakfast
Recreation: Hiking, rafting, arts & crafts
Amenities & Services: Complete spa treatments avail., including full-body massage, face massage, pedicure, full-body cleansing

Accommodations

Units: 1 upstairs suite; main house plus log cabin w/ upstairs loft
Some Rooms: Barbecue grill, microwave, CD player, featherbed, whirlpool & steam room
Bed & Bath: King & twin, sleeper sofa; private baths
Favorites: None
Comfort & Decor: Modern suite in main house, rustic cabin

Rates, Reservations, & Restrictions

Deposit: 1 night
Discounts: None
Credit Cards: None
Check-in/Out: 3 p.m. (spa treatment at 4:30 p.m.)/11 a.m.
Smoking: No
Pets: No
Kids: No
Minimum Stay: None
Open: All year
Hosts: Nena Parkerson-Smith & Jody MacSmith
Rt. 3, Box 312A
Burnsville, NC 28714
(828) 682-4157
thepanes@ioa.com
www.geocities.com/EnchantedForest/Palace/6215

MILLSTONE INN, Cashiers

Overall: ★★★★ | Room Quality: B | Value: C | Price: $130–$198

One enduring image we have here is of a white-haired visitor in an Adirondack chair on the back sloping lawn of the Millstone Inn, lost in the view of a seemingly infinite forest in front of him. This rustic inn inspires daydreaming. And hiking—few areas of the country have as many waterfalls per capita as Cashiers. The glass-enclosed porch is an ideal spot to breakfast on woodland views. The owners are new, so we hope they maintain the wonderful casual atmosphere that the former owners did so well. Don't miss Cashiers' many funky restaurants, such as the Market Basket, a grocery store where they serve dinner and may roll out a piano at the end of the aisles where a singer and pianist perform for your supper. More bread and the Irving Berlin, please. *Note:* When you make reservations, be sure to get precise directions to the best, fastest route. Some guests mistakenly take the "scenic" mountain route recommended by some locals. But some of these twisty-turny routes turn necks and backs into aching corkscrews.

Setting & Facilities

Location: 0.5 mile from Hwy. 84, a mile west of Cashiers intersection w/ Hwy. 107
Near: Nantahala Nat'l Forest, Whiteside Mountain, Silver Slip waterfalls, Lake Glenville, Lake Toxaway, many waterfalls nearby
Building: Shingled U shape, 1933
Grounds: Large sloping lawn adjoins national forest
Public Space: Sitting room, library
Food & Drink: Full breakfast w/ breads, juices, fruits, & hot dishes; tea, coffee, soda, sherry, cookies, fruit, & candy in guest refreshment area
Recreation: Hiking to waterfalls, horseback riding, golf, tennis, fishing
Amenities & Services: Newspapers, maps, trail guides, local restaurant menus; makes restaurant reservations for guests

Accommodations

Units: 7 guest rooms, 4 suites
All Rooms: Fridge, TV, hair dryer, mountain & forest views
Some Rooms: Kitchen, dining area, balcony
Bed & Bath: Queen or king; private baths
Favorites: Rooms 7 & 8—large w/ mountain views, exposed beam ceilings
Comfort & Decor: Antique furnishings, artwork

Rates, Reservations, & Restrictions

Deposit: Credit card; 7-day cancellation
Discounts: Nov.–May
Credit Cards: V, MC, D
Check-in/Out: 3–10 p.m./11 a.m.
Smoking: No
Pets: No
Kids: Teenagers welcome
Minimum Stay: 2 nights preferred on weekends
Open: Mar.–Dec.
Hosts: Doug & Beverly Woock
Hwy. 64 W., P.O. Box 949
Cashiers, NC 28717
(828) 743-2737 or (888) 645-5786
Fax: (828) 743-0208
office@millstoneinn.com
www.millstoneinn.com

WINDSONG, Clyde

Overall: ★★★★½ Room Quality: A Value: C Price: $120–$175

Most of the time we look askance at poetic phrases in bed-and-breakfast brochures, often penned by writers using more salary-inspired imagination than hard fact. But the cover of the "Windsong—A Mountain Inn" folder comes close to capturing the relaxation of this beautiful place: "A place removed where time moves at a different pace, slower, somehow richer." Each room has a different theme that is certainly a place removed. A "different pace"? How about a hike with llamas to a waterfall or a walk with Mindy, the dog, who keeps guests from getting lost. We have only a few quibbles with this beautiful place. The room TV/VCR gets no TV channels; it's strictly for playing tapes. And don't speed down the gravel road unless your car paint job needs sanding. But couples relaxing in a tub for two with a log fire glowing may not be terribly interested in our pedestrian qualms. It is a very romantic place.

Setting & Facilities

Location: From I-40 North, take Exit 24, go 2.8 mi. on NC 209, turn right on Riverside Dr., turn right at Ferguson Cove Loop & Windsong sign, & follow Windsong signs
Near: Biltmore Estate, Great Smoky Mountains Nat'l Park, Cherokee Indian Reservation, Great Smoky Mountain Railway
Building: Modern log cabin
Grounds: 24 acres w/ llama pastures, forests, herb & flower gardens

Public Space: Game room, deck, DR
Food & Drink: Full breakfast w/ strawberries Vinaigrette, Kahlua caramel French toast, or Mexican frittata
Recreation: Swimming, tennis, hiking, bird-watching, white-water rafting
Amenities & Services: Video library, swimming pool, hot tub, tennis court

Accommodations

Units: 5 guest rooms in main inn, separate Pond Lodge w/ 2 suites
All Rooms: TV/VCR
Bed & Bath: Private baths
Favorites: Country Room w/ corner location & mountain view
Comfort & Decor: Each room has a different motif: Safari Room (African masks, antiques), Garden Room (water fountain, paintings, and mirrors), Santa Fe Room (log bed and Santa Fe–style art); high-beamed ceilings.

Rates, Reservations, & Restrictions

Deposit: 1 night
Discounts: 10% 7 or more days, 10% seniors Sun.–Thurs.
Credit Cards: V, MC, D
Check-in/Out: 3–6 p.m./11 a.m.
Smoking: No
Pets: No
Kids: Children any age in Pond Lodge, 12 & older in Main Inn
Minimum Stay: None
Open: All year
Hosts: Russ & Barbara Mancini
459 Rockcliffe Ln.
Clyde, NC 28721
(828) 627-6111
Fax: (828) 627-8080
Russ@windsongbb.com
www.windsongbb.com

OLDE TOWN INN, Dillsboro

Overall: ★★½ Room Quality: C Value: A Price: $65–$125

Host Lera Chitwood is learning the ropes of running a bed-and-breakfast but doing her best to accommodate guests and their needs. Each evening she serves complimentary wine and beer. Staying here is like visiting a relative who has a homey place in the country. The station of the Great Smoky Mountain Scenic Railroad is only a block away; this train is a "must" ride for mountain sight-seeing. The best restaurant in the craft shop–crowded little town is Jarrett House. This bed-and-breakfast is a bit too close to the highway, so road sounds can be a problem. Ask for directions about parking, which is behind the inn. As the host herself advises, the steep driveway can be tough to negotiate in wet conditions. In case of snow, park in the railroad parking area overnight.

Setting & Facilities

Location: Exit 21 Hwy. 441 (45 min. from Asheville)
Near: Great Smoky Mountain Nat'l Park, Scenic Railroad, Cherokee Indian Reservation & Casino, Nantahala River

Building: Typical large farmhouse w/ long columned porch
Grounds: About .75 acre on hill
Public Space: Porch, LR
Food & Drink: Full breakfast
Recreation: Hiking, fishing, casino gambling
Amenities & Services: None

Accommodations

Units: 5 guest rooms
All Rooms: Attractive pastel colors
Some Rooms: White wicker furniture, fireplace
Bed & Bath: Queen, double, or trundle; private baths; claw-foot tub, shower
Favorites: New Dogwood Suite, sleeps family of 4
Comfort & Decor: Very homey and comfortable—nothing fancy

Rates, Reservations, & Restrictions

Deposit: 50% for 1-night stay, 1 night for longer stays
Discounts: None
Credit Cards: AE, V, MC, D
Check-in/Out: 3:30 p.m./10:30 a.m.
Smoking: No
Pets: Some accepted (ask—there are 2 large resident dogs)
Kids: Welcome
Minimum Stay: None
Open: All year
Hosts: Lera Chitwood
P.O. Box 485, 300 Haywood Rd.
Dillsboro, NC 28725
(828) 586-3461
oldetown@gte.net

INN AT WINTERSUN, Fairview

Overall: ★★★★★ Room Quality: A Value: B Price: $190–$385

We hate to sound too much like a gushy travel brochure, but this place is absolutely exquisite. Everything expresses quality, careful planning, and a supreme regard for the beauty of nature. There are no TVs in the rooms, but who needs the Travel Channel when there is a real 25-foot waterfall nearby? The spa is pure romance with a huge whirlpool in marble next to a fireplace. Small wonder that Robin Williams rented this whole inn for himself and his family when *Patch Adams* was being filmed nearby. This inn deserves an Academy Award for natural elegance.

SETTING & FACILITIES

Location: Take I-40 to 74A East 6 mi., turn left on Miller Rd., then right on Wintersun Lane (call ahead for access code to activate electric gate)
Near: Biltmore Estate, mountain recreation
Building: Country lodge
Grounds: 80 acres w/ trout stream
Public Space: LR, DR, covered porch overlooking waterfall
Food & Drink: Full breakfast; specialties: wild mushroom quiche, blueberry muffins, fruit compote w/ yogurt
Recreation: Hiking, mountain biking, guided trail riding, river rafting
Amenities & Services: Concierge booking services for outdoor excursions, tickets to Biltmore, local festivals, etc.

ACCOMMODATIONS

Units: 4 guest rooms, 1 suite
All Rooms: Large windows w/ mountain views, hardwood floors, wood-burning fireplace, robes
Some Rooms: Corner location w/ woodland garden views
Bed & Bath: Beds vary; private baths
Favorites: Wintersun Suite & Spa w/ private entrance to waterfall garden
Comfort & Decor: 10-foot ceilings, country ambiance, and comfortable furnishings

RATES, RESERVATIONS, & RESTRICTIONS

Deposit: Credit card
Discounts: No
Credit Cards: V, MC
Check-in/Out: 3–6 p.m./11 a.m.
Smoking: Outdoors only
Pets: No
Kids: No
Minimum Stay: 2 nights weekends
Open: All year
Hosts: Judy Carter & Susan Sluyter
One Wintersun Ln.
Fairview, NC 28730
(828) 628-7890 or (888) 628-1628
Fax: (828) 628-7891
www.innatwintersun.com

CLADDAGH INN, Hendersonville

Overall: ★★★½ Room Quality: B Value: C Price: $80–$135

"Claddagh" at first seems a strange Irish name to give to what seems to be a Victorian inn. But the Irish meanings of the word "love" and "ring of friendship" make more sense when you meet the hosts, August and Geraldine, and become acquainted with the inviting and cozy bed-and-breakfast they have created. The Irish theme throughout is actually a welcome relief from the heavy dose of ye olde Victorian themes throughout many bed-and-breakfasts in this area. In fact, we found the Claddagh to be more inviting than the Waverly Inn next door, which seems to get most of the recognition. On St. Patrick's Day, the Claddagh really waves the shillelagh to the beat of an Irish band. The beautiful porch is the best seat in town for the Apple Festival Parade every Labor Day. Hendersonville does not lack in culture either, with the Brevard Music Center and Flat Rock Playhouse nearby.

SETTING & FACILITIES

Location: Downtown Hendersonville off I-64
Near: Carl Sandburg Home (5 mi.), Biltmore House (18 mi.), Chimney Rock (8 mi.)
Building: 1888 Classic Revival Victorian
Grounds: None
Public Space: Parlor, library, veranda
Food & Drink: Full breakfast w/ eggs, bacon, ham, sausage, grits, quiche, baked apples; evening sherry
Recreation: Antiques & craft shopping, hiking, fishing
Amenities & Services: Irish gift shop on premises (Irish knits, porcelains, etc.), games in parlor

ACCOMMODATIONS

Units: 16 guest rooms
All Rooms: AC, phone, TV
Some Rooms: Stained-glass archway, decorative fireplace
Bed & Bath: King, queen, or twins; private baths
Favorites: None
Comfort & Decor: This old inn has been completely renovated with modern touches.

RATES, RESERVATIONS, & RESTRICTIONS

Deposit: Credit card; 7-day cancellation
Discounts: 7th night free for weekly stays (except in fall foliage season)
Credit Cards: AE, V, MC, D
Check-in/Out: 3 p.m./11 a.m.
Smoking: No
Pets: No
Kids: Welcome
Minimum Stay: None
Open: All year
Hosts: August & Geraldine Emmanuel
755 North Main St.
Hendersonville, NC 28792
(828) 697-7778 or (800) 225-4700
Innkeepers@claddaghinn.com
www.claddaghinn.com

WAVERLY INN, Hendersonville

Overall: ★★★ Room Quality: B Value: C Price: $109–$195

Be cautious when you check in to this bed-and-breakfast. The person next to you could be a murderer. Well, not exactly. It could be one of the actors participating in the inn's murder mystery weekends. He or she pretends to be a regular guest until the plot thickens, along with the soup. We wouldn't use the word *cozy* for this bed-and-breakfast (like the Claddagh Inn next door). The reception area is more like a hotel. However, the rooms have some very nice antique beds and baths. Golfers take note: There are five courses a few minutes from the inn's front door. The inn's location on Main Street makes it very convenient to restaurants.

Setting & Facilities

Location: Right in Hendersonville, 20 mi. south of Asheville
Near: Carl Sandburg Home, Flat Rock Playhouse, Chimney Rock, Pisgah National Forest, Thomas Wolfe House
Building: 1898 Victorian Inn (continuously open since that year)
Grounds: None
Public Space: Parlor, porches
Food & Drink: Full breakfast w/ eggs, ground grits, French toast, or pancakes; complimentary refreshments; cookies avail. throughout day
Recreation: Antiques shopping, fishing, hiking, golf
Amenities & Services: Help w/ restaurant & tour plans, rocking chairs on porch

Accommodations

Units: 14 guest rooms, 1 suite
All Rooms: Named for native wildflowers, TV, AC, phone
Some Rooms: Sun porch
Bed & Bath: Four-poster canopy & brass beds; private baths w/ claw-foot tubs & antique pedestal sinks
Favorites: None
Comfort & Decor: Turn-of-the-century touches and comfortable features such as sitting areas on all three floors

Rates, Reservations, & Restrictions

Deposit: 1 night
Discounts: None
Credit Cards: AE, V, MC, DC, CB, D
Check-in/Out: 1–10 p.m./11 a.m.
Smoking: No
Pets: No
Kids: Welcome
Minimum Stay: 2 nights on weekends
Open: All year
Host: Darla Olmstead
783 N. Main St.
Hendersonville, NC 28792
(828) 693-9193 or (800) 537-8195
Fax: (828) 692-1010
info@waverlyinn.com
www.waverlyinn.com

ESEEOLA LODGE, Linville

Overall: ★★★★ Room Quality: B Value: D Price: $290–$500

At first glance, the Eseeola Lodge seems a little stuffy with coat and tie required at dinner. But on further acquaintance, guests find so much to see and do here that they quickly forget the more formal aspects of one of the most highly honored inns in this part of North Carolina. It's been the local hub of social activities since the 1890s. When the original inn burned down, a new long wooden structure with cedar bark was built to replace it in 1926. Since that time, the inn has won a wall full of awards: National Register of Historic Places, four stars from Mobil, and a silver medal from *Golf Magazine* for the Linville Golf Course. In addition to exploring all the high-country attractions of North Carolina, guests can also be perfectly happy staying all day at this resort—playing golf, tennis, swimming, and letting the kids burn energy at a special day camp.

Setting & Facilities

Location: Base of Grandfather Mountain
Near: Blue Ridge Parkway, Moses H. Cone Park, Blowing Rock
Building: 1926 2-story wooden building w/ chestnut bark
Grounds: Hiking trails & winding streams
Public Space: DR, lobby
Food & Drink: Full breakfast w/ omelets & waffles; dinner also included in rate
Recreation: Swimming, golf, croquet, fishing, tennis
Amenities & Services: Heated swimming pool, croquet court, 8 Har-Tru tennis courts, playground, children's day camp, fresh flowers & fruit basket in room

Accommodations

Units: 19 guest rooms & 5 suites in main building plus 2-BR cottage
All Rooms: AC, phone, cable TV, hair dryer
Some Rooms: Porch w/ garden view
Bed & Bath: King or twins; private baths
Favorites: None
Comfort & Decor: Being redecorated in English Country style

Rates, Reservations, & Restrictions

Deposit: Credit card; 1 night
Discounts: Golf packages include 18 holes, cart, breakfast & dinner, & 2 nights' lodging and start at $400 in spring
Credit Cards: MC,V
Check-in/Out: 4 p.m./11 a.m.
Smoking: Not in DR; smoking rooms avail.
Pets: No
Kids: Welcome
Minimum Stay: 3 nights
Open: Mid-May–late-Oct.
Host: John Blackburn
Box 99, 175 Linville Ave.
Linville, NC 28646
(828) 733-4311 or (800) 742-6717
Fax: (828) 733-3227
www.eseeola.com

CATALOOCHEE RANCH, Maggie Valley

Overall: ★★★ | Room Quality: D | Value: C | Price: $140–$355

Standing on top of the mountain here you can see abutting ranges of the Great Smoky and Blue Ridge Mountains that look like approaching dark waves. In fact, this dude ranch's Indian name, Cataloochee, means "wave after wave" in Cherokee. The rooms in the main ranch building and in the cabins and lodges are as plain, simple, and comfortable as an old Western boot—nothing very fancy but comfortable to slip into. The main attraction here during the warmer months is horseback riding, and from November to March snow skiing is king at the nearby Cataloochee Ski Area. The whole area is a great rural treat to walk through or to throw a fishing line into the pond at the bottom of the hill. It's a delightful dude ranch experience. There's only one sour note: Some horseback-riding guests we talked with complained about bees on the trail, stirred up by their horses and in turn spooking the animals. This may be a rare occurrence, but it's worth asking the wrangler du jour if the problem currently exists before you mount Old Paint. Don't forget to ask for specific directions when you make reservations, especially where to turn in at Maggie Valley (we got lost!). The ranch can be a little complicated to find but is definitely worth the effort.

SETTING & FACILITIES

Location: Exit 40 off I-40 to 276, turn right on Hwy. 19 through Maggie Valley; turn right on Fie Top Rd. (3 mi. to top)
Near: Appalachian Trail, Grandfather Mountain, Tweetsie Railroad, Cataloochee Ski Area
Building: Rustic ranch–style main building & cabins
Grounds: 1,000-acre mountaintop w/ fishing pond & woods
Public Space: Swim/spa, large common room in main building
Food & Drink: Full breakfast w/ eggs, bacon, sausage, pancakes, French toast; refreshments
Recreation: Horseback riding, hiking, fishing, hay rides, white-water rafting
Amenities & Services: Videos, books

ACCOMMODATIONS

Units: 6 guest rooms, 13 cabins, 6 suites
Some Rooms: Fireplace, cathedral ceiling, kitchen, private entrance, mountain view, TV/VCR, porch
Bed & Bath: Beds vary; private baths; some w/ whirlpool tub
Favorites: Miss Judy's House—2-story cabin w/ 3 BRs, kitchenette; good for families or friends traveling together
Comfort & Decor: Plain and rustic

RATES, RESERVATIONS, & RESTRICTIONS

Deposit: 1 night for 1–3 night reservation, 2 nights for 4–6 night reservation, 3 nights for 7 nights or more; 2-week cancellation
Discounts: No
Credit Cards: AE, MC, V
Check-in/Out: 3 p.m./11 a.m.
Smoking: No
Pets: No
Kids: Welcome
Minimum Stay: 1-night stays accepted but not encouraged; required during peak travel months
Open: All year; from Apr.–Nov. all activities & meals; from Dec. 26–Feb., lodging only for guests going to Cataloochee Ski Area
Hosts: Alex & Ashli Aumen, plus other family members
119 Ranch Dr.
Maggie Valley, NC 28751
(828) 926-1401 or (800) 868-1401
Fax: (828) 926-9249
info@cataloochee-ranch.com
www.cataloochee-ranch.com

PINE CREST INN, Tryon

Overall: ★★★★ Room Quality: B Value: C Price: $160–$200

Pine Crest has already won its share of accolades, ranging from a four-diamond AAA rating to the National Register of Historic Places. Guests have a choice of accommodations in the main inn, a log cabin, stone cottage, or woodcutter's cottage. You wonder how Ernest Hemingway might have described the place. He stayed here, and his super-masculine side would have liked the horse and steeplechase themes throughout the rooms. Scott Fitzgerald did, too. If the Fox & Hounds nook (where liquor is served) had existed at the time, he might have spent more time there. If Zelda, his wife, were here today, she'd probably be at the Colonial-style restaurant ordering the pork tenderloin cassis or the potato-crusted salmon. She would also have dressed to the nines for the annual social event of the year, the Block Horse Steeplechase at the nearby Foothills Equestrian Nature Center. There is also an excellent conference center for boards of directors and small business meetings.

SETTING & FACILITIES

Location: 2 blocks from intersection of Hwy. 176 & New Market Rd.
Near: Foothills Equestrian Nature Center
Building: 1917 mountain inn w/ cottages
Grounds: 9-acre estate
Public Space: Large reception area, award-winning restaurant on premises
Food & Drink: Choice of cont'l plus or full breakfast; early coffee or tea; dinner & picnic lunches avail.
Recreation: Jogging, hiking, putting, fishing, antiques shopping
Amenities & Services: AC, phone, TV, VCR; fax & copier; putting green

Accommodations

Units: 17 guest rooms, 18 suites
All Rooms: Equestrian theme, Ralph Lauren linens
Bed & Bath: King or queen; private baths
Favorites: None
Comfort & Decor: Rich, elegant look with unusual whimsical touches (e.g., host Jennifer's collection of teddy bears).

Rates, Reservations, & Restrictions

Deposit: Credit card
Discounts: Corp.
Credit Cards: AE, V, MC
Check-in/Out: 3 p.m./11 a.m.
Smoking: Nonsmoking rooms avail.
Pets: No
Kids: Welcome
Minimum Stay: 2 nights during Oct. weekends
Open: All year except Jan.
Hosts: Jeremy & Jennifer Wainwright
200 Pinecrest Ln.
Tryon, NC 28782-3427
(828) 859-9135 or (800) 633-3001
Fax: (828) 859-9135
info@pinecrestinn.com
www.pinecrestinn.com

INN AT THE TAYLOR HOUSE, Valle Crucis

Overall: ★★★★ Room Quality: B Value: C Price: $150–$265

If you were flying a private plane close to the ground near Boone, North Carolina, and banked toward the west, you would see two small rivers that flowed toward each other, creating a cross and giving the tiny nearby town the Latin name for "Vale of the cross," or Valle Crucis. In 1911 Henry Taylor built a farmhouse in this town established by Scottish immigrants. He may also have created the area's first bed-and-breakfast inn. His wife took in guests for $7 a day, including three meals. Host/owner Chip Schwab can't match that, but she does provide plush accommodations and has found unusual ways to make use of the farm's outbuildings. A barn has become a honeymoon cottage. A pump house has become the Massage Cottage, where guests can receive a chair or full-body massage by a licensed therapist. The milk house is now a gift shop. But our favorite place still serves its original function—a long front porch with comfortable seating.

Setting & Facilities

Location: Near Boone; take Hwy. 194 off Hwy. 421 to reach Valle Crucis
Near: Blowing Rock, Old Mission School, Banner Elk, Linville
Building: 1911 farmhouse
Grounds: Garden and shade trees

Public Space: DR, LR, porch w/ wicker chairs
Food & Drink: Full breakfast w/ egg dishes & pancakes
Recreation: Hiking, rafting, horseback riding, golf, antiques shopping
Amenities & Services: Massage avail., gift shop

Accommodations

Units: 8 guest rooms
All Rooms: Beautifully decorated in excellent taste
Bed & Bath: King, queen, or twins; private baths
Favorites: None
Comfort & Decor: Decorated with paintings by local artists

Rates, Reservations, & Restrictions

Deposit: 1 night; 7-day cancellation
Discounts: None
Credit Cards: V, MC; cash or personal check preferred
Check-in/Out: 3 p.m./11 a.m.
Smoking: No
Pets: No
Kids: Welcome (by prior arrangement)
Minimum Stay: 2 nights weekends
Open: Apr.–Dec. 1
Host: Chip Schwab
4584 Hwy. 194, P.O. Box 713
Valle Crucis, NC 28691
(828) 963-5581
Fax: (828) 963-5818
taylorhouse@highsouth.com
www.highsouth.com/taylorhouse

GRANDVIEW LODGE, Waynesville

Overall: ★★★ Room Quality: C Value: A Price: $80–$115

How would you like to have your breakfast cooked by the "Chef of the South"? That is what the *Atlanta Journal-Constitution* once named host Linda Arnold. She trained at the Culinary Institute of America, and each morning you can sample her graduate achievements. Husband Stan is a former corporate executive who speaks Polish, Russian, and German in addition to English. And leave it to a corporate type to come up with big-time marketing ideas. Every year each guest that spends $500 for food and lodging at the Grandview will receive $50 in credit toward future stays. Since breakfast and dinner are already included in rates that hover around $100 for couples ($80 for single occupancy), the new "Frequent Guest Dollars" program makes this lodge even more of a super bargain.

Setting & Facilities

Location: Exit 27 off I-40 to Hwy. 23-74; look for Waynesville signs
Near: Great Smoky Mountains Nat'l Park, Maggie Valley, Blue Ridge Parkway
Building: Century-old country lodge
Grounds: 2.5 acres w/ apple orchards & grape arbors
Public Space: Porch, DR

Food & Drink: Full breakfast; special treats: Linda's homemade jams, "Grandview Chocoholic Tart"; dinner included in rate; special dietary requests honored
Recreation: Hiking, tennis, golf
Amenities & Services: Cooking tips

ACCOMMODATIONS

Units: 9 guest rooms in lodge, 2 apts.
All Rooms: Color cable TV, gas-burning fireplace
Bed & Bath: King or queen plus 2nd bed in each room; private baths
Favorites: Mary Todd Room, light & airy
Comfort & Decor: Bright, light rooms

RATES, RESERVATIONS, & RESTRICTIONS

Deposit: Credit card, but personal check preferred
Discounts: None
Credit Cards: V, MC
Check-in/Out: 1 p.m./10 a.m.
Smoking: No
Pets: No
Kids: Welcome
Minimum Stay: None
Open: All year
Hosts: Stan & Linda Arnold
466 Lickstone Rd.
Waynesville, NC 28786
(828) 456-5212 or (800) 255-7826
innkeeper@grandviewlodgenc.com
www.bbonline.com/nc/grandview

SWAG COUNTRY INN, Waynesville

Overall: ★★★★½ Room Quality: B Value: D Price: $240–$510

Ordinarily we do not include inns that serve three meals a day; this begins to cross over that always fuzzy definition of bed-and-breakfast and full-service hotel. However, not to report on some extraordinary lodging alternatives in an area just because they sometimes serve three meals would be a disservice to readers. That's why we are including the Swag Country Inn, three wonderful meals a day and all. The history of the inn is fascinating, like a frontier jigsaw puzzle. The common room was once a fieldstone country church, reconstructed stone by stone on this site. Logs and stones, some more than 150 years old, were brought from all over Tennessee and North Carolina and reassembled into the log guest rooms. Then host/owner Deener Mathews added luxurious new touches to these great old settings, from steam showers and private balconies to coffee beans and grinders. You will be staying at a 5,000-foot elevation, which could bother some people, and the gravel road leading to the inn is 2.5 miles long; drive slowly to avoid car pings. But the view from the Swag is absolutely spectacular. Because of all the meals and luxury, the rates are pretty spectacular for this part of North Carolina. If you're traveling on a budget, choose the Grandview Lodge (see profile). If your mutual funds have been doing very well, choose a vacation at the Swag Country Inn.

SETTING & FACILITIES

Location: 6 mi. from Waynesville on back roads; call for directions
Near: Great Smoky Mountains Nat'l Park, Cherokee Indian Reservation
Building: 6 log buildings
Grounds: 250 acres w/ nature trails, a pond, & forests
Public Space: Common room w/ fireplace
Food & Drink: Full breakfast; lunch & dinner included; hors d'oeuvres before dinner; dinner is special w/ cider chicken or cumin-crusted pork w/ raspberry sauce; high tea
Recreation: Hiking, workshops in photography, bird-watching, quilting, etc.
Amenities & Services: Badminton & croquet areas

ACCOMMODATIONS

Units: 12 guest rooms
All Rooms: Fireplace or wood stove, phone
Some Rooms: Wet bar (bring own liquor; this is a dry county)
Bed & Bath: King, queen, or twin; private baths—steam shower, tub/shower
Favorites: Cabin suite w/ steam shower & whirlpool tub, small deck, "tree" bed
Comfort & Decor: Rustic elegance

RATES, RESERVATIONS, & RESTRICTIONS

Deposit: 50% of total stay
Discounts: None
Credit Cards: AE, V, MC, D
Check-in/Out: 3 p.m./11 a.m.
Smoking: No
Pets: No
Kids: Welcome
Minimum Stay: 2 nights
Open: May 1–mid-Nov.
Host: Deener Mathews
2300 Swag Rd.
Waynesville, NC 28786
(828) 926-0430 or (800) 789-7672
Fax: (828) 926-2036
letters@theswag.com
www.theswag.com

DRY RIDGE INN, Weaverville

Overall: ★★★ Room Quality: C Value: B Price: $90–$130

Imagine living in a typical mountain village home in the nineteenth century. Now you can experience some of the same feeling at Dry Ridge Inn. Travelers have been staying here for more than a hundred years. If they returned today, they would find such modern surprises as a hot tub on a backyard deck and artwork throughout the home by host/artist Mary Lou. If you see something you like, you can probably buy it in the small gift shop downstairs. We found the hosts very eager to please. For example, although they don't take pets, they will try to board guests' Rover or Fluffy at a friend's house.

SETTING & FACILITIES

Location: Take Hwy. 19/23 north from Asheville, take exit for New Stock Rd., go north on Bus. 19 for 2 mi., turn right on Brown St.
Near: Blue Ridge Parkway, Biltmore Estate, Smoky Mountains, Grandfather Mountain
Building: 3½-story village style, 1886
Grounds: Acre yard w/ flowers
Public Space: Parlor, sitting area
Food & Drink: Full breakfast by candlelight; specialty: gingerbread pancakes w/ lemon sauce
Recreation: Hiking to mountain streams, sight-seeing in Asheville
Amenities & Services: Newspapers, local maps, large library, local menus, "guest comment" book (w/ restaurant reviews)

ACCOMMODATIONS

Units: 7 guest rooms
All Rooms: Individually decorated, hardwood floors
Some Rooms: Fireplace
Bed & Bath: Beds vary; private baths
Favorites: Gibson Room w/ water garden view & fireplace w/ love seat
Comfort & Decor: Filled with antiques and the host's artwork

RATES, RESERVATIONS, & RESTRICTIONS

Deposit: 50% of total stay; 7-day cancellation
Discounts: 10% 3-night stays, AARP, 20% corp. Sun.–Thur.
Credit Cards: MC, V, AE, D
Check-in/Out: 3–8 p.m./11 a.m.
Smoking: No
Pets: No
Kids: 8 years & older
Minimum Stay: 2 nights on weekends
Open: All year
Hosts: Paul & Mary Lou Gibson
26 Brown St.
Weaverville, NC 28787
(800) 839-3899
Fax: (868) 658-8022
dryridgeinn@msn.com

INN ON MAIN STREET, Weaverville

Overall: ★★★ Room Quality: C Value: C Price: $95–$125

You almost expect Dr. Zebulon Robinson to walk in the door of this Victorian home he built in 1900, perhaps stopping in the parlor to read the local newspaper and then going upstairs to the master bedroom where he might store his thermometers and stethoscope in a large medical instrument cabinet. He would still feel right at home if he made the same entrance today. The present owners have tried to maintain this same Victorian ambiance. He might be puzzled by the TV in the parlor (the only one in the house), but if he went up to the "Robinson" room he would still find his old medical instrument cabinet, now a vanity. He probably would also have approved of an old-fashioned medical treatment nearby—a hot springs mineral bath for $15.

Setting & Facilities

Location: Block from downtown, at corner of Main & East Sts.
Near: Biltmore Estate, Asheville antiques & nightlife, Blue Ridge Parkway, Hot Springs spa
Building: 1900 Country Victorian
Grounds: Landscaped lot
Public Space: Front & back porches, parlor, DR
Food & Drink: Full breakfast w/ homemade bread, muffins, fruit, juice plus specialties—egg frittatas, spinach quiche; "bottomless" cookie jar for daytime snacks
Recreation: Golf, hiking, trail rides, canoeing, mountain biking, kayaking
Amenities & Services: Newspapers, magazines, TV in parlor, local restaurant menus

Accommodations

Units: 7 guest rooms
All Rooms: AC, hardwood floors w/ area rugs, antiques
Some Rooms: Fireplace, mountain view; 2 w/ private access
Bed & Bath: King, twin; private baths
Favorites: Robinson w/ brass queen & antique tub
Comfort & Decor: Early Victorian

Rates, Reservations, & Restrictions

Deposit: 1 night; 7-day cancellation
Discounts: Extended stay, singles, frequent business travelers
Credit Cards: V, MC, D
Check-in/Out: 3–7 p.m./11 a.m.
Smoking: No
Pets: No
Kids: No small children
Minimum Stay: 2 nights on peak season weekends
Open: All year (except breaks in Jan.)
Hosts: Dan & Nancy Ward
88 S. Main St.
Weaverville, NC 28787
(828) 645-4935 or (877) 873-6074
relax@innonmain.com
www.innonmain.com

South Carolina

The Spanish were the first to favor this area, and they explored much of the coast in 1521. They, and later the French, decided they liked the land so much that they would settle here. But their early attempts failed, and France's Charles II promptly gave the land to eight English noblemen.

South Carolina has been sought and fought over ever since, witnessing bloody battles between the English and American Revolutionary armies at Kings Mountain, Cowpens, Eutaw Springs, and the Guildford Courthouse. Later South Carolina again became a battleground between Yankees and Southerners, with the Confederacy igniting the war in their own backyard at Fort Sumter in Charleston's harbor.

Today tourists go into battle on the golf fairways of Hilton Head. They overrun the historic streets of Charleston like a straw-hatted invading army, devouring she-crab soup and roasted oysters and lining up for country music shows in Myrtle Beach.

South Carolina has some wonderful bed-and-breakfasts, and we'll point you toward some of the better ones. We recommend that you first decide what you want to see in the state, and then pick the most convenient bed-and-breakfasts near them. The more you can reduce your driving the more time you can have to enjoy all the pleasures of the Palmetto State.

Here are some worthwhile attractions: Historic Charleston (of course), Sumter National Monument, the Charleston Museum (America's oldest museum), the Riverbanks and Zoo in Columbia, border-to-border golf courses throughout the state (particularly around Myrtle Beach and Hilton Head), the cool retreats of the Georgia Mountains, and the gardens at Cypress Gardens, Brookgreen, and Glencairn.

For More Information

South Carolina Department of Tourism
(803) 734-0122

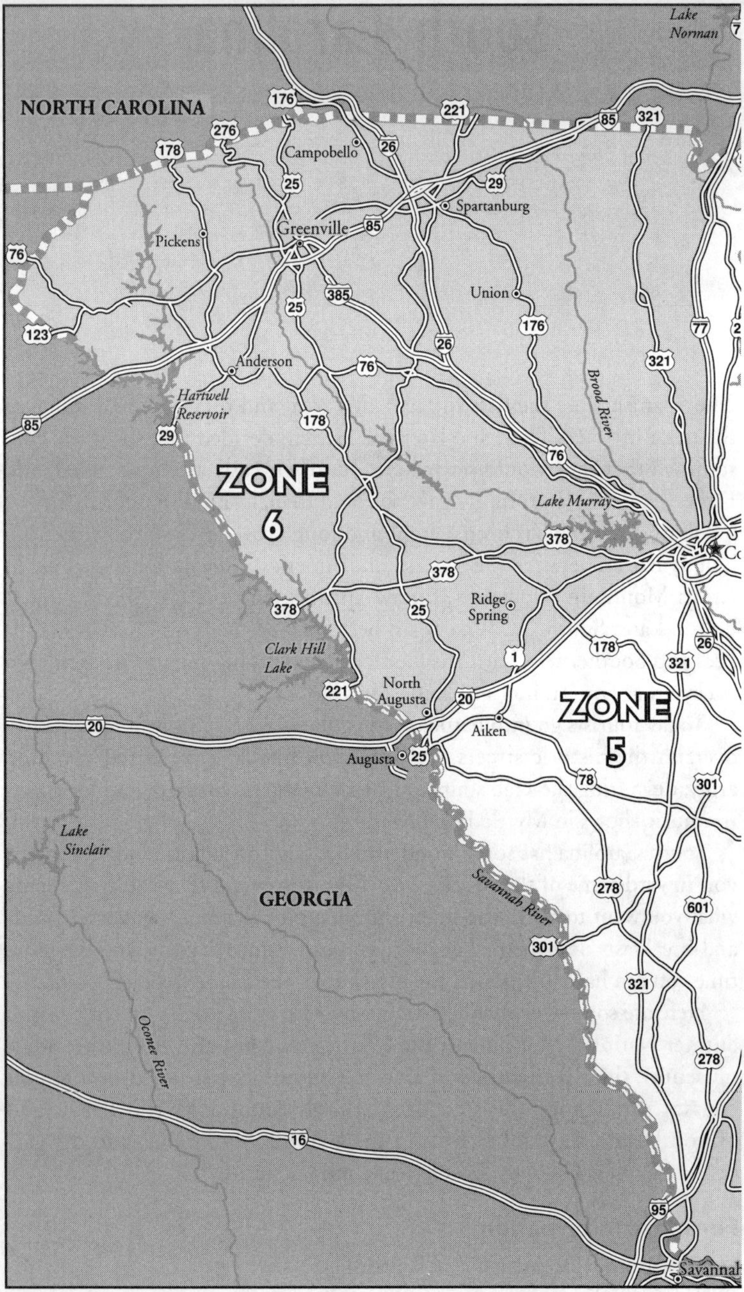

NORTH CAROLINA
Lake Norman
Campobello
Spartanburg
Greenville
Pickens
Union
Anderson
Hartwell Reservoir
Brood River
Lake Murray
ZONE 6
Ridge Spring
Clark Hill Lake
North Augusta
Aiken
Augusta
ZONE 5
Lake Sinclair
GEORGIA
Savannah River
Oconee River
Savannah

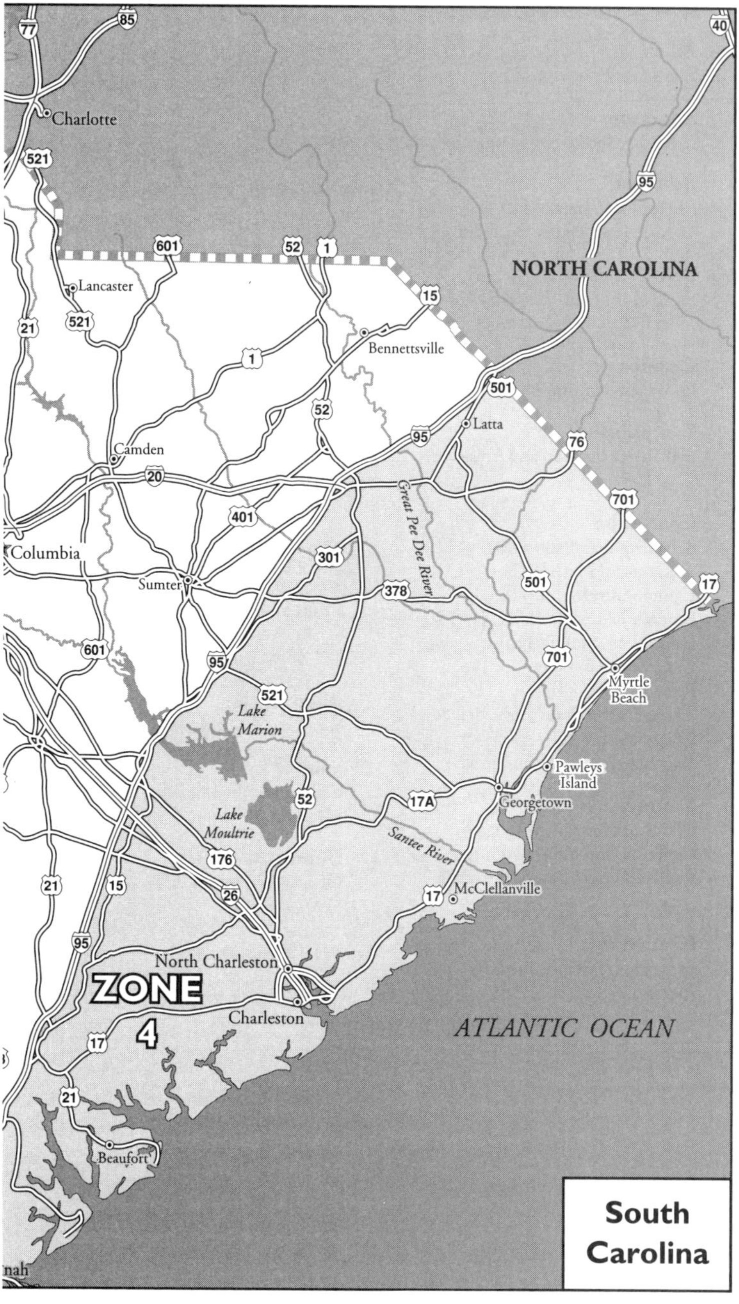
Charlotte
NORTH CAROLINA
Lancaster
Bennettsville
Latta
Camden
Columbia
Sumter
Great Pee Dee River
Lake Marion
Lake Moultrie
Santee River
Myrtle Beach
Pawleys Island
Georgetown
McClellanville
North Charleston
ZONE 4
Charleston
ATLANTIC OCEAN
Beaufort
South Carolina

Zone 4
Coastal South Carolina

With apologies to Tony Bennett, we believe that almost as many travelers have left their heart in Charleston as in San Francisco. Walk down cobblestone streets past some of the 73 buildings constructed before the American Revolution. Take a tour of Fort Sumter, where the first shots of the Civil War were fired in anger and confusion. Come in late spring for one of the great cultural event of the Americas, the Spoleto Festival.

Up the coast the Grand Strand begins at historic Georgetown and stretches 60 miles to the North Carolina border, a glorious beach of golden and white sand. Along the way are the trendy new restaurants and shows of Myrtle Beach and some 100 golf courses and 200 tennis courts.

You'll find some of the world's most elegant and expensive bed-and-breakfasts in Charleston. Our rule of thumb is the higher the price, the skimpier the continental breakfast served. But for unbelievable, unimaginable luxury, Two Meeting Street Inn and Rutledge House are the cream of the crop.

It's hard to imagine that the real development of Hilton Head Island at the very southern end of the Carolina coast began as recently as 1956. The island's "plantation" resorts have lured new residents, golfers, and nature lovers from all over the world.

For More Information

Charleston Trident Convention and Visitors Bureau
(803) 853-8000

Myrtle Beach Convention and Visitors Bureau
(800) 488-8998

RHETT HOUSE INN, Beaufort

Overall: ★★★★★ Room Quality: A Value: C Price: $150–$250

If this place looks familiar, you're probably a movie buff—*Forrest Gump*, *Prince of Tides*, and other movies were filmed here. Barbra Streisand stayed here. So did Nick Nolte and other movie stars. One reason is evident at first glance—"sheer luxury." The Rhett House Inn is where you can come to indulge yourself in Southern charm, planned for you by owner/hosts who, ironically, were Yankee-born. *Convenience* is another word that comes to mind. Guests stay right on the Intracoastal Waterway in the historic district of Beaufort. This is a very romantic inn. For extra privacy, request the guest cottage. Sea Island cotton was responsible for the immense wealth generated in this little community in the eighteenth century, and you can see how this money was spent on splendid old mansions in Old Point. Ask about house tours held every spring and fall in Beaufort.

Setting & Facilities

Location: A block from the Intracoastal Waterway in downtown Beaufort
Near: George Elliot House Museum, John Mark Verdier House Museum, 1724 St. Helena's Episcopal Church
Building: 1820 Antebellum plantation house & guest cottage
Grounds: Gardens
Public Space: Veranda
Food & Drink: Full breakfast w/ pancakes, eggs, or French toast, and "true Southern grits"; evening hors d'oeuvres
Recreation: Sight-seeing in the low country
Amenities & Services: Picnic baskets on request, conf. facil. for 20

Accommodations

Units: 17 guest rooms
All Rooms: Cable TV, phone, robes, hair dryer, bicycles
Some Rooms: Fireplace, private porch, whirlpool tub
Bed & Bath: Beds vary; private baths
Favorites: None
Comfort & Decor: Oriental rugs complement the English and American antiques.

Rates, Reservations, & Restrictions

Deposit: Credit card, 1 night
Discounts: AAA
Credit Cards: AE, V, MC
Check-in/Out: 3 p.m./11 a.m.
Smoking: No
Pets: No
Kids: 5 & older
Minimum Stay: 2 nights weekends
Open: All year
Hosts: Steve & Marianne Harrison
100 Craven St.
Beaufort, SC 29902
(843) 524-9030 or (888) 480-9530
Fax: (843) 524-1310
rhetthse@hargray.com
www.innbook.com/rhett.html

TWOSUNS INN BED & BREAKFAST, Beaufort

Overall: ★★★½ Room Quality: B Value: B Price: $105–$151

In historic Beaufort you might expect a bed-and-breakfast that resonates with dignity and history, but hardly one that has gone bananas! In many ways the TwoSuns Inn is conventional, with bay views from the veranda, casual furniture that sometimes borders on "attic modern," and wonderful breakfasts. But what really sets this inn apart is the enthusiasm and sense of humor of Ron and Carol Key. Their diligence in restoring and maintaining the house has earned them the South Carolina Honor Award for Historic Preservation. Their quirky side has encouraged them to create a "Mini-Banana Museum" in their home (as loyal members of the International Banana Club—ask them about it). Go to their Web site, memorize and use the current banana phrase when you make your reservation, and you will "save a bunch" on your bill. The current phrase when this book went to print was: "Time flies like an arrow but fruit flies like a banana." As humorist Dave Barry likes to say, we are not making this up!

SETTING & FACILITIES

Location: Right on Hwy. 21 at Beaufort Plaza, left on Bay St.
Near: Hunting Island State Park, Hilton Head, Savannah (45 mi.)
Building: 1917 Neoclassic Revival
Grounds: On the Intracoastal Waterway
Public Space: LR, DR, veranda
Food & Drink: Full breakfast; afternoon "Tea & Toddy"
Recreation: Carriage & walking tours
Amenities & Services: Hair dryers, book of menus

ACCOMMODATIONS

Units: 6 guest rooms
All Rooms: TV, radio, alarm clock, phone
Bed & Bath: King or queen; private baths
Favorites: None
Comfort & Decor: Informal

RATES, RESERVATIONS, & RESTRICTIONS

Deposit: Credit card
Discounts: "Banana" discount (see comments above)
Credit Cards: AE, V, MC, D, DC
Check-in/Out: 3–9 p.m./noon
Smoking: No
Pets: No
Kids: 12 & older
Minimum Stay: None
Open: All year
Hosts: Ron & Carroll Key
1705 Bay St.
Beaufort, SC 29902
(843) 522-1122 or (800) 532-4244
Fax: (843) 522-1122
twosuns@islc.net
www.twosunsinn.com

BELVEDERE BED & BREAKFAST, Charleston

Overall: ★★★½ Room Quality: B Value: C Price: $150–$175

Belvedere is beautiful, inside and out. The huge front columns are particularly impressive. The interior woodwork is a century older than the house itself, rescued from the old Belvedere Plantation in the 1920s. The inn is right across the street from Colonial Lake, which is an easy walk or rickshaw ride from the downtown area. Try the semicircular piazza on the second floor; a wonderful place to watch sunsets over the lake. The owner, David Spell, used to own the famous 2 Meeting Street Inn in Charleston, which he sold in 1990, but he brought along his collections of books, blue canton china and crystal, and his innate sense of hospitality to Belvedere. Parking is on the street, but a little easier than at some Charleston bed-and-breakfasts because this is a residential area.

SETTING & FACILITIES

Location: Exit I-26 & proceed down Rutledge Ave.
Near: Fort Sumter, historic homes
Building: 1900 Colonial Revival
Grounds: Formal garden w/ patio
Public Space: Den w/ cable & VCR, LR, DR, piazza w/ lake view
Food & Drink: Cont'l breakfast plus w/ sweet potato–pineapple walnut bread; afternoon sherry & cookies
Recreation: Walking tours, house tours
Amenities & Services: Newspaper, restaurant & tour guides, including videos of Charleston

ACCOMMODATIONS

Units: 3 guest rooms
All Rooms: Poster canopied bed, AC
Some Rooms: Colonial Lake view, marble bathroom, ornamental fireplace
Bed & Bath: Beds vary; private baths
Favorites: None
Comfort & Decor: This place resonates with history; 1800s woodwork.

RATES, RESERVATIONS, & RESTRICTIONS

Deposit: 1 night; 14-day cancellation
Discounts: AAA, members of Nat'l Trust for Preservation; discounts not applicable during summer
Credit Cards: None; personal check or cash
Check-in/Out: 4–6 p.m./10 a.m. (flexible)
Smoking: No
Pets: No, but can arrange for kennel
Kids: 8 & older
Minimum Stay: 2 nights weekends, 3 nights holiday weekends
Open: All year (except Christmas week)
Hosts: David Spell & Joanne Kuhn
40 Rutledge Ave.
Charleston, SC 29401
(843) 722-0973 or (800) 816-1664
www.belvedereinn.com

BRASINGTON HOUSE BED & BREAKFAST, Charleston

Overall: ★★★½ | Room Quality: C | Value: B | Price: $134–$154

Brasington House offers some advantages over other bed-and-breakfasts in Charleston. First, the hosts are personally involved with their guests. This is their home. At other area bed-and-breakfasts the owners frequently live elsewhere and hire hosts (some great, some not). Another advantage is off-street parking. This is very important in a city as busy as Charleston. And compared to other Charleston rates, Brasington House offers good value. Some unusual services here include an unpublished toll-free number, which will be given to you when you make a reservation, and help with dining reservations. Your hosts will send you a list of recommended restaurants when you arrive and then suggest you make your dining reservations immediately to avoid disappointment, or call them and they will make the reservations for you.

SETTING & FACILITIES

Location: Historic District
Near: Waterfront Park, City Market, Museum Houses
Building: 200-year-old Antebellum
Grounds: None
Public Space: Sitting room
Food & Drink: Full breakfast; complimentary afternoon wine; evening liqueurs
Recreation: Sight-seeing
Amenities & Services: Help w/ restaurant reservations

ACCOMMODATIONS

Units: 4 guest rooms
All Rooms: Coffee & tea facil., antiques, hearts-of-pine floors
Some Rooms: Nonworking fireplace
Bed & Bath: Beds vary; private baths
Favorites: None
Comfort & Decor: Beautiful antiques fill the house.

RATES, RESERVATIONS, & RESTRICTIONS

Deposit: 1 night
Discounts: None
Credit Cards: V, MC
Check-in/Out: Call (flexible)/11 a.m.
Smoking: No
Pets: No
Kids: No
Minimum Stay: 2 nights spring, fall, & all weekends
Open: Closed Dec. & Jan.
Hosts: Dalton & Judy Brasington
328 E. Bay St.
Charleston, SC 29401
(843) 722-1274

CANNONBORO INN, Charleston

Overall: ★★★½ Room Quality: B Value: C Price: $79–$200

The staff prides themselves on knowing everything there is to know about Charleston. They are all members of the local concierge association, so they have the inside scoop on activities, events, and tour sites. They also have two large albums with detailed information about tours and restaurants, the best organization of information we've seen in any bed-and-breakfast. On Thursday afternoons a local historian drops by to talk about the city's history. The rooms are big and comfortable, but the bathrooms are a little worn. Breakfast is a special treat, especially when they serve artichoke pie or stuffed waffles.

Setting & Facilities

Location: From I-26 East take 2nd Meeting St. exit (221B) & turn right on Calhoun to Ashley
Near: Rainbow Row, Colonial Lake, beaches, parks
Building: Single house w/ Victorian touches
Grounds: English garden w/ fish pond
Public Space: Parlor, 2 piazzas
Food & Drink: Full breakfast; afternoon tea; evening sherry in parlor
Recreation: Sightseeing, carriage rides
Amenities & Services: Full concierge service, restaurant directory in room, loaner bikes

Accommodations

Units: 6 guest rooms
All Rooms: Poster or canopy bed, period furnishings, hearts-of-pine floors, area rugs, cable TV
Bed & Bath: King or queen; private baths
Favorites: None
Comfort & Decor: All rooms have comfortable seating.

Rates, Reservations, & Restrictions

Deposit: Credit card; full amount; 7-day cancellation
Discounts: Off-season rates (Nov.–Feb.)
Credit Cards: AE, V, MC, D
Check-in/Out: 3 p.m./10 a.m.
Smoking: No
Pets: No
Kids: 10 & older
Minimum Stay: 2 or 3 nights major holidays
Open: All year
Hosts: Lynn Bartosh, Bud & Sally Allen
184 Ashley Ave.
Charleston, SC 29403
(843) 723-8527 or (800) 235-8039
Fax: (843) 723-8007
cannonboroinn@aol.com
www.charleston-sc-inns.com/cannonboro

FANTASIA BED & BREAKFAST, Charleston

Overall: ★★★ | Room Quality: C | Value: C | Price: $75–$195

The "Single House" is a famous house plan that dates back to the crowded streets of Europe, where every foot was at a premium. So that is what Mary Scott built in 1813, a house that was one room wide with additional rooms behind it and the narrow part facing the street. The owner has wisely chosen to stress comfort over ye olde antique feel and has picked reproductions that are also easy to sit on. Many of the bed-and-breakfasts in Charleston serve continental breakfasts, but Fantasia serves a gourmet feast every morning. Free off-street parking is available here, a tremendous advantage in the car-crowded historic district.

SETTING & FACILITIES

Location: Exit 221B off I-26; go south on Meeting St. & turn left on George
Near: Charleston Historic District
Building: Charleston Single House
Grounds: None
Public Space: DR, LR, piazza
Food & Drink: Full breakfast w/ peach cobbler, pecan waffles w/ bananas, homemade breakfast sausage
Recreation: Historic walking tours, harbor cruises
Amenities & Services: Concierge service

ACCOMMODATIONS

Units: 6 guest rooms
All Rooms: On-site parking
Some Rooms: Whirlpool tub, private piazza, fireplace
Bed & Bath: Queens; private baths
Favorites: Magnolia Suite w/ whirlpool tub, fireplace, sitting room
Comfort & Decor: Eclectic decor

RATES, RESERVATIONS, & RESTRICTIONS

Deposit: 1 night
Discounts: None
Credit Cards: AE, MC, V, D
Check-in/Out: 3 p.m./10 a.m.
Smoking: No
Pets: No
Kids: 12 & older
Minimum Stay: 2 nights on weekends
Open: All year
Hosts: Martin & Catherine Riccio
11 George St.
Charleston, SC 29401
(843) 853-0201 or (800) 852-4466
Fax: (843) 853-1441
mail@fantasiabb.com
www.fantasiabb.com

FULTON LANE INN, Charleston

Overall: ★★½ | Room Quality: C | Value: D | Price: $140–$285

Fulton Lane is a handsome inn, but we believe the Four Diamonds awarded by AAA may be one or even two stars too many. Here are some guest comments: "The location off Broad Street is excellent but the inn can be difficult to find." "Getting in is a little awkward. Must carry bags from back lot behind the inn to the alley where entrance is located." The inn brochure promises "soaring windows frame captivating vistas of the city's historic skyline." That may be true of most of the windows, but a guest commented, "Some rooms look into hotel walls. We had a closed-in feeling." This is a highly rated inn, and we do recommend it. It is very convenient and parking is available for $5 a day. However, it could be worthwhile to check out your room whenever possible before you move your suitcases out of the car.

SETTING & FACILITIES

Location: On King St. several blocks up from the Battery
Near: Charleston Harbor, famous homes, Saks Fifth Ave., antiques shops
Building: 1870 Victorian inn
Grounds: None
Public Space: Lobby
Food & Drink: Cont'l breakfast served in room; evening wine & sherry in lobby
Recreation: Sight-seeing, shopping
Amenities & Services: Morning newspaper, nightly turn-down w/ chocolates, hot tubs, conf. facil., concierge service

ACCOMMODATIONS

Units: 27 guest rooms including 5 1-BR suites
All Rooms: Stocked guest fridge
Some Rooms: Fireplace, canopied bed, whirlpool tub, cathedral ceiling
Bed & Bath: Beds vary; private baths
Favorites: None
Comfort & Decor: Light and airy with pastel colors and louvered shades

RATES, RESERVATIONS, & RESTRICTIONS

Deposit: 1 night
Discounts: AAA, AARP, corp.
Credit Cards: Most major cards
Check-in/Out: 3 p.m./noon
Smoking: No
Pets: No
Kids: Welcome
Minimum Stay: 2 nights certain times of year; ask
Open: All year
Host: Michelle Woodhull
202 King St.
Charleston, SC 29401
(843) 720-2600 or (800) 720-2688
Fax: (843) 720-2940
fli@charminginns.com
www.charminginns.com

GOVERNOR'S HOUSE INN, Charleston

Overall: ★★★★ Room Quality: B Value: D Price: $165–$340

Two Meeting Street Inn, created by the Spell family, is one of the best-known bed-and-breakfast inns in the South, and when the daughter of the family develops her own inn, you can expect someplace pretty special. And that is what you will find at the Governor's House Inn. Everything is in gorgeous excess here, including the prices. Rooms are steeped in colonial history; Edward Rutledge, youngest signer of the Declaration of Independence, lived here. The staff of this large home is exceedingly helpful. We do feel, however, that the rates are too steep, and the fact that they don't accept any credit cards can be an inconvenience. But all the rooms were booked when we visited, including the one costing $340 a night. We're among the penny-pinchers who think that spending that much for a room and bed puts lumps in our mattress.

Setting & Facilities

Location: From I-26 take Meeting St. exit, 1.5 mi. to Broad St., right on Broad, 1.5 blocks
Near: City Market, The Battery, Four Corners of Law
Building: Federal
Grounds: Yard & gardens
Public Space: Parlor, LR, DR, verandas, sun porch
Food & Drink: Cont'l breakfast w/ oversized muffins & local fruit (blueberries, kiwi w/ low country sauce, strawberries); afternoon tea w/ sweets & cheese
Recreation: Sight-seeing historic homes, antiques shopping, golf, swimming
Amenities & Services: Menus for Charleston's great restaurants; will arrange everything from carriage rides to 3-masted schooner trips

Accommodations

Units: 9 guest rooms
All Rooms: Hardwood floors, Oriental rug, cable TV, phone
Some Rooms: Porch, working fireplace, canopy bed, wet bar
Bed & Bath: King or queen; private baths
Favorites: None
Comfort & Decor: There are nine fireplaces, crystal chandeliers, and rooms filled with magnificent antiques.

Rates, Reservations, & Restrictions

Deposit: 1 night for 3-day reservation, 2 nights for 4 or more days
Discounts: Off-season (July, Aug., Jan., Feb.)
Credit Cards: None
Check-in/Out: 2:30 p.m./11 a.m.
Smoking: No; on porches only
Pets: No
Kids: 13 & over
Minimum Stay: 2 days on weekends
Open: All year except Christmas Day & the day before/after
Host: Karen Spell Shaw
117 Broad St.
Charleston, SC 29401
(843) 720-2070 or (800) 720-9812
www.governorshouse.com

RUTLEDGE HOUSE INN, Charleston

Overall: ★★★★★ Room Quality: A Value: D Price: $185–$365

George Washington probably slept here, or at least his diary records he had breakfast here. Good thing he was a guest, because he may not have been able to pay the bill today. But in fairness, we have to say that those with significant travel budgets will be buying a lot of luxury and historic memories with their money at this incredibly beautiful inn. The top price of $365 is for the Grand Suite (described below). You will be staying in the former home of John Rutledge, one of the original signers of the Declaration of Independence. The inn is a National Historic Landmark on the National Register of Historic and a Charleston treasure.

SETTING & FACILITIES

Location: Exit 221 off I-26 to Meeting St. & turn right on King St.; B&B 1.5 blocks down on right
Near: In Historic District, 15-min. walk to the Battery & City Market
Building: 1763 main house, 2-story carriage house, & reproduction carriage house
Grounds: Buildings surround a courtyard w/ seating
Public Space: Ballroom, adjoining balcony
Food & Drink: Afternoon tea in ballroom; cont'l breakfast delivered to rooms: Southern biscuits w/ hot sherried fruit, muffins; full breakfast also avail. w/ shrimp, grits, eggs Benedict; wine, sherry, & brandy in ballroom
Recreation: Walking, jogging, biking through Charleston's historic streets
Amenities & Services: Guest memberships to local health club, local newspapers, complimentary on-site parking (very important in Charleston!), free local calls, concierge service, nightly turn-down w/ chocolates

ACCOMMODATIONS

Units: 19 guest rooms
All Rooms: Color cable TV, fridge stocked w/ refreshments, iron & ironing board, robes, phone
Some Rooms: 14-ft. ceiling, carved Italian marble fireplaces, hand-laid parquet floor, courtyard view
Bed & Bath: Beds vary; private baths (tub/shower, whirlpool, or glass-walled shower)
Favorites: Grand Suite—900 square feet of luxury w/ 2 carved Italian marble fireplaces & parquet floors
Comfort & Decor: Blend of eighteenth- and nineteenth-century styles

RATES, RESERVATIONS, & RESTRICTIONS

Deposit: Credit card; 1 night charged a month before arrival
Discounts: Low-season discounts for midweek stays
Credit Cards: AE, V, MC, D, DC
Check-in/Out: 4 p.m./noon
Smoking: 2 rooms of Cooper Carriage House, ballroom, balcony of main house ballroom
Pets: No
Kids: Welcome; add'l fee of $20 for children 13 & older
Minimum Stay: Varies by season

Open: All year
Host: Linda Bishop
116 Broad St.
Charleston, SC 29401
(843) 723-7999 or (800) 476-9741
Fax: (843) 720-2615
jrh@charminginns.com
www.charminginns.com

TWENTY-SEVEN STATE STREET BED & BREAKFAST, Charleston

Overall: ★★★½ Room Quality: B Value: C Price: $110–$180

Twenty-Seven State Street has been rated as "valuable to the city" in terms of historical importance (the second highest rating given). Almost everything Charleston has to offer is within walking distance. Theaters abound in this area, making it one of the best located inns in the city. However, there is a penalty for all this convenience—$4.25 a day for parking if you can find a place. If you choose not to have breakfast, $15 a day is taken off the bill for couples; $7.50 a day from singles—money you can apply to your parking costs all over town.

SETTING & FACILITIES

Location: 2 blocks south of South Market St.
Near: Waterfront Park, City Market, Museum Houses
Building: 1800 Town House
Grounds: Courtyard & veranda
Public Space: Courtyard, common room
Food & Drink: Cont'l plus w/ fruit, breads, cheese
Recreation: Touring historic sights, shopping
Amenities & Services: Fresh flowers, lists of restaurants, loaner bicycles

ACCOMMODATIONS

Units: 5 guest rooms (2 Carriage House, 3 main house)
All Rooms: private entrance, kitchenette, Oriental rugs, hardwood floors, cable TV, phone w/ answering machine, coffeemaker
Bed & Bath: Queens; private baths
Favorites: None
Comfort & Decor: Extra comfortable beds

RATES, RESERVATIONS, & RESTRICTIONS

Deposit: Credit card to secure reservation, then mail check for 1 night's payment
Discounts: Off-season rates
Credit Cards: Prefer cash & checks
Check-in/Out: 9 a.m./2 p.m. ; flexible
Smoking: No
Pets: No
Kids: Welcome
Minimum Stay: 2 nights weekends, special events, holidays
Open: All year
Hosts: Paul & Joye Craven
27 State St.
Charleston, SC 29401
(843) 722-4243
Fax: (843) 722-6030
www.charleston-bb.com

TWO MEETING STREET INN, Charleston

Overall: ★★★★½ Room Quality: A Value: C Price: $165–$265

It's easy to go overboard in describing Two Meeting Street Inn. Its wide two-story porches provide a great view of Charleston's famous harbor, and its beautiful rooms whisper of countless wedding and anniversary secrets. The whole house was initially a $75,000 wedding present in 1890 from father to daughter (he put the check on her bed on her wedding day). Nothing was spared to create the home, with even Louis Comfort Tiffany himself installing his namesake windows. Anastasia, or at least the woman who claimed to be the only surviving daughter of Czar Nicholas II, stayed here. So have thousands of honeymooners and anniversary celebrants. Singles might feel a little out of place here unless they're just coming to indulge in some personal luxury time and are not too concerned with meeting others. The continental breakfast, like those served by many Charleston bed-and-breakfasts, may not be hearty enough to last until lunch. The cost is high, but the inn is an extraordinary experience. One annoyance is that the inn does not accept credit cards, which means you have to pay for everything on the spot with a personal or travelers' check. And don't forget that South Carolina slaps a whopping 12 percent "sales and accommodations" charge on your final bill. If you stayed in the $265 Grand Victorian Room, that's another $31 a night! Better put another muffin in your pocket for lunch. You've paid for it.

SETTING & FACILITIES

Location: At the Battery, Charleston's Historic Harbor
Near: Historic District
Building: 1892 Queen Anne mansion
Grounds: Formal gardens w/ curved brick walkways
Public Space: Parlor, porches
Food & Drink: Cont'l breakfast, afternoon tea & sherry
Recreation: Sight-seeing, antiques shopping
Amenities & Services: Restaurant reservations

ACCOMMODATIONS

Units: 9 guest rooms
All Rooms: Beautiful antiques, four-poster canopied bed, fresh flowers
Some Rooms: Bay window
Bed & Bath: Beds vary; private baths
Favorites: None
Comfort & Decor: Luxurious Southern furnishings

RATES, RESERVATIONS, & RESTRICTIONS

Deposit: 1 night
Discounts: None
Credit Cards: None
Check-in/Out: 2:30 p.m./11 a.m.
Smoking: No
Pets: No
Kids: 12 & older
Minimum Stay: 2 nights weekends, 3 nights holidays
Open: All year

Hosts: Pete & Jean Spell,
Karen Spell Shaw
2 Meeting St.
Charleston, SC 29401
(803) 723-7322
www.twomeetingstreet.com

1790 HOUSE BED & BREAKFAST, Georgetown

Overall: ★★★½ Room Quality: B Value: B Price: $95–$135

The house itself is a historical treasure, decorated in excellent taste. The innkeepers do an excellent job and really want to please guests but don't hover over them as in some other bed-and-breakfasts. The inn is within walking distance of good restaurants. And Georgetown itself is a historical treasure. The Spanish were the first would-be settlers back in 1526. The first permanent English settlers came in the early 1700s, and some of their houses are still standing. Take some time just to drive back to other centuries on some of the streets around here.

Setting & Facilities

Location: On Hwy. 521, which becomes Highmarket St. in Georgetown
Near: Rice Museum, several plantations open to public
Building: West Indies–style plantation house
Grounds: Gardens
Public Space: Long porch, parlor, keeping room, DR
Food & Drink: Full breakfast; evening refreshments
Recreation: Sight-seeing
Amenities & Services: Harbor & river cruises, shopping, restaurants; bicycles, Ping-Pong table

Accommodations

Units: 5 guest rooms, detached cottage
All Rooms: Extra large
Some Rooms: Rice Planter's canopy bed, fireplace, sleigh bed, cable TV
Bed & Bath: Private baths
Favorites: Dependency Cottage w/ private patio
Comfort & Decor: Number of comfortable seating areas and sofas

Rates, Reservations, & Restrictions

Deposit: Credit card; 1 night's payment 7 days in advance
Discounts: Corp., others (ask)
Credit Cards: AE, D, V, MC
Check-in/Out: 3–7 p.m./11 a.m.
Smoking: No
Pets: Yes
Kids: Welcome—$10 charge for age 10 & under; $20 for age 11 & older
Minimum Stay: None
Open: All year
Host: Patricia & John Wiley
630 Highmarket St.
Georgetown, SC 29440
(843) 546-4821 or (800) 890-7432
Fax: (843) 520-0609
jwiley5211@aol.com
www.1790house.com

ALEXANDRA'S INN, Georgetown

Overall: ★★★ Room Quality: B Value: B Price: $95–$120

Innkeepers Vit and Diane invite guests into what they call the "quiet zone." Georgetown can provide a nice hiatus from sometimes frantic Myrtle Beach and too-much-to-see Charleston. You may even have a sense of déjà vu from the great old movie, *Gone with the Wind.* The front of the inn resembles "Tara," and the antebellum feeling is carried throughout the house in furnishings, decor, and movie memorabilia. When you think it's getting too quiet, the innkeepers can arrange golf, kayaking, or nature tours. April is a good month to visit Georgetown. That's when 32 plantations go on display for a week of tours.

Setting & Facilities

Location: Between Myrtle Beach & Charleston on Rt. 17
Near: Brookgreen Gardens, Huntington Beach State Park, Atlantic Ocean
Building: 1890 Victorian
Grounds: Garden w/ swimming pool & 300-year-old pecan tree
Public Space: DR, parlor, porches
Food & Drink: Full breakfast w/ pastry, Belgian waffles; complimentary soda & bottled water
Recreation: Antiques shopping, historic tours, kayaking, beach activities
Amenities & Services: Newspapers, magazines, golf maps, restaurant menus

Accommodations

Units: 5 guest rooms main house plus separate carriage house
All Rooms: TV, phone, fireplace
Some Rooms: Whirlpool tub
Bed & Bath: King or queen; private baths
Favorites: Scarlett's Room w/ whirlpool tub
Comfort & Decor: Comfortable loveseats and chairs plus antiques

Rates, Reservations, & Restrictions

Deposit: Credit card; 7-day cancellation
Discounts: None
Credit Cards: AE, V
Check-in/Out: 3–7 p.m./11 a.m.
Smoking: No
Pets: No
Kids: No
Minimum Stay: 2 nights during holidays & peak season
Open: All year
Hosts: Diane & Vit Visbaras
620 Prince St.
Georgetown, SC 29440
(843) 527-0233 or (888) 557-0233
Fax: (843) 520-0718
alexinn@sccoast.net
www.alexandrasinn.com

MANSFIELD PLANTATION BED & BREAKFAST COUNTRY INN, Georgetown

Overall: ★★★½ Room Quality: B Value: B Price: $95–$150

Who was that guy out by the live oak, shooting at red coats? It could have been Mel Gibson, who was here filming the Revolutionary War epic, *The Patriot*, due for release on July 4, 2000. The inn makes a perfect setting for such a movie, and it's spacious and comfortable to boot. The main house contains several common rooms. Guests stay in three outer buildings (the former kitchen house, school house, and guest house), but have breakfast in the main house. There is also a slave village on the grounds with six buildings. Fascinating as the old plantation and its history are, the real show is put on by Mother Nature. Walk through old rice fields. Watch for ducks, woodpeckers, owls, and birds. Bring along your pet, but watch out—yes, there are alligators here. Then, later, you can see where you've been as you watch Mel on screen, dashing around those moss-draped trees—perhaps on his way to those great Belgian waffles.

Setting & Facilities

Location: From Hwys. 17 & 701 intersection, take 701 north 3.5 mi.
Near: Atlantic Ocean, nature preserve, museums
Building: 1800 Federal-style plantation house & pre–Civil War buildings
Grounds: 900 acres w/ 200 live oaks & gardens
Public Space: Dbl. sitting rooms w/ fireplaces
Food & Drink: Full breakfast; specialties: French toast, Belgian waffles, venison sausage; complimentary sodas, ice, spring water
Recreation: Boating, canoeing, kayaking, bird-watching, golf, dock fishing
Amenities & Services: Bikes

Accommodations

Units: 8 guest rooms
All Rooms: Fireplace, hardwood floors, AC, private entrance
Some Rooms: Porch, rocking chairs, brick terrace
Bed & Bath: Beds vary (roll-away beds for children); private baths
Favorites: 2 rooms w/ brick terrace & goldfish pond
Comfort & Decor: Antiques, oil portraits of ancestors, and gas chandeliers create a romantic atmosphere.

Rates, Reservations, & Restrictions

Deposit: 1 night; 7-day cancellation
Discounts: Singles, 3rd person
Credit Cards: None
Check-in/Out: 3–7 p.m./11 a.m.
Smoking: No
Pets: Welcome; no size limitation or extra charge
Kids: Welcome
Minimum Stay: 2 nights on Valentine's Day, Memorial Day, Fourth of July, Labor Day
Open: All year
Hosts: Jim & Sally Cahalan
1776 Mansfield Rd.
Georgetown, SC 29440
(843) 546-6961 or (800) 355-3223
Fax: (843) 546-5235
mansfield_plantation@prodigy.net
www.bbonline.com/sc/mansfield

SHAW HOUSE, Georgetown

Overall: ★★½ Room Quality: C Value: B Price: $55–$75

Gushed one recent guest: "Mary and Joe Shaw are just about the nicest people you'll ever meet. They opened Georgetown's first bed-and-breakfast 16 years ago and are still going strong. They absolutely love people, and guests become friends the instant they walk through the door." Okay, but here's just the facts, ma'am. The three guest bedrooms are huge. Unlike some bed-and-breakfast owners who look on children as resident aliens, Mary loves kids and keeps a stash of toys and games on hand for them. And she sends everyone off with a hearty Southern breakfast, complete with grits and sausage. The inn is right next to a marsh that is perfect for bird-watching.

Setting & Facilities

Location: In Georgetown, go north at Orange St., turn left on Palmetto, then right on Cypress St.
Near: Beach (30 mi. to Myrtle Beach)
Building: 1974 Colonial (Williamsburg style)
Grounds: An acre of grassy lawn w/ pine trees & flowering shrubbery
Public Space: Den, family room, sun porch
Food & Drink: Full breakfast w/ quiche, casserole, shrimp, & crab meat; complimentary beverages include tea, juices, wine
Recreation: Beach activities, golf, tennis, boating, bird-watching
Amenities & Services: Daily paper, bicycles, nightly turn-down w/ chocolates, piano, game

Accommodations

Units: 3 guest rooms
All Rooms: Antiques, phone, TV
Some Rooms: Four-poster rice bed
Bed & Bath: Beds vary; private baths
Favorites: None
Comfort & Decor: Filled with interesting French provincial touches

Rates, Reservations, & Restrictions

Deposit: 50% of total stay
Discounts: 10% AAA, 1-week stays, singles
Credit Cards: AE, V, MC
Check-in/Out: Noon/11 a.m.
Smoking: No
Pets: No; lodging avail. nearby
Kids: Welcome
Minimum Stay: None
Open: All year
Hosts: Joe & Mary Shaw
613 Cypress Ct.
Georgetown, SC 29440
(843) 546-9663
Fax: (843) 546-9663
jeshaw@sccoast.net

ABINGDON MANOR, Latta

Overall: ★★★★ Room Quality: B Value: C Price: $105–$150

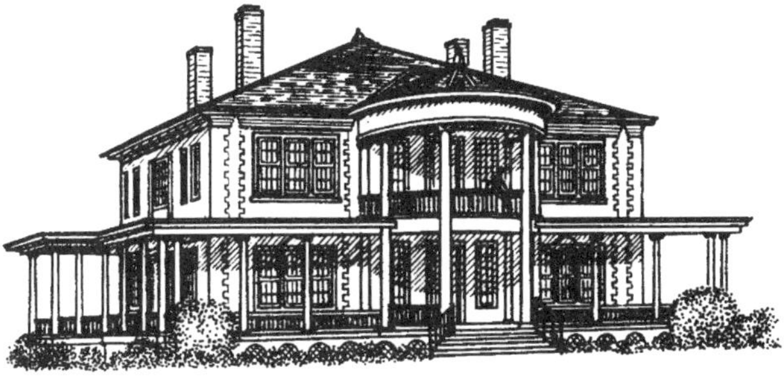

Abingdon Manor offers a pleasant oasis in a small-town atmosphere. But Latta may surprise you, with 16 antiques stores in town and the surrounding areas and a flourishing art colony. Don't miss the great little Dillon County Museum, one of the best in South Carolina, free to the public, and only three blocks from Abingdon Manor. Our only disappointment with this bed-and-breakfast was the breakfast, which was rather ordinary and not that tasteful. However the cook has been taking lessons and probably has improved by the time you read this. A small bicarbonate gripe about a very attractive bed-and-breakfast.

Setting & Facilities

Location: From I-95 take Exit 181, go east 1 mi. on Rt. 38 to Rt. 917, & follow signs to Latta
Near: Florence, Myrtle Beach
Building: Greek Revival
Grounds: 3 acres in historic district
Public Space: 3 parlors, veranda, library, DR, porches
Food & Drink: Complimentary evening wine & hors d'oeuvres; full breakfast w/ cooked entrees
Recreation: Museums, guided canoe/kayak trips, bird-watching, art galleries
Amenities & Services: Dry cleaning, local restaurant menus & reservations, bicycles, whirlpool tub, guest fridge, games

Accommodations

Units: 6 guest rooms, 1 2-room suite
All Rooms: Oversized, fireplace
Bed & Bath: Private baths; 4 w/ tub/shower combo, terry robes
Favorites: Senator Manning Suite w/ working fireplaces & panoramic view
Comfort & Decor: Antiques and fresh flowers

Rates, Reservations, & Restrictions

Deposit: Credit card; 78-hour cancellation
Discounts: 10% AAA, corp.
Credit Cards: AE, V, MC, D
Check-in/Out: 3 p.m./11 a.m.
Smoking: Outdoors only
Pets: No
Kids: 12 & over
Minimum Stay: None
Open: All year
Hosts: Michael & Patty Griffey
307 Church St.
Latta, SC 29565
(843) 752-5090 or (888) 752-5090
Fax: (843) 752-6034
abingdon@southtech.net
www.bbonline.com/sc/abingdon

LAUREL HILL PLANTATION BED & BREAKFAST, McClellanville

Overall: ★★★½ Room Quality: B Value: C Price: $95–$125

The original plantation house was destroyed by Hurricane Hugo and carefully restored. Want to write or read a book? Admire or shop for antiques? This may be the place to stay. You'll have plenty of peace and isolation in this rural retreat. You can browse among some great antiques in the house, which is decorated with excellent taste. There is even an antiques shop right in the house. There are also some great parks and national forest areas to visit. However, if you're looking for city-style entertainment and great restaurants, this away-from-everything bed-and-breakfast may be a little *too* away from everything for some people. You will have to drive some distance for really good meals (after the one meal, breakfast, is served). Watch where you step if you go out walking. Unfortunately Hugo didn't flood out the fire ants and other critters. Being city folks ourselves, we recommend enjoying the great views of the salt marshes, islands, and Atlantic Ocean from that great wraparound porch.

SETTING & FACILITIES

Location: On Hwy. 17 30 mi. north of Charleston
Near: Buck Hill Recreation Area, beaches, Butterfly Barn, Sewee Visitor & Environmental Education Center
Building: Reconstructed 1850 Plantation House
Grounds: Overlooks salt marshes, islands, & Atlantic Ocean
Public Space: Porches, parlor
Food & Drink: Full breakfast; afternoon refreshments
Recreation: Birding, fishing, hiking
Amenities & Services: Antiques & gift shop

ACCOMMODATIONS

Units: 4 guest rooms
All Rooms: Marsh & creek views
Bed & Bath: Beds vary; private baths
Favorites: None
Comfort & Decor: Country antiques

RATES, RESERVATIONS, & RESTRICTIONS

Deposit: Credit card; 1 night; 7-day cancellation
Discounts: None
Credit Cards: AE, V, MC, D
Check-in/Out: 4–7 p.m./11 a.m.
Smoking: No
Pets: No
Kids: Sometimes; ask
Minimum Stay: Ask; changes w/ seasons
Open: All year
Hosts: Jackie & Lee Morrison
P.O. Box 190, 891 N. Hwy. 17
McClellanville, SC 29458
(843) 887-3708 or (888) 887-3708
www.bbonline.com/sc/laurelhill

SERENDIPITY, Myrtle Beach

Overall: ★★	Room Quality: C	Value: B	Price: $55–$139

Surprisingly, tourist-bustling Myrtle Beach has only a few scattered bed-and-breakfasts. This is high-rise hotel and condo country. At first glance, Serendipity is a little disappointing from the outside—more like a motel, which it once was in the 1950s. However, the rooms have been furnished handsomely in a more traditional bed-and-breakfast style. The inn is only about 300 yards from the beach—a nice plus—and offers a swimming pool and hot tub. It's a pleasant alternative to high-rise city and a good place for groups to gather.

Setting & Facilities

Location: Between Bus. Rt. 17 & the ocean
Near: Ocean Music Theaters, Brookgreen Gardens, aquarium
Building: Spanish Mission-style complex
Grounds: Courtyard
Public Space: Courtyard, garden room
Food & Drink: Expanded cont'l w/ scrambled or boiled eggs, yogurt, fresh fruit
Recreation: Swimming, tennis, golf, hot-air ballooning, horseback riding
Amenities & Services: Daily newspaper, portable baby crib, restaurant reservations

Accommodations

Units: 15 guest rooms
All Rooms: Individually designed, courtyard access, AC, color TV
Some Rooms: Full kitchen, fridge, LR
Bed & Bath: Beds vary; private baths
Favorites: London Bridge Room w/ queen bed under lace canopy, kitchen
Comfort & Decor: Comfortable furnishings with art prints

Rates, Reservations, & Restrictions

Deposit: 1 night, 7-day cancellation
Discounts: Honeymooners, return guests, AAAP, AAA
Credit Cards: AE, V, MC
Check-in/Out: 2 p.m./11 a.m.
Smoking: No
Pets: No
Kids: Welcome; age 11 & over $10 nightly in parents' room
Minimum Stay: Suites, 5 nights; guest rooms, 2 nights
Open: All year
Hosts: Phil & Kay Mullins
407 71st Ave. N.
Myrtle Beach, SC 29572
(843) 449-5268 or (800) 762-3229
Fax: (843) 449-1998
serendipity-inn@worldnet.att.net
www.serendipityinn.com

LITCHFIELD PLANTATION, Pawleys Island

Overall: ★★★★★ | Room Quality: A | Value: B | Price: $66–$358

The only word that comes to mind about Litchfield Plantation is *perfection.* You drive toward the original Plantation House through a tunnel of live oak trees. Or dock your boat at the private marina. All of this elegance is a little overwhelming at first because the inn has ten separate buildings, including a Carriage House Club for dining, suites, and retreat cabins—all exquisitely furnished. Donald Trump would feel at home in the three-bedroom villa ($457 in high season). The rest of us could still do quite nicely in the Classic Rooms ($66 in low season). Special packages are available with golf or four-course gourmet dinners included. Keep the Litchfield Inn in mind for really special occasions in your life. It is one of the South's finest.

SETTING & FACILITIES

Location: 30 mi. south of Myrtle Beach; take I-95 to Hwy. 17
Near: Myrtle Beach, Charleston, Brookgreen Gardens
Building: 10 buildings total w/ 1750 Low-Country plantation house at center
Grounds: 600 acres original plantation, manicured lawns
Public Space: Carriage House w/ bar & library
Food & Drink: Complimentary cont'l breakfast; full breakfast avail. at extra charge; dinner by reservation
Recreation: Deep-sea fishing, kayaking, horseback riding, bird-watching
Amenities & Services: Heated swimming pool w/ cabanas, private beach facil., tennis courts, 3-story oceanfront beach house with private parking, showers, and picnic facil.

ACCOMMODATIONS

Units: 38 guest rooms
All Rooms: DR, LR, kitchen, robes, phone w/ data port, cable TV
Some Rooms: Balcony, whirlpool tub, fireplace
Bed & Bath: Beds vary; private baths
Favorites: None
Comfort & Decor: Incredible Southern elegance

RATES, RESERVATIONS, & RESTRICTIONS

Deposit: Credit card; 1–2 nights; 14-day cancellation
Discounts: None
Credit Cards: AE, V, MC, D, CB, Eurocard
Check-in/Out: 3 p.m./11 a.m.
Smoking: Limited to certain rooms; not permitted in Plantation House
Pets: No
Kids: 12 & older
Minimum Stay: 2 nights on weekends
Open: All year
Host: Karl Friedrich
P.O. Box 290, Kings River Rd.
Pawleys Island, SC 29585
(843) 237-9121 or (800) 869-1410
Fax: (843) 237-1041
vacation@litchfieldplantation.com
www.litchfieldplantation.com

Zone 5
Central South Carolina

Like many Southern states bordering the ocean or the Gulf of Mexico, South Carolina terrain gradually climbs from the low-land beaches to an interior dotted with farms and large national and state forests.

Columbia is near the center of this heartland, the capital of the state. The great zoo is one of the highlights of a visit to this area, especially for parents traveling with their kids. What child doesn't delight in spotting a polar bear or a Siberian tiger in surroundings similar to their native lands?

Everyone can enjoy Japanese irises at Swan Lake Iris Gardens in Sumter, visited by seven species of swans. The black Pee Dee River teams with bream fish and offers great canoe adventures. In Orangeburg take a tour of the National Fish Hatchery.

For More Information

Columbia Metropolitan Convention and Visitors Bureau
(800) 264-4884

SANDHURST ESTATE, Aiken

Overall: ★★★★ Room Quality: B Value: B Price: $75–$200

Sandhurst is certainly not your typical country inn. Rather, it is a 12,000-square-foot mansion that is as elegant as it is large. If you love horses, you've come to the perfect area. You can go horseback riding, take polo lessons, or simply ride in a carriage. You can even bring your own horse; there are extra stalls in the stable. If horses aren't your thing, bring your clubs; there are dozens of golf courses in this part of South Carolina. Or if you want to do nothing at all, you can slip into one of the robes provided with each room and open your welcoming bottle of wine. Or wait until the host serves high tea and hors d'oeuvres in the afternoon. A very civilized place to become Scarlett or Rhett for a few days without worrying where your next radish is coming from.

Setting & Facilities

Location: Aiken historic district, near North Augusta
Near: Hitchcock Woods, Palmetto Golf Course, Masters Golf Tournament (Augusta, GA)
Building: 1883 mansion designed by Stanford White
Grounds: 5 acres
Public Space: LR, music hall, sunroom, library
Food & Drink: Full breakfast w/ eggs Benedict; low-cholesterol diets
Recreation: Thoroughbred racing, golf, horseback riding
Amenities & Services: Newspapers, same-day laundry & valet services, computer & modem/fax/copier, exercise equip., bikes

Accommodations

Units: 10 guest rooms
All Rooms: Antiques & authentic Oriental rugs
Some Rooms: Fireplace, marble bath, antique four-poster bed, dbl. whirlpool tub, private veranda
Bed & Bath: Beds vary; private baths except Twin Room has shared bath
Favorites: None
Comfort & Decor: Elegant antiques

Rates, Reservations, & Restrictions

Deposit: Credit card
Discounts: Group, corp., gov't.
Credit Cards: All major cards
Check-in/Out: 3 p.m./noon
Smoking: No
Pets: Not in house; kennels avail. in barn
Kids: Welcome
Minimum Stay: None
Open: All year
Host: Sandy Croy
215 Dupree Place
Aiken, SC 29801
(803) 642-9259
sandhurst@scescape.net
www.sandhurstestate.com

BREEDEN INN AND CARRIAGE HOUSE, Bennettsville

Overall: ★★★★ Room Quality: B Value: B Price: $85–$135

You can tell a lot about bed-and-breakfasts by what their guests say and write. Some journal entries from this inn: "It was immediately peaceful inside your doors." "The part of the house we enjoy the most is the front porch. Sipping lemonade there takes us back in time." "It's so refreshing to be with people with huge hearts." We weren't quite that overwhelmed, but we really enjoyed the hosts and the setting. And we were really impressed by the grounds as well, certified by the National Wildlife Federation as a Backyard Wildlife Habitat. There are numerous trees, many over a hundred years old, plus sitting areas where you can contemplate nature, or perhaps pen yet another gushy note of thanks to Wes and Bonnie.

SETTING & FACILITIES

Location: From Bus. 9 to Main St.
Near: Museums, Cotton Trail, courthouse, library
Building: 1886 Beaux Arts Southern mansion
Grounds: 3 acres of historic district
Public Space: Parlor, music parlor, DR, veranda, pool area, porches
Food & Drink: Full breakfast w/ fresh fruit sampler (8–10 fruits), various egg dishes w/ meats; refreshments on arrival: garden or peach tea or soda
Recreation: Swimming, walking, birdwatching, boating, fishing, tennis
Amenities & Services: Bicycles, inground swimming pool, restaurant lists, binoculars & guidebook for birdwatching

ACCOMMODATIONS

Units: 6 guest rooms (10 when Garden Cottage is completed)
All Rooms: Cable TV, phone, collectibles dating back to 1800s, desk, period light fixtures
Bed & Bath: Beds vary; private baths
Favorites: Heart Room in main house; Savannah Room in carriage house
Comfort & Decor: Filled with family heirlooms, antiques, needlepoint, and collectibles

Rates, Reservations, & Restrictions

Deposit: 1 night
Discounts: AAA, corp., gov't.
Credit Cards: AE,V, MC
Check-in/Out: 4–10 p.m./11 a.m.
Smoking: No
Pets: No; kennels nearby
Kids: Welcome
Minimum Stay: None
Open: All year
Hosts: Wesley & Bonnie Park
404 E. Main St.
Bennettsville, SC 29512
(843) 479-3665 or (888) 335-2996
Fax: (843) 479-7998
breedeninn@att.net
www.bbonline.com/sc/breeden

LORD CAMDEN INN, Camden

Overall:★★★	Room Quality: B	Value: C	Price: $75–$110

General Sherman, as you might imagine, is not a poster boy in the South. He burned down whole towns as his armies marched through. His army reportedly tried to burn down Camden and all its houses, but a heavy rainstorm made everything too wet too burn. That allowed the 1852 building that now houses the Lord Camden Inn to survive. Guests can enjoy the swimming pool, badminton, horseshoes, and an herb garden. You can arrange to be picked up at the inn by a horse-drawn carriage for a tour of the historic parts of town. This is a very attractive bed-and-breakfast, but we were a little annoyed by too many extra charges ($10 per night for a pet, $10 for breakfast in your room, $18 for a poolside barbecue). Don't miss the Revolutionary War Site about 1.5 miles south. And if the weather turns bad, remember that rain isn't always bad.

Setting & Facilities

Location: On Hwy. 521, 2.5 blocks to North Hwy. 1
Near: Camden Revolutionary War Site, Steeplechase Museum, Darlington Race Track
Building: 1832 Greek Revival/Federal

Grounds: Fish pond, gardens
Public Space: Lounge, DR, balconies, porch
Food & Drink: Full breakfast w/ quiche, sausages, scones; cookies, wet bar, soft drinks
Recreation: Swimming, golf, fishing, horseback riding
Amenities & Services: Guest fridge, swimming pool, badminton, horseshoes, local restaurant lists

ACCOMMODATIONS

Units: 4 guest rooms
All Rooms: TV, phone, hardwood floors, fireplace
Some Rooms: Balcony
Bed & Bath: Beds vary; 3 w/ private baths
Favorites: Honeymoon Room w/ Eastlake bed & dressers; Owl Room w/ soft colors
Comfort & Decor: Many Victorian antiques

RATES, RESERVATIONS, & RESTRICTIONS

Deposit: 1 night
Discounts: Singles ($5 off), 7-day stays
Credit Cards: AE, V, MC, D
Check-in/Out: 3–6 p.m./11 a.m.
Smoking: No
Pets: Small pets only; $10 extra per night
Kids: Welcome
Minimum Stay: None
Open: All year
Hosts: John & Juliette Swenson
1502 Broad St.
Camden, SC 29020
(803) 713-9050 or (800) 737-9971
Fax: (803) 425-4603
lady@camden.net
www.lordcamden-inn.com

CHESTNUT COTTAGE, Columbia

Overall: ★★★ Room Quality: C Value: B Price: $125–$200

From the outside, this small cottage looks like a modest, well-kept home of a maiden aunt and "isn't it nice that the poor dear found something at her age?" But don't judge it too quickly. History buffs will go wild here.

From that small porch, Jefferson Davis, president of the Confederacy, once addressed the local citizenry. This was the home of Mary Boykin Chestnut, who wrote about her life in the Deep South, an account that was later published as *Diary from Dixie*. When the *Diary* was revised and reissued in 1982, it won a Pulitzer Prize. You may want to read this book before coming here. The room named for Mary Boykin Chestnut is a very feminine room, but it's not the best for late-morning sleep-ins; it's right next to the kitchen. The Jefferson Davis Room has its own whirlpool and a view of the piazza.

SETTING & FACILITIES

Location: From I-27 take Exit 126 to downtown Columbia; Elmwood to right on Bull Street, then left on Hampton St.
Near: Fort Jackson Museum, Riverfront Park, State House
Building: 1850 cottage
Grounds: Garden w/ fountain
Public Space: Parlor, porch
Food & Drink: Full breakfast served in room, parlor, or on porch
Recreation: Sight-seeing
Amenities & Services: VCR on request, computer w/ Internet access (for rent), printer, fax, Civil War library

ACCOMMODATIONS

Units: 5 guest rooms
All Rooms: Jacuzzi, TV, phone
Some Rooms: Pencil post & cannon ball beds, garden view
Bed & Bath: Beds vary; private baths
Favorites: None
Comfort & Decor: Appointed with Georgian & Victorian furniture

RATES, RESERVATIONS, & RESTRICTIONS

Deposit: Credit card; 14-day cancellation
Discounts: Corp., extended stay
Credit Cards: AE, V, MC, D, DC
Check-in/Out: 4–6 p.m./11 a.m.
Smoking: No
Pets: No
Kids: 12 & older; ask host about younger children
Minimum Stay: None
Open: All year
Host: Gale Garrett
1718 Hampton St.
Columbia, SC 29201
(803) 256-1718
Fax: (803) 779-3157 (call first)
ggarrett@logicsouth.com
www.bbonline/sc/chestnut

CLAUSSEN'S INN AT FIVE POINTS, Columbia

Overall: ★★★½ Room Quality: B Value: B Price: $100–$130

This inn is very popular with business travelers, who get discounts of $25 or more per night. They also like being so close to the government and corporate offices of Columbia. The two-story loft suites are particularly interesting for travelers who like space and privacy, with a living room with a sleeper sofa and wet bar downstairs and a bedroom upstairs. But these lofts are not recommended for any travelers who may have trouble with the steps. Choose one of the other guest rooms.

Setting & Facilities

Location: Take Harden St., then turn right on Greene St.
Near: Downtown Columbia
Building: 62-year-old bakery building restored to modern inn
Grounds: None
Public Space: 2-story lobby
Food & Drink: Cont'l breakfast; afternoon fruit, sherry
Recreation: USC is right next door w/ a swimming pool & tennis courts avail. to public
Amenities & Services: Dinner reservations at local restaurants, disabled access

Accommodations

Units: 21 guest rooms plus 8 loft suites
All Rooms: Phone, TV, desk, AC, fan, balcony
Some Rooms: Four-poster & brass beds, whirlpool tub, courtyard access
Bed & Bath: Beds vary; private baths
Favorites: Loft suites
Comfort & Decor: Attractive antique reproductions

Rates, Reservations, & Restrictions

Deposit: Credit card
Discounts: Corp., AAA, AARP, children under 12 free
Credit Cards: AE, V, MC, D, DC
Check-in/Out: 3 p.m./noon
Smoking: Nonsmoking rooms avail.
Pets: No
Kids: Welcome
Minimum Stay: 2 nights football weekends
Open: All year
Hosts: Rick Widney
2003 Greene St.
Columbia, SC 29205
(803) 765-0440 or (800) 622-3382
Fax: (803) 799-7924

RICHLAND STREET BED & BREAKFAST, Columbia

Overall: ★★★★ Room Quality: B Value: B Price: $79–$110

The Richland Street Bed & Breakfast is sort of an ersatz Victorian, built in 1992 to resemble houses from another century. We prefer the real thing, but one advantage of new construction is the opportunity to build in modern conveniences right from the start, and particularly, to create larger rooms. Many of the original Victorian homes were built for generations of men and women who were five feet tall. We were particularly impressed by the spaciousness and cleanliness of the rooms in this award-winning bed-and-breakfast. Breakfast served in the room for an additional $10 seemed like an unnecessarily high charge. Unless you need the privacy, we suggest dining with the other guests in the breakfast room. There are also extra charges if you check in early or leave late. This is a popular bed-and-breakfast with corporate travelers, and it's close to the government center.

Setting & Facilities

Location: From Hwy. 277 turn right on Richland St. (1st house on right)
Near: State gov't offices, house museums, Riverbanks Zoological Park
Building: Victorian-style home
Grounds: Small yard & garden
Public Space: Breakfast room, porch
Food & Drink: Cont'l plus w/ hot casserole; afternoon refreshments
Recreation: Sight-seeing
Amenities & Services: Assist w/ dinner reservations; fax avail.

Accommodations

Units: 7 guest rooms
All Rooms: Phone, TV, AC
Some Rooms: Whirlpool tub
Bed & Bath: King or queen; private baths
Favorites: None
Comfort & Decor: Quiet elegance—rooms vary considerably, from Victorian to an almost all-white honeymoon suite.

Rates, Reservations, & Restrictions

Deposit: Credit card; 1 night
Discounts: None
Credit Cards: AE, V, MC
Check-in/Out: 4 p.m./11 a.m. (extra charge if you arrive early or check out late)
Smoking: No
Pets: No
Kids: 12 & older
Minimum Stay: None
Open: All year
Host: Naomi Perryman
1425 Richland St.
Columbia, SC 29201
(803) 779-7001

WADE-BECKHAM HOUSE BED & BREAKFAST, Lancaster

Overall: ★★★½ Room Quality: B Value: A Price: $75

The Wade-Beckham House is full of historic surprises. Some of the window panes and doors date back to the start of the nineteenth century. A hand-painted rose plate in the Rose Room survived General Sherman's march through the South. Of more contemporary interest is a small South Carolina flag that went to the moon. It was carried there by astronaut Charles Duke, who is the twin brother of Dr. William Duke, one of your hosts. The bathroom situation here is a little complicated. The host wants everyone to have a private bathroom ("the public demands it now"). But there are only two bathrooms upstairs and three guest rooms. Their unusual solution: The host will rent to only one party, the first to reserve. The other two guest rooms upstairs will then remain vacant during their stay so the first guests will have the whole top floor to themselves and the two bathrooms. Jan

Duke is an engagingly honest woman. "I want people to know exactly what they are getting. There are no whirlpool tubs in the rooms. We are out in the country, and there is no Wal-Mart on the corner. It's several miles to restaurants." What she does offer is a comfortable home and hospitality at a modest rate. Good enough for us when we have a couple of new books and a need for "quality time" with ourselves and our significant others.

SETTING & FACILITIES

Location: Outside Lancaster on Hwy. 200
Near: Heritage USA, Carowinds, Revolutionary & Civil War sites
Building: Circa 1801 Plantation Home
Grounds: 450 acres w/ horses, cows, chickens
Public Space: Front porch
Food & Drink: Full breakfast
Recreation: Sight-seeing, hiking
Amenities & Services: None

ACCOMMODATIONS

Units: 3 guest rooms
All Rooms: Numerous antiques
Some Rooms: Hearts-of-pine floors, military artifacts, canopy bed, lace fans
Bed & Bath: Beds vary; 2 w/ private baths, 1 shared (see comments)
Favorites: Wade Hampton Room w/ early nineteenth-century furniture
Comfort & Decor: Family collection of numerous original antiques

RATES, RESERVATIONS, & RESTRICTIONS

Deposit: None
Discounts: AARP
Credit Cards: None
Check-in/Out: Flexible; ask
Smoking: No
Pets: No
Kids: 16 & older
Minimum Stay: None
Open: All year; closed at some times for hosts' travels
Host: Jan Beckham Duke
3385 Great Falls Hwy.
Lancaster, SC 29720
(803) 285-1105
www.bbonline.com/sc/wadebeckham

CALHOUN ST. BED & BREAKFAST, Sumter

Overall: ★★ | Room Quality: D | Value: D | Price: $75–$85

At first sight we were not terribly impressed with this bed-and-breakfast. The house is rather ordinary and in some disorder when we arrived (which, of course, could be a one-time thing). But on closer examination, there are several things to like about the place—including interesting family heirlooms and collectibles throughout the house gathered from all over the world, from Japan to Africa. Two thirteenth-century French sculptures are really extraordinary. Breakfast is also handled in a very thoughtful way. Guests can make their selections from a menu on their pillow and choose their breakfast time from 6 to 10 a.m.

SETTING & FACILITIES

Location: Call for directions; numerous turns in Sumter
Near: Swan Lake/Iris Gardens, Poinsette State Park, Santee Lakes, Columbia (state capitol), State Museum Riverbanks Museum, 2 hrs. to Charleston or Myrtle Beach
Building: 1892 Victorian stick-style clapboard w/ wraparound front porch
Grounds: .75 acre w/ rose garden
Public Space: Entry foyer, LR w/ fireplace, DR w/ fireplace, TV area, upstairs foyer w/ games
Food & Drink: Full breakfast w/ eggs, cereal, muffins; complimentary beverages include wine & sherry
Recreation: Jogging, tennis, kayaking, swimming
Amenities & Services: Newspapers, TV w/ VCR & videos

ACCOMMODATIONS

Units: 4 guest rooms
Some Rooms: Audubon bird prints, English leather trunk, desk
Bed & Bath: Beds vary; private baths
Favorites: Audubon Room is largest room w/ windows on 3 sides & more privacy
Comfort & Decor: Numerous antiques and family heirlooms

RATES, RESERVATIONS, & RESTRICTIONS

Deposit: Credit card, 1 night; 24-hour cancellation
Discounts: AAA, corp., military
Credit Cards: AE, V, MC, D
Check-in/Out: 4–7 p.m./11 a.m.
Smoking: No
Pets: No
Kids: Welcome (toys, games, & swings & jungle gym behind house)
Minimum Stay: None
Open: All year
Hosts: David & Mackenzie Sholtz
302 West Calhoun St.
Sumter, SC 29150
(803) 665-7035 or (800) 355-8119
Fax: (803) 778-0934
calhnbb@mindspring.com
calhnbb.home.mindspring.com

MAGNOLIA HOUSE, Sumter

Overall: ★★★½ | Room Quality: B | Value: B | Price: $75–$135

If you're traveling with a pet, you have both found a home here. Your host, Pierre, is a good-natured French-Canadian who likes animals and has a poodle and two cats of his own as permanent guests. He even lets your Fido or Fifi stay right in the room with you. He speaks fluent French, making his home very popular with many Canadians passing through. While you are in Sumter, visit Swan Lake and the Irish Gardens. You will see eight varieties of swans and a multitude of Canada geese who must have heard about Pierre.

SETTING & FACILITIES

Location: 1.5 hours from Charleston & Myrtle Beach
Near: Swan Lake, Iris Gardens
Building: 1907 Greek Revival
Grounds: English walled gardens

Public Space: LR, DR, porches
Food & Drink: Full breakfast; evening refreshments on back porch
Recreation: Sight-seeing, shopping
Amenities & Services: Local restaurant list

Accommodations

Units: 4 guest rooms
All Rooms: Antiques, phone, color cable TV
Bed & Bath: Beds vary; private baths
Favorites: None
Comfort & Decor: Highlights include a liberal display of arts, stained-glass windows, and five fireplaces. Luta's Chambre features a French theme with a four-poster bed, a beautiful antique mahogany wardrobe, a fireplace, and a 105-year-old pillbox toilet.

Rates, Reservations, & Restrictions

Deposit: Credit card
Discounts: Corp.
Credit Cards: AE, V, MC
Check-in/Out: Ask
Smoking: No
Pets: Dogs & cats
Kids: 9 & older ($10 extra per night)
Minimum Stay: 2 nights on Memorial Day, Iris Festival, & Labor Day weekends
Open: All year
Hosts: Pierre & Liz Tremblay
230 Church St.
Sumter, SC 29150
(804) 775-6694 or (888) 666-0296
www.bbonline.com/sc/magnolia

Zone 6
Western South Carolina

The gradual rise in elevation that began at the sea coast ultimately climaxes in the Blue Ridge Mountains and a profusion of lakes, waterfalls, and forestland. There is kayaking and white-water rafting on the Chattooga National Wild and Scenic River. Abbeville is the site of the birth and death of the Confederacy. The first secessionist movement began here. Several years later, in 1865, Jefferson Davis officially said goodbye to the defeated remnants of the Confederate Army.

The huge national forests in the western part of the state offer unlimited recreation opportunities for swimming, hiking, and fishing. For a bird's-eye view of the mountains, drive the Cherokee Foothills Scenic Highway. The western part of the state also harbors some surprisingly elegant bed-and-breakfast inns. In north Augusta (right across the border from Augusta, Georgia), you will find such incredibly beautiful bed-and-breakfasts as Rosemary Hall and Lookaway Hall.

For More Information

Upcountry Carolina Association
(800) 849-4766

JEFFERSON HOUSE, Anderson

Overall: ★★★ Room Quality: B Value: C Price: $65–$110

The house looks deceptively small from the outside, but the parlors and guest rooms are surprisingly large, furnished with country Victorian items. This is not one of those "showcase" bed-and-breakfasts, but the warm welcome provided by Vaughnde (pronounced Von-da) is much bigger than the house. Several minutes from town, the Jefferson is rural enough to attract some roaming deer and wild turkey. Cobb's Glen Golf and Country Club is right across the street. Your host will be happy to make arrangements for guests to play there. If you are allergic to cats, be aware that Vaughnde has one furry friend resident indoors and several outdoors.

SETTING & FACILITIES

Location: Hwy. 29 to right on Old Williamston Rd.
Near: Lake Hartwell, Cobb's Glen Golf Course, mountains, Charlotte
Building: Greek Revival
Grounds: 4 rural acres
Public Space: 2 libraries, 2 sitting areas
Food & Drink: Full breakfast Mon.–Fri.; specialties: blueberry pancakes, potato casserole; extended cont'l Sat. & Sun w/ coffee cakes, yogurt, one hot item (e.g., quiche)
Recreation: Golfing, boating, skiing (water & snow), hiking, swimming
Amenities & Services: Local newspaper, restaurant lists, hair dryers

ACCOMMODATIONS

Units: 7 guest rooms
Some Rooms: Woodland view, cable TV, phone
Bed & Bath: Beds vary; private baths
Favorites: Elizabeth room w/ original pecanwood ceiling & wall
Comfort & Decor: Rooms are individually decorated with quilts, pictures, and chandeliers.

Rates, Reservations, & Restrictions

Deposit: Credit card; 2-week cancellation on Clemson football weekends
Discounts: 3rd person for $10
Credit Cards: AE, V, MC, D
Check-in/Out: Ask
Smoking: No
Pets: No
Kids: Welcome
Minimum Stay: None
Open: All year
Host: Vaughnde Morris
2835 Old Williamston Rd.
Anderson, SC 29621
(864) 224-0678
Fax: (864) 224-1618

BELL TOWER INN BED & BREAKFAST, Campobello

Overall: ★★★½ Room Quality: B Value: B Price: $75–$95

The Bell Tower Inn has relatively new owners (since 1998) who are very eager to make this old schoolhouse a successful bed-and-breakfast. One of the rooms has a country Italian feeling and the other a lighter, more colorful look. Pleasant and inviting, but it brings on a little bed-and-breakfast déjà vu, in that it's similar to others we had seen in so many other homes. But we lost all sense of boredom in the Tower Room. It is extraordinary, with a high ceiling and a carved wood rail loft with a round, antique stained-glass window. It also has a fireplace, satellite TV, and a private covered sitting deck looking out on the woods. The bathroom is extra large with two sinks, a private "necessary" room, and a claw-foot tub. You have to see this room to believe it. Book this room if it's available! Probably one of the more spectacular rooms we've seen on our appointed rounds.

Setting & Facilities

Location: In Cherokee Foothills close to I-85 or I-26
Near: Antiques shops of Landrum, Inman, Tryon; Biltmore Estate; Carl Sandberg Home; Cowpens Rev. Battlefield
Building: Remodeled 102-year-old school
Grounds: English garden w/ butterflies & birds
Public Space: Porch, LR
Food & Drink: Full breakfast
Recreation: Sight-seeing, antiques shopping
Amenities & Services: Picnic basket provided on request for a fee

Accommodations

Units: 3 guest rooms
All Rooms: AC & heating
Some Rooms: Stained-glass window, fireplace, covered sitting deck, TV, VCR, whirlpool tub
Bed & Bath: Beds vary; private baths
Favorites: Tower Room
Comfort & Decor: Italian country and Victorian styles

Rates, Reservations, & Restrictions

Deposit: 50% of total stay
Discounts: 10% seniors, gov't., 25% for 7 days or more
Credit Cards: AE, V, MC, D
Check-in/Out: 3 p.m./11 a.m. (flexible)
Smoking: No
Pets: No
Kids: 12 & older; ask about younger children
Minimum Stay: None
Open: All year
Hosts: Bob & Candy Payne
501 Depot St.
Campobello, SC 29322
(864) 468-4266 or (877) 235 5869
Fax: Same as phone
belltowr@greenville.infi.net
www.bbonline.com/sc/belltower

LOOKAWAY HALL, North Augusta

Overall: ★★★★½ Room Quality: A Value: C Price: $75–$145

Business travelers seem to gravitate to Lookaway Hall, with its ample meeting space for up to 125 overachievers. There is the Courtyard and Sunken Garden for outdoor celebrations, accommodating up to 200 people. The views of the Savannah River are so impressive they gave this building its "Lookaway" name. If you're traveling with a spouse, choose the more romantic Rosemary Hall across the street. With your boss, choose Lookaway Hall for business meetings with a real touch of class. *Note:* Check in at Rosemary Hall for either bed-and-breakfast.

Setting & Facilities

Location: From downtown Augusta, Georgia, cross the Savannah River (13th St. bridge); st. becomes Georgia Ave., then turn left on Carolina Ave.
Near: Augusta (Georgia) Riverwalk & Amphitheatre, Augusta Nat'l, downtown shops
Building: 1895 Victorian
Grounds: Manicured grounds w/ camellia garden & river views
Public Space: DR, foyer, sitting parlor
Food & Drink: Full breakfast (at reg. rates) or cont'l (at group rates), usually served across from St. Rosemary Hall; evening hors d'oeuvres during cocktail hour
Recreation: Ball fields, walking trails, new bike trail
Amenities & Services: Daily newspapers, list of local restaurants, fax & copy services avail.

Accommodations

Units: 15 guest rooms
All Rooms: Period antiques, large, cable TV, phone
Some Rooms: Private veranda, whirlpool tub
Bed & Bath: Beds vary; private baths
Favorites: None
Comfort & Decor: Period antiques

Rates, Reservations, & Restrictions

Deposit: Credit card or 50% down; 72-hour cancellation
Discounts: AARP, groups
Credit Cards: AE, V, MC, other major cards
Check-in/Out: 3 p.m./11 a.m.
Smoking: No
Pets: No; local kennel avail.
Kids: Welcome
No-Nos: No guest kitchen privileges
Minimum Stay: None
Open: All year
Host: Geneva Robinson
804 Carolina Ave.
North Augusta, SC 29841
(803) 278-6222 or (800) 531-5578
Fax: (803) 278-4877

ROSEMARY HALL, North Augusta

Overall: ★★★★½ Room Quality: A Value: C Price: $75–$195

Blink when you drive up to 804 Carolina Avenue and you'll think you are seeing double. Two incredibly gorgeous bed-and-breakfast inns are right across the street from each other, both gleaming white Victorian mansions with white columns right out of *Gone with the Wind.* In fact, both Rosemary and Lookaway Halls were in the movies, a Disney remake of *Darn that Cat.* A recent guest waxed eloquent about Rosemary Hall: "Magnificent—reminded me of the mansions of Newport, Rhode Island." Rosemary is definitely the place for romantic weekends and wedding anniversaries. But, frankly Scarlett, the breakfasts were not that hot—literally—lukewarm coffee, eggs, and bacon had a precooked, warmed-over taste (opinion of two guests). Journalistic honesty requires us to report this flaw, but it's not fair to turn away from such a beautiful place because of one lukewarm dining experience. Reviewers from AAA gave both inns the Four Diamond Award. So you and your taste buds will have to decide for yourself.

Setting & Facilities

Location: From downtown Augusta, Georgia, cross the Savannah River (13th St. bridge); st. becomes Georgia Ave., turn left on Carolina Ave., & Rosemary Hall is on left
Near: Augusta (GA) Riverwalk & Amphitheatre, Augusta Nat'l, downtown shops
Building: Victorian
Grounds: Wide green lawn
Public Space: DR, foyer, sitting parlor
Food & Drink: Full breakfast (at reg. rates) or cont'l (at group rates); evening hors d'oeuvres during cocktail hour
Recreation: Ball fields, walking trails, new bike trail
Amenities & Services: Daily newspapers, list of local restaurants

ACCOMMODATIONS

Units: 8 guest rooms
All Rooms: Period antiques, large, cable TV, phones
Some Rooms: Private veranda, whirlpool tub
Bed & Bath: Beds vary; private baths
Favorites: None
Comfort & Decor: Period antiques create a romantic ambiance.

RATES, RESERVATIONS, & RESTRICTIONS

Deposit: Credit card or 50% down; 72-hour cancellation
Discounts: AARP, groups
Credit Cards: AE, V, MC, other major cards
Check-in/Out: 3 p.m./11 a.m.
Smoking: No
Pets: No; local kennel available
Kids: Welcome
No-Nos: No guest kitchen privileges
Minimum Stay: None
Open: All year
Host: Geneva Robinson
804 Carolina Ave.
North Augusta, SC 29841
(803) 278-6222 or (800) 531-5578
Fax: (803) 278-4877

SCHELL HAUS BED & BREAKFAST AND CONFERENCE CENTER, Pickens

Overall: ★★★½ Room Quality: B Value: B Price: $90–$160

The biggest draw of this bed-and-breakfast: back-to-nature getaways among the four state parks that are within minutes of the home. Park activities range from hiking and swimming to guided nature walks. For fishing enthusiasts, Keowee and Jocassee—also a short drive away—are aquatic paradises. Trout, bass, and pan fish are typical catches. The hosts offer special packages that include everything from anniversary celebrations to hot-air ballooning and golf programs. Although romantic and secluded, this bed-and-breakfast is also a good setting for conferences, business travelers, and church retreats for up to 75 people (but 25 is a more comfortable range).

SETTING & FACILITIES

Location: Foothills of Blue Ridge Mountains, scenic Hwy. 11
Near: 4 state parks including Table Rock & Caesars Head, Furman & Clemson Universities
Building: Victorian-style mountain retreat
Grounds: Surrounding woods w/ full view of Table Rock
Public Space: Parlor, decks
Food & Drink: Full breakfast w/ local fruits ("heart-healthy" breakfasts avail.); afternoon refreshments
Recreation: Fishing, boating, hiking, golf
Amenities & Services: Swimming pool, picnic baskets avail. by advance request, conf. center w/ AV equipment and fax/Internet access

ACCOMMODATIONS

Units: 6 guest rooms
All Rooms: TV, coffeemaker
Some Rooms: VCR, whirlpool tub
Bed & Bath: Beds vary; private baths
Favorites: None
Comfort & Decor: Antique reproductions

RATES, RESERVATIONS, & RESTRICTIONS

Deposit: 50% of total stay; 7-day cancellation
Discounts: Corp. Sun.–Thurs.
Credit Cards: V, MC, D
Check-in/Out: 3 p.m./11 a.m.
Smoking: No
Pets: Kennel on premises; $15 per day
Kids: Ask
Minimum Stay: 2 nights during special holidays
Open: All year
Hosts: Jim & Sharon Mahanes
117 Hiawatha Trail
Pickens, SC 29671
(864) 878-0078
Fax: (864) 878-0066
schellhs@bellsouth.net
www.bbonline.com/sc/schellhaus

SOUTHWOOD MANOR, Ridge Spring

Overall: ★★★½ Room Quality: B Value: B Price: $65–$125

It's hard to imagine a more unusual bed-and-breakfast. The rooms include the brightly colored Monet's Pad (with pictures actually painted by your host Judy Adamick when she was in Monet's gardens in France) and the aviation-themed Beach Dormer. The latter is a tribute to Mike Adamick's days as an open-cockpit biplane ride operator in Myrtle Beach, pictured on the wall. Mike is still an aviation buff and maintains a 2,000-foot grass airstrip on the grounds for guests with private planes who want to fly in. This area is best known for fox hunting and raising horses. The hosts have two horses of their own. You can even bring your own and stable it at their "horse motel." We told you this place is different and fun.

Setting & Facilities

Location: Rt. 392 or 23 to Ridge Spring
Near: Aiken ("horse training capitol of the South"), golf courses, Montmorenci Vineyards
Building: Georgian Colonial Plantation
Grounds: 20 acres
Public Space: LR, solarium, porch
Food & Drink: Full country breakfast; specialty: cheese strata
Recreation: Horseback riding, polo
Amenities & Services: Swimming pool

Accommodations

Units: 4 guest rooms
All Rooms: Individually decorated w/ different themes, fireplace
Bed & Bath: 3 w/ private bath
Favorites: None
Comfort & Decor: Nineteenth-century, relaxed ambiance

Rates, Reservations, & Restrictions

Deposit: Credit card
Discounts: AARP, corp.
Credit Cards: V, MC
Check-in/Out: 1 p.m./11 a.m. (flexible)
Smoking: No
Pets: Yes
Kids: 6 & older ("babies accepted if there are no other guests")
Minimum Stay: None
Open: All year
Hosts: Mike & Judy Adamick
100 E. Main St., P.O. Box 434
Ridge Spring, SC 29129
(803) 685-5100 or (800) 931-1786
Fax: (803) 685-5263
sothent@pbtcomm.net

INN AT MERRIDUN, Union

Overall: ★★★½ Room Quality: B Value: C Price: $89–$125

The house has an imposing, beautiful facade, but the furnishings don't quite live up to the grandeur of the building. However, one of the great treats here is breakfast, because both the husband and wife hosts love to cook. Guests can also book a dinner cooked to order by Peggy and Jim. You can participate in a number of special events, including Murder Mystery Weekends and Sunday afternoon teas.

Setting & Facilities

Location: From Charlotte, take I-77 South to Carowinds Blvd., exit right to Hwy. 49 South to Union
Near: Rose Hill Plantation State Park, Carowinds Amusement Park, Historic Brattonsville
Building: 1855 Greek Revival
Grounds: 9 wooded acres
Public Space: Parlor, porches
Food & Drink: 3-course breakfast includes fresh pineapple & strawberries w/ crème fraîche, baked eggs w/ Bearnaise sauce, cheddar-basil biscuit bites; tea & dinner also served

Recreation: Walking, horseback riding, auto races, water sports
Amenities & Services: Morning newspapers, video library, local restaurant menus

ACCOMMODATIONS

Units: 5 guest rooms
All Rooms: Phone w/ dataport, cable TV w/ VCR
Some Rooms: Dbl. whirlpool tub
Bed & Bath: King or queen; private baths
Favorites: Sisters' Boudoir w/ Victorian decor & claw-foot tub
Comfort & Decor: Antiques, reproductions, and floral artwork

RATES, RESERVATIONS, & RESTRICTIONS

Deposit: 1 night; 72-hour cancellation
Discounts: AAA, military, extended stays
Credit Cards: AE, V, MC, D
Check-in/Out: Ask
Smoking: No
Pets: No
Kids: 12 & older
Minimum Stay: 2 nights when Sun. booked
Open: All year
Hosts: Jim & Peggy Waller
100 Merridun Pl.
Union, SC 29379
(864) 427-7052 or (864) 892-0373
Fax: (864) 429-0373
info@merridun.com
www.merridun.com

Georgia

At 59,441 square miles, Georgia is the largest state east of the Mississippi River. From the Appalachian Mountains on the north border to its beautiful beaches on the Atlantic, it is filled with festivals, antebellum mansions, golf courses, fishing lakes, sporting events, and history by the mile. If you were to helicopter through the state, dropping down at random times and places, here are a few of the pleasures you'd experience.

On the Blue and Gray Trail through the mountains you could see annual Civil War reenactments at Tunnel Hill or visit a Confederate camp at Pickett's Mill State Park. Drop down on the "Top of Georgia" into such counties as Rabun and Union where you can fish, swim, or boat. Watch an Atlanta Braves game or dip into Underground Atlanta to sample 12 acres of music and food and shopping. In Plains you could see a former president of the United States teaching a Sunday School class, or in Warms Springs, the simple quarters of another president who led the country through the Great Depression and World War II. It's all here, along with a fair or festival almost every day of the year. What? You haven't been to the Cotton Pickin' Fair in October or the Georgia Peach Festival in June?

Along the way you'll experience the sights and marks of Georgia's history. The Cherokee Native Americans were among the first settlers of the region, until they were forced to move to Oklahoma on the sad, infamous Trail of Tears. In 1773 Gen. James Oglethorpe established a colony for the poor and the persecuted at Savannah. Georgia's red earth felt the pounding feet of Cornwallis's British troops during the American Revolution and Sherman's "march to the sea" during the Civil War. Georgia rejoined the Union in 1870.

There are a few commonsense precautions when traveling through Georgia. Keep your eye on the weather. Although Georgia is a Southern state, polar air masses can still sweep down from Canada, chilling the unwary or the summer-underdressed in fall and spring. Hurricanes can and do hit Georgia, particularly along the southern areas. We were traveling through the state in 1999 when Hurricane Floyd veered toward the coast, forcing the largest evacuation of Savannah and other eastern areas in history.

As we have suggested before, plan your stays in bed-and-breakfasts after you have selected the Georgia attractions, events, and activities that interest you. You have much to choose from, including such prominent sites as Stone Mountain Park, Martin Luther King Jr. National Historic Site, Chickamauga National Military Park, Callaway Gardens, Okefenokee Swamp, St. Simons Island, and the Cumberland National Seashore.

Drive carefully and watch out for the other fellow. Georgia ranked third among all the states we visited for arrests for "driving under the influence" (20,414 arrests in 1998).

For More Information

Free "Georgia on my mind" Guide
(800) VISIT GA (847-4842)
www.gomm.com

Note: This line can get very busy. You may have a long wait but at least you're not paying telephone charges.

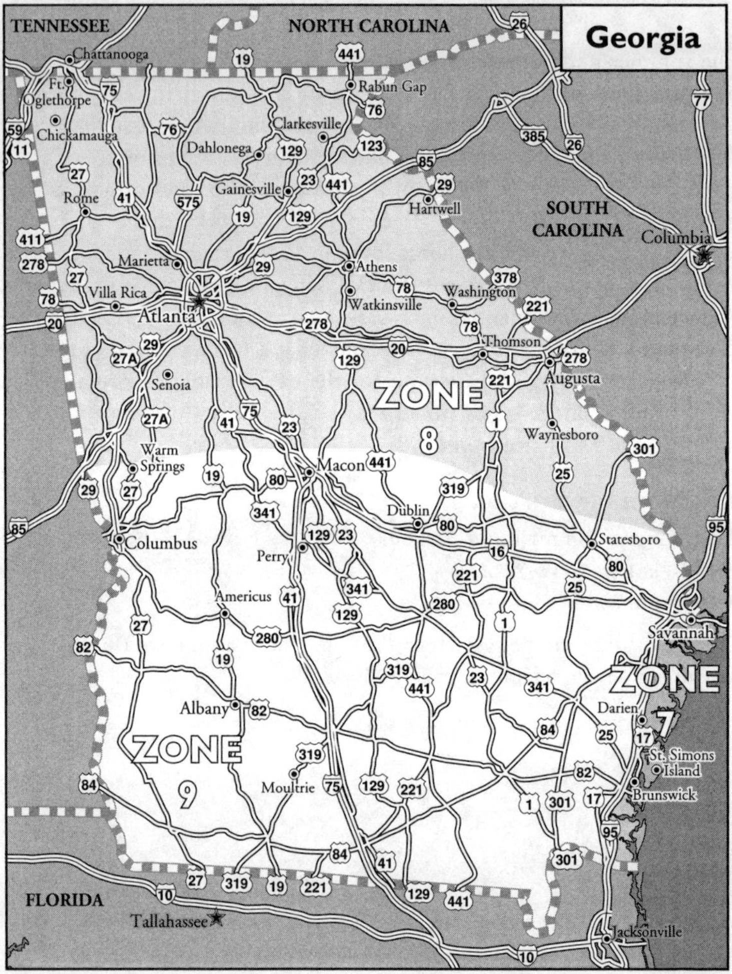
Georgia
TENNESSEE
NORTH CAROLINA
SOUTH CAROLINA
FLORIDA
Chattanooga
Ft. Oglethorpe
Chickamauga
Rome
Marietta
Villa Rica
Atlanta
Senoia
Warm Springs
Columbus
Dahlonega
Gainesville
Clarkesville
Rabun Gap
Hartwell
Athens
Watkinsville
Washington
Thomson
Augusta
Waynesboro
Columbia
Macon
Dublin
Statesboro
Perry
Americus
Albany
Moultrie
Savannah
Darien
St. Simons Island
Brunswick
Jacksonville
Tallahassee
ZONE 8
ZONE 9
ZONE 7

Zone 7
Coastal Georgia

Interstate 95 parallels the long Atlantic coastline of Georgia from the South Carolina border near Savannah to the Florida state-line close to Jacksonville. The narrow strip of land and beaches it defines contain countless riches for travelers.

The crown jewel is Savannah. Founder Gen. James Oglethorpe had a different vision for this city, not based on the European pattern of one central town center but instead a community growing around 26 parklike squares (24 of these original squares survive today). For better or for worse, the best-selling novel *Midnight in the Garden of Good and Evil* brought this graceful city to the attention of thousands of reader/travelers. The tourist office was delighted with the incredible influx of new visitors; many of the residents less so, turned off by the depiction of local inhabitants who lived free in vacant mansions or took flies for walks on thread leashes!

The barrier islands provide a heady mixture of sun and leisure pursuits. These include Cumberland Island, visited by more than 300 species of birds; Jekyll Island, with a ten-mile beach and a Music Theatre Festival (Broadway productions outdoors); and St. Simons Island, with a lighthouse and miles of bike trails.

For More Information

Brunswick–Golden Isles Visitors Bureau
(800) 933-2627

MCKINNON HOUSE BED & BREAKFAST, Brunswick

Overall: ★★★½ Room Quality: B Value: C Price: $85–$125

Lumber magnate L. T. McKinnon built this turn-of-the-century home, and there's no other like it in Brunswick. Seventeen Corinthian columns adorn the front and side porches, a feature continued in the reception hall and several of the nine fireplaces. Future plans include opening a fourth bedroom and bath for guest use. The host says proudly that the house was featured in the movie *Conrack* (which we never saw or even heard of). The front porch is a handsome place to pose for the inevitable travel snapshots. The two upstairs bedrooms have private baths, but they are in adjoining rooms. The host provides robes, but it's still not the most convenient arrangement for guests in the night. Take the room on the first floor when available.

SETTING & FACILITIES

Location: On coast off I-95
Near: St. Simons, Sea, and Jekyll Islands
Building: 1902 Queen Anne
Grounds: None
Public Space: 4 porches, 2 parlors
Food & Drink: Full breakfast w/ fruit & egg, cheese, & sausage casserole; specialty: egg cups (egg, cheese, & bread baked in a muffin tin—a great hit w/ guests)
Recreation: Fishing, beaches, boat tours, horseback riding
Amenities & Services: Local sightseeing information

ACCOMMODATIONS

Units: 3 guest rooms
All Rooms: Hardwood floors, Oriental rug
Bed & Bath: 1 king, 2 doubles; private baths
Favorites: Downstairs room—large w/ 4 windows, romantic, king bed
Comfort & Decor: Victorian pieces are mixed with antiques from New Orleans and Charleston, where the host once lived. White ash paneling, ceiling beams, and intricate carving make this a special place.

RATES, RESERVATIONS, & RESTRICTIONS

Deposit: 1 night
Discounts: Seasonal
Credit Cards: None
Check-in/Out: 4 p.m./11 a.m.
Smoking: No; "by order of the fire marshal"
Pets: Yes
Kids: Welcome, but no rollaway beds or cribs
Minimum Stay: None
Open: All year
Host: Jo Miller
1001 Egmont St.
Brunswick, GA 31520
(912) 261-9100

WATERSHILL BED & BREAKFAST, Brunswick

Overall: ★★ Room Quality: D Value: D Price: $85–$115

When Jack Waters and Matthew Hill purchased this 1875 house in December 1998, it had been cut up into four apartments. After five intensive months of removing aging kitchens and baths and designing new bedrooms, baths, lounges, and their own kitchen, they opened for business. It's not your average Southern mansion bed-and-breakfast. It is the home of consummate collectors who have given their decorating urges full rein. The hosts are very convivial and welcome guests with refreshments and a chat on the porch or in the living room. The next morning they have breakfast with their guests. The five accommodations and public spaces reflect their years of travel and gathering. There's not much to see in Brunswick, but the islands are fascinating.

Setting & Facilities

Location: Historic District
Near: St. Simons, Sea, and Jekyll Islands
Building: 1889 Folk Victorian
Grounds: Lawns & gardens
Public Space: Parlors upstairs & down, porches
Food & Drink: Full breakfast; afternoon wine & cheese
Recreation: Swimming, fishing, golf, tennis
Amenities & Services: Newspapers, restaurant & local events lists

Accommodations

Units: 5 guest rooms
All Rooms: TV, sitting area
Some Rooms: private porch, daybed
Bed & Bath: Queens, private baths
Favorites: Bridal suite w/ claw-foot tub, four-poster bed
Comfort & Decor: Antiques, collectibles, and local artwork and crafts blend to create an inviting atmosphere.

Rates, Reservations, & Restrictions

Deposit: Credit card
Discounts: AARP, corp., stays over 3 days
Credit Cards: AE, V, MC, D
Check-in/Out: Flexible
Smoking: No
Pets: Some, with size limits; ask
Kids: Ask
Minimum Stay: None
Open: All year
Hosts: Jack Waters & Mathew Hill
728 Union St.
Brunswick, GA 31520
(912) 264-4262
jack@watershill.com
www.watershill.com

OPEN GATES BED & BREAKFAST, Darien

Overall: ★★	Room Quality: D	Value: A	Price: $64–$88

This bed-and-breakfast is in the midst of a prime natural wonderland of bird and wildlife habitats. Host C. Wayne Davis regularly offers guests boat tours to Butler Island, Blackbeard Island, rice fields, and surrounding marshes. Because this area has no beaches, it is mercifully undeveloped and almost industry-free. Children are welcome if they are of a "discerning nature," as the former host put it. Translation: Our house is filled with family pieces and delicate collectibles, and we don't need any young home-wreckers.

Setting & Facilities

Location: In Darien 1.5 mi. east on I-95 (Exits 9, 10)
Near: Migratory flyaway, Altamaha Waterfowl Management Area, marshes, islands
Building: 1876 Southern home
Grounds: Beautiful gardens
Public Space: Front porch
Food & Drink: Full breakfast includes Plantation Pan Cake
Recreation: Sight-seeing, bird- & wildlife watching, boat tours
Amenities & Services: Antique children's books, free tours of surrounding area library

Accommodations

Units: 4 guest rooms
Some Rooms: Historic quilts, botanical prints, herbarium
Bed & Bath: Beds vary; 2 w/ private baths, 2 w/ adjacent baths
Favorites: Timber Baron's Room w/ sleigh bed, antique dresser sets, doll clothes
Comfort & Decor: Each room is decorated differently with unique prints.

Rates, Reservations, & Restrictions

Deposit: 1 night
Discounts: None
Credit Cards: Cash or checks only
Check-in/Out: Ask; flexible
Smoking: No
Pets: No
Kids: Welcome
Minimum Stay: 2 days during major holiday weekends
Open: All year
Host: C. Wayne Davis
Vernon Square
Darien, GA 31305
(912) 437-6985

BALLASTONE, Savannah

Overall: ★★★★★	Room Quality: A	Value: C	Price: $215–$415

If you haven't been to this superb inn in the past several years, you will be pleasantly surprised at the renovations and amenities that have made the

Ballastone even more special. A not-so-pleasant surprise will be the increase in rates, about $100 or more above quoted rates just two years ago. Still, if you can afford it, this is the most luxurious bed-and-breakfast in Savannah. Everything works together to make guests relaxed, from the terry robes and private balconies to the antique bar and attractive courtyard. Want your clothes pressed, to have a massage, play a round of golf, or visit a local health club? Say the word and the staff will make all arrangements. Luxury, relaxation, a carefree vacation—all at the Ballastone Inn. We just hope the management won't take this glowing review as a cue to raise the rates again.

Setting & Facilities

Location: Historic District
Near: Telfair Museum of Fine Art, many good Savannah restaurants
Building: Restored 1838 mansion
Grounds: None
Public Space: Parlor, courtyard
Food & Drink: Full breakfast; evening hors d'oeuvres
Recreation: Shopping, sight-seeing
Amenities & Services: Elevator, off-street parking, bicycles, tennis equipment, access to nearby health club

Accommodations

Units: 17 guest rooms & suites
All Rooms: Regional motif, TV, VCR
Some Rooms: Fireplace, sitting area, whirlpool tub, rice poster or canopy bed
Bed & Bath: Beds vary; private baths
Favorites: None
Comfort & Decor: Elegance from different eras is on display.

Rates, Reservations, & Restrictions

Deposit: 1 night
Discounts: None
Credit Cards: None
Check-in/Out: 3 p.m./11 a.m.
Smoking: Bar & courtyard only
Pets: No
Kids: 16 & over
Minimum Stay: 2 nights on weekends
Open: All year
Hosts: Staff
14 East Oglethorpe Ave.
Savannah, GA 31401
(912) 236-1484 or (800) 822-4553
Fax: (912) 236-4626
info@ballastone.com
www.ballastone.com

ELIZA THOMPSON HOUSE, Savannah

Overall: ★★★★ Room Quality: B Value: D Price: $109–$250

The Eliza Thompson House is a beautiful Southern mansion dating back to 1847. Here are some of the things we believe you will really enjoy about this gracious inn (and a couple things that may bug you). You will certainly like the antiques-filled decor, the four-poster beds, and the heated and covered portion of the great courtyard where you can have your breakfast in rain or shine comfort. Tennis great Martina

Navratilova called this place "a sweet inn," which it can be until you try to park. The inn staff was unfailingly helpful in making dinner reservations and even providing a free 48-hour parking pass you can post on your car. But there's the rub. Finding even a metered place on the streets near the inn can be a trick worthy of David Copperfield. Meters are free on Saturdays and Sundays, but you still have that parking search every time you return after dinner, sight-seeing, etc. The lighting could be better in the rooms for reading. Picky, picky, picky.

Setting & Facilities

Location: East on I-16 to Exit 16 (Montgomery St.), right on Liberty St., right on Whitaker St., left on Jones St.
Near: Historic District, River St., Mansion Museum, Telfair Museum of Fine Art
Building: 1847 Federal-style mansion
Grounds: Courtyard
Public Space: Breakfast room, courtyard, parlor
Food & Drink: Coffee, juice, cereal, bagels, muffins, & hot-baked entree (e.g., stuffed French toast); evening wine & cheese
Recreation: Trolley & horse & buggy tours, "Garden of Evil" tours, garden visits
Amenities & Services: Reservations for tours, local restaurant menus

Accommodations

Units: 25 guest rooms
All Rooms: Phone, color TV, robes, hair dryer, four-poster bed, antiques
Some Rooms: Fireplace
Bed & Bath: King; private baths
Favorites: R. Bruce w/ 300 yards of materials on ceiling selected by famous designers
Comfort & Decor: Antiques of the era are used throughout.

Rates, Reservations, & Restrictions

Deposit: No
Discounts: No
Credit Cards: MC, V
Check-in/Out: 3 p.m./11 a.m.
Smoking: No
Pets: No
Kids: Welcome; age 12 & under stay free
No-Nos: No kitchen privileges
Minimum Stay: 2 nights on weekends during peak seasons, 3 nights some holidays
Open: All year
Hosts: Carol & Steve Day
5 W. Jones St.
Savannah, GA 31405
(912) 236-3620 or (800) 348-9378
Fax: (912) 238-1920
elizath@aol.com
www.elizathompsonhouse.com

GASTONIAN, Savannah

Overall: ★★★★½ Room Quality: A Value: D Price: $225–$375

The Gastonian is opulence plus, but unfortunately, like most bed-and-breakfasts in Savannah, it's opulence at a high price. The Caracalla Suite was named for the Roman emperor who invented bathing, and when you see it you'll know why. One room in the suite is for sleeping, the other for bathing with a whirlpool tub that could almost be used for Olympic freestyle tryouts. It can bubble up to five people! Most major magazine reviewers have gone gaga over the Gastonian. Everything from the afternoon tea and concierge services that make tour and restaurant reservations run like a well-oiled hospitality machine. To enjoy some of this elegance at the lowest possible cost, come during low season (November–January or July and August) or visit the Gastonian's Internet site where they often offer special rates you won't find anywhere else. You must mention you saw the deal on the Internet.

Setting & Facilities

Location: Historic District
Near: Forsyth Park, restaurants on the river
Building: Two side-by-side 1868 Regency Italianate mansions
Grounds: Gardens, sundeck
Public Space: Courtyard
Food & Drink: 3-course breakfast; complimentary wines
Recreation: Sight-seeing, tennis
Amenities & Services: Staff of 18

Accommodations

Units: 17 guest rooms
All Rooms: Eighteenth- & nineteenth-century antiques, working fireplace, phone, cable TV, individual temperature control
Some Rooms: Whirlpool tub, wheelchair access
Bed & Bath: Beds vary; private baths
Favorites: None
Comfort & Decor: Super elegant antiques and rich hues create a luxurious atmosphere.

Rates, Reservations, & Restrictions

Deposit: 1 night
Discounts: None
Credit Cards: AE, V, MC, D
Check-in/Out: 3 p.m./noon
Smoking: No
Pets: No
Kids: 12 & older
Minimum Stay: None
Open: All year
Host: Anne Landers
220 E. Gaston St.
Savannah, GA 31401
(912) 232-2869 or (800) 322-6603
Fax: (912) 232-0710
www.gastonian.com

HAMILTON-TURNER INN, Savannah

Overall: ★★★★½ Room Quality: A Value: D Price: $135–$275

If you read *Midnight in the Garden of Good and Evil*, you may remember a blonde girl named Mandy. Keep this under your hat, but the real "Mandy" originally owned the Hamilton-Turner Inn. Now she is the night innkeeper here. If you bring along a copy of the book, she will personalize it for you. That's just one of the surprises waiting for you at this handsome inn on one of the famous squares in the city. We found the rooms to be exquisite. Afternoon tea is sweet fun, with young, pretty girls filling three tables with high-calorie no-no's. Traffic sounds are a little loud at night. And a nearby church is undergoing a 15-month restoration. That means construction workers arrive around 7 a.m. and fill many of the parking places on this square. But parking problems or not, this is a wonderful inn experience. Maybe you should leave your car and fly to Savannah. The inn provides free pick-up at the airport.

Setting & Facilities

Location: I-16 East to Savannah, follow signs to downtown, right on Liberty St. to Abercorn St.
Near: Historic district; about 3 blocks from river & 2 blocks from Forsyth Park
Building: Second French Empire
Grounds: Private courtyard & gardens overlooking Lafayette Square
Public Space: Large parlor, separate tea room
Food & Drink: Full Southern breakfast of scrambled eggs, grits, hash browns, fresh fruit, orange pecan sauce, & sausage, bacon, or ham; evening sherry & coffee
Recreation: Tours of historic district, golf, ocean, river nearby
Amenities & Services: Free airport pick-up 7 a.m.–6 p.m.

Accommodations

Units: 14 guest rooms
All Rooms: Robes, hair dryer, TV/VCR, phone, computer hook-up
Some Rooms: Fireplace, balcony, whirlpool tub
Bed & Bath: Beds vary; private baths
Favorites: Room 304 w/ bay window & easy access to courtyard; room 321 w/ king bed, whirlpool, fireplace, balcony
Comfort & Decor: Victorian antiques and original oils create an atmosphere of romantic elegance.

Rates, Reservations, & Restrictions

Deposit: Credit card; 72-hour cancellation
Discounts: None
Credit Cards: AE, V, MC, DC, D
Check-in/Out: 2 p.m./10 a.m.; exceptions on request
Smoking: No
Pets: In carriage house only
Kids: Welcome
Minimum Stay: 2 nights on weekends (unless single room is avail.)
Open: All year
Hosts: Charlie & Sue Strickland
330 Abercom St.
Savannah, GA 31401
(212) 233-1833 or (888) 448-8849
Fax: (912) 233-0291
homemaid@worldnet.attnet
www.hamilton-turnerinn.com

MAGNOLIA PLACE INN, Savannah

Overall: ★★★★★ Room Quality: A Value: D Price: $145–$270

"Quiet elegance" is one of those travel brochure terms that actually could have been invented for the Magnolia Place Inn. Breakfast is served on a silver tray in the room, or guests can choose to dine in the parlor, garden, or on the veranda. Christmas is a particularly festive time to visit with poinsettias and decorations everywhere. The rates are high, although not as bad as some other Savannah bed-and-breakfast graduates of the robber-baron school of inn-keeping. This would be an ideal honeymoon retreat. Consider giving a gift certificate from the inn to the happy couple to help prevent their first argument over money.

SETTING & FACILITIES

Location: Historic District overlooking Forsyth Park
Near: Historic homes, Savannah Visitors Center, Telfair Mansion & Art Museum
Building: Building: 1878 Steamboat Gothic
Grounds: Garden
Public Space: Parlor, veranda
Food & Drink: Cont'l breakfast; afternoon wine & tea; sweets & coffee at night
Recreation: Sight-seeing
Amenities & Services: Gift certificates avail., video library

ACCOMMODATIONS

Units: 13 guest rooms, 2 suites
All Rooms: Period prints, antiques, TV & VCR
Some Rooms: Fireplace, dbl. whirlpool tub
Bed & Bath: Beds vary; private baths
Favorites: None
Comfort & Decor: Genteel riches are evident in beautiful porcelains, English antiques, and prints.

RATES, RESERVATIONS, & RESTRICTIONS

Deposit: Credit card
Discounts: Corp.
Credit Cards: AE, V, MC, D, DC
Check-in/Out: 2:30 p.m./11 a.m.
Smoking: No
Pets: No
Kids: 12 & older; ask about younger kids—exceptions are sometimes made
Minimum Stay: 3 nights during New Year's Eve, St. Patrick's Day
Open: All year
Hosts: Rob & Jane Sales, Kathy Medlock
503 Whitaker St.
Savannah, GA 31401
(912) 236-7674 or (800) 238-7674
Fax: (912) 236-1145
info@magnoliaplaceinn.com
www.magnoliaplaceinn.com

PRESIDENT'S QUARTERS, Savannah

Overall: ★★★½ Room Quality: B Value: C Price: $185–$225

This elegant bed-and-breakfast's major attributes are personal service and convenience. Savannah, as noted elsewhere, is a very tough town in which to park. But you will have access to a private parking facility at this bed-and-breakfast. You can decide to have breakfast served in your room or in the courtyard. Walk to great restaurants on River Street, only three blocks away. There is 24-hour concierge service for reservations and advice. All of the rooms are named for Presidents who have visited Savannah, so guests can sleep in a four-poster bed in the Lyndon B. Johnson Room, a king four-poster in the Richard Nixon room, or a queen bed in the Chester A. Arthur Room (which would not have been big enough for the room's namesake). Ask about joining the Corporate Cabinet Club to qualify for corporate rates.

SETTING & FACILITIES

Location: Heart of Savannah's Historic District
Near: Savannah Visitors Center, River Street Train Museum, Telfair Mansion & Art Museum, many historic homes
Building: Twin Federal-style townhouses
Grounds: None
Public Space: Courtyard, sitting rooms
Food & Drink: Full breakfast w/ Belgian waffles, quiche, fruit; afternoon tea w/ cakes, cheeses, wine
Recreation: Sight-seeing, tennis, golf
Amenities & Services: Reservations for tours & restaurants, help w/ luggage, extensive video library

ACCOMMODATIONS

Units: 11 guest rooms, 9 suites
All Rooms: Robes, high ceiling (up to 13 feet), fruit & wine
Some Rooms: Working fireplace, loft BR, four-poster bed
Bed & Bath: Beds vary; private baths
Favorites: None
Comfort & Decor: Elegant and posh throughout

RATES, RESERVATIONS, & RESTRICTIONS

Deposit: Credit card, 1 night
Discounts: AAA, AARP
Credit Cards: V, MC, DC, D
Check-in/Out: 2 p.m./11 a.m.
Smoking: Only in certain restricted areas; ask
Pets: No
Kids: Welcome
Minimum Stay: 2 nights on weekends
Open: All year
Hosts: Stacy Stephens & Hank Smalling
225 East President St.
Savannah, GA 31401
(912) 233-1600 or (800) 233-1776
Fax: (912) 238-0849
pquinn@aol.com
www.presidentsquarters.com

LODGE ON LITTLE ST. SIMONS ISLAND, St. Simons Island

Overall: ★★½ Room Quality: D Value: D Price: $325–$850

This place isn't technically a bed-and-breakfast inn because it serves three meals a day on the American plan. It isn't even a single building, but a collection of cottages of various conditions. But we're including it because of its extraordinary natural setting. It was hard to rate the rooms because they vary from cottage to cottage, from modern and attractive to getting a little too old for this kind of work. Ahh, but the setting—a whole island almost to yourself with deer, armadillos, buntings, piping plovers, and more, glimpsed on beach hikes or morning horseback rides. All meals and almost all activities are included in the daily rates, which nevertheless still seem high to us. As the old jokes goes, we just want to "rent" the island for a few days, not buy it. But then we found you can buy the whole island and all its facilities for a day if you are having a really big family reunion or business meeting, for $6,200 in high season (winter/spring).

Setting & Facilities

Location: Accessible only by boat from marina on neighboring St. Simon; ask for directions
Near: Beach, Sea Island
Building: Group of guest cottages
Grounds: 10,000 acres of coastal wilderness w/ tidal creeks, salt marshes, 7 mi. of beaches
Public Space: Hunting Lodge (site of meals, cocktail hour)
Food & Drink: Choice of cont'l or full breakfast; American plan: 3 meals daily, plus snacks & beverages
Recreation: Swimming, shelling, bicycling, horseback riding, boating
Amenities & Services: Spring-fed pool; rates include gear, sporting equipment

Accommodations

Units: 15 guest rooms in cottages
All Rooms: Marsh or forest view, washer/dryer access, coffeemaker, hair dryer; cottages have shared room w/ fireplace
Bed & Bath: Beds vary; private baths
Favorites: Michael Cottage in private setting on edge of forest
Comfort & Decor: Decor ranges from rustic with pine bough and antique wicker furnishings in the Hunting Lodge to light and airy in the Michael Cottage; cottages feature local art.

RATES, RESERVATIONS, & RESTRICTIONS

Deposit: 50%
Discounts: None
Credit Cards: AE, V, MC, D
Check-in/Out: 10 a.m.–4 p.m./10 a.m.
Smoking: No
Pets: No
Kids: All ages welcome Jun.–Sept.; 8 or older all year
Minimum Stay: 2 nights
Open: All year
Host: Bo Taylor
P.O. Box 21078
Little St. Simons Island, GA 31522
(912) 638-7472 or (888) 733-5774
Fax: (912) 638-1811
issi@mindspring.com
www.LittleStSimonsIsland.com

Zone 8
Northern Georgia

For many vacationers and business travelers, Atlanta *is* Georgia. Atlanta is a proud, bustling city, where many streets seem to be named Peachtree (get a good map or you will get lost), that is home of one of the nation's busiest airports as well as headquarters of several Fortune 500 corporations, such as Coca-Cola and United Parcel Service. The city also has many links to America's civil rights movement through Martin Luther King Jr. The King Center with a museum is now located in a National Historic District. Take a tour of CNN Center and see where so many "crisis" stories on TV are shaped.

But don't miss the many other interesting cities and towns in this zone. The upper northeastern portion of this zone includes "Mother Nature's playground," the beautiful mountains of Georgia. You can see Amicalola Falls, the Dahlonega Gold Museum (gold was mined in Dahlonega before the Civil War began), and the Georgia Mountain Fair.

For More Information

Atlanta Convention and Visitors Bureau
(800) 285-2682

Georgia State Visitor Center (Lavonia)
(706) 356-4019

NICHOLSON HOUSE INN, Athens

Overall: ★★½ | Room Quality: C | Value: C | Price: $75–$85

The Nicholson House Inn was actually built around a log cabin erected in 1820. The suites in the two carriage houses would be perfect for honeymoon or anniversary couples who prefer privacy to meeting with other guests. One of the carriage houses offers a small sitting room and bedroom. Another offers a kitchenette and sitting room. On sunny days the porch of the main house offers a quiet retreat with distant deer frequently sighted. On cooler days, move inside to the library with a wood stove and reading materials about the fascinating early history of the house.

SETTING & FACILITIES

Location: 75 mi. north of Atlanta; Exit 50 off I-85; stay on US 129 to reach B&B
Near: University of Georgia, State Botanical Garden, Morton Theatre, Butts-Mehre Heritage Hall Sports Museum
Building: 1947 Colonial Revival plus 2 carriage houses
Grounds: 6 wooded acres
Public Space: Formal parlor, library
Food & Drink: Cont'l plus
Recreation: Tennis, golf
Amenities & Services: Phones w/ computer lines avail., meeting facil. (16)

ACCOMMODATIONS

Units: 6 guest rooms, 2 suites in carriage house
Some Rooms: Fireplace, carved four-poster bed, private deck or balcony
Bed & Bath: Beds vary; private baths
Favorites: None
Comfort & Decor: Comfortable overstuffed furniture

RATES, RESERVATIONS, & RESTRICTIONS

Deposit: Credit Card
Discounts: None
Credit Cards: AE, V, MC, D
Check-in/Out: Ask
Smoking: No
Pets: No
Kids: Welcome, but ask
Minimum Stay: None
Open: All year
Host: Stu Kelley
6295 Jefferson Rd.
Athens, GA 30607
(706) 353-7799
Fax: (706) 353-7799
www.virtualcities.com/ons/ga

SHELLMONT BED & BREAKFAST LODGE, Atlanta

Overall: ★★★★½ | Room Quality: B | Value: A | Price: $95–$415

This bed-and-breakfast is covered with kudos, ranging from the Atlanta's "Mayors Award" for historic preservation to three diamonds from AAA and three stars from Mobil. Judge for yourself the quality of the restoration of the Tiffany windows and the woodwork. For a private retreat, select the three-room carriage house. Everything is very convenient, including some of Atlanta's top restaurants and cultural attractions. Before visiting the High Museum, read Thomas Wolf's *A Man in Full*, with one chapter set at the High, a hilarious send-up of cultural pretensions in Atlanta (and elsewhere). But don't take this book with you when you go there. It's definitely not popular in some quarters of the city.

SETTING & FACILITIES

Location: Corner of Piedmont & Sixth St.
Near: Margaret Mitchell House, Atlanta Botanical Gardens, High Museum of Art
Building: 1891Colonial Revival & Carriage House
Grounds: Gardens, specimen trees
Public Space: Several parlors, LRs, verandas
Food & Drink: Full breakfast w/ Belgian waffles; "health" meals; complimentary beverages; fruit basket
Recreation: Tennis, jogging, walking
Amenities & Services: Computer, Internet, fax, copier, & laundry services avail.; safe deposit box

ACCOMMODATIONS

Units: 5 guest rooms, 2 suites
All Rooms: TV, phone w/ data port, clock radio
Some Rooms: Whirlpool tub, steam shower
Bed & Bath: Beds vary; private baths
Favorites: None
Comfort & Decor: Antiques and Victorian wall treatments are found throughout.

RATES, RESERVATIONS, & RESTRICTIONS

Deposit: 1st & last night; 7-day cancellation
Discounts: None
Credit Cards: AE, V, MC, D, DC
Check-in/Out: 3 p.m./11 a.m.
Smoking: No
Pets: No
Kids: Welcome; under age 12 in carriage house only
Minimum Stay: 2 nights on weekends, 3 nights during some holidays
Open: All year
Hosts: Ed & Debbie McCord
821 Piedmont Ave. NE
Atlanta, GA 30308
(404) 872-9290
Fax: (404) 872-5379
innkeeper@shellmont.com
www.shellmont.com

AZALEA INN, Augusta

Overall: ★★½ | Room Quality: C | Value: D | Price: $79–$150

In 1999 when David Tremain and Andrew Harney bought their two-building bed-and-breakfast and adjacent residence, the contract stipulated that Masters golf fans continue to have access to their favorite rooms.

"That's guaranteed occupancy," reasoned David, as they moved into the residence/reception building and reopened the Azalea Inn. David has expanded his interest in the Masters, offering a variety of golf packages during the tournament at other homes and apartments. These packages also include tickets. The guest buildings, 1895 and 1902 duplexes, have dividing walls, making guest lounges impractical, but porches fill some of that need. Four rooms have private back porches; four others share two porches, which provide a perfect setting for the basket breakfasts delivered each morning. Tip: If you're traveling with kids, don't miss Fort Discovery on the Riverwalk, a high-tech wonderland of exhibits and shows.

SETTING & FACILITIES

Location: Off I-20 on Greene St.
Near: Gertrude Herbert Institute of Art, Fort Discovery on Riverwalk, Masters Golf Tournament, Savannah River
Building: 1895 Victorian
Grounds: None
Public Space: Porches
Food & Drink: Breakfast served in room; note: lower-priced rooms don't include breakfast, add $10
Recreation: Sight-seeing, golf
Amenities & Services: Golf information

ACCOMMODATIONS

Units: 21 guest rooms
All Rooms: Fireplace, whirlpool tub, 11-foot ceiling, desk/table
Some Rooms: Glass sun porch
Bed & Bath: 11 kings, 10 queens; private baths
Favorites: Room 334B Honeymoon suite w/ fireplace in BR & bath, king canopy bed
Comfort & Decor: Period, elegant antiques and gilded mirrors set the scene; most rooms are open and airy, and knickknacks are few.

RATES, RESERVATIONS, & RESTRICTIONS

Deposit: Credit card
Discounts: None
Credit Cards: AE, V, MC
Check-in/Out: 3–6 p.m./11 a.m.
Smoking: No
Pets: No
Kids: Welcome
Minimum Stay: None
Open: All year
Hosts: David Tremaine & Andrew Harney
312–316 Greene St.
Augusta, GA 30901
(706) 724-3454
www.theazaleainn.com

GORDON-LEE MANSION, Chickamauga

Overall: ★★★½	Room Quality: B	Value: A	Price: $75–$110

The Confederacy was already in desperate straits in 1863 when the Union Army prepared to march on the vital railroad center at Chattanooga, Tennessee. General Rosecrans massed his troops at Chickamauga in Georgia and rolled out his war maps in the Gordon-Lee Mansion. He breakfasted here, too, and so can you. The house is now one of the most historic bed-and-breakfasts in the South. Take a stroll over grounds once heavily trod by cavalry and soldiers. Glimpse life as it was once lived in the Old South. You have a choice of staying in the mansion or in a nearby Log House with two bedrooms and a kitchen (no breakfast is served at the Log House; you fix your own in the full kitchen there). The Chickamauga Military Park is only a short drive and more than a century away.

Setting & Facilities

Location: Off I-93, 6 mi. on Hwy. 341 to Chickamauga
Near: Chickamauga Military Park, Lookout Mountain, Rock City, Ft. Oglethorpe
Building: 1847 Antebellum mansion
Grounds: 7 acres, formal gardens, gazebo
Public Space: Verandas, gardens
Food & Drink: Full breakfast
Recreation: Sight-seeing
Amenities & Services: None

Accommodations

Units: 5 guest rooms, plus 2-BR log house
All Rooms: Antique furnishings
Some Rooms: Four-poster bed, canopy bed
Bed & Bath: Beds vary; private baths
Favorites: None
Comfort & Decor: This careful restoration of the early pre–Civil War period features crystal chandeliers and Oriental floor coverings.

Rates, Reservations, & Restrictions

Deposit: Credit card
Discounts: Corp. rate $60 Mon.–Thur., 10% for seniors (60 & older)
Credit Cards: AE, V, MC, D
Check-in/Out: 3 p.m./11:30 a.m.
Smoking: No
Pets: No
Kids: 12 & older
Minimum Stay: 2 nights on weekends
Open: All year
Host: Richard Darclift
217 Cove Rd.
Chickamauga, GA 30707
(706) 375-4728 or (800) 487-4728
glmbb@aol.com

GLEN-ELLA SPRINGS, Clarkesville

Overall: ★★★★½ Room Quality: A Value: B Price: $145–$195

Glen-Ella Springs Inn is a genuine oasis, appearing suddenly beside a meandering gravel road—two floors, rustic, peaceful. We're not big fans of gravel roads because of what they can do to car finishes, so drive slowly. Owners Bobby and Barrie Aycock rescued the property in 1986, adding an inviting swimming pool and sun deck, with a cheerful garden nearby. "Food is my reason for doing this. I run the kitchen; Bobby manages the inn and dining room," says Barrie. "He has the perfect personality and gets along with everyone." Conferences come for two to three days and use a private, fully equipped building. Guests plan day trips, relax on site, and enjoy the hearty fireplace and a good evening meal. Request suites early for fall and winter weekends, as they are usually the first to be reserved when temperatures drop because of the cozy fireplaces in the rooms.

SETTING & FACILITIES

Location: 90 mi. north of Atlanta between Clarkesville & Clayton
Near: Orchard Golf Course, Chatooga River (white-water rafting)
Building: Large historic inn (on Nat'l Register of Historic Places)
Grounds: 18 landscaped acres
Public Space: Decks
Food & Drink: Full breakfast; dinner avail. most evenings
Recreation: Swimming, hiking, white-water rafting, trout fishing, tennis, golf
Amenities & Services: Access to private golf course, conf. center, wedding coordinator, swimming pool

ACCOMMODATIONS

Units: 21 guest rooms, including 2 penthouse rooms & 2 suites
All Rooms: AC, phone, voice mail, porch w/ woodland views, heart-pine walls
Some Rooms: Whirlpool tub, fireplace
Bed & Bath: Queen or king; private baths
Favorites: Suites w/ king beds, whirlpool tubs
Comfort & Decor: Period antiques and local handicrafts adorn this property.

RATES, RESERVATIONS, & RESTRICTIONS

Deposit: 1 night; 7-day cancellation
Discounts: None
Credit Cards: AE, V, MC, D
Check-in/Out: 2 p.m./11 a.m.
Smoking: No
Pets: No
Kids: 6 & older
Minimum Stay: None
Open: All year
Hosts: Bobby & Barrie Aycock
1789 Bear Gap Rd.
Clarkesville, GA 30523
(706) 754-7295 or (877) 456-7527
Fax: (706) 754-1560
info@glenella.com
www.glenella.com

LILY CREEK LODGE, Dahlonega

Overall: ★★½ | Room Quality: C | Value: B | Price: $85–$145

Each of the guest rooms here has a theme, but some of them don't come off well. The themes are a little jarring in this beautiful forest setting where we were expecting a handsomely rustic ambience. However, there are some unusual rewards for staying here. You can have breakfast in the "tree house," actually a raised gazebo. Then take a walk through the woods (some distance) to a swimming pool filled with mountain spring water and a pavilion with wicker furniture, a huge hot tub, a refrigerator, and a telescope for spotting the many birds and butterflies.

Setting & Facilities

Location: Blue Ridge Mountain foothills
Near: Amicalola Falls (highest in eastern U.S.), Gold Museum
Building: European-style chalet
Grounds: 7 acres; wildlife sanctuary
Public Space: Great Room, DR, woods
Food & Drink: Cont'l breakfast
Recreation: Swimming, games, hiking
Amenities & Services: Swimming pool, bocce ball court, tree house

Accommodations

Units: 12 guest rooms including 1 suite
All Rooms: Themed
Some Rooms: Kitchen facil.
Bed & Bath: Beds vary; private baths
Favorites: None
Comfort & Decor: The Lohengrin room is Bavarian, Moonglow is Cole Porter, and the Left Bank is Parisian.

Rates, Reservations, & Restrictions

Deposit: Credit card; 72-hour cancellation
Discounts: None
Credit Cards: AE, V, MC
Check-in/Out: 3 p.m./11 a.m.
Smoking: Smoking parlor & outside
Pets: No
Kids: Welcome
Minimum Stay: 2 nights during Oct. weekends
Open: All year
Hosts: Don & Sharon Bacek
2608 Auraria Rd.
Dahlonega, GA 30533
(706) 864-6848 or (888) 844-2694
Fax: (706) 864-6848
baceks@stc.net
www.virtualcities.com/ons/ga

MOUNTAIN TOP LODGE B&B, Dahlonega

Overall: ★★★ Room Quality: C Value: C Price: $70–$145

If you enjoy meeting fellow travelers, the communal breakfast is the place to do it. Or later, talk with them from your rocker on a great front porch that runs the entire length of the lodge. The atmosphere of this lodge is rustic, inside and out. If you have a choice, stay in one of the annex rooms, which are usually larger than those in the main house. If you are a repeat visitor, you get your first name printed on a mug—we saw many personalized mugs. However, of the two main inns in Dahlonega, we'd choose the Lily Creek Lodge first and this as a close runner-up.

Setting & Facilities

Location: An hour north of Atlanta
Near: Amicalola Falls (highest in eastern U.S.), Appalachian Trail
Building: Rustic mountain lodge
Grounds: 40 acres

Public Space: DR, deck, porch, great room
Food & Drink: Full country breakfast w/ cheese muffins; guest kitchen fridge stocked w/ complimentary snacks & beverages
Recreation: Hiking, fishing, horseback riding, rafting
Amenities & Services: Books, games, puzzles

Accommodations

Units: 9 guest rooms in main building, 4 in annex
Some Rooms: Gas-log fireplace, in-room whirlpool
Bed & Bath: Beds vary; private baths
Favorites: None
Comfort & Decor: Filled with mountain crafts, flea market finds, and antiques

Rates, Reservations, & Restrictions

Deposit: 50% of entire stay or 1 night (whichever greater)
Discounts: None
Credit Cards: AE, V, MC
Check-in/Out: Ask
Smoking: Deck, porch only
Pets: No
Kids: 12 & older
Minimum Stay: 2 nights during fall weekends, holidays, & special events
Open: All year
Host: Karen Lewan
447 Mountain Top Lodge Rd.
Dahlonega, GA 30533
(706) 864-5257 or (800) 526-9754
Fax: (706) 864-8265
www.bbonline.com/ca/mtntop_index

PAGE HOUSE BED & BREAKFAST, Dublin

Overall: ★★★★½ Room Quality: B Value: A Price: $90–$120

Prominently positioned on what once was termed "millionaire's row," the white, four-pillared Page House is magnificent. Innkeepers Kelly and Janice Canady call it "a peek at the past when cotton was king. You can still recapture that grandeur today." The front porch leads to a 60-foot entrance hall with a 56-foot ballroom to its right. A first-floor bedroom and bath offer disabled access, while five bedrooms and a roomy guest lounge are on the second floor. Now what exactly do tourists do in Dublin? Not much. There really isn't much to see or do, but it is a good one-night stop on the way to Savannah. Most of the inn's business comes from corporate travelers because there is a lot of industry in Dublin. One long-standing afternoon tradition of the inn we like: homemade hot pecan pie served warm with ice cream.

Setting & Facilities

Location: Hwy. 80 West, 7 blocks from downtown Dublin
Near: Laurens County Library (resources for researching genealogy), Theater Dublin, Dublin-Laurens Museum
Building: Greek Revival house
Grounds: Several flower gardens
Public Space: Library, ballroom, 2nd-floor lounge

Food & Drink: Full country breakfast w/ eggs, bacon, grits; specialties: sausage, egg, & cheese casserole & Belgian waffles w/ banana & pecans

Recreation: Tennis, walking

Amenities & Services: Local restaurant listings

Accommodations

Units: 6 guest rooms

All Rooms: Cable TV, phone w/ data port

Some Rooms: Kitchenette, private balcony, wheelchair ramp

Bed & Bath: Beds vary; private baths

Favorites: King Suite

Comfort & Decor: Soft shades of green, wine, and yellow provide attractive backgrounds for well-coordinated furnishings; antiques, artwork, and numbered prints abound.

Rates, Reservations, & Restrictions

Deposit: Credit card

Discounts: No charge 3rd person in room; 10% corp.

Credit Cards: AE, V, MC

Check-in/Out: 3 p.m./noon

Smoking: No

Pets: No; local kennel avail.

Kids: 12 & older

No-Nos: Open bars; guests can have alcoholic beverages in their own rooms

Minimum Stay: None

Open: All year except Christmas Eve & Day, New Year's Eve & Day

Hosts: Kelly & Janice Canady
711 Bellevue Ave.
Dublin, GA 31021
(912) 275-4551
Fax: (912) 275-4551
pagehous@accucomm.net
www.pagehousebb.com

CAPTAIN'S QUARTERS INN, Ft. Oglethorpe

Overall: ★★½ Room Quality: C Value: B Price: $99–$139

Travelers interested in the Civil War have found their place. This inn is located directly across from the Chickamauga National Battlefield. When the U.S. Army established Ft. Oglethorpe in 1902, they constructed some home quarters for married officers and their families, handsome duplexes. Over time, since 1946 when the fort was closed, these duplexes have been restored. Today they are handsome bed-and-breakfast quarters with four-poster beds and claw-foot tubs. The inn attracts many women business travelers.

Setting & Facilities

Location: NW Georgia, near Chattanooga, TN

Near: Civil War battlefields, Lookout Mountain, Tennessee River

Building: 1902 Classic Revival Home

Grounds: Open public green in front (former army parade field)

Public Space: Library, parlor, porches, large common room

Food & Drink: 3-course breakfast buffet
Recreation: Sight-seeing, white-water rafting, hang gliding (Lookout Mountain)
Amenities & Services: Steinway piano that guests can play

Accommodations

Units: 7 guest rooms
All Rooms: Phone w/ data port
Some Rooms: Working fireplace, wicker chairs
Bed & Bath: Beds vary; private baths
Favorites: None
Comfort & Decor: Country English antiques; elegantly decorated with personal collectibles of the innkeepers

Rates, Reservations, & Restrictions

Deposit: 1 night; 3-day cancellation
Discounts: None
Credit Cards: V, D
Check-in/Out: 3–7 p.m./11 a.m.
Smoking: No
Pets: No
Kids: Ask
Minimum Stay: 2 nights during certain holiday weekends; ask
Open: All year
Hosts: Daniel & Betty McKenzie
13 Barnhardt Circle
Ft. Oglethorpe, GA 30742
(706) 858-0624 or (800) 710-6816
Fax: (706) 861-4053
innkeeper@captains-qtrs-inn.com
www.virtualcities.com/ons/ga

DUNLAP HOUSE, Gainesville

Overall: ★★★★ Room Quality: B Value: B Price: $75–$155

The owners are relatively new but are certainly catching on fast. They provide guests with terry robes, large towels, and bottled water. The water will come in handy when you hike the Appalachian Trail or the Elachee Nature Center. If you are interested in boats, you have the perfect topic for breakfast conversation with the hosts. David and Karen have owned boats over the years and can recount the trials and pleasures of boating. While they don't accept pets, you won't be animal-lonely—a resident Labrador named Maverick and seven cockatiels will keep you company.

Setting & Facilities

Location: 2 mi. from Rt. 983
Near: Olympic Rowing Venue Lake Lanier, Mall of Georgia, Riverside Academy, Brenau College & Academy
Building: 1910 cottage
Grounds: Lawn
Public Space: Veranda
Food & Drink: Full breakfast w/ egg or hash browns/ham casserole, yogurt, fresh fruit; dinner delivered from restaurant across street
Recreation: Fishing, outlet shopping, hiking
Amenities & Services: Terry robes

Accommodations

Units: 10 guest rooms
All Rooms: Antique reproductions, phone w/ data port, fresh flowers, cable TV, 9-ft. ceiling
Some Rooms: Fireplace
Bed & Bath: Beds vary; private baths
Favorites: King Room w/ fireplace
Comfort & Decor: Numerous nautical prints, lighthouses, and seascapes

Rates, Reservations, & Restrictions

Deposit: Credit card; 7-day cancellation
Discounts: Corp., group, seasonal, senior (ask!), AAA
Credit Cards: AE, V, MC
Check-in/Out: 3 p.m./11 a.m.
Smoking: No
Pets: No
Kids: Welcome
Minimum Stay: None
Open: All year
Hosts: David & Karen Peters
635 Green St.
Gainesville, GA 30501
(770) 536-0200 or (800) 276-2935
Fax: (770) 503-7857
innkeepers@dunlaphouse.com
www.dunlaphouse.com

SKELTON HOUSE BED & BREAKFAST, Hartwell

Overall: ★★★★ Room Quality: B Value: B Price: $85–$100

Skelton House, a delightful Victorian home restored and remodeled in 1997, is hosted with warmth and grace by John and Ruth Skelton. "We're a family enterprise," Ruth declares. "Our son, Parke, and his wife, Terri, operate a gourmet restaurant in town. He's the chef, but John and I bake the bread, pies, and cakes in our kitchen." Seven themed bedrooms, three porches, and a lovely garden create a genteel atmosphere in a small-town environment. Across the intersection, a Laundromat is convenient, although not a visual asset. Businessmen stay here while calling on Hartwell's manufacturing community; tourists come seeking lakefront property or to enjoy a quiet weekend, a wedding, or family reunion.

Setting & Facilities

Location: Exit 59 off I-85 to Hwy. 77 to Hartwell, right on Benson St.
Near: Lake Hartwell, 2 golf courses, speedway
Building: 2-story Victorian
Grounds: 2 acres of landscaped gardens
Public Space: Morning room, parlor, DR
Food & Drink: Full breakfast
Recreation: Golfing, theater, music
Amenities & Services: Free newspapers, restaurant lists

Accommodations

Units: 7 guest rooms
All Rooms: Individual temperature controls, TV, phone w/ data port
Some Rooms: Disabled access, Jacuzzi tub, private balcony & entrance

Bed & Bath: Beds vary; private baths
Favorites: Parke's room w/ private balcony, garden tub
Comfort & Decor: Antiques are found throughout the house.

Rates, Reservations, & Restrictions

Deposit: 1 night; 72-hour cancellation
Discounts: Multiple nights, corp.
Credit Cards: All major cards
Check-in/Out: 4 p.m./11 a.m.
Smoking: No
Pets: No
Kids: Welcome
Minimum Stay: None
Open: All year
Hosts: John & Ruth Skelton
97 Benson St.
Hartwell, GA 30643
(706) 376-7969 or (877) 556-3790
Fax: (706) 856-3139
skeltonhouse@hartcom.net
www.theskeltonhouse.com

SIXTY POLK STREET, Marietta

Overall: ★★★½ Room Quality: B Value: C Price: $85–$125

Joe and Glenda call their four-bedroom bed-and-breakfast "our home, and we extend our hospitality to our guests." They also own an antiques shop, and their bed-and-breakfast displays many pieces appropriate to the Victorian period. Visual treats include seven handsome chandeliers, six gas fireplaces, a library with full-height shelves with lendable books for guests, and a dining room with a distinctive tray ceiling 14 feet in height. Breakfast includes good popovers.

Setting & Facilities

Location: 18 mi. north of Atlanta; I-70 North to Exit 112
Near: Marietta Square, Kennesaw Mountain Nat'l Civil War Battlefield, Marietta City Club
Building: 1872 Victorian French Regency
Grounds: None

Public Space: Parlor, DR, library, porches
Food & Drink: Full breakfast; complimentary soft drinks & juices, afternoon snack
Recreation: Sight-seeing, golf, carriage rides, walking tours
Amenities & Services: Books

Accommodations

Units: 4 guest rooms
All Rooms: Hardwood floors
Some Rooms: Fireplace, sleigh bed, claw-foot tub, sitting room
Bed & Bath: Beds vary; private baths; Canopy Room's bath is next door
Favorites: Wood Suite w/ sitting area & orig. horizontal paneling
Comfort & Decor: Period antiques and antique lighting

Rates, Reservations, & Restrictions

Deposit: 1 night
Discounts: AAA, seniors over 65
Credit Cards: AE, V, MC
Check-in/Out: 3–7 p.m./11 a.m.
Smoking: No
Pets: Ask
Kids: 12 & over
Minimum Stay: None
Open: All year
Hosts: Joe & Glenda Mertes
60 Polk St.
Marietta, GA 30064
(770) 419-1688 or (800) 845-7266

STANLEY HOUSE, Marietta

Overall: ★★★½ | Room Quality: B | Value: C | Price: $100

The Stanley House offers a special third-floor bedroom lit by skylights. At one end a ladder leads to a loft and daybed—perfect for a youngster. Owner Bridget Matarrese's front patio and porch offer tables and chairs, and the front room has been opened up to provide wide spaces for receptions, weddings, and other functions. There are five ample and tastefully decorated bedrooms and a large second-floor back deck for guests. The 100-year-old Victorian home's downstairs fireplaces provide enjoyable ambience and warmth. Located within easy walking distance of the downtown square antiques and specialty shops.

Setting & Facilities

Location: Exit 113 off I-75 (N. Marietta Parkway), west to Church St.
Near: Kennesaw Battlefield, White Water Park, Town Center Mall, Marietta Square
Building: Queen Anne Victorian
Grounds: Garden, courtyard
Public Space: LR, DR, front parlor, ballroom
Food & Drink: Cont'l plus
Recreation: Swimming, hiking
Amenities & Services: Daily newspaper, restaurant recommendations

ACCOMMODATIONS

Units: 5 guest rooms
All Rooms: Antiques
Some Rooms: Canopy bed, loft w/ daybed
Bed & Bath: Beds vary; private baths (4 in room, 1 across hall)
Favorites: None
Comfort & Decor: Victorian furniture and wallpapers; scenic murals decorate the walls.

RATES, RESERVATIONS, & RESTRICTIONS

Deposit: Credit card
Discounts: None
Credit Cards: AE, V, MC, D
Check-in/Out: 3 p.m./11 a.m.
Smoking: No
Pets: No
Kids: Welcome
Minimum Stay: None
Open: All year (no breakfast on Thanksgiving, Christmas, New Year's, Easter)
Host: Bridget K. Matarrese
236 Church St.
Marietta, GA 30060
(770) 426-1881
Fax: (770) 426-1881
bmatarrese@yahoo.com

WHITLOCK INN, Marietta

Overall: ★★★★ Room Quality: B Value: C Price: $145

Innkeeper Alexis Edwards describes her inn as "a genuine turn-of-the-century Southern home with period furnishings and full Southern hospitality." Meticulously restored and elegantly furnished in 1994, the inn offers five spacious, attractive bedrooms and a comfortable sun deck. Downstairs, bright and friendly public spaces open to an inviting rocker-lined porch. Nearby Marietta Square (three blocks away) provides excellent shopping and dining, and there are plenty of day-trip opportunities such as Kennesaw Mountain, Six Flags over Georgia, and Atlanta itself. Guests may be annoyed by the train whistle at night, so the host thoughtfully provides a small package containing soft foam ear plugs.

Setting & Facilities

Location: Block from Marietta Square
Near: Antebellum homes, Kennesaw Mountain Nat'l Park, Marietta City Club public course
Building: 1900 Victorian mansion
Grounds: Gardens
Public Space: Sundeck, porches
Food & Drink: Cont'l breakfast; afternoon sweets
Recreation: Golfing, sight-seeing
Amenities & Services: Makes dinner & theater reservations, fax & copier access

Accommodations

Units: 5 guest rooms
All Rooms: Ceiling fan, cable TV, phone
Some Rooms: Canopy or poster bed
Bed & Bath: Beds vary; private baths
Favorites: None
Comfort & Decor: Southern antiques

Rates, Reservations, & Restrictions

Deposit: 1 night; 48-hour cancellation
Discounts: None
Credit Cards: AE, V, MC, D
Check-in/Out: 3 p.m./11 a.m.
Smoking: No
Pets: No; kennel avail. at local vet
Kids: 12 & older
Minimum Stay: 1 night
Open: All year
Host: Alexis Edwards
57 Whitlock Ave.
Marietta, GA 30064
(770) 428-1495
Fax: (770) 919-9620
alexis@whitlockinn.com
www.whitlockinn.com

SYLVAN FALLS MILL, Rabun Gap

Overall: ★★ Room Quality: D Value: A Price: $85–$95

Bring your camera. Sylvan Falls Mill grist mill is powered by a spectacular 100-foot waterfall. The water flows right under you when you sit on the deck. For another view, ask for the Waterfall Room with a bay window that frames the falls; book this room if it's available. Black Rock State Park is right at the foot of this property. This is rustic country, so don't worry about dressing up.

Setting & Facilities

Location: I-441 near Clayton, GA (close to the SC & NC state lines)
Near: Black Rock State Park
Building: Restored old grist mill
Grounds: The falls & nearby trails
Public Space: Common sitting room, porch

Food & Drink: Full breakfast w/ emphasis on healthy, organic ingredients
Recreation: Hiking, white-water rafting
Amenities & Services: None

Accommodations

Units: 4 guest rooms
Some Rooms: Fireplace, bay window
Bed & Bath: Beds vary; private baths
Favorites: Waterfall Room
Comfort & Decor: The Cherub Fireplace Room has a gas-log wood stove and private porch; the Valley View Room has a microwave and fridge; antique reproductions are found throughout.

Rates, Reservations, & Restrictions

Deposit: Credit card
Discounts: Reduced rates winter, discount coupons for return guests
Credit Cards: V, MC
Check-in/Out: Flexible; ask
Smoking: No
Pets: Sometimes; depends on type of pet
Kids: Welcome
Minimum Stay: 2 nights during fall weekends & major holidays
Open: All year
Hosts: Marion & Deborah Brown
156 Taylor Chapel Rd.
Rabun Gap, GA 30568
(706) 746-7183
jmb@dnet.net
www.sylvanfallsmill.com

CLAREMONT HOUSE BED & BREAKFAST, Rome

Overall: ★★★★½ Room Quality: A Value: A Price: $88–$125

Proclaimed Georgia's finest example of Victorian Gothic architecture, this bed-and-breakfast dazzles its guests with 14-foot ceilings, 11 fireplaces, and exquisitely carved woodwork. Trompe l'oeil or faux painted wood to simulate marble is a rarity that can be seen here, and the floors and wainscoting of alternating patterns of walnut and chestnut are worthy of serious study. Innkeepers Gwen and George Kastanias say, "The magnificent woodwork and carpentry that have survived puts us in awe. Many original fixtures, pulls, and service buttons are still here." Gwen has explored the attic and "found treasures. We have a million ideas." She glows when talking about the house. You may, too.

Setting & Facilities

Location: Downtown Historic District
Near: Clock Tower Museum, Chieftain's Museum, Barnsley Gardens, Berry College, Cave Spring
Building: 1882 Victorian Gothic
Grounds: 1 acre w/ 117-year-old oak trees
Public Space: Library, DR, parlors (1 w/ baby grand piano), porch

Food & Drink: Full breakfast; specialties: waffles, French toast, 3-egg omelet; afternoon snack Fri. & Sat.
Recreation: Hiking, bicycling, fishing, boating
Amenities & Services: Local restaurant list & reservations, fax avail.

Accommodations

Units: 4 guest rooms in main house & cottage
All Rooms: Cable TV, phone, 14-foot ceiling, fireplace
Some Rooms: Claw-foot tub, poster canopy bed
Bed & Bath: Beds vary; private baths
Favorites: Victoria Room w/ king four-poster bed
Comfort & Decor: Airy, open rooms are superbly decorated and feature classic woodwork.

Rates, Reservations, & Restrictions

Deposit: Credit card; 7-day cancellation
Discounts: Weekly & monthly stays, corp.
Credit Cards: AE, V, MC
Check-in/Out: 4–7 p.m./11 a.m.
Smoking: No
Pets: No
Kids: Welcome
Minimum Stay: None
Open: All year except Thanksgiving, Christmas
Hosts: Gwen, George, & Holly Kastanias, Richard Pecha
906 East Second Ave.
Rome, GA 30161
(706) 291-0900 or (800) 254-4797
Fax: (706) 232-9865
clarinnrome@aol.com
www.bbonline.com/ga/claremont

VERANDA, Senoia

Overall: ★★★ Room Quality: C Value: C Price: $99–$150

You could call this a breakfast-and-bed. The host loves to cook, and it shows every morning. Each of the guest rooms has a theme and numerous surprises. The Walking Stick Room holds more than 100 walking sticks. There is a drum in the Civil War Room that was carried during that war. Want to read? Book the Mystery Room, with its choice of several hundred crime/mystery paperbacks. The inn has a small gift shop with an unusual specialty—kaleidoscopes, on sale from $2.50 to $7,000! Nearby are some 113 sites in Senoia on the National Register of Historic Places, which must be close to a record for a town this small. One of the Internet sites lists this bed-and-breakfast as "near" Callaway Gardens. Maybe "near" by private jet; these world-famous gardens are still 50 miles away.

Setting & Facilities

Location: 37 mi. from Atlanta
Near: Buggy Shop Museum, antiques stores, numerous historic homes
Building: Restored turn-of-the-century columned inn (originally Holberg Hotel)
Grounds: Landscaped lawn
Public Space: Front porch

Food & Drink: Full breakfast; specialties: sherbet, omelets, poached eggs, sourdough bread; dinner served by advance reservation; specialties: broccoli & chicken casserole, shrimp mousse

Recreation: Sight-seeing, tennis, fishing

Amenities & Services: Turn-down service, chocolates, treats on bed, walking canes, games

ACCOMMODATIONS

Units: 9 guest rooms

All Rooms: Themed w/ appropriate antiques

Some Rooms: Park view, claw-foot tub, paperbacks

Bed & Bath: 1 king, rest queen; private baths

Favorites: None

Comfort & Decor: Early 1900s antiques

RATES, RESERVATIONS, & RESTRICTIONS

Deposit: 1 night; credit card

Discounts: None

Credit Cards: AE, V, MC, D

Check-in/Out: Ask

Smoking: No

Pets: No

Kids: Welcome

No-Nos: Alcoholic beverages in guest rooms only

Minimum Stay: 2 nights on weekends

Open: All year

Hosts: Bobby & Jan Boal
252 Seavy St.
Senoia, GA 30276-0177
(770) 599-3905
Fax: (770) 599-0806
www.stay-in-ga.com/inns/veranda

FOUR CHIMNEYS, Thomson

Overall: ★★½	Room Quality: C	Value: B	Price: $55–$105

Ralph Zieger has always been interested in the history of his "two-on-two" plantation house (two rooms over two) that he had dated back to 1820. While opening a wall for a door, he recently found evidence of Quaker post-and-beam construction that would date it prior to 1803.

SETTING & FACILITIES

Location: Off I-20 near Augusta

Near: Washington (historic town), Augusta & Masters Tournament

Building: Plantation Plain

Grounds: Rural; gardens, wildlife sanctuary

Public Space: LR, DR, porches

Food & Drink: Family-style full breakfast

Recreation: Hiking, reading

Amenities & Services: Champagne, sparkling beverages for honeymooners

ACCOMMODATIONS

Units: 4 guest rooms

All Rooms: Fireplace

Bed & Bath: Beds vary; 2 w/ private baths, 2 share bath

Favorites: None

Comfort & Decor: Each room is themed to a flower color.

Rates, Reservations, & Restrictions

Deposit: 1 night during Dec., Masters Tournament in Apr.
Discounts: Senior (ask if you're 60 or older), AARP
Credit Cards: V, MC
Check-in/Out: 4 p.m./noon
Smoking: Designated areas
Pets: No
Kids: 14 & older
Minimum Stay: None
Open: All year
Hosts: Ralph & Maggie Zieger
2316 Wire Rd. SE
Thomson, GA 302824
(706) 597-0220

TWIN OAKS B&B AND COTTAGES, Villa Rica

Overall: ★★★★ Room Quality: B Value: B Price: $125–$155

Ideal for a honeymoon, anniversary, or special occasion. The three cottages have a maximum amount of space around them for privacy and are actually one large room plus a bath. If you like the idea of a quick morning swim, ask for the Pool House Cottage—a log house overlooking the pool with a garden view. Like animals? You will find black swans here, as well as Canada geese, dogs, cats, and even a pot-bellied pig named Elmer Leroy. There are nature trails to explore and a three-level pond with waterfalls and goldfish. This is an unusual country retreat many people with city-malaise would really enjoy, made even more special because of the good natures of the hosts.

Setting & Facilities

Location: Exit 6 off I-20 West (Villa Rica—Liberty Road)
Near: 20 mi. from Six Flags over Georgia, antiques shops
Building: Modern main building & cottages
Grounds: 23-acre farm
Public Space: Nature trails
Food & Drink: Full breakfast; lunch & dinner served on request
Recreation: Walking, horseback riding, golf, swimming
Amenities & Services: Swimming pool

Accommodations

Units: 2 suites, 3 cottages
Some Rooms: Dbl. whirlpool tub, VCR, CD player, fireplace, fully equipped kitchen
Bed & Bath: Beds vary; private baths
Favorites: None
Comfort & Decor: Modern, sophisticated interiors have a sleek city penthouse look; sexy black marble bathrooms are a focal point.

Rates, Reservations, & Restrictions

Deposit: 1 night
Discounts: Corp.
Credit Cards: None
Check-in/Out: 3 p.m./noon
Smoking: No; on decks only
Pets: No
Kids: 1 child, 12 or older, allowed per family

Minimum Stay: 2 nights on weekends
Open: All year
Hosts: Earl & Carol Turner
9565 East Liberty Rd.
Villa Rica, GA 30180
(770) 459-4374
Fax: (770) 459-4374
www.bbonline.com

MAYNARD'S MANOR, Washington

Overall: ★★★½ Room Quality: B Value: B Price: $85

When Louise and Ross Maynard first saw the 1820 house they wanted for a bed-and-breakfast, it was shrouded in brush. The interior had been gutted, and there was no stairway to the second floor. Ross began the daunting task of rebuilding walls, floors, doors, adding bathrooms, and preparing six airy guest bedrooms for service. The finished woodwork, electrical, and plumbing needs were his responsibility. Louise followed with wallboard, painting, and trim; sewing draperies; and furnishing the house. Now, with Maynard's Manor offering a bright welcome, Louise is busy creating a variety of delicious breakfast menus: "Folks staying here several nights shouldn't have the same breakfast every day."

SETTING & FACILITIES

Location: On Hwy. 78 in downtown Washington
Near: Robert Toombs House (state museum), City Museum
Building: Antebellum home w/ Greek Revival columns
Grounds: Gardens w/ gazebo & historic plants
Public Space: Parlor, library, 2 DRs, porches
Food & Drink: Wine & hors d'oeuvres on arrival; full breakfast; specialties: sweet potato muffins, baked orange croissants w/ strawberries, bacon
Recreation: Sight-seeing
Amenities & Services: Booklet w/ walking tour of historic sights

ACCOMMODATIONS

Units: 6 guest rooms
All Rooms: Antiques
Bed & Bath: Queens; private baths
Favorites: None
Comfort & Decor: Each room is individually decorated.

RATES, RESERVATIONS, & RESTRICTIONS

Deposit: Credit card; 24-hour cancellation
Discounts: None
Credit Cards: MC,V
Check-in/Out: 4–6 p.m./10:30 a.m.
Smoking: No
Pets: No; boarding avail. nearby
Kids: 12 & over
Minimum Stay: None
Open: All year
Hosts: Ross & Louise Maynard
219 East Robert Toombs Ave.
Washington, GA 30673
(706) 678-4303
www.kudcom.com/maynard

ASHFORD MANOR BED & BREAKFAST, Watkinsville

Overall: ★★★★ Room Quality: B Value: A Price: $95

This dynamic, spectacular property is unlike any ordinary Victorian bed-and-breakfast, offering six very different eye-popping bedrooms and eight acres of exceptional grounds. Thirteen triple-sash windows give guests easy access to the porch. The breakfast room features changing local exhibits. Three Midwesterners remodeled and furnished the building and adjacent cottage in six months. A large Italianate swimming pool and four flowered terraces make the outdoors special. The only problem: The area seems to be very restaurant poor.

Setting & Facilities

Location: Bus. Rt. 441 (Main St.), left on Harden Hill Rd.
Near: State Botanical Gardens, Happy Valley Pottery (artists' community), Athens
Building: 1893 Victorian manor house
Grounds: 5-acre estate w/ landscaped gardens, pool, open woods
Public Space: Drawing room w/ fireplace, music room w/ grand piano, DR, porch, gardens
Food & Drink: Full breakfast; specialties: Belgian waffles w/ pecan syrup, herbed eggs, stuffed French toast, sherried mushroom & goat-cheese omelet; call for special dietary needs
Recreation: Swimming, walking, horseback riding, golf
Amenities & Services: Swimming pool, local newspapers, classical music piped through house

Accommodations

Units: 6 guest rooms
All Rooms: Phone, robes, hair dryer
Bed & Bath: Beds vary; private baths
Favorites: None
Comfort & Decor: Unusual and interesting decor features antique mirrors and chandeliers. The White Room (a honeymoon suite) is all white with a canopy depicting the Sistine Chapel and a painting of Niagara Falls. The garden room, done in latticework and plants, has a disappearing bed.

Rates, Reservations, & Restrictions

Deposit: Credit card; 7-day cancellation
Discounts: Sun.–Thurs.
Credit Cards: AE, V, MC, D, DC
Check-in/Out: 3 p.m./noon
Smoking: No
Pets: 1 room for 1 large dog or 2 small ones
Kids: Age 16 & older
Minimum Stay: None
Open: All year
Hosts: Jim Shearon, Dave Shearon, & Mario Castro
5 Warden Hill Rd.
Watkinsville, GA 36077
(706) 769-2633
Fax: (706) 769-2633
dshearon@ambedandbreakfast.com
www.ambedandbreakfast.com

STEADMAN HOUSE, Waynesboro

Overall: ★★★★	Room Quality: B	Value: B	Price: $70

Some travel notes from a recent guest at this bed-and-breakfast says it all: "Town is small and not tourist-oriented, about 30 minutes from Augusta. The house was warm and inviting, like visiting a favorite relative. Breakfast was superb and beautifully served. The hosts were a very 'hands-on' couple who did their best to make our stay fun and give us background information about the town." Your host, Janice, recommends a walking tour of the many historic homes in the area, and she can provide directions and a map. One unusual event held here each January is the Georgia Field Trials, with competition among top bird dogs. In fact, Waynesboro proudly proclaims itself the "Bird-Dog Capital of the World."

SETTING & FACILITIES

Location: Take Hwy. 25 from Augusta to Waynesboro
Near: Augusta, Masters Golf Tournament, historic homes
Building: Spanish Mission style
Grounds: Water garden
Public Space: DR, LR, patio
Food & Drink: Full breakfast w/ waffles, French toast
Recreation: Sight-seeing
Amenities & Services: Restaurant lists & menus

ACCOMMODATIONS

Units: 4 guest rooms
All Rooms: Hardwood floors
Bed & Bath: Beds vary; private baths
Favorites: None
Comfort & Decor: Comfortable furniture

RATES, RESERVATIONS, & RESTRICTIONS

Deposit: Credit card
Discounts: Corp.
Credit Cards: AE, V, MC
Check-in/Out: 3–6 p.m./11 a.m.
Smoking: No
Pets: Yes
Kids: Welcome
Minimum Stay: None
Open: All year
Hosts: Christopher & Janice Szuflita
828 Liberty St.
Waynesboro, GA 30830
(706) 437-1228

Zone 9
Southern Georgia

A number of things come to many people's minds when they think of traveling to this portion of Georgia: *Gone with the Wind* plantation homes (some now converted to bed-and-breakfasts), former President Jimmy Carter's humble beginning in Plains, the memories of former President Franklin D. Roosevelt in Warm Springs, magnificent Callaway Gardens (don't miss the Day Butterfly Center here—home to more than 1,000 color-saturated butterflies), and typical small Southern towns, where a breakfast without grits is a day without sunshine.

Columbus on the western border of the state is a pleasant surprise not mentioned in some travel guidebooks. A number of upscale bed-and-breakfast homes and inns here offer everything from the perfect settings for a wedding to quiet retreats for business travelers. The restored Springer Opera House once provided a stage for Oscar Wilde and Irving Berlin.

Valdosta has three historic districts that re-create the Victorian era. And there's much more to see and do, including visits to the Georgia Agrirama, the 36 historic sites in Thomasville, the bass fishing at Lake Seminole, and much more—as long as your car and sight-seeing urge last.

March is definitely the time to visit Macon if you love flowers. During the Cherry Blossom Festival some 200,000 Yoshino cherry trees create a cloud of blooms; eat your heart out, Washington, D.C.

For More Information

Numerous state convention centers and bureaus and welcome centers are located throughout this area, listed in "Georgia on My Mind"
(800) VISIT GA (847-4682)
www.gomm.com

Note: This line can get very busy. You may have a long wait but at least you're not paying telephone charges.

COTTAGE INN BED & BREAKFAST, Americus

Overall: ★★ | Room Quality: D | Value: A | Price: $65–$75

This Antebellum cottage was transplanted from Cuthbert to Americus and still retains much of its early Southern comfort. There are some poignant places to visit nearby, including the infamous Andersonville, the Civil War prisoner-of-war camp that claimed so many lives. The restored Rylander Theater in Americus is a glittering jewel that now presents live entertainment. Or, if you prefer, take a swim in the bed-and-breakfast's pool, play tennis on the clay court, or sit in comfortable rockers on the porch as inquisitive peacocks stare at you briefly and then strut on by.

Setting & Facilities

Location: Just outside Americus
Near: Andersonville, Jimmy Carter Nat'l Historic Site in Plains, Camellia Gardens
Building: 1852 raised cottage
Grounds: 5 acres
Public Space: Porch, pool
Food & Drink: Cont'l plus breakfast
Recreation: Sight-seeing, antiques shopping
Amenities & Services: Swimming pool, clay tennis court

Accommodations

Units: 5 guest rooms
All Rooms: Cable TV
Some Rooms: Hardwood floors, carpet
Bed & Bath: Beds vary; private baths
Favorites: None
Comfort & Decor: An eclectic mix of Oriental and English items

Rates, Reservations, & Restrictions

Deposit: None
Discounts: AAA, AARP, corp., 7-day stays
Credit Cards: V, MC
Check-in/Out: Flexible; ask
Smoking: No
Pets: Yes
Kids: Welcome
Minimum Stay: None
Open: All year
Hosts: Jimmy & Billy Gatewood
Hwy. 49 North
Americus, GA 31709
(912) 924-8995
Fax: (912) 924-6248

GATES HOUSE, Columbus

Overall: ★★★★½ | Room Quality: A | Value: B | Price: $85–$135

A Persian cat sits on an elegant couch, seeming to step right out of black-and-gold cushions embroidered with outlines of different animals. The image is striking, like many of the rooms in the Gates House bed-and-breakfast. On warm days ask to dine outside in the garden. The fountain and gazebo have seen countless weddings and wedding photographs. This is a convenient place to stay when visiting Columbus. Couples and singles alike will feel at home here.

Setting & Facilities

Location: Exit 1 off I-185 to 2nd Ave. to 8th St., right on Broadway
Near: Riverwalk (a block away), River Center for Performing Arts, convention center, Springer Opera House
Building: 1880 Colonial Empire house
Grounds: Large backyard & outdoor dining area
Public Space: LR, DR, backyard, library, screened porch
Food & Drink: Full breakfast; specialties: sourdough French toast w/ brown sugar, pecans, cinnamon; wine, soft drinks served in afternoon; call for special dietary needs
Recreation: Museums, walking the river trail
Amenities & Services: Membership privileges at health club

Accommodations

Units: 3 guest rooms
All Rooms: Victorian, French furnishings
Some Rooms: Whirlpool tub
Bed & Bath: Beds vary; private baths
Favorites: Peacock Room w/ four-poster bed, whirlpool tub
Comfort & Decor: Beautiful antiques create a soft elegance.

Rates, Reservations, & Restrictions

Deposit: Credit card
Discounts: None
Credit Cards: AE, V, MC
Check-in/Out: 3 p.m./11 a.m.
Smoking: No
Pets: No
Kids: Welcome "with some limitations"; ask
Minimum Stay: None
Open: All year
Hosts: Thomas & Carol Gates
737 Broadway
Columbus, GA 31901
(706) 324-6464 or (800) 891-3187
Fax: (706) 324-2070
info@gateshouse.com
www.gateshouse.com

MANSION BED & BREAKFAST INN, Columbus

Overall: ★★★½ | Room Quality: B | Value: C | Price: $125–$185

Side by side with a second inn operated by the same company (see comments about the Woodruff House), the Mansion seems to attract many women who love the romanticism of the Victorian antiques and fireplaces. Many weddings and receptions are held here, and many brides and grooms pose for pictures in front of the building. You can rent the entire house for the night for $450.

Setting & Facilities

Location: I-185 S to Exit 6 or 7, left into downtown
Near: Civic Center, Iron Works Trade & Convention Center, Golden Park, Springer Opera
Building: 1881 Queen Anne
Grounds: Large lawn
Public Space: Parlor
Food & Drink: Full breakfast; specialty: quiche
Recreation: Sight-seeing
Amenities & Services: 24-hour concierge service

Accommodations

Units: 5 rooms
All Rooms: High ceiling, hardwood floors, fireplaces
Bed & Bath: Beds vary; private baths
Favorites: None
Comfort & Decor: Rooms are spacious and feature handsome antiques and high ceilings.

Rates, Reservations, & Restrictions

Deposit: Credit card
Discounts: Corp.
Credit Cards: AE, V, MC, D
Check-in/Out: 3 p.m./noon
Smoking: No
Pets: No
Kids: Welcome
Minimum Stay: None
Open: All year
Host: Susan Parmiter Poe
1414 2nd Ave.
Columbus, GA 31901
(706) 320-9300 or (888) 320-9309
Fax: (706) 320-9304
lbussey@mindspring.com

ROTHSCHILD-POUND HOUSE INN, Columbus

Overall: ★★★★ Room Quality: B Value: C Price: $97–$165

The Pounds began to restore this house in 1995, and just in time. For many of its 120 years, the house had been abused and neglected, becoming a derelict far from its elegant beginnings as the home of Columbus business tycoons. But the new owners stepped in before the wrecking ball hit and created a handsome bed-and-breakfast that is a livable mixture of beautiful decor and furnishings and comfortable living. This place is a great favorite among business travelers. Come in time for the evening conversations among the hosts and fellow guests over cocktails and hors d'oeuvres.

Setting & Facilities

Location: Corner of 2nd & 7th Sts. in downtown Columbus (historic district)
Near: Springer Opera House, Chattahoochee Riverwalk, convention center, Central Business District
Building: 1876 Empire Victorian
Grounds: None
Public Space: Large LR, DR

Food & Drink: Full Southern breakfast w/ specialty pancakes, gourmet grits, quiches; served in room on request

Recreation: Sight-seeing

Amenities & Services: Concierge services (restaurant reservations)

ACCOMMODATIONS

Units: 10 guest suites

All Rooms: Hardwood floors, fireplace, cable TV, stocked mini-fridge, coffeemaker, fresh flowers

Some Rooms: Full private kitchen

Bed & Bath: Beds vary; private baths (period or whirlpool)

Favorites: Thomas Room w/ steam shower, king bed, 1878 draperies

Comfort & Decor: Elegant antiques and soft couches

RATES, RESERVATIONS, & RESTRICTIONS

Deposit: Credit card

Discounts: None

Credit Cards: AE,V, MC, DC

Check-in/Out: 1 p.m./noon

Smoking: No

Pets: In individual cases; ask

Kids: Sometimes; ask

Minimum Stay: None

Open: All year

Hosts: Gary & Mamie Pound
201 Seventh St.
Columbus, GA 31901
(706) 322-4075 or (800) 585-4075
mpound@awts.com

WOODRUFF HOUSE, Columbus

Overall: ★★★½ Room Quality: B Value: C Price: $90–$160

The Woodruff House and the Mansion are two side-by-side bed-and-breakfast inns in the heart of Columbus, operated by the same company with the same reservation number. The Woodruff House attracts many business travelers, particularly men who like to relax in the "sports center" with a pool table, grab a beer and sandwich from the kitchen, and watch baseball or football in the TV parlor. The separate cottage and coach house between the two buildings are convenient for people who want privacy. If you check into the Woodruff House, you may want to drink a toast with a Coca-Cola. You're staying in the birthplace of Robert Woodruff, the business leader who made this soft drink a household beverage worldwide. You have your choice at breakfast—if you're late for a business appointment, you can have a quick continental breakfast, or walk right next door for a full breakfast served at the Mansion.

SETTING & FACILITIES

Location: I-185 S to Exit 6 or 7, left into downtown

Near: Civic Center, Iron Works Trade & Convention Center, Golden Park, Springer Opera

Building: 1885 mansion

Grounds: None

Public Space: TV/game room
Food & Drink: Cont'l or full breakfast
Recreation: Sight-seeing
Amenities & Services: 24-hour concierge service, full kitchen avail., billiards

Accommodations

Units: 5 rooms plus separate cottage, coach house
All Rooms: Fireplace, cable TV, phone, 12-foot ceiling
Bed & Bath: Beds vary; private baths
Favorites: None
Comfort & Decor: Handsome antiques

Rates, Reservations, & Restrictions

Deposit: Credit card
Discounts: Corp.
Credit Cards: AE, V, MC, D
Check-in/Out: 3 p.m./noon
Smoking: No
Pets: No
Kids: Welcome
Minimum Stay: None
Open: All year
Host: Susan Parmiter Poe
1414 2nd Ave.
Columbus, GA 31901
(706) 320-9300 or (888) 320-9309
Fax: (706) 324-0282
lbussey@mindspring.com

1842 INN, Macon

Overall: ★★★★★ Room Quality: A Value: C Price: $140–$235

This is truly one of the great inns of the South, with an elegant building and magnificent interiors, and it has been so recognized by a number of awards. But most striking of all is the attention paid to guests who stay either in the Antebellum mansion or the Victorian house right across the courtyard. This interior description from *Country Inns* magazine gives you a small idea of what to expect: "A Portuguese crystal chandelier illuminates a walnut table topped with tropical flowers in the center hall, also brightened through French doors capped by a fanlight." It's another world—another century to enjoy.

Setting & Facilities

Location: Exit 52 off I-75, Hardeman Ave. to College St.
Near: Hay House (famous 1861 Italianate villa), downtown, Museum of Arts & Sciences, Georgia Music Hall of Fame
Building: 1842 Greek Revival
Grounds: 1.75 acres
Public Space: Lobby, veranda, courtyard
Food & Drink: Cont'l
Recreation: Sight-seeing
Amenities & Services: Morning newspaper, overnight shoe shines, nearby private dining & health club, concierge service, conf. facil. (20)

Accommodations

Units: 21 guest rooms
All Rooms: Magnificent antiques, desks that become dining tables
Some Rooms: Fireplace, canopied four-poster bed, whirlpool tub
Bed & Bath: Beds vary; private baths
Favorites: None
Comfort & Decor: Antique tapestries, oil paintings, and crystal chandeliers create an elegant atmosphere.

Rates, Reservations, & Restrictions

Deposit: Credit card; 7-day cancellation
Discounts: Off-season
Credit Cards: All major cards
Check-in/Out: 3 p.m./11 a.m.
Smoking: No
Pets: No
Kids: 13 & older
Minimum Stay: None
Open: All year
Host: Nazario Filipponi
353 College St.
Macon, GA 31201
(912) 741-1842 or (800) 336-1842
Fax: (912) 741-1842
The1842inn@worldnet.att.net
www.innbook.com/inns/1842

BARBARA TUCKER CRAWFORD INN, Moultrie

Overall: ★★★★ Room Quality: B Value: B Price: $85–$125

This white-pillared 1905 mansion is cheerful and airy, with large, attractive rooms flanking the entry hallway, and a handsome staircase to four spacious, tastefully furnished guest rooms. It's difficult to choose one as a favorite, for they are all winners. Benches in a shaded garden and a free-form swimming pool welcome all guests. Innkeeper Sharon Herndon's breakfasts of fresh fruits, casseroles, and home-baked breads are tempting. "We offer an opportunity to enjoy an elegant old house with many modern comforts," she says. "I hope our guests will feel our history, learn about the people who lived here. You can't get that in a chain motel." We agree. That's why we're writing this guide.

Setting & Facilities

Location: South on Bus. 319, right on 7th Ave. SW
Near: Colquitt County Arts Center, Odom Genealogy Library, Reed Bigham State Park
Building: Neoclassical
Grounds: Landscaped gardens
Public Space: Parlor, library, DR
Food & Drink: Choice of full or cont'l breakfast; dinner avail. w/ advance notice; bedtime snacks
Recreation: Museums, sight-seeing, swimming
Amenities & Services: Robes, bath gels, swimming pool

ACCOMMODATIONS

Units: 4 guest rooms
All Rooms: Comfortable seating
Bed & Bath: Beds vary; private baths
Favorites: None
Comfort & Decor: Tasteful mixture of antiques, reproductions, and modern furnishings

RATES, RESERVATIONS, & RESTRICTIONS

Deposit: None except Expo week
Discounts: None
Credit Cards: None; checks & cash only
Check-in/Out: 4–7 p.m./11 a.m.
Smoking: No
Pets: No
Kids: 12 & over
No-Nos: No alcohol on premises without special arrangement, no loud music
Minimum Stay: None
Open: All year
Host: Sharon Herndon
704 3rd St.
Moultrie, GA 31768
(912) 890-0714
Fax: (912) 890-0714

HENDERSON VILLAGE, Perry

Overall: ★★★★½	Room Quality: A	Value: B	Price: $145–$245

This 18-acre retreat offers more ambience, luxury, and things to do than most travelers can absorb during a brief holiday. A dozen nineteenth-century homes and cottages, original to the property or moved from nearby, comprise a delightful village. Gardens, porches and rockers, a swimming pool, an aviary with exotic birds, a few mules, a goat, and a pair of ostriches provide diversion enough. But, on adjacent land are fishing ponds; biking, walking, and riding trails; the opportunity for skeet shooting; turkey, deer, quail, and wild boar hunting. And tennis and golf are not far away. Whew! Besides breakfast, Langston House offers a pleasant pub and dinners of the highest order.

SETTING & FACILITIES

Location: Exit 41 off I-75, 10 mi. south to Perry
Near: Andersonville Trail (marked route of antiques stores, museums, President Jimmy Carter's home), Museum of Aviation, Georgia Music Hall of Fame
Building: Collection of nineteenth-century homes, cottages
Grounds: 18 acres w/ pecan, cypress, dogwood trees
Public Space: Private porches
Food & Drink: Full Southern breakfast at Langston House Restaurant (on premises) or delivered to guest quarters (on request)
Recreation: Walking, horseback riding, fishing (9 stocked ponds), golf
Amenities & Services: Guest library w/ videos, CDs, books; swimming pool

Accommodations

Units: 24 guest rooms
All Rooms: TV, VCR, terry robes, CD stereo system
Some Rooms: Whirlpool tub, private porch
Bed & Bath: Feather beds; private baths
Favorites: Master Suite in Hodge House
Comfort & Decor: Antique reproductions and designer fabrics

Rates, Reservations, & Restrictions

Deposit: 1 night
Discounts: For long stays; ask
Credit Cards: AE, V, MC
Check-in/Out: 3 p.m./noon
Smoking: No
Pets: No
Kids: Welcome
Minimum Stay: None
Open: All year
Host: Stuart Macpherson
125 South Langston Circle
Perry, GA 31069
(912) 988-8696 or (888) 615-9722
Fax: (912) 988-9009
info@hendersonvillage.com
www.hendersonvillage.com

STATESBORO INN & RESTAURANT, Statesboro

Overall: ★★★★½ Room Quality: A Value: A Price: $85–$135

A rambling two-story 1904 building and two annexes make up this cheerful country inn. The entry hall, two dining rooms, and picturesque English mini-pub quickly establish the ambience with hearts-of-pine ceilings, paneling, wainscoting, and doors. Lush garden patios provide quiet relaxation spots. In five years the Garges family has developed a comfortable, tasteful inn with excellent meals and amenities. Many repeat customers come annually. We like the attitude of the management. When an emergency evacuation of coastal areas was ordered in 1999 as Hurricane Floyd approached, some inland inns got greedy and raised their rates because they knew so many people had no other alternatives. Kudos to the Statesboro Inn for not raising their rates during this emergency. When some people refused to leave their pets behind, the innkeeper said, "bring 'em along," and soon had an innful of gerbils, birds, dogs, cats, and grateful pet owners.

Setting & Facilities

Location: 301 North from I-16
Near: Savannah, Georgia Southern University, the "Antique Trail" (map avail.)
Building: 1900 Victorian home
Grounds: Gardens, ponds
Public Space: Front porch, veranda, DR, guest lounges

Food & Drink: Full breakfast; homemade cookies, fudge always avail.; on-site restaurant serves dinner
Recreation: Sight-seeing nearby historic homes that usually aren't open to public
Amenities & Services: 24-hour data port phones

ACCOMMODATIONS

Units: 18 guest rooms
All Rooms: Hardwood floors, ceiling fan, restaurant recommendation book
Some Rooms: Working fireplace, whirlpool tub, private porch
Bed & Bath: Beds vary; private baths
Favorites: Bridal suite
Comfort & Decor: Large and pleasant rooms have a Victorian feel.

RATES, RESERVATIONS, & RESTRICTIONS

Deposit: Credit card
Discounts: AAA, AARP, corp.
Credit Cards: AE, V, MC
Check-in/Out: 2 p.m./11 a.m.
Smoking: No
Pets: Small
Kids: Welcome
Minimum Stay: None
Open: All year
Hosts: Tony & Michele Garges, John & Melissa Garges
106 South Main St.
Statesboro, GA 30458
(912) 489-8628 or (800) 846-9466
frontdesk@statesboroinn.com
www.statesboroinn.com

HOTEL WARM SPRINGS BED & BREAKFAST, Warm Springs

Overall: ★★ Room Quality: D Value: B Price: $60–$175

Back in the 1940s a black limousine would pull to a stop in front of the Hotel Warm Springs and a chauffeur would enter the ice cream parlor on the first floor. He would emerge a few moments later carrying an ice cream cone to a man in the back seat of the car, President Franklin D. Roosevelt—in residence at the Little White House just a few miles away. FDR's presence is felt throughout Hotel Warm Springs, now a bed-and-breakfast. A color portrait hangs in one room. News photos of his activities line the lobby walls. And the staff loves to talk about the times the president came in to play chess with local people. The building and furnishings certainly look historic (or put another way, showing signs of age). But the host, Gerrie, keeps everything spotless. And the ice cream parlor is still there, serving wonderful treats.

SETTING & FACILITIES

Location: Downtown Warm Springs
Near: President Roosevelt's Little White House, Callaway Gardens
Building: 1907 brick hotel
Grounds: None

Public Space: Seating area on second floor, ice cream parlor
Food & Drink: Full Southern breakfast
Recreation: Sight-seeing, shopping in Warm Springs' small stores
Amenities & Services: Shopping tips

Accommodations

Units: 14 guest rooms
All Rooms: Cable TV, individual A/C, period antiques from Roosevelt era
Bed & Bath: Beds vary; private baths
Favorites: None
Comfort & Decor: Comfortable and homelike atmosphere makes you feel you're at Grandmother's house.

Rates, Reservations, & Restrictions

Deposit: Credit card
Discounts: None
Credit Cards: All major cards
Check-in/Out: 2 p.m./noon
Smoking: No
Pets: No
Kids: Welcome
Minimum Stay: None
Open: All year
Host: Gerrie Thompson
Box 351
Warm Springs, GA 31930
(706) 655-2114 or (800) 366-7616
Fax: (706) 655-2114
hotelwarmspings@alltell.net

Florida

When the first chill winds begin to blow across North America, thousands upon thousands of Americans and Canadians start to have one word on their minds: *Florida*. These generally middle-aged and senior "snowbirds" join "spring break" college kids and all other manner of travelers from all over Europe and South America to celebrate the sun on this generally flat 500-mile-long finger of land separating the Atlantic Ocean from the Gulf of Mexico.

For some, Florida is a floating cruise port to sail from Miami, Port Everglades, Tampa, and Canaveral to destinations all over the world. For others it's the perfect rental- or family-car trip to more than 1,200 miles of beaches; world-famous amusement extravaganzas, such as Walt Disney World, Sea World Orlando, Universal Studios Escape, and Busch Gardens Tampa; through natural worlds of citrus groves, swamps, and cypress trees; to golf courses designed by Arnold Palmer and Pete Dye.

Many people think of the Seminoles as the original inhabitants of Florida. But they were preceded by the Timucua, Apalachee, and Calusa tribes. In 1513 Spanish explorer Ponce de Leon was the first European to feel the rays of what would some day become the "Sunshine State." In the years that followed the Spanish, French, British, and American forces warred over and through this peninsula until one of the last "owners" of the land ceded Florida to America in 1819.

However, the clear victors today are tourists from around the world who have claimed their piece of Florida land and sea to fish from, dine on Atlantic shrimp and Apalachiola oysters, golf over, scuba, snorkel, or kayak through, and generally have a wonderful suntan-coated time.

However, like every place in the world, all that sunshine does have some clouds. These range from monster hurricanes to interstates clogged with teenagers who sometimes drive too fast and cataract-challenged senior citizens who drive too slow.

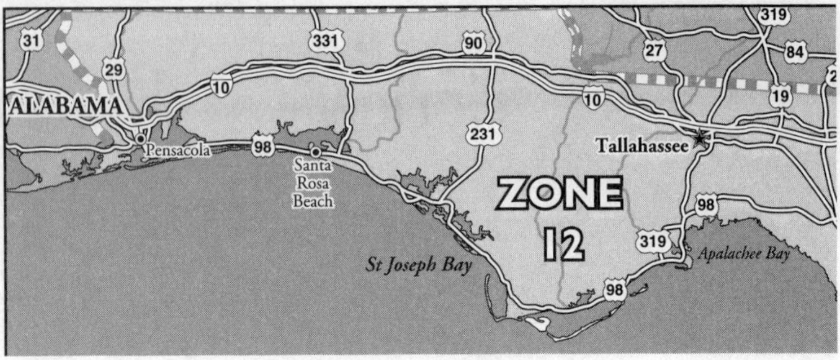
319
31
331
90
27
84
29
10
10
19
ALABAMA
231
Tallahassee
Pensacola
98
Santa
Rosa
Beach
ZONE
12
98
319
Apalachee Bay
St Joseph Bay
98

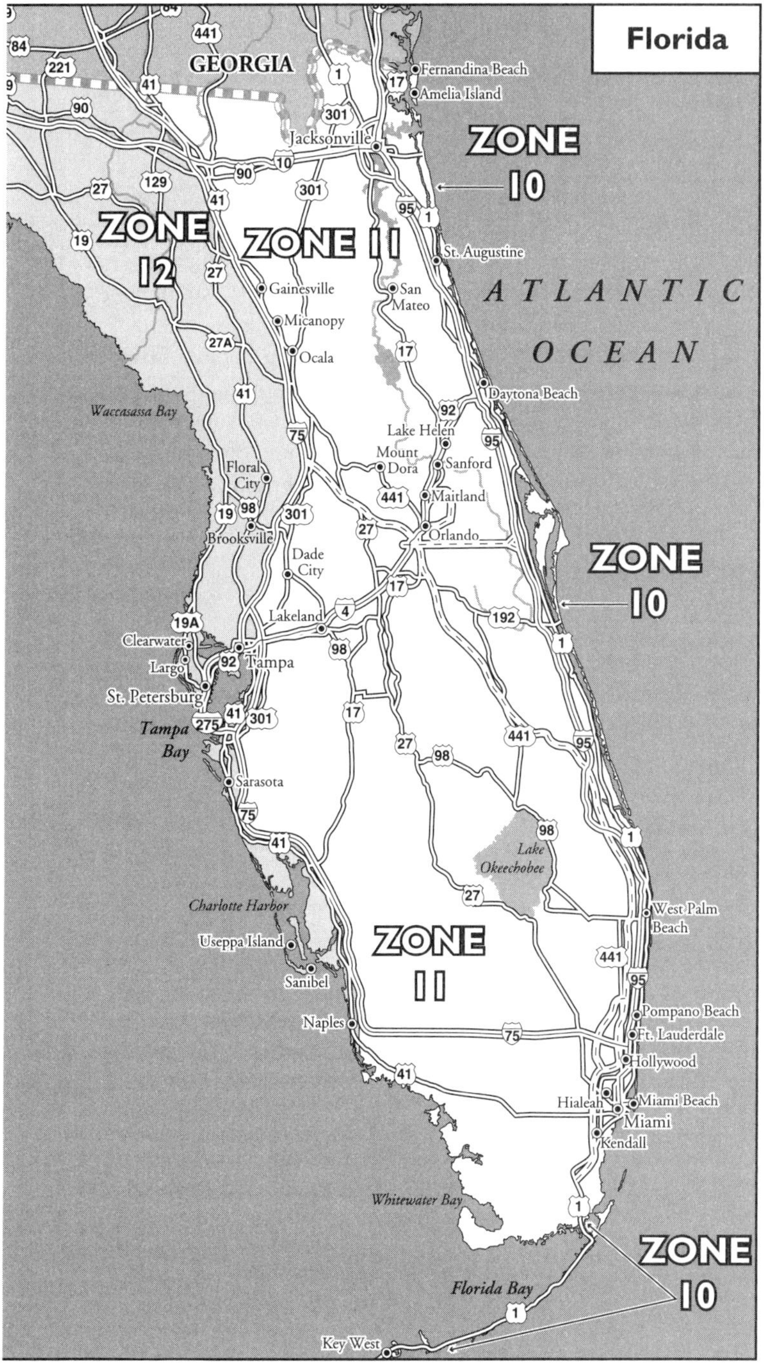
Florida
GEORGIA
Fernandina Beach
Amelia Island
Jacksonville
ZONE 10
ZONE 12
ZONE 11
St. Augustine
ATLANTIC OCEAN
Gainesville
San Mateo
Micanopy
Ocala
Daytona Beach
Waccasassa Bay
Lake Helen
Mount Dora
Sanford
Floral City
Maitland
Brooksville
Orlando
Dade City
ZONE 10
Lakeland
Clearwater
Largo
Tampa
St. Petersburg
Tampa Bay
Sarasota
Lake Okeechobee
Charlotte Harbor
West Palm Beach
Useppa Island
ZONE 11
Sanibel
Pompano Beach
Naples
Ft. Lauderdale
Hollywood
Hialeah
Miami Beach
Miami
Kendall
Whitewater Bay
ZONE 10
Florida Bay
Key West

According to the U.S. Department of Justice statistics, Florida is the Southern capital of car theft (more than 92,000 arrests in 1998) and runner-up to North Carolina in "driving under the influence" arrests (more than 53,000 arrests in 1998).

These are not reasons to avoid one of the most beautiful resort states in the South. They are reasons to be a prudent traveler who packs a good deal of common sense for every trip. That starts with planning your trip carefully so you know which areas and attractions you want to visit, avoiding unnecessary driving, and parking in well-lit areas.

Look at just a few of the attractions you can include in your plans. Miami and Miami Beach, Orlando's theme park worlds, the Kennedy Space Center, the Ringling Circus Museum in Sarasota, the "sunset" ceremonies in the Keys, and St. Augustine—America's oldest European settlement.

Choose your fun. Then select the bed-and-breakfast that is most convenient or affordable.

For More Information

Visit Florida
(888) 7FLA USA
www.flausa

Tourist Assistance
(800) 656-8777

State Parks
(850) 488-9872
www.dep.state.fl.us/parks

Historic Sites
(850) 488-1480
www.dos.state.fl.us

Zone 10
East Coast

This zone is a deceptively narrow strip of land and beaches lying along the Atlantic Ocean side of Interstate 95, but it contains many of the "big" names in Florida tourism: Miami and Miami Beach, Palm Beach, Fort Lauderdale, and Daytona Beach. It sticks out like a wagging finger of islands between the Atlantic Ocean and Gulf of Mexico—the Florida Keys.

Miami has become a mirror image of parts of Cuba and South America as thousands of immigrants have settled here, bringing along their culture and foods and joining retirees from all over the United States. It has also become a palm tree–lined business capital with modern high-rises sprouting everywhere. Across Biscayne Bay, Miami Beach offers a more touristy, Art Deco atmosphere and, of course, a world-famous beach.

Palm Beach still has the reputation of being the Grand Dame of the East Coast, although some of the super-rich are now heading for less conspicuous places of consumption to park their Porches. Daytona Beach is still "spring break" country for class-weary students from all over America, as well as the home of the Daytona 500 race and Bike Week. The hotels and motels along this coast range from mildew-seedy to spectacular extravaganzas. We found some wonderful bed-and-breakfasts here.

The Florida Keys evoke their own images—Ernest Hemingway hunched over a typewriter creating *For Whom the Bell Tolls* (in a handsome house museum you can visit now on Key West), porpoises that leap from the water and kiss visitors on the forehead, and the Sunset ceremony in Key West, where cats jump through flaming hoops, street theater people juggle and walk on stilts, and everyone politely applauds a well-done sunset.

For more information

Greater Miami Convention and Visitors Bureau
(800) 283-2707; www.miamiandmiamibeaches.com

See FLAUSA Visit Florida Guide (free); (888) 7FLA USA

ADDISON HOUSE BED & BREAKFAST, Amelia Island

Overall: ★★★★½ Room Quality: B Value: B Price: $99–$175

Let's say it flat out. This is a terrific bed-and-breakfast. The main Historic House with a wraparound porch is the centerpiece. In the last several years two new buildings have been added around a courtyard, the Garden House and Coulter Cottage. The ambience is definitely resort casual at the bed-and-breakfast and in nearby Fernandina. The courtyard itself seems lifted out of a small mountain village in Mexico. This place was perfect for President Bill Clinton's advance guard and Secret Service people when he was in the area because the Addison House is very conscious of rules. Guests sign a formal agreement when they check in that they understand the bed-and-breakfast is a completely smoke-free environment, inside and out. Some guests have been fined $100 for smoking in the rooms.

SETTING & FACILITIES

Location: I-95 to Exit 129, east on A1A over Intracoastal Waterway Bridge to Amelia Island
Near: Fernandina Beach, Historic District of Fernandina, golf courses
Building: 1886 mansion
Grounds: Courtyard w/ garden
Public Space: Porches, courtyard
Food & Drink: Full breakfast served in DR or on porch
Recreation: Sailing, fishing, kayaking
Amenities & Services: Free local calls, meetings (12), fax & copier access

ACCOMMODATIONS

Units: 5 guest rooms in main Historic House, 4 each in Coulter Cottage & Garden House
All Rooms: Cable TV, phone
Some Rooms: VCR, CD player, whirlpool or soaking tub
Bed & Bath: Beds vary; private baths
Favorites: Camellia Room in Historic House; rooms in cottages for privacy
Comfort & Decor: Plush, attractive linens, high-quality period reproductions, and attention to details create a feeling of luxury.

RATES, RESERVATIONS, & RESTRICTIONS

Deposit: Credit card; 1 night
Discounts: Dec. & Jan. specials; see Web site
Credit Cards: AE, V, MC
Check-in/Out: 3 p.m./11 a.m.
Smoking: No
Pets: No
Kids: No
Minimum Stay: 2 nights on weekends, 3 nights during special events
Open: All year
Hosts: John, Donna, & Jennifer Gibson
614 Ash St.
Amelia Island, FL 32034
(904) 277-1604 or (800) 943-1604
www.addisonhousebb.com

COQUINA INN BED & BREAKFAST, Daytona Beach

Overall: ★★★★ Room Quality: B Value: A Price: $80–$110

The Coquina Inn is a handsome old house that offers reasonably priced accommodations. The innkeeper is helpful and responsive when needed but operates on a "hands-off" basis to give guests maximum privacy. Need a bike to ride to the beach? It's yours. Don't feel like pedaling? A complimentary shuttle service to the beach and marinas is available. Want to play lazy and have breakfast in bed? It's on the way. The breakfast, by the way, is plentiful and good.

SETTING & FACILITIES

Location: Corner of Palmetto Ave. & Cedar St.
Near: "World's most famous beach," Halifax Harbor Marina, Daytona Internat'l Speedway, Klassix Auto Attraction, Adventure Landing (water park)
Building: 1912 mansion constructed of coquina limestone
Grounds: Corner lot w/ gazebo hot tub, hibiscus, & azalea
Public Space: DR, LR parlor, sunroom
Food & Drink: Full breakfast; specialties: eggs Benedict, eggs Foxworthy, French toast; call for special dietary needs
Recreation: Swimming (ocean less than 1 mi. away), surfing, scuba diving, fishing, tennis, golf, sight-seeing, parasailing, ice skating
Amenities & Services: Local newspapers, lists of local restaurants & attractions, guest phone in sunroom

ACCOMMODATIONS

Units: 4 guest rooms
All Rooms: On second floor, cable TV, ceiling fan, clock/radio
Some Rooms: Coquina rock fireplace, private balcony
Bed & Bath: Queen or full; private baths include claw-foot tub w/ shower & Victorian soaking tub
Favorites: Jasmine—romantic w/ fireplace, canopy bed
Comfort & Decor: A variety of Florida artwork is featured w/ Key West, Hemingway, and St. Augustine themes; comfortable furniture: "We didn't want anything that looked fragile enough that you wouldn't want to sit on it."

RATES, RESERVATIONS, & RESTRICTIONS

Deposit: Only during special event weeks (race & bike weeks); note: these weeks are sometimes booked up a year in advance
Discounts: AAA., corp. Sun.–Thur.
Credit Cards: AE, MC, V
Check-in/Out: 3–7 p.m./11 a.m.
Smoking: No
Pets: No
Kids: 7 & older
Minimum Stay: Only during special events; 5-night minimum in Feb. & bike week in March
Open: All year
Hosts: Dennis Haight & Ann Christoffersen
544 South Palmetto Ave.
Daytona Beach, FL 32114
(904) 254-4969 or (800) 805-7533
Fax: (904) 254-4959
CoquinaBnB@aol.com

VILLA, Daytona Beach

Overall: ★★★★★ Room Quality: A Value: B Price: $100–$190

Often you can tell a lot about a bed-and-breakfast in the first fifteen minutes. Here are the Villa's 15 minutes of fame: a very attractive pool and sunning area, large rooms decorated with unique antiques, closets lined with cedar with guest bathrobes, bold bathroom fixtures and a shower with seven shower heads, and original woodwork imported from Spain. But enough of this slavish blathering. We loved this place and think you will, too. P.S. Airport pick-ups are sometimes possible in the host's 1971 Rolls Royce, a nice news item for your postcard to the office gang.

Setting & Facilities

Location: Heart of Daytona Beach
Near: 3–4 blocks to beach, Boardwalk—Arcade area, Daytona nightlife
Building: 70-year-old Spanish mansion
Grounds: 1.25 acres
Public Space: Formal LR, DR, breakfast rooms, library/entertainment room
Food & Drink: Cont'l breakfast; complimentary soft drinks
Recreation: Sight-seeing, swimming
Amenities & Services: Swimming pool, off-street parking, newspapers, movie rentals

Accommodations

Units: 17 guest rooms
All Rooms: Cable TV, VCR, writing desk
Some Rooms: Canopy bed, couch
Bed & Bath: Beds vary; private baths
Favorites: King Juan Carlos
Comfort & Decor: Decor features Chinese jade, Oriental rugs, and Russian icons.

Rates, Reservations, & Restrictions

Deposit: Credit card
Discounts: 1 night; ask about special packages
Credit Cards: AE, V, MC
Check-in/Out: 3–6 p.m./noon
Smoking: No
Pets: No, but owner may make exceptions; ask
Kids: Some restrictions; ask
Minimum Stay: Only during Daytona 500 (Feb.) & Bike Week (mid-March), 5-night minimum
Open: All year
Host: Jim Camp
801 N. Peninsula
Daytona Beach, FL 32118
(904) 248-2020
www.thevillabb.com
jim@thevilla.com

1735 HOUSE, Fernandina Beach

Overall: ★★	Room Quality: D	Value: C	Price: $101–$161

How to say this delicately; this bed-and-breakfast is not for everyone. The guest rooms, bathrooms, and furnishings have seen better days. The hallways are narrow and steep. In a heartbeat we'd select the nearby classy Addison House for couples looking for something special. But for college kids looking for a place to hang out right on the beach or families who don't want to worry about their kids writing on a Van Gogh and who may want to economize by cooking some of their meals, this bed-and-breakfast could be a possibility. Just don't expect too much and you won't be disappointed.

SETTING & FACILITIES

Location: On Fernandina Beach
Near: Beach, 40 restaurants
Building: Beach-style home
Grounds: Right on beach
Public Space: None
Food & Drink: Cont'l breakfast
Recreation: Swimming, beach activities
Amenities & Services: None

ACCOMMODATIONS

Units: 5 guest rooms
Some Rooms: Separate BR for parents, built-in bunk-beds for kids, kitchen facil.
Bed & Bath: Beds vary; private baths
Favorites: None
Comfort & Decor: Nautical theme

RATES, RESERVATIONS, & RESTRICTIONS

Deposit: Credit card
Discounts: AAA, AARP
Credit Cards: AE, MC, V, D
Check-in/Out: 4 p.m./11 a.m.
Smoking: No
Pets: No
Kids: Welcome
Minimum Stay: None
Open: All year
Hosts: Managers vary
584 S. Fletcher Ave.
Fernandina, FL 32034
(904) 261-5878

A LITTLE INN BY THE SEA, Ft. Lauderdale

Overall: ★★	Room Quality: C	Value: C	Price: $79–$298

Florida's beaches and Intercoastal Waterways are lined with hundreds of inns that all look remarkably alike: aging pink or gray/white stucco buildings with color brochures that make you feel they are ready to accommodate rock celebrities in complete comfort and style. After a while, disappointed travelers develop a knee-jerk response to the sight of these buildings and speed up. That's unfortunate, because they could miss some gems among the dross. That's what we found at A Little Inn by the Sea. On the outside the two pink side-by-side buildings look rather unimposing. But inside rooms are comfortable and attractively decorated. Several types of accommodations are available: single, efficiencies, or apartments with separate rooms for children. You can walk to restaurants and pubs nearby or to a long fishing pier. A few steps from virtually every room is a wide white-sand beach. This is a good place for families run by a large family (among them they speak German, French, Spanish, and English).

SETTING & FACILITIES

Location: From I-95 take Oakland Park Blvd. east, left on A1A; call for directions from A1A; there's much road construction in the area; on wide, clean beach
Near: Internat'l Swimming Hall of Fame, Ocean World
Building: 2 separate buildings, Florida casual
Grounds: Islandlike setting
Public Space: Large dining/lobby area, veranda overlooking beach
Food & Drink: Cont'l plus w/ fruit, pastries, muffins, juice, coffee, tea, & (occasionally) waffles
Recreation: Swimming, kayaking, windsurfing, fishing
Amenities & Services: Morning newspaper, small library in lobby, beach chairs, swimming pool, high-speed phone lines for modems w/ Internet access

ACCOMMODATIONS

Units: 29 guest rooms
All Rooms: Tropical decor, sea shells, AC, ceiling fan
Some Rooms: Balcony, complete kitchen w/ fridge, stove, dishes
Bed & Bath: Queen or double; private baths
Favorites: Rooms on first floor of main building w/ direct beach access
Comfort & Decor: A tropical ambience and soft beds lend themselves to a relaxed atmosphere.

RATES, RESERVATIONS, & RESTRICTIONS

Deposit: 1 night for stays up to 1 week, 2 nights for longer stays
Discounts: AAA, AARP; ask about senior discount
Credit Cards: AE, V, MC, D, DC
Check-in/Out: 2 p.m./11 a.m.
Smoking: No
Pets: No
Kids: Welcome; teenagers unaccompanied by adults are not welcome, especially during spring breaks
No-Nos: Not returning borrowed chairs from beach
Minimum Stay: None
Open: All year
Hosts: Various family members
4546 El Mar Dr.
Lauderdale by the Sea, FL 33308
(954) 772-2450 or (800) 492-0311
Fax: (954) 938-9354
alinn@icnect.net
www.alittleinn.com

HOUSE ON CHERRY STREET, Jacksonville

Overall: ★★★★ Room Quality: B Value: B Price: $79–$109

This is a house that loves ducks. You will find duck decoys, duck mugs, and duck prints mixed in with a wonderful collection of old furniture that includes everything from Queen Anne chairs to a slant-front desk (both made around 1760). The house is located in a quiet neighborhood on a cul de sac where the noisiest neighbor is the quiet-flowing St. John's River. You will want to talk with Carol if you're a tennis buff—she has umpired some great matches. This bed-and-breakfast seems to attract more of a business and professional group rather than weekenders. But that doesn't mean it wouldn't be just right for vacationers who want a quiet retreat by a pretty river.

SETTING & FACILITIES

Location: Off I-95 to Riverside Ave. S, 1.5 mi. to left on Cherry St.
Near: Gator Bowl, Cummer Museum, Historic Avondale
Building: 2-story Federal
Grounds: Yard, right on St. John's River
Public Space: Sitting room, porches, LR
Food & Drink: Cont'l w/ baked goods & yogurt
Recreation: Fishing, walking, tennis, canoeing, kayaking
Amenities & Services: None

ACCOMMODATIONS

Units: 4 guest rooms
All Rooms: Canopy bed, flowers
Some Rooms: 3 have water views
Bed & Bath: Queens; private baths
Favorites: Avondale Room is the largest
Comfort & Decor: Furnished with antiques and collectibles

RATES, RESERVATIONS, & RESTRICTIONS

Deposit: Credit card
Discounts: 7th night free
Credit Cards: AE, V, MC
Check-in/Out: 3 p.m./noon
Smoking: No
Pets: No; resident dog
Kids: 10 & older
Minimum Stay: 2 nights during special events
Open: All year
Host: Carol Anderson
1844 Cherry St.
Jacksonville, FL 32205
(904) 384-1999
Fax: (904) 384-5013
houseoncherry@compuserve.com

PLANTATION MANOR INN, Jacksonville

Overall: ★★★★ Room Quality: B Value: B Price: $125–$175

One male guest commented, "Somewhat overwrought in gilt and frills." But others, particularly women and couples seeking a romantic escape from city life, enjoy the great Southern facade of the Plantation Manor Inn. Still others stay here because of the inn's convenience for sight-seeing or business (two blocks from the St. John's River and the Historic Riverside District, 18 blocks from the Civic Auditorium, and less than a five-minute walk to some good restaurants). One of the original owners of the house was a bank president. We believe he spent his money wisely here.

Setting & Facilities

Location: From east, I-10 to I-95 South, right on Riverside Ave., right on Copeland St.
Near: Jacksonville Landing, Cummer Art Gallery, Alltel Football Stadium, St. John's River
Building: Greek Revival
Grounds: Walled garden w/ lap pool
Public Space: Board room, parlor, porches
Food & Drink: Country breakfast w/ ham, sausage, eggs cooked to order, French toast, pancakes; complimentary refreshments
Recreation: Swimming, shopping
Amenities & Services: Outdoor spa

Accommodations

Units: 9 guest rooms
All Rooms: Cable TV, hair dryer, iron & ironing board, robes
Some Rooms: Fireplace, canopy bed, swimming pool view
Bed & Bath: King, full, or queen; private baths
Favorites: None
Comfort & Decor: Elegant atmosphere with crystal chandeliers and Oriental rugs.

Rates, Reservations, & Restrictions

Deposit: Credit card; 1 night
Discounts: 10% AAA
Credit Cards: AE, V, MC, DC
Check-in/Out: 3 p.m./11 a.m.
Smoking: No
Pets: No
Kids: 12 & older
No-Nos: No kitchen privileges
Minimum Stay: Special events only
Open: All year
Hosts: Jerry & Kathy Ray
1630 Copeland St.
Jacksonville, FL 32204
(904) 354-4630
Fax: (904) 387-0960
pmijaxfl@aol.com
www.bbonline.com/fl/plantation

KEY WEST BED & BREAKFAST, Key West

Overall: ★★★½ Room Quality: B Value: A Price: $39–$250

The emphasis here is definitely on romance, with kids and TV banned (the kid ban is occasionally waived during summer when business may be slow). Host Jody was an art major and colorist, and her place is sexy in a free-spirited Caribbean manner. And talk about laid-back. If a guest has to cancel, whether they get a refund or not depends (in judge Jody's decision) on whether "they are nice or really snotty." One drawback is the lack of on-site parking. The neighborhood is convenient but also a little worrisome because of some rundown homes and empty bottles on the streets. Still, the local police reports indicate modest crime problems (a vagrant sleeping in the visitor center and a public pot-smoking arrest). The best bargains at this bed-and-breakfast, as in almost all (count 'em) 60 bed-and-breakfasts on Key West, are during the summer off-season.

Setting & Facilities

Location: From Truman Ave. (US 1), right on William St.
Near: Mallory Square, docks
Building: 1898 Victorian
Grounds: Garden w/ tropical plants, hanging orchids
Public Space: Lounge
Food & Drink: Expanded cont'l, heavy on fruits (pineapple, melon, bananas)
Recreation: Close to Duval St. & all its activities
Amenities & Services: Free local calls, will book activities

Accommodations

Units: 8 guest rooms
All Rooms: AC, local art
Some Rooms: Canopy bed, veranda
Bed & Bath: Beds vary; 4 w/ private baths, 4 share bath
Favorites: None
Comfort & Decor: Dade County Pine walls and an island feeling with Carribean-Afro-Mexican art

Rates, Reservations, & Restrictions

Deposit: 1 night
Discounts: 10% airline employees
Credit Cards: All major cards
Check-in/Out: 2 p.m./11 a.m.
Smoking: No
Pets: No
Kids: 18 & older
Minimum Stay: 3 nights on weekends (if stay includes Sat.)
Open: All year
Host: Jody Carlson
415 Williams St.
Key West, FL 33040
(305) 296-7274 or (800) 438-6155
Fax: (305) 293-0306
relax@keywestbandb.com

LIGHTBOURN INN, Key West

Overall: ★★★★ | Room Quality: B | Value: A | Price: $98–$218

The Lightbourn Inn is as casual and easygoing as Key West itself with two great pluses: a wonderful hot breakfast and off-street parking on this car-crowded island. And don't worry about dressing up; the hosts usually greet you in tank tops and shorts. One unusual amenity: an outdoors juke box loaded with 45s. At breakfast it plays "Good Morning" sung by Gene Kelly and Debbie Reynolds, followed by Jimmy Buffett and other older odes to Key West. There are no screens on the windows, but that's normal on Key West due to benign breezes and a take-no-prisoners suppression of mosquitoes. The clientele consists mostly of couples—gay and straight. The $98 poolside room (off season—summer) is a great bargain on this popular island, the most southern part of the United States.

SETTING & FACILITIES

Location: Stay on US 1 (becomes Truman Ave.)
Near: Mallory Square, Hemingway House, everything
Building: Restored Queen Anne mansion
Grounds: Tropical gardens surround swimming pool
Public Space: Lounge
Food & Drink: Full breakfast w/ different entrees daily: eggs Florentine, strata, quiche, bread pudding w/ glazed pecans (wonderful!)
Recreation: Sight-seeing, beaches, boating
Amenities & Services: Books, excursions

ACCOMMODATIONS

Units: 10 guest rooms
All Rooms: Cable TV, phone, reading chair
Some Rooms: Private veranda
Bed & Bath: Queen or king; private baths
Favorites: None
Comfort & Decor: Each room has its own restful color scheme and comfortable beds; antiques and signed celebrity photos.

RATES, RESERVATIONS, & RESTRICTIONS

Deposit: 1 night; 14-day cancellation
Discounts: AAA
Credit Cards: AE, V, MC, DC, CB
Check-in/Out: 2–6 p.m./11 a.m.
Smoking: No
Pets: No
Kids: Usually, no; sometimes 12 or older allowed in slow summer months
Minimum Stay: 2 days during winter season & weekends
Open: All year
Hosts: Kelly Summers & Scott Fuhriman
907 Truman Ave.
Key West, FL 33040
(305) 296-5152 or (800) 352-6011
Fax: (305) 294-9490
lightbourn@sprynet.com
www.lightbourn.com

MIAMI AREA BED & BREAKFAST, Miami

Overall: ★★★★½ Room Quality: A Value: B Price: $115–$175

Imagine spending the night at New York's Museum of Modern Art, sleeping and browsing amidst your favorite art. That's the feeling you get at this bed-and-breakfast in greater Miami, a beautiful environment created by the host, who is an award-winning artist. You enter a living room filled with her striking modern art; write notes beneath another extraordinary black, blue, and white oil; and bathe in a two-person Jacuzzi controlled by an electronic timer on the wall. Her hand-painted tablecloth brightens the dining room (with matching hand-painted napkins), and bright painted soap dishes and glasses adorn the marble sinks in the bathrooms. This bed-and-breakfast is a masterpiece. *Note:* We can't list the address or host of this bed-and-breakfast (some exclusive properties keep this information confidential to discourage drive-by traffice). If you are serious about staying here, call the toll-free number for details.

Setting & Facilities

Location: Greater Miami area
Near: Miami Seaquarium, Fairchild Tropical Gardens, Key Biscayne beaches, Parrot Jungle, University of Miami
Building: Key West–style historic home
Grounds: Tropical; largest banyan tree on east coast of Florida
Public Space: DR, sunroom, LR, garden, & verandas
Food & Drink: Fresh-ground Colombian coffee, orange juice, strawberry pancakes w/ pure maple syrup
Recreation: Swimming beaches, boating, golf, tennis, fishing, snorkeling, hang-gliding, shopping
Amenities & Services: Welcome drink, lists of attractions & restaurants, free local phone calls, guest membership in island resort, beach towels, newspapers

Accommodations

Units: 3 guest suites
All Rooms: AC, color cable TV, private phone line, full-size desk
Some Rooms: Private covered sitting veranda, double marble sink & Jacuzzi for 2
Bed & Bath: Queen or king beds
Favorites: Banyan Room—large & bright, overlooking garden
Comfort & Decor: The modern decor showcases beautiful rooms with contemporary original oils or unique photographs and open, wide public spaces.

Rates, Reservations, & Restrictions

Deposit: 1 night; 14-day cancellation
Discounts: 7 days or more
Credit Cards: V, MC, AE
Check-in/Out: 3 p.m./11 a.m.
Smoking: No; on outside grounds only
Pets: No
Kids: 7 & older
No-Nos: Use of electric range
Minimum Stay: None
Open: All year
Hosts: Unlisted
(305) 665-2274 or (800) 339-9430
Fax: (305) 666-1186
cocoBandB@aol.com
www.kwflorida.com/coconut.html

HOTEL LEON, Miami Beach

Overall: ★★ Room Quality: D Value: D Price: $110–$395

Imagine Humphrey Bogart sidling up to Peter Lorre in a small Havana bar. That's the feeling we got about this bed-and-breakfast. We had a terrible time finding a place to park on streets that are jammed day and night, finally feeding quarters (for 15 minutes!) into a meter three blocks away.

We later learned we should have used the hotel's valet parking, available by stopping along a tiny yellow strip in front of the entrance. The dining area is in the bar and rather crowded. The best examples of Miami Beach's Art Deco buildings are not on this street. Walk one block over toward the ocean for much better examples. The rooms are clean, and the location is convenient, but staying here is much more of a hotel/motel experience than a stay in a true bed-and-breakfast.

Setting & Facilities

Location: On Collins Ave. in the heart of the Art Deco district
Near: Miami Beach Convention Center, Colony Theater, Jackie Gleason Theater of the Performing Arts, Lummus Park Beach
Building: White/green Spanish Art Deco
Grounds: None
Public Space: Lobby, bar, dining area (all small)
Food & Drink: Eggs, croissants, juice, coffee served buffet style
Recreation: Swimming, shopping
Amenities & Services: Valet parking ($16/day), 24-hour concierge, reduced rates at nearby gym

Accommodations

Units: 18 guest rooms
All Rooms: Cable TV, AC, CD stereo, robes
Some Rooms: Suites & penthouse avail.
Bed & Bath: Beds vary; private baths w/ tub
Favorites: None
Comfort & Decor: Standard motel modern with Spanish ambience

Rates, Reservations, & Restrictions

Deposit: Credit card
Discounts: None
Credit Cards: AE, V, MC, DC
Check-in/Out: 4 p.m./noon
Smoking: Yes
Pets: Yes
Kids: Welcome
Minimum Stay: 2 nights on weekends
Open: All year
Hosts: Various managers
841 Collins Ave.
Miami Beach, FL 33139
(305) 673-3767
Fax: (305) 673-3767
hotel-leon@travelbase.com
www.hotel-leon@travelbase.com

VILLA NINA ISLAND INN, North Hutchinson Island

Overall: ★★★★½ Room Quality: B Value: B Price: $105–$195

"I really prefer not to cook," said Nina Rapport somewhat brusquely. "We do serve a continental breakfast, but many guests prefer a hot meal, so we give them a $10 discount on their rate and they can eat at a good restaurant nearby." Uh-oh, we thought—another bed-and-breakfast hostess who may have chosen the wrong profession. But her manner quickly lightened as she showed us the rooms she had decorated, each more beautiful and luxurious than the last. This is a truly outstanding bed-and-breakfast, a romantic setting for a honeymoon or anniversary. There are many things to do without leaving "home"—with a heated swimming pool, a private pond, a path through a tunnel of trees to a beach on the Atlantic, and a short walk to a large state recreation area. Everything in the rooms promotes relaxation—from the soft blue-and-white color schemes to a refrigerator for storing wine and sodas and a sitting area with thick notebooks filled with information about area attractions and restaurant suggestions. Everything seems planned for the guests' convenience. Soon Nina, like the science teacher she is, was enthusiastically pointing out mounds on the beach where turtles lay their eggs. Her parting comment was, "Come back and we'll do some fishing on the river." Our first impression of her was completely wrong. She turns out to be a lady as lovely as the bed-and-breakfast experience she and her husband, Glenn, have created for their fortunate guests.

Setting & Facilities

Location: Exit 67 off I-95 East to US-1; east on AIA, 3 mi. to traffic light, left in 1.3 mi.
Near: Navy Seal Museum, Fort Pierce Jai-Alai, Dodgers' & Mets' spring training camps, miles of beaches
Building: Modern Mediterranean style
Grounds: 8 barrier island acres w/ direct beach access across road, landscaped areas w/ plant ID stakes.
Public Space: Wide lawn, paths to state recreation area & Atlantic beach
Food & Drink: Cont'l w/ coffee, orange juice, muffins, Danishes, pastries
Recreation: Swimming, fishing in pond or river or ocean, hiking, shopping, antiques hunting
Amenities & Services: Heated pool overlooking river; free canoe, rowboat, bicycle, and snorkel gear rentals; free newspapers, coffee, wine, & snacks in room

Accommodations

Units: 5 guest rooms
All Rooms: Wicker furniture, fridge, coffeemaker, guest-controlled heating & AC, phone, private entrance
Some Rooms: Water views of Wildcat Cove on Indian River, marble bath & shower
Bed & Bath: King or queen; private baths
Favorites: Riomar Suite w/ 2 entrances, 2 TVs, wet bar, 11-foot ceilings—fabulous!
Comfort & Decor: Modern, cool pastel colors, unique decorations such as shell baskets, local artwork, and area rugs combine to create a luxurious tropical atmosphere.

Rates, Reservations, & Restrictions

Deposit: 1 night
Discounts: Monthly stays
Credit Cards: MC, V, D
Check-in/Out: 4 p.m./11 a.m.
Smoking: No
Pets: No
Kids: No
No-Nos: Smoking inside or out (completely smoke-free facil.)

Minimum Stay: 2 nights on weekends
Open: All year
Hosts: Glenn & Nina Rappaport
3851 North A1A
North Hutchinson Island, FL 34949
(561) 467-8673
Fax: (561) 467-8673
villanina@villanina.com
www.villanina.com

BAYFRONT WESTCOTT HOUSE INN, St. Augustine

Overall: ★★★★½ Room Quality: B Value: D Price: $95–$225

We nominate this property as one of the best bed-and-breakfasts in St. Augustine (a hard decision with all the excellent ones here). The rooms are luxurious without all the busy Victorian frou-frou you find in some bed-and-breakfasts in the South. Take breakfast in bed and your afternoon wine on the veranda. Walk out the door and you're right at the bayfront. Take some early morning photographs of boats in Matanzas Bay backlit by the sun. You'll also take home some nice memories from this lovely bed-and-breakfast.

SETTING & FACILITIES

Location: From I-95 exit at Rt. 16, right on San Marco Ave. (becomes Avenida Menendez)
Near: City marina, historic Bridge of Lions, beach, state park
Building: 3-story Victorian house w/ view of Mantanzas Bay & Bridge of Lions
Grounds: Courtyard
Public Space: Courtyard, porches, parlor, kitchen
Food & Drink: Cont'l breakfast served in room; complimentary wine in afternoon, brandy in evening
Recreation: Walking, swimming, bird-watching
Amenities & Services: Newspapers, daily menus, restaurant & city tour recommendations

ACCOMMODATIONS

Units: 9 guest rooms
All Rooms: Large
Some Rooms: Views, fireplace, whirlpool tub
Bed & Bath: King or 2 queens; private baths (several w/ shower & tub)
Favorites: Menendez for grandeur, Rosalina for romance, Elisa Maria & Esmerelda for families
Comfort & Decor: Showcases local and historic art and antiques.

RATES, RESERVATIONS, & RESTRICTIONS

Deposit: 1 night
Discounts: AAA, summer season
Credit Cards: AE, V, MC, D, DC
Check-in/Out: 3 p.m./11 a.m.
Smoking: No
Pets: No
Kids: Welcome
Minimum Stay: 2 nights on weekends
Open: All year

Hosts: Robert & Janice Graubard
146 Avenida Menendez
St. Augustine, FL 32084
(904) 824-4301 or (800) 513-9814
Fax: (904) 824-4301
westcott@aug.com
www.westcotthouse.com

SECRET GARDEN INN, St. Augustine

Overall: ★★ Room Quality: D Value: B Price: $105–$145

Breakfast is on the light, healthy side and is delivered to your room. You can dine at a window table or take your tray out on the patio where you will be surrounded by banana trees, ginger plants, and hibiscus flowers. St. Augustine, with its many historic sights, is a wonderful walking city. The inn can be a little difficult to find. It's located "off" Charlotte Street, down a little lane. Ask for specific directions when you call or you may have a much longer walking tour than you planned. In addition to the Wisteria Room, check out the Moonflower Room, with its high vaulted ceiling and large deck.

Setting & Facilities

Location: Downtown St. Augustine
Near: Castilla de San Marcos (old Spanish fort), a block from bayfront, carriage rides
Building: Cottage-style
Grounds: Garden
Public Space: Garden
Food & Drink: Cont'l plus w/ fresh fruit, breads, pastries, jams, juices
Recreation: Beach activities (10-min. drive) include windsurfing, kayaking; tennis courts nearby
Amenities & Services: Maps & restaurant guides, communal TV

Accommodations

Units: 3 guest rooms
All Rooms: Large, kitchen, deck or patio
Some Rooms: Sitting room
Bed & Bath: Queens; private baths
Favorites: Wisteria Room for privacy
Comfort & Decor: Each room is decorated with different themes—Victorian, country, etc.; enjoy the many original works of art.

Rates, Reservations, & Restrictions

Deposit: 1 night
Discounts: Midweek (rates down to $85–$105) except in holiday season
Credit Cards: V, MC, D
Check-in/Out: 2 p.m./11 a.m.
Smoking: No
Pets: No
Kids: Welcome
Minimum Stay: 2 nights on weekends, 3 nights during some holidays
Open: All year
Host: Nancy Noloboff
56½ Charlotte St.
St. Augustine, FL 32084
(904) 829-3678
www.secretgardeninn.com

ST. FRANCIS INN, St. Augustine

Overall: ★★★ Room Quality: C Value: B Price: $79–$189

Imagine if you were a traveler in Florida in 1845, the year the state entered the Union. You would have probably arrived at the St. Francis Inn by carriage or horseback. The inn had just opened its doors to boarders, becoming one of the oldest continuously operating inns in America. Then you might have carried a basic spoon in your saddlebag to dip into a common pot at the dinner table. Today you would need a full complement of silverware as you tackle the lavish buffet breakfast. Your horse would be replaced by a loaner bicycle for touring the old, fascinating streets of St. Augustine. The inn's slogan is "Come visit the past," and that is certainly what you can do in this attractive inn with amenities that include a swimming pool (small) and an evening get-together with fellow guests and complimentary wine and beer. A few of the rooms are on the small side and a little dark. If size is important to you, look before you book. But these are minor quarrels. This is a fine inn we think you will enjoy.

SETTING & FACILITIES

Location: Historic District, 5 mi. east on I-95
Near: Castillo San Marcos, Lightner Museum, Flagler College, bayfront
Building: 1791 Spanish Colonial
Grounds: Courtyards, swimming pool
Public Space: Lobby, sitting room, DR
Food & Drink: Full buffet-style breakfast w/ stuffed French toast, bread pudding, strawberry soup, blueberry pancakes; complimentary refreshments & cookies avail. all day
Recreation: Golf, tennis, ocean & pool swimming
Amenities & Services: Restaurant menus, free pass to The Oldest House (museum), private parking, swimming pool

ACCOMMODATIONS

Units: 14 guest rooms
All Rooms: Color TV, phone, individually controlled AC & heat
Some Rooms: Fireplace, private balcony, whirlpool tub
Bed & Bath: Beds vary; private baths
Favorites: Balcony Room w/ queen four-poster bed, dbl. whirlpool tub, fireplace, private balcony, beautiful view of St. Francis Park
Comfort & Decor: A large collection of paintings and other artwork by local artists is the highlight.

RATES, RESERVATIONS, & RESTRICTIONS

Deposit: 1 night
Discounts: Midweek AAA, AARP, military
Credit Cards: AE, V, MC, D
Check-in/Out: 3 p.m./noon
Smoking: No
Pets: No
Kids: 10 & older

Minimum Stay: 2 nights on certain holiday weekends
Open: All year
Host: Joe Finnegan
279 St. George St.
St. Augustine, FL 32084
(904) 824-6068 or (800) 824-6062
Fax: (904) 810-5525
innceasd@aug.com
www.stfrancisinn.com

HIBISCUS HOUSE BED & BREAKFAST, West Palm Beach

Overall: ★★★½ Room Quality: B Value: A Price: $65–$240

The hosts have decorated this home with highly personal antiques. It works because one of them is a prominent Palm Beach decorator. Talk with them about the best dining spots in the area. Don't miss the beautiful tropical garden and breakfast served on fine china with Waterford crystal.

SETTING & FACILITIES

Location: East from I-95 on Palm Beach Lakes Blvd., left on Flagler to 30th St., left on 30th to 501
Near: Palm Beach, downtown West Palm Beach, 4 beaches within 10-min. drive
Building: 1922 frame vernacular Mayor's Mansion
Grounds: Gardens & tropical pool area
Public Space: LR, DR, library, Florida room
Food & Drink: Full breakfast; specialities: Hibiscus House eggs Benedict, banana French toast; complimentary sunset cocktails
Recreation: Swimming, bicycling
Amenities & Services: Daily newspaper, swimming pool, bicycles avail.

ACCOMMODATIONS

Units: 8 guest rooms
All Rooms: TV, phone
Some Rooms: Sitting room, fireplace, four-poster bed
Bed & Bath: Queens; private baths
Favorites: Burgundy Suite w/ private staircase; sitting room w/ oversized chairs, ottomans & wet bar; four-poster rice bed
Comfort & Decor: Mixture of antiques and traditional furniture

RATES, RESERVATIONS, & RESTRICTIONS

Deposit: Credit card; 14-day cancellation
Discounts: 10% AAA, 20% stays 7 days or more
Credit Cards: AE, V, MC
Check-in/Out: 2 p.m./noon
Smoking: No
Pets: Dogs, cats welcome
Kids: Welcome
Minimum Stay: None
Open: All year
Hosts: Raleigh Hill & Colin Rayner
501 30th St.
W. Palm Beach, FL 33407
(561) 863-5633 or (800) 203-4927
Fax: (561) 863-5633
www.hibiscushouse.com
hibiscushouse@mymailstation.com

Zone 11
Central Florida

Yes, it costs an arm and a leg, but almost everybody does it sooner or later, often kidnapped by their children: Walt Disney World. The Orlando area also means Universal Studios, Sea World, and other get-out-your-wallet attractions. Fortunately there is also a ring of lakes throughout the central area for the less costly pursuit of bass.

After Mickey, many parents set out for Silver Springs and the fascinating glass-bottom boat rides. If you're more adventurous, head south to the largest subtropical wilderness in the United States, Everglades National Park. The Everglades is a slow-moving, 50-mile river that harbors and feeds thousands of birds and alligators. Suddenly seeing a gator's nonblinking eye staring at you through the weeds a few feet away is a great adventure, safe when viewed from a moving sight-seeing tram. Lakeland, Ocala, and Winter Park are other destinations worth exploring.

For More Information

Central Florida Visitors and Convention Bureau
(800) 828-7655

Tropical Everglades Visitors Center
(305) 245-9180
www.fla_keys.com

See FLAUSA Visit Florida Guide (free); (888) 7FLA USA

AZALEA HOUSE BED & BREAKFAST, Dade City

Overall: ★★★½ Room Quality: B Value: B Price: $65–$79

The Azalea House has several unusual claims to fame. It has been featured as the "Minute Maid bed-and-breakfast" on orange juice cartons. It also has an unusual fellow guest who may make faces at you and steal an occasional banana. It is Joey, a 28-year-old Javanese macaque monkey. Palako itself is historic but does not offer much to do. However, there are some good hiking areas. Tip to parents: If you're traveling with your kids, consider the Green Room. It has two beds in the main room and two twin beds in a separate porch area.

Setting & Facilities

Location: Exit 59 off I-75; take Hwy. 52 to Dade City (8.5 mi.)
Near: Florida Aquarium, Busch Gardens (40-min. drive), Pioneer Florida Museum, Withlacoochee State Park
Building: Post Victorian (eclectic architecture)
Grounds: Garden
Public Space: Library
Food & Drink: Full breakfast w/ eggs, cereal, fruit
Recreation: Golf, hiking, biking, canoeing
Amenities & Services: None

Accommodations

Units: 3 guest rooms, 1 family suite
All Rooms: TV, phone, iron, ironing board, pine floors
Bed & Bath: Kings; private baths
Favorites: Blue Room w/ claw-foot Victorian bath
Comfort & Decor: Traditional and Oriental furnishings

Rates, Reservations, & Restrictions

Deposit: Credit card; 48-hour cancellation
Discounts: 5% singles, seniors (65 & older) when paying cash
Credit Cards: AE, V, MC, D
Check-in/Out: 2 p.m./11:30 a.m.
Smoking: No
Pets: No

Kids: 5 & older
Minimum Stay: None
Open: All year
Hosts: Nancy Bryant, owner; Grace Bryant, manager
37719 Meridian Ave.
Dade City, FL 33523
(352) 523-1773

CLAUSER'S BED & BREAKFAST, Lake Helen

Overall: ★★★½	Room Quality: B	Value: B	Price: $95–$140

Have you ever wanted to be a detective? Or perhaps a sniveling rat that tries to blame the cook for poisoning Aunt Martha? Or perhaps—well, as you've probably guessed, you could be chosen to play any of several different parts during one of this bed-and-breakfast's mystery weekends, with the play written by your hosts. These programs are designed for a group that books all eight rooms and includes breakfasts and dinners. It's a great party idea for a company meeting (a once-in-a-lifetime opportunity to arrest your boss). Other functions can be planned for family reunions, retreats, and small weddings. This is a beautiful area to explore. The rooms vary from Holiday Inn–plus quality in the older building to Hyatt quality in the newer carriage house. A favorite gathering place for guests is "Sherlock's"—an English-style pub in the lobby with a full liquor license.

SETTING & FACILITIES

Location: East on Hwy. 44 past Volusia Country Fairgrounds, right on Prevatt Ave., right on Kicklighter
Near: Orlando (1 hour), Atlantic beaches (30 min.), Cassadaga (village known for psychics & mediums, 5 min.), National Wildlife Area
Building: 1895 Victorian & 1994 Carriage House
Grounds: 3 acres of gardens & trees surrounded by 100 acres of wooded property
Public Space: Parlor, porches
Food & Drink: Full breakfast; specialties: omelets, crème brûlée French toast, Dutch apple pancakes

Recreation: Walking to lake & natural springs
Amenities & Services: Bicycles, basket of menus & area map, books, games, movies, services of massage therapist available

ACCOMMODATIONS

Units: 8 guest rooms
All Rooms: Forest & garden views, central heat & A/C, ceiling fan, phone
Some Rooms: Screened porch, fireplace, whirlpool or soaking tub
Bed & Bath: King or queen; 3 queen BRs also have twin to sleep 3rd person; private baths
Favorites: Charlevoix Room w/ king bed, fireplace, travertine marble tile floor
Comfort & Decor: Designed for comfort; parlor has overstuffed sofa, loveseat, and wing-back chairs around fireplace.

RATES, RESERVATIONS, & RESTRICTIONS

Deposit: 1–3 night stays, 1 night deposit; 4 or more, 50% total cost; 7-day cancellation, 21-day cancellation for holidays or special events
Discounts: 10% seniors, $10 singles, seasonal specials
Credit Cards: AE, V, MC, D
Check-in/Out: 3–6 p.m./11 a.m.
Smoking: No
Pets: No
Kids: 15 & older
Minimum Stay: 2–3 nights for some holidays, special events
Open: All year
Hosts: Tom & Marge Clauser
201 E. Kicklighter Rd.
Lake Helen, FL 32744
(904) 228-0310 or (800) 220-0310
Fax: (904) 228-2337
ClauserInn@totcon.com
www.ClauserInn.com

LAKE MORTON BED & BREAKFAST, Lakeland

Overall: ★★½ Room Quality: D Value: A Price: $55–$65

Just two blocks from the Lake Morton Bed & Breakfast you will find a visual feast of Frank Lloyd Wright designs—seven buildings on the campus of Florida Southern College. Walk to the lake a half block away and you will see up to 60 swans swimming in their year-round home. In winter you can see what kind of season the Detroit Tigers may have as they warm up and play ball at their winter home. Those are just some of the surprises Lakeland offers. This bed-and-breakfast has some surprises of its own, including a host who was once a Rhodes scholar in Russia and a collection of 1920s, '30s, and '50s furnishings for which the word *eclectic* was born. This is not the fanciest bed-and-breakfast in Florida, but its rates are super reasonable at $55–$65, especially when senior travelers take another 10 percent off that.

Setting & Facilities

Location: Travel around Lake Morton (either direction) to pick up South Blvd. on other side
Near: Florida Southern College, Lakeland's downtown antiques center, Detroit Tigers' winter home
Building: 1926 Prairie-style house
Grounds: Landscaped w/ azalea bushes, ferns
Public Space: LR, DR, porch, patio
Food & Drink: Full breakfast w/ eggs, fresh fruit, Florida juices or health breakfast w/ fruit, muffins, juice
Recreation: Walking around lake, bicycling, tennis, golf, swimming
Amenities & Services: Local restaurant list, local newspaper, dining & touring recommendations

Accommodations

Units: 4 guest rooms
All Rooms: Phone, sitting room, small kitchen facil., cable TV, soda, juices, popcorn
Bed & Bath: Full or queens; private baths w/ combination tub/shower
Favorites: Eicker Suite w/ sitting area & BR divided by obelisk pillars, oak fireplace
Comfort & Decor: 1920–30s furniture includes a Mission-style dining room set and ruby red depression glass in the living room.

Rates, Reservations, & Restrictions

Deposit: 1 night
Discounts: 10% seniors
Credit Cards: None
Check-in/Out: 1 p.m./10 a.m.
Smoking: No
Pets: No
Kids: Welcome
Minimum Stay: None
Open: All year
Hosts: Bryce & Mary Ann Zender
817 South Blvd.
Lakeland, FL 33801
(863) 688-6788
Fax: (863) 687-6291
orycez@aol.com

THURSTON HOUSE, Maitland

Overall: ★★★ Room Quality: B Value: C Price: $130–$140

Fleeing cold Minnesota winters, wealthy businessman Cyrus Thurston sought the warmth of Florida, the tranquility of a lake, and acres of land that could be transformed into flower and herb gardens. He found all that in Maitland, Florida, and built a large farmhouse in the Queen Anne style. Now guests of the Thurston House can enjoy all this peace and beauty with some extras Cyrus never dreamed of, such as neighboring Walt Disney World. Let's face it: Orlando can become a zoo in peak winter months, but these human animals have cars and horns. But Thurston House sits on a quiet street by a quiet lake, at peace with the world.

Setting & Facilities

Location: I-4 to Lee Rd. (Exit 46); east on Lee Rd, left on Wymore, right on Kennedy (becomes Lake Ave.) overlooking Lake Eulalia
Near: 5 mi. to downtown Orlando, 10-min. walk to Audubon Society Birds of Prey Center, 2 mi. to Winter Park, 30 min. to Walt Disney World
Building: 1885 Queen Anne Victorian farmhouse
Grounds: 5 acres of woodlands
Public Space: Front & back parlors, porch
Food & Drink: Expanded cont'l weekdays, full breakfast weekends (e.g., herb cheese omelet)
Recreation: Hiking, biking, numerous area attractions
Amenities & Services: Newspapers, local restaurant menus

Accommodations

Units: 4 guest rooms
All Rooms: Desk w/ phone, separate AC/heat control
Some Rooms: Lake view
Bed & Bath: Beds vary; private baths
Favorites: Hirsh Room w/ four-poster bed, claw-foot tub
Comfort & Decor: Antiques and reproductions

Rates, Reservations, & Restrictions

Deposit: 1 night; 5-day cancellation
Discounts: AARP, AAA, corp., 1 week or longer—10%
Credit Cards: AE, V, MC
Check-in/Out: 3–7 p.m./11 a.m.
Smoking: No
Pets: No
Kids: 13 & older
Minimum Stay: Varies some holidays, Feb. & Mar. weekends
Open: All year
Host: Carole Ballard
851 Lake Ave.
Maitland, FL 32751
(407) 539-1911 or (800) 843-2721
Fax: (407) 539-0365
turstonbb@aol.com
www.thurstonhouse.com

HERLONG MANSION, Micanopy

Overall: ★★★★	Room Quality: B	Value: B	Price: $70–$175

If you're planning a wedding, Herlong Mansion provides an attractive setting. The wide front porch with white wicker furniture is a pleasant place for wedding guests to wait and gossip about the groom's lack of dependability. And Meg's Suite is a romantic place for the honeymoon. If you and your spouse have been quarreling lately, consider adding a special occasion package (birthdays and anniversaries) that includes a bottle of champagne, half a dozen roses, fruit, cheese, crackers, and chocolates—and at $50, much more reasonable than marriage counseling. For less special occasions, the Mansion is a good headquarters for exploring Micanopy's 18 antiques shops and the Museum of Retired Cars (we're not kidding—that's its name!)

SETTING & FACILITIES

Location: 1 mi. east of Exit 73 off I-75
Near: Gainesville, Payne's Prairie State Park, University of Florida
Building: 1845 Greek Revival w/ 4 Corinthian columns
Grounds: 2 acres w/ large oak, magnolia, & pecan trees
Public Space: Parlor, library, music room, 2 verandas, gazebo, patio
Food & Drink: Full breakfast; specialty: hash brown quiche
Recreation: Walking, sight-seeing
Amenities & Services: Newspapers, local restaurant menus

ACCOMMODATIONS

Units: 11 guest rooms including 4 suites & 2 cottages
All Rooms: Antiques
Some Rooms: Fireplace, whirlpool tub
Bed & Bath: King, queen, or double; private baths
Favorites: Mae's Room for those who don't mind an occasional ghost
Comfort & Decor: The first floor showcases traditional Victorian furniture, while the second floor has family heirlooms and photos.

RATES, RESERVATIONS, & RESTRICTIONS

Deposit: 50% of room rate or 1 night; 7-day cancellation
Discounts: Sun.–Thur., 3rd night free
Credit Cards: V, MC
Check-in/Out: 3–6 p.m./11 a.m.
Smoking: No
Pets: Not in main house, okay in cottages
Kids: Welcome
Minimum Stay: 2 nights during University of Florida football weekends
Open: All year
Host: H.C. (Sonny) Howard Jr.
402 N.E. Cholokka Blvd, P.O. Box 667
Micanopy, FL 32667
(352) 466-3322 or (800) 437-5664
info@herlong.com
www.herlong.com

EMERALD HILL INN, Mount Dora

Overall: ★★★½	Room Quality: C	Value: B	Price: $99–$149

We wouldn't exactly apply the word *romantic* to the Emerald Hill Inn. Instead, we would say "therapeutic." The lakeside setting and unhurried roads lend themselves to daydreaming and peaceful walks. One of the real bonuses is the big buffet breakfast (see just a few of the specials listed below) and that 30 percent discount to business travelers during the week (the largest discount we've come across in Florida).

Setting & Facilities

Location: From Hwy. 441 go west on Sadler Ave., right on East Lake Jem Rd.
Near: Renninger's Twin Markets, Orlando, Walt Disney World, Sea World, Universal Florida, Ocala Nat'l Forest, Wekiva Springs State Park
Building: 1941 ranch-style limestone
Grounds: 2.3 acres of rural lakefront w/ hickory, cypress, magnolia, & dogwood trees
Public Space: LR w/ cathedral ceiling, Florida room w/ lake view; coquina rock fireplaces in both rooms
Food & Drink: Full breakfast; specialties: Suzette French toast, artichoke & roasted red pepper egg casserole, mushroom-herb quiche, blintz soufflé w/ blueberry syrup & more!; complimentary beverages & snacks
Recreation: Lake fishing, picnics, bird-watching, walking, jogging, bicycling
Amenities & Services: Local restaurant menus

Accommodations

Units: 4 guest rooms
All Rooms: AC, ceiling fan, clock radio
Some Rooms: Patio, lake view, TV/VCR, sitting room
Bed & Bath: 3 rooms w/ queen, 1 w/ king & twin; private baths
Favorites: Diamond Room w/ lake view from bed
Comfort & Decor: Comfortable upholstered furniture, vintage furniture, original artwork, and photography; the innkeeper is also an interior designer, and it shows.

Rates, Reservations, & Restrictions

Deposit: 50%
Discounts: 10% AAA; single business travelers 30% Sun.–Thurs.
Credit Cards: V, MC, D
Check-in/Out: 3–6 p.m./11 a.m.
Smoking: No
Pets: No
Kids: 10 & older
No-Nos: No kitchen privileges
Minimum Stay: 2 nights on weekends, holidays, festival weekends
Open: All year
Hosts: Michael & Diane Wiseman
27751 Lake Jem Rd.
Mount Dora, FL 32757
(352) 383-2777 or (800) 366-9387
Emeraldhill@aol.com
www.bbonline.com/fl/emeraldhill

HERITAGE COUNTRY INN, Ocala

Overall: ★★★ | Room Quality: B | Value: A | Price: $59–$94

One of the problems with some of the wonderful historic Victorian bed-and-breakfasts is that some of the features that make them charming don't meet the needs of older or disabled travelers. The Heritage Country Inn was designed and built by Harold and Lao as a modern one-floor bed-and-breakfast with many built-in conveniences and necessities for travelers of all abilities. These include doors wide enough for wheelchairs, extra-large bathrooms, and lower wall switches. All these thoughtful touches add up to a bed-and-breakfast experience that everyone can enjoy.

SETTING & FACILITIES

Location: 10.5 mi. west of I-75 on Hwy. 40, Exit 69; look for yellow flags
Near: Rainbow Springs, Rainbow River plus many parks, museums
Building: Built as B&B; owner calls it "Country Carpenter Gothic"
Grounds: Landscaped area in midst of rolling hills w/ view of horse farms
Public Space: Large courtyard w/ gazebo
Food & Drink: Full 3-course breakfast; specialties: yeast rolls, fresh fruit muffins; call for special dietary needs
Recreation: Walking, hiking, bird-watching on trails behind inn, canoeing, boating, scuba diving, swimming in Rainbow Springs
Amenities & Services: Special area maps, help in planning activities, 1st-floor disabled access

ACCOMMODATIONS

Units: 6 guest rooms
All Rooms: Extra large (500 sq. ft.), wood-burning fireplace (usable in winter), sitting area
Some Rooms: Canopy bed, Jacuzzi tub
Bed & Bath: Beds vary; private baths
Favorites: None
Comfort & Decor: Handcrafted furniture, 10-foot ceilings, and comfortable seating combine for an open, relaxed atmosphere.

RATES, RESERVATIONS, & RESTRICTIONS

Deposit: Credit card
Discounts: $5 seniors (over 60), children 6 & under free
Credit Cards: AE, V, MC
Check-in/Out: 4 p.m./11 a.m.
Smoking: No
Pets: No
Kids: Welcome
Minimum Stay: 2 nights during major holidays & weekends
Open: All year
Host: Lao Coutts
14343 W. Hwy. 40
Ocala, FL 34481
(352) 489-0023 or (888) 240-2233
www.heritagecountryinn.com

SEVEN SISTERS INN, Ocala

Overall: ★★★★½ Room Quality: B Value: B Price: $95–$145

A recent guest commented, "We had breakfast and dinner here. All of the food was absolutely fantastic. The room was rather small but very clean." The awards this bed-and-breakfast has won would support her comments. Our only complaint—the Victorian style is attractive but sometimes results in clutter. Less is sometimes more. The inn is very promotion-minded and creates a number of special packages and events, including murder mystery weekends, candlelight dinners, and a "pamper" package with massages by a professional masseur.

Setting & Facilities

Location: Corner Ft. King & Wenona Sts.
Near: Historic district old restored homes, antiques & gift shops, Silver Springs
Building: Restored Queen Anne Victorian
Grounds: None
Public Space: Club Room w/ TV, cordless phone
Food & Drink: Full breakfast; specialties: 3-cheese French toast w/ apricots, pesto eggs; try "crummy muffins"; tea & cookies, early morning coffee
Recreation: Sight-seeing, shopping
Amenities & Services: Newspapers, guest bikes, fax avail.

Accommodations

Units: 6 guest rooms, 2 suites
Some Rooms: Cable TV, fireplace, desk, phone
Bed & Bath: King, four-poster queen, double, canopied bed; private baths
Favorites: None
Comfort & Decor: Room sizes vary, but Victorian furnishings are found throughout.

Rates, Reservations, & Restrictions

Deposit: Credit card; 1 night; 7-day cancellation
Discounts: AARP, corp.
Credit Cards: AE, V, MC, D
Check-in/Out: 3–6 p.m./11 a.m.
Smoking: No
Pets: Pet care avail. nearby
Kids: 12 & older
Minimum Stay: 2 nights on some weekends
Open: All year
Hosts: Ken & Bonnie Olden
820 S.E. Fort King St.
Ocala, FL 34471
(352) 867-1170 or (800) 250-3496
Fax: (352) 867-5266
sistersinn@aol.com
www.7sistersinn.com

CYPRESS GLEN, Orlando

Overall: ★★★★★ | Room Quality: A | Value: C | Price: $230–$335

Cypress Glen is one of the most beautiful, most convenient, and most expensive bed-and-breakfasts in the Orlando area. But let the hostess herself make a case as to why the best suite, Sophia, is worth $335 big ones a night. "This very Art Deco suite is furnished with a unique silver wrought-iron king bed. The custom duvet cover, draperies, and piles of pillows are sumptuous in clouds of cream silks and pale-green velvets. The bedchamber with French doors has direct access to the pool and lanai. The sitting room has a fully equipped office. And there is one of the most breathtaking private bathrooms anywhere, measuring 430 square feet with a whirlpool tub for two, walk-in shower, exercise bike, mini bar, stereo, and . . ." Stop! We're only mortals. This place is drop-dead gorgeous. Is it worth all that money? If your Silicon Valley stock has done well recently, go for it!

SETTING & FACILITIES

Location: From Hwy. 535 take a right on Centurion Court
Near: Downtown Disney, Walt Disney World, Universal Florida, Sea World, downtown Orlando, Kennedy Space Center (1 hour)
Building: Art Deco
Grounds: 2 acres of Florida pine woods w/ enclosed, landscaped swimming pool
Public Space: Full use of house
Food & Drink: Breakfast buffet—cont'l plus w/ breads, fruits, pastries, juices
Recreation: Swimming, hiking
Amenities & Services: Heated spa, swimming pool, liqueur & chocolates at turn-down, free local calls

ACCOMMODATIONS

Units: 2 suites
All Rooms: TV & VCR, robes, hair dryer, portable phone w/ message line, data port & fax on dedicated line, fully stocked complimentary refreshment center
Some Rooms: Direct pool access, dbl. whirlpool tub, stereo w/ CD player
Bed & Bath: Kings; private baths
Favorites: Sophia Suite
Comfort & Decor: This grand contemporary house with Art Deco interiors is a comfortable place to work or play.

RATES, RESERVATIONS, & RESTRICTIONS

Deposit: 50% of cost of entire stay
Discounts: Honeymooners, extended stays
Credit Cards: All major cards
Check-in/Out: 3 p.m./11 a.m.
Smoking: In taproom only
Pets: No; resident dog Whoopie will help fill void
Kids: No
No-Nos: "No no-nos," says host
Minimum Stay: None
Open: All year
Host: Sandy Sarillo
10336 Centurion Ct.
Orlando, FL 32836
(407) 909-0338 or (888) 909-0338
Fax: (407) 909-0345
cypglen@aol.com
www.cypressglen.com

MEADOW MARSH BED & BREAKFAST, Orlando

Overall: ★★★★	Room Quality: B	Value: B	Price: $95–$199

Walt Disney World and Universal Florida are fun for adults, too, and within easy driving distances of this bed-and-breakfast. Your host, Cavelle, also wants you to enjoy the "true Florida." That's why she likes to brief guests about where to find natural springs, museums, and other fun activities that cost little or nothing and pay off in hours of relaxation. She also likes to arrange unusual things for her guests, such as a picnic on the lawn or a candlelight dinner in her lovely Southern home.

Setting & Facilities

Location: Just west of downtown Orlando
Near: Close to Universal (20 min.), Walt Disney World (30 min.), Cape Canaveral (60 min.)
Building: 1877 Victorian farmhouse
Grounds: 12 acres w/ 100-year-old oaks; meadow to 20-mi.-long bike trail
Public Space: Parlor, library area, music room w/ baby grand, TV room, 2 porches w/ swings
Food & Drink: 3-course breakfast
Recreation: "Rails to Trails" next to property for biking, jogging, walking
Amenities & Services: Lawn & parlor games, make dinner reservations

Accommodations

Units: 4 guest rooms in main house, cottage in rear
All Rooms: View of grounds
Some Rooms: 100-year-old bed w/ inlaid headboard, access to screened porch
Bed & Bath: Queen or double; private baths; 3 w/ dbl. whirlpool tubs, others w/ claw-foot or apron-style tubs
Favorites: Edith's Rose Room—a suite w/ separate sitting area, fireplace, & whirlpool tub
Comfort & Decor: Early pictures from the original owners hang on the walls; antiques and traditional furniture.

Rates, Reservations, & Restrictions

Deposit: Full payment for 1 night stay; 50% of total stay for 2 nights or more
Discounts: 10% for guests staying any 3 nights Mon.–Thurs.
Credit Cards: V, MC
Check-in/Out: 3–5 p.m./11 a.m.
Smoking: No
Pets: No
Kids: 12 & older, but owner advises against bringing children to this "romantic getaway."
Minimum Stay: 2 or 3 nights for special holidays & events
Open: All year
Hosts: John & Cavelle Pawlack
940 Tildenville School Rd.
Orlando, FL 34787
(407) 656-2064 or (888) 656-2064
Fax: (407) 654-0656
Cavelle5@aol.com
www.meadowmarshbnb.com

PERRIHOUSE BED & BREAKFAST INN, Orlando

Overall: ★★★ Room Quality: C Value: C Price: $99–$139

It would be hard to find accommodations more convenient to Downtown Disney (three-minute drive) and the Walt Disney World Resort. Guests also escape the concrete sterility of many of the area's motels and hotels. They can wander through 16 tranquil acres where traffic sounds are replaced by dozens of bird songs. New facilities may be available by the time this book is published. These include some glamorous new

Birdhouse Cottages, with everything from see-through fireplaces to his-and-her marble vanities, and a PerriHouse Vacation Home for families and groups. Two heady moments: Order a Mimosa to sip in the hot tub, and visit the inn's Web site to be greeted by scratchy calls that seem to come from sore-throated birds.

SETTING & FACILITIES

Location: 3 mi. north on I-4, Exit 27 on SR 535
Near: Downtown Disney, Walt Disney World, Universal Florida
Building: Ranch-style w/ wraparound porch
Grounds: 16 acres of woodlands (listed as BackYard Wildlife Habitat by National Wildlife Federation)
Public Space: Grounds, patio
Food & Drink: Cont'l plus breakfast; specialty: banana bread
Recreation: Bird-watching, sightseeing, horseback riding, guided fishing trips
Amenities & Services: Renew marriage vows at BirdHouse Wedding Chapel, binoculars for bird-watching, pools, hot tub, laundry facil., gift shop, fax avail., gift certificates

ACCOMMODATIONS

Units: 8 guest rooms
All Rooms: Mini-bar, voice mail, data port
Some Rooms: Fireplace, private entrance
Bed & Bath: 5 kings, 4 queens, twins, cribs avail.; private baths (small)
Favorites: None
Comfort & Decor: Rooms are pleasant—we rated them about Holiday Inn style.

RATES, RESERVATIONS, & RESTRICTIONS

Deposit: Credit card; 1 night
Discounts: None
Credit Cards: AE, V, MC, D, DC
Check-in/Out: Ask
Smoking: No
Pets: No
Kids: Welcome
Minimum Stay: None
Open: All year
Hosts: Nick & Angi Perretti
10417 Centurion Court
Orlando, FL 32836
(407) 876-4830 or (800) 876-4830
Fax: (407) 876-0241
birds@perrihouse.com
www.perrihouse.com

FERNCOURT BED & BREAKFAST, San Mateo

Overall: ★★★ Room Quality: B Value: A Price: $65–$135

Do you harbor a secret dream to run a bed-and-breakfast ? Want to restore an old home? Your hosts Jack and Dee Dee will be happy to talk to you about their personal experiences doing both. You may also want to talk to them about local things to see and do. It is difficult to get any advance information about San Mateo. We reviewed a number of Florida guidebooks and can't even find the town listed. Check out that breakfast menu (below), certainly one of the more extensive and exotic in Florida. This bed-and-breakfast also has a sixth guest room (without bath) that can be rented with an adjoining room by a family that doesn't mind sharing a bath. Otherwise, the hosts don't rent out the sixth room.

SETTING & FACILITIES

Location: 30 mi. west of St. Augustine
Near: St. John's River; day outings to Daytona Beach, Kennedy Space Center, Walt Disney World
Building: 1889 Queen Anne Victorian
Grounds: 2 acres
Public Space: 2 DRs, 2 parlors, wraparound veranda w/ swings
Food & Drink: Full breakfast "always includes some form of eggs"; specialties: soft scrambled eggs w/ cream cheese & dill, poached fruit, sugar-crusted scones w/ bourbon-soaked currants, French Vienna coffee cake
Recreation: Bicycling, sight-seeing, fishing
Amenities & Services: Bicycles avail.

ACCOMMODATIONS

Units: 5 guest rooms
All Rooms: On 2nd floor, ceiling fan, central heat & air
Bed & Bath: King, queen, or double; private baths
Favorites: Morgan Room w/ large brass king bed, writing desk, walk-in shower
Comfort & Decor: Turn-of-the-century antiques, period wallpaper, and some objects handcrafted by the hosts

RATES, RESERVATIONS, & RESTRICTIONS

Deposit: 1 night
Discounts: 20% on stays of 3 days or longer
Credit Cards: AE, V, MC
Check-in/Out: 2 p.m./11 a.m.
Smoking: No
Pets: No dogs or cats; occasional exceptions for birds, caged animals
Kids: 12 & older, but hosts won't put third person in any room
Minimum Stay: 2–3 nights during holiday periods
Open: All year
Hosts: Jack & Dee Dee Morgan
150 Central Ave. P.O. Box 32187
San Mateo, FL 32187
(904) 329-9755
ferncourt@gvso.net

HIGGINS HOUSE BED & BREAKFAST, Sanford

Overall: ★★★ Room Quality: C Value: B Price: $80–$150

Higgins House was the first and best bed-and-breakfast in Sanford's historic district. The home is more modest than grand but has a comfortable feel about it. Take the time to see the beautiful flower garden behind the home. Then take a ten-minute walk to the historic district, which has some of the most affordable food in all of Florida. Ask your hosts for dining recommendations.

Setting & Facilities

Location: Exit 51 off I-4, east to Sanford
Near: St. Johns River, Central Florida Zoo, Sanford antiques district, beaches, Sea World, Blue Springs State Park
Building: 1894 Queen Anne Victorian
Grounds: Corner lot across from Centennial Park; Victorian garden in back
Public Space: Parlor, TV room
Food & Drink: Cont'l, sometimes serve omelets; specialty: bread pudding supreme; complimentary wine & cheese; beer brewed on site
Recreation: Boating, fishing, sailing, hiking, birding, canoeing, horseback riding
Amenities & Services: Newspapers, restaurant menus, hot tub

Accommodations

Units: 3 guest rooms, large cottage
All Rooms: Sitting area
Bed & Bath: Queen or double; private baths; claw-foot tubs w/ or w/o showers
Favorites: Wicker & Queen Anne, romantic & private
Comfort & Decor: Everything in this house has been restored in Victorian manner.

Rates, Reservations, & Restrictions

Deposit: 1 night
Discounts: None
Credit Cards: AE, V, MC, D
Check-in/Out: 3–6 p.m./11 a.m.
Smoking: No
Pets: No
Kids: Welcome in cottage
Minimum Stay: None
Open: All year
Hosts: Walter & Roberta Padget
420 Oak Ave.
Sanford, FL 32771
(407) 324-9238 or (800) 584-0014
Fax: (407) 324-5060
reservations@higginshouse.com
www.higginshouse.com

Zone 12
Gulf Coast

Interstate 75 is one of our zone markers. It runs parallel to the Gulf Coast in the south, then pares off the Florida Panhandle and a western hunk of the state to the north. Tampa, with its busy international airport and bustling high-rises, is just about dead center in this zone. While Tampa is business-oriented, it also offers some great tourist attractions: the glass-domed Florida Aquarium (don't miss it!) and Busch Gardens Tampa. Neighboring St. Pete is much more laid back with a resort/beach community attitude.

Naples is where shoppers from New York's Fifth Avenue and Chicago's Miracle Mile go to shop, browse in art galleries, and to see and be seen in fashionable restaurants and stores. Sanibel is a resort island where just about everybody goes for sun and sea shells.

Sarasota is one of Florida's truly beautiful cities, with a view of Sarasota Bay and a long string of beach-covered barrier islands in the Gulf of Mexico. The city's Ringling Museum of Art boasts some outstanding Renaissance art for adults and a circus museum that's three-ring fun for everyone. One of the most charming bed-and-breakfasts in the area is the Cypress, with a front yard view of the bay.

The panhandle offers vacationers long stretches of white-sand beaches and extraordinarily green water, perfect for snorkeling and scuba diving. Adventurous souls may want to know about Usseppa Island, once used by the CIA to train Cuban Bay of Pigs invaders. Collier Inn in the center of the island has a hefty price tag but offers unique privacy and glorious bedrooms.

For More Information

Florida's Nature Coast Coalition
(800) 257-8881
www.naturecoastcoalition.com

Emerald Coast Convention and Visitors Bureau
(800) 322-3319

See FLAUSA Visit Florida Guide (free); (888) 7FLA USA

VERONA HOUSE BED & BREAKFAST, Brooksville

Overall: ★★½	Room Quality: C	Value: B	Price: $65–$100

Yes, you may have shopped Sears and bought "big-ticket" items such as a Kenmore range, Kitchenaid refrigerator, or Craftsman power saw. But if you lived in the early part of the last century, you also could have shopped a Sears catalog for a whole house. That's what the first owners of Verona House did in 1925. The ready-to-assemble building arrived in two box cars, along with a 76-page instruction book. Prices started at $500. The remaining "catalog" houses have become famous landmarks in many communities. Ask Bob or Joyce to recount the history of their house. Save some time to visit downtown Brooksville, where you will find some good restaurants and coffee houses, antiques and crafts shops, and a whole lot of history at the Hernando County Historical Museum.

SETTING & FACILITIES

Location: At historical Brooksville Course House on 98, turn left (south) on Main St.
Near: Roger's Christmas House, Weeki Wachee Springs, & Homosassa Springs State Park (home of manatees)
Building: Sears Roebuck Catalog House Dutch Colonial style
Grounds: Garden area w/ large oaks
Public Space: Sitting area, LR w/ TV & stereo, covered porch w/ swings
Food & Drink: Full breakfast; specialties: French toast, potato casserole; candlelight dinner by reservation
Recreation: Walking & biking trails, golf, tennis, bird-watching
Amenities & Services: Newspapers, lists of local attractions

ACCOMMODATIONS

Units: 4 guest rooms plus bungalow
All Rooms: Desk, phone
Bed & Bath: Queen, king, extra-long single bed; private baths
Favorites: Magnolia Room, larger w/ bigger closet
Comfort & Decor: Numerous family heirlooms and collectibles make it feel like visiting Grandma's house years ago. All rooms are light and airy.

RATES, RESERVATIONS, & RESTRICTIONS

Deposit: Credit card; 1 night; 7-day cancellation
Discounts: Singles, seniors
Credit Cards: AE, V, MC, D, DC
Check-in/Out: 3 p.m./11 a.m.
Smoking: No
Pets: No
Kids: Ask
Minimum Stay: 2 nights during holidays
Open: All year
Hosts: Bob & Jan Boyd
201 South Main St.
Brooksville, FL 34601
(352) 796-4001 or (800) 355-6717
Fax: (352) 799-0612
veronabb@gate.net
www.bbhost.com/veronabb

COTTAGE AT SHADOWBRIGHT, Floral City

Overall: ★★★★ Room Quality: B Value: A Price: $65

If you're like us, meeting other people is one of the pleasures of travel. However, if you're planning a quiet romantic weekend with a significant other, listening to a bed-and-breakfast host describing recent surgery or a funny visit to her aunt may not be your morning cup of tea. Even that charming couple from Nashville, Indiana, who wants to teach you how to play canasta, is not exactly what you had in mind. Then the total privacy of the very romantic Cottage at Shadowbright was made for you. In fact, you and your S.O. will be the only guests in this one-bedroom bed-and-breakfast. You can prepare snacks or your own gourmet dinner in the cottage's fully equipped kitchen or sip wine in bed and watch the fire in the stone fireplace go to sleep. On top of all this romantic privacy, Shadowbright is one of those outstanding bargains that fortunately not everybody coming to Florida knows about. If you stay here and really enjoy it, keep it under your hat so you'll be able to get reservations again next year.

SETTING & FACILITIES

Location: East on Hwy. 48 to Floral City, right on Daniels Rd.
Near: Floral City historic district, World Woods Golf Club, Withlacoochee River, Crystal River State Archaeological Museum, Coastal Heritage Museum
Building: 1930s stone cottage
Grounds: 2 parklike acres w/ 100-year-old oaks
Public Space: Surrounding park acres
Food & Drink: Cont'l breakfast basket Sat. & Sun.
Recreation: Golf, Rails-to-Trails biking & hiking path, antiquing
Amenities & Services: None

ACCOMMODATIONS

Units: 1-BR cottage
All Rooms: Stone fireplace, TV/VCR, central air & heat, fridge, microwave
Bed & Bath: Double; private bath w/ shower
Favorites: N/A
Comfort & Decor: Simple, clean appearance with antiques and artwork

RATES, RESERVATIONS, & RESTRICTIONS

Deposit: 1 night; 48-hour cancellation
Discounts: None
Credit Cards: V, MC
Check-in/Out: 3–9 p.m./noon
Smoking: No
Pets: No
Kids: No; adults only
Minimum Stay: 2 nights on holidays, special event weekends
Open: All year
Hosts: Barry Pendry & Cathi Ayers
8140 S. Shadowbright Place
Floral City, FL 34436
(352) 341-0546
shadowbright@juno.com
www.bbonline.com/fl/shadowbright

INN BY THE SEA, Naples

Overall: ★★★ Room Quality: C Value: B Price: $94–$189

Connie and Maas van den Top are world travelers who are new to the bed-and-breakfast business but learning fast. They are friendly people who between them speak English, Dutch, Italian, German, and Russian. You can have great conversations with them. Maas was a UN official and an international financial consultant. Connie continues to be active in education. They are now constantly making changes to improve the quality of their bed-and-breakfast, offering guests the use of bicycles, beach towels, and providing local restaurant menus. The rooms are small but comfortable and homelike. All rooms have private baths, but we prefer the two rooms on the first floor because the bathrooms are located in the rooms. On the second floor you have to walk across the hall to your bath, a little inconvenient at night. We also take issue with the name "Inn by the Sea" (which, of course, the new owners had nothing to do with). It implies that this small home is right on the Gulf when it is actually in a residential area two blocks from the beach. But these are minor quibbles. We really felt comfortable in this small bed-and-breakfast, a pleasant homelike retreat in the midst of elegant Naples.

Setting & Facilities

Location: From US 41 take 5th Ave. south to 11th Ave.; Inn by the Sea is on the corner
Near: Within 2 blocks of beach, upscale restaurants, shops; Collier County Museum; Conservancy Briggs Nature Center; Teddy Bear Museum
Building: Florida casual circa 1937
Grounds: Yard, garden
Public Space: Sitting area w/ TV & phone, DR
Food & Drink: Cont'l plus w/ juice, muffins, fruit w/ yogurt, cereals, coffee
Recreation: Beach, swimming, good tennis courts, nearby public park
Amenities & Services: Daily newspaper, free local calls

Accommodations

Units: 6 guest rooms plus 3-room cottage in back (long-term rentals)
All Rooms: Antique wicker furniture
Some Rooms: Day bed
Bed & Bath: Beds vary; private baths
Favorites: Captiva—bright room on first floor
Comfort & Decor: It's nothing fancy, but this homey lodging provides comfortable couches and beds.

Rates, Reservations, & Restrictions

Deposit: Credit card
Discounts: None
Credit Cards: AE, V, MC, D
Check-in/Out: 3 p.m./11 a.m.
Smoking: No
Pets: No
Kids: 13 & over
Minimum Stay: 2-days on weekends, Dec. 15–Apr. 15

Open: All year
Hosts: Connie & Maas van den Top
287 Eleventh Ave.
South Naples, FL 34102-7022
(941) 649-4124 or (800) 584-1268
Fax: (941) 434-2842
cvdtop@aol.com

SONG OF THE SEA, Sanibel Island

Overall: ★★★½ Room Quality: B Value: C Price: $190–$410

A hotel fact sheet refers to Song of the Sea as a "romantic European-style seaside inn." Not quite. At first glance it looks like a modern motel to us. But you can't always judge a bed-and-breakfast by its cover. The inn has won numerous awards for excellence. The rooms are the real attraction here, plus a glorious three-mile beach (ideal for shelling, right after the tide has gone out). All suites have complete kitchens with a microwave, stove, and refrigerator—and the maid cleans dishes every day. Many couples return here every year to celebrate anniversaries. Teenagers are actively discouraged from coming, but younger children are welcome.

Setting & Facilities

Location: Eastern end of Sanibel Island, a few minutes' drive from Sanibel Causeway
Near: 23-mile paved bike path, J.N. Ding Darling National Wildlife Refuge, beaches
Building: Motel modern
Grounds: Tropical vegetation, on beach w/ swimming pool
Public Space: Lobby breakfast area, patio
Food & Drink: Expanded cont'l w/ juices, fruit, French pastries, yogurt, bagels
Recreation: Swimming, shelling, fishing, all water sports, golf
Amenities & Services: Bottle of wine, fresh flowers on arrival, heated pool, whirlpool, laundry room (coin-operated machines), charge privileges at nearby resorts, golf club

Accommodations

Units: 22 guest rooms, 8 suites
All Rooms: Fully equipped kitchen, private screened patio
Some Rooms: Front Gulf
Bed & Bath: Beds vary; private baths
Favorites: Rooms fronting Gulf
Comfort & Decor: The overall feel is casual Mediterranean. Rooms have a pleasant, light decor with Thomasville pine furniture.

Rates, Reservations, & Restrictions

Deposit: 7 days (low season); 14 days (high season)
Discounts: AAA, AARP
Credit Cards: V, MC, AE, D
Check-in/Out: 4 p.m./11 a.m.
Smoking: Yes
Pets: No
Kids: 6 & older

Minimum Stay: None
Open: All year
Hosts: Staff
863 East Gulf Dr.
Sanibel Island, FL 33957
(941) 481-3636 or (800) 965-7772
Fax: (941) 481-4947
www.southseas.com

HIGHLANDS HOUSE BED & BREAKFAST INN, Santa Rosa Beach

Overall: ★★★ Room Quality: C Value: C Price: $90–$160

Rooms here are pleasant if somewhat standard, designed for people who don't want a lot of ye olde gee-gaws. Guests come here mainly for the proximity to the beach. They can follow a path right to the Gulf without a road intervening, which is a good thing because the road here, once a sleepy back-panhandle road, is now grossly commercialized. The good news is that commercialization has also brought some outstanding restaurants to the area. Ask your host for recommendations and directions.

Setting & Facilities

Location: Take CR 393 to end, left on C30A, 0.25 mi. to B&B on beach side of road.
Near: Grayton Beach State Park, Topsail park
Building: Antebellum home
Grounds: Yard, garden, & wetlands
Public Space: Parlor, meeting room, veranda
Food & Drink: Full breakfast
Recreation: Golfing, biking & walking trails, swimming, tennis
Amenities & Services: Lists of local restaurants & attractions, meetings (10) w/ coffee breaks & lunch provided

Accommodations

Units: 8 guest rooms
Some Rooms: 4 rooms w/ Gulf view, fireplace, disabled access, whirlpool tub
Bed & Bath: King, queen, double, or full; private baths
Favorites: None
Comfort & Decor: Several rooms are furnished with antiques; most have white pine rice beds.

Rates, Reservations, & Restrictions

Deposit: 1 night
Discounts: 10% AAA (must present card)
Credit Cards: V, MC, D
Check-in/Out: 3 p.m./11 a.m.
Smoking: No
Pets: No
Kids: Welcome; children 10 & younger stay free w/ parents
Minimum Stay: 2 nights on weekends, 3 nights during holidays
Open: Open 11 months of the year; closed after Thanksgiving until day after Christmas
Hosts: Ray & Joan Robins
4195 W. Scenic Highway 30A
Santa Rosa Beach, FL 32459
(850) 267-0110
Fax: (850) 267-3602
www.ahighlandshousebbinn.com

CYPRESS . . . A BED & BREAKFAST INN, Sarasota

Overall: ★★★★½ Room Quality: B Value: B Price: $150–$210

One night we drove three hours through the rainy streets of Sarasota looking for Gulfstream Avenue, finally finding the entrance on the back through Palm Avenue. The Cypress was worth all the travail. The hosts greet you with a glass of wine and hors d'oeuvres. Two are former New Jersey teachers, and the other is a successful photographer from New York (his tinted photos hang on the walls). One of the great delights of this place is the eclectic collection of art and objets d'art gathered by all three hosts during their travels. The collection is displayed in all the rooms; this menagerie shouldn't work but it does. This beautiful retreat right on the bay has hosts who just can't stop being friendly. It's wonderful!

SETTING & FACILITIES

Location: Exit 39 off I-75, west 5.7 mi., left on Tamiami Trail, left on Ringling Blvd., 2nd right on Palm Ave. (Look for Denny's on left, park behind inn on Palm; look for Cypress sign)
Near: Selby Botantical Gardens (half-block away), Bayfront Park, historic arts & theater district
Building: Frame 1940 2-story Florida vernacular
Grounds: Yard w/ fountain, parking area
Public Space: LR, dining porch, kitchen
Food & Drink: Full breakfast w/ fresh fruit, orange juice, egg & Canadian bacon w/ special sauce on English muffin, mango muffins; early morning coffee; sunset cocktails
Recreation: Bicycling, shopping, gallery-hopping, fishing
Amenities & Services: Discount restaurant coupons

ACCOMMODATIONS

Units: 4 guest rooms including 2 suites
All Rooms: Flowers, hardwood floors
Some Rooms: Private entrance
Bed & Bath: Queens; private baths w/ whirlpool, tub, or shower
Favorites: Elizabeth Brittany Suite—2-BR Victorian, marble-tiled bathroom
Comfort & Decor: An eclectic mixture of antiques, accent pieces, and photographs (hand-colored seaside scenes) creates a unique decor.

RATES, RESERVATIONS, & RESTRICTIONS

Deposit: 1 night full amount; extended stays 50% of total
Discounts: Corp., off-season, midweek; ask!
Credit Cards: V, MC, AE, D, DC
Check-in/Out: 3 p.m./11 a.m.
Smoking: No, outside only
Pets: No
Kids: No
Minimum Stay: None
Open: All year
Hosts: Vicki Hadley, Nina Belott, & Robert Belott
621 Gulfstream Ave. South
Sarasota, FL 34236
(941) 955-4683

MANSION HOUSE, St. Petersburg

Overall: ★★★★★ Room Quality: B Value: B Price: $95–$165

This is an exceptional bed-and-breakfast. There are more beautiful places to stay in Florida (although the Mansion is certainly no slacker in looks and elegance), but what really stands out here is the quality of the service. Here are some examples of what the host, Rose, does for guests, starting with an orientation session about local attractions, best restaurants, and best places to shop for antiques. She sometimes invites guests to join the family for dinner without charge (that's really unusual in a bed-and-breakfast !). When guests need to borrow a bike, a beach chair, or umbrella, they help themselves. Another unique feature: When someone is in town for surgery or medical treatment, Rose can help arrange transportation to the hospital, prepare special foods to meet dietary needs for the recovering patient, and even customize rates to meet the needs of the individual. All of this adds up to exceptional caring and service. Hats off to Ron and Rose!

Setting & Facilities

Location: Corner of First St. & Fifth Ave.
Near: Busch Gardens, the Pier, Festival of States, Devil Rays baseball, Lightning hockey, Buccaneer football
Building: 2 Arts & Crafts–style homes & carriage house, built in early 1900 by St. Petersburg's first mayor
Grounds: Landscaping by Robert Davies w/ numerous palm trees plus a large garden area (The Courtyard) suitable for receptions, weddings
Public Space: 10 common areas include garden, library (shared by all guests of 2 houses)
Food & Drink: Excellent full breakfast; try host Rob's blueberry pancakes or orange French toast; complimentary snacks, soft drinks, wine
Recreation: Hiking, swimming, beach activities
Amenities & Services: Swimming pool, recommendations for area restaurants & activities

Accommodations

Units: 12 guest rooms
All Rooms: Phone w/ data port, robes, fresh flowers
Some Rooms: Four-poster bed
Bed & Bath: Beds vary; private baths; private label soaps & shampoo
Favorites: Pembroke Room w/ four-poster bed, cathedral ceiling—elegant!
Comfort & Decor: Fine antiques and paintings

Rates, Reservations, & Restrictions

Deposit: Credit card; 1 night; 72-hour cancellation for business travelers, 2 weeks for leisure travelers
Discounts: AAA, frequent visitors, stays of 5 days or more
Credit Cards: AE, V, MC, CB
Check-in/Out: Flexible/11 a.m.
Smoking: No

Pets: No "officially," but may make exceptions; ask; if lonesome for pet, can take resident Black Lab, Sasha, for a walk
Kids: Welcome
Minimum Stay: None
Open: All year

Hosts: Robert & Rose Marie Ray
105 Fifth Ave. NE
St. Petersburg, FL 33701
(727) 821-9391 or (800) 274-7520
Fax: (727) 821-6906
mansion1@ix.netcom.com
www.mansionbandb.com

COLLIER INN, Useppa Island

Overall: ★★★★★ Room Quality: A Value: B Price: $150–$230

Collier Inn is at the center of 100 acres of history and privacy, savored by everyone from mystery writers and presidents to Thomas Edison and Henry Ford. Long ago Calusa Indians fished for trout, king mackeral, and redfish—just as fishing enthusiasts do today. Collier Inn, an imposing island mansion with white columns, was originally a fishing club. As a guest, you are invited to enjoy the privileges and pleasures of the Usseppa Island Club, playing croquet on internationally recognized tournament grounds, taking tennis lessons, or walking the "Pink Promenade" that wends through gardens and homes. One disadvantage: The Inn restaurant is the only one on the island. But the good news: It is superb. This is one bed-and-breakfast with strong appeal for men, with numerous sports fishing pictures and trophies covering the walls. The Isaak Walton suite was practically made for a man. But the light, white Centennial Suite delights many women. The tiny museum behind the inn contains memorabilia of a fascinating island secret: Useppa was once an outpost of the CIA, used to train Cubans for the unsuccessful Bay of Pigs invasion.

SETTING & FACILITIES

Location: Motor ferry from Pine Island (accessible from I-75, Fort Myers)
Near: Deep-sea fishing port
Building: Late-nineteenth century sports club
Grounds: Extensive landscaped lawns
Public Space: DR, bar lounge, outdoor recreation areas, Useppa Island Historic Museum
Food & Drink: Cont'l plus w/ fruit juices, fruit, muffins, pastries, coffee, tea; dinner w/ rich, varied menu; sample entree: Mondongo snapper (fresh sautéed snapper w/ blue crab, garlic, shallots, brown butter)
Recreation: Swimming, tennis, outdoor chess w/ huge push-around pieces, fishing, hiking, world-class croquet court
Amenities & Services: Heated towel racks, arrangements for water taxi, library, fitness center

Accommodations

Units: 7 guest rooms
All Rooms: Unique decor
Some Rooms: Water views
Bed & Bath: Queen or double; private baths, some whirlpool tubs, walk-in showers (gloriously big bathrooms!)
Favorites: Centennial Suite
Comfort & Decor: Island elegant

Rates, Reservations, & Restrictions

Deposit: Credit card
Discounts: None
Credit Cards: AE,V, MC
Check-in/Out: 3 p.m./11 a.m.
Smoking: No
Pets: No
Kids: Welcome
Minimum Stay: 2 nights on weekend, 3 nights during holidays
Open: All year
Hosts: Managers vary
P.O. Box 640
Bokeelia, FL 33922
(941) 283-1061
Fax: (941) 283-0290
www.useppa.com

Alabama

On the map Alabama looks like a square-shaped person standing with two short legs in the Gulf of Mexico. Surrounded by Florida, Tennessee, and Mississippi, Alabama is practically the poster state for the Deep South.

The first Europeans to arrive were the Spanish in the early sixteenth century, but it was the French 200 years later who established the first permanent settlement (Mobile Bay). But then France had to cede the whole area to England, who quickly lost it to the Spanish, who liked what they had seen the first time around. Then U.S. forces captured the Mobile area, and Alabama was admitted to the Union in 1819, only to secede from that same Union at the beginning of the Civil War in 1861.

Today you can still find many traces of this history throughout Alabama. Each spring many Alabama towns hold "pilgrimages" back to the past, taking visitors on tours of Antebellum homes, churches, and plantations. If you're lucky enough to be in one of those towns at the time, join the parade.

The state geography begins at its small toehold in the Gulf of Mexico, with low-lying white-sand beaches. As you travel further north, the land gradually begins to rise and you encounter many lakes and wide rivers until you reach the rocky highlands of the Northeast. Interstate 20 runs like a loosely hung belt across the center of the state, looping around the principal city of Birmingham, so we've used it as our marker between Zones 13 and 14. Right on this boundary line, Birmingham has been arbitrarily assigned to the northern zone, possibly to future letters of protest by its residents.

Alabama has many things to see and do. Start by drawing up your list of "must-sees" and then choose your bed-and-breakfasts along the way. Some candidates for this list could include Helen Keller's birthplace, the First White House of the Confederacy, the *USS Alabama* Memorial Park, the Russell Cave National Monument, the Alabama Memorial Park, the

Alabama Space and Rocket Center, the Moundville State Monument, the Pike Pioneer Museum, and the W.C. Handy Home & Museum. Who was W.C. Handy? Well, youngsters, he was the Father of the Blues ("St. Louis Blues," "Memphis Blues," for starters).

Alabama has relatively few bed-and-breakfasts compared with other Southern states we visited. But what the state lacked in quantity, they more than made up for in the quality of the bed-and-breakfast homes we found.

For More Information

Alabama Bureau of Tourism and Travel
(800) ALABAMA
www.touralabama.org

Alabama Society of Traditional Bed and Breakfasts
(334) 875-9967

Alabama State Parks
(334) 242-3333
www.vten.com

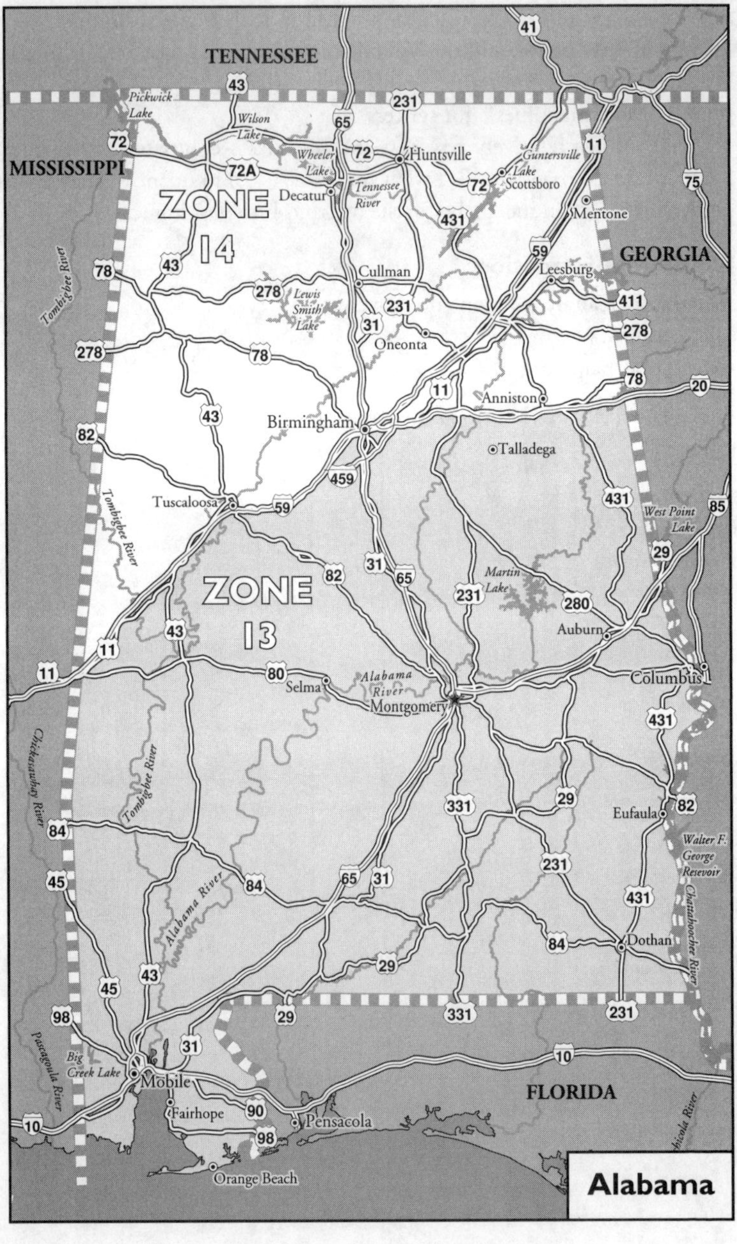
TENNESSEE
MISSISSIPPI
GEORGIA
FLORIDA
ZONE 14
ZONE 13
Pickwick Lake
Wilson Lake
Wheeler Lake
Huntsville
Guntersville Lake
Scottsboro
Decatur
Tennessee River
Mentone
Cullman
Leesburg
Lewis Smith Lake
Oneonta
Anniston
Birmingham
Talladega
Tuscaloosa
Tombigbee River
West Point Lake
Martin Lake
Auburn
Alabama River
Selma
Montgomery
Columbus
Chickasawhay River
Eufaula
Walter F. George Resevoir
Alabama River
Chattahoochee River
Dothan
Pascagoula River
Big Creek Lake
Mobile
Fairhope
Pensacola
Orange Beach
Alabama

Zone 13
Southern Alabama

A good place to start is in Montgomery, the state capital, with dome murals depicting milestones in the history of the state. Montgomery is also the site of the internationally known Shakespeare Festival. At an unlikely place, Union Station, you can relive the days of country music star Hank Williams and of the 1920s personification of glamour and zaniness, Scott and Zelda Fitzgerald, in two museums.

Football fans won't want to miss the Paul W. ("Bear") Bryant Museum at the University of Alabama in Tuscaloosa. You'll see video replays of the Crimson Tide's most famous plays. Near Analusia you'll find great hiking trails in the Conecuh National Forest.

Bellingrath Gardens and Home in Mobile is worth a day or more. Definitely more during the spring Azalea Trail Festival, when more than a quarter of a million bushes bloom. Golfers will find plenty of playing room on 16 courses in the Gulf Coast area, along with virtually unlimited fishing opportunities by chartered boat or simply by throwing a line into one of the omnipresent lakes or bayous.

Our all-time favorite bed-and-breakfasts in this Southern zone are the Kendall Manor Inn, with a 75-foot-high belvedere and 16-foot high ceilings, and Grace Hall Bed & Breakfast (ask to see the hosts' photograph of Miz Eliza, a ghost guest who appears from time to time).

For More Information

Lower Alabama Tourism and Retiree Assn.
(800) 235-4730
www.chamberentercomp.com

KENDALL MANOR INN, Eufaula

Overall: ★★★★★ Room Quality: A Value: A Price: $79–$129

What's the fun of having money if you can't show it off? That seemed to be the philosophy of the nineteenth-century cotton merchant who built Kendall Manor. How else to explain the 75-foot belvedere, the ruby glass windows, and the gold leaf cornices? Your visit may start with refreshments on the wide veranda. A butler's pantry is stocked with drinks for guests. Every bedroom is more stunning than the last one, filled with exquisite antiques. Guests are encouraged to become part of the history of Kendall Manor by writing their own message on the walls leading to the belvedere (okay, we didn't know what that was until we looked it up—a turret or cupola looking out over a pleasant view). There's even a resident ghost, Annie, the nanny of the Kendall children. Or it could be that cotton merchant coming to see how much he couldn't take with him. The new owners are already planning improvements on perfection. In the works—a swimming pool, wine cellar, and renovated carriage house with two more guest rooms. The Kendall Manor Inn would be outstanding in Eufaula or Savannah or Charleston for that matter. A wonderfully pleasant surprise.

Setting & Facilities

Location: In Eufaula turn right on Broad St. & go to top of hill
Near: Calloway Gardens, Lake Eufaula
Building: 1872 Italianate
Grounds: 2.7 acres in town w/ gardens
Public Space: Library, parlor, DR, family room
Food & Drink: Full breakfast; dinner also served
Recreation: Walking, swimming, boating, fishing, antiques shopping
Amenities & Services: Fax, copier, excercise facil. within walking distance

Accommodations

Units: 6 guest rooms
All Rooms: Large w/ 16-foot ceilings, sitting area, phone w/ data port
Some Rooms: Antiques
Bed & Bath: 1 king, 4 queens, 2 doubles; private baths
Favorites: Alabama Room w/ 4 large windows & king bed
Comfort & Decor: Antiques with signed art and Persian rugs

Rates, Reservations, & Restrictions

Deposit: Ask
Discounts: 5% over 65
Credit Cards: AE, V, MC, D
Check-in/Out: 4 p.m./11 a.m.
Smoking: No
Pets: No
Kids: 14 & older
No-Nos: Kitchen privileges
Minimum Stay: None

Open: All year
Hosts: David & Judy Ray
684 West Broad St.
Eufala, AL 36027
(334) 687-8847
Fax: (334) 616-0678
kmanorinn@mindspring.com
www.bbonline/al/eufala

BAY BREEZE GUEST HOUSE, Fairhope

Overall: ★★★½ Room Quality: C Value: B Price: $100–$225

The Bay Breeze Guest House sits high on a bluff overlooking Mobile Bay, well set back from the road. The furnishings of this stucco house have grown through the years, and every wicker chair, quilt, and Oriental rug tells a story. A 462-foot-long pier stretches out to deep water in Mobile Bay. Wild and domestic ducks and geese come calling. There are goldfish in a pond, dogs (in the house and yard), and visiting cats—thankfully for those with allergies, only in the yard. You can bicycle, feed the ducks, swim from the private beach, fish or crab from the dock, sail a Sunfish sailboat, or row a handmade skiff, all there for the guests to enjoy. Later visit the large open kitchen stocked with ice cream, snacks, and drinks. The Camellia Room is large and comfortable. However, it lacks sufficient window shades, and the early morning light can awaken sleepers.

Setting & Facilities

Location: On S. Mobile St. at Municipal Pier
Near: Mobile Bay, Gulf of Mexico, historic sites
Building: 1930s "California-style" beach house
Grounds: 3 acres of landscaped gardens, waterfront
Public Space: LR, sitting room, deck
Food & Drink: Full breakfast
Recreation: Swimming, boating, bicycling, crabbing, fishing
Amenities & Services: Local restaurant guides, maps

Accommodations

Units: 3 guest rooms, 1 suite (separate cottage
Some Rooms: Oriental rugs, disabled access, full kitchen
Bed & Bath: Queens; private baths
Favorites: None
Comfort & Decor: The main house is decorated with five generations of family antiques. The Cottage Suite showcases beautiful rugs, brick floors, and white pine paneling.

Rates, Reservations, & Restrictions

Deposit: Credit card; 72-hour cancellation, 2 weeks for special events
Discounts: Singles, certain months; ask
Credit Cards: AE, V, MC
Check-in/Out: 3 p.m./11 a.m.
Smoking: No
Pets: "Very limited"
Kids: "Very limited"
No-Nos: Don't dive or jump off pier

Minimum Stay: 2 nights in March & Oct./Nov. weekends
Open: All year
Hosts: Bill & Becky Jones
742 South Mobile St.
Fairhope, AL 36533
(334) 928-8976
Fax: (334) 928-0360
www.bbonline.com/al/baybreeze

CHURCH STREET INN, Fairhope

Overall: ★★★ Room Quality: C Value: B Price: $85

Church Street Inn is adjacent to the business district of the perfect Southern town of Fairhope. This secluded village overlooks Mobile Bay and attracts tourists to its boutiques, art galleries, antiques shops, and restaurants in a town with all-year-blooming hanging flower baskets. The inn offers all the comforts of a small home with a comfortable living room and ice cream and other snacks waiting in the kitchen. There's even an ironing board on call for pressing needs. All the bedrooms are large, named for the great-granddaughters in the family. Ashley Anne's bedroom has a queen and twin bed and a claw-foot tub. For guests who like a little mystery, look for the "secret passage" in this room. The same people who own Bay Breeze also own Church Street Inn.

SETTING & FACILITIES

Location: Exit Hwy. 98 at scenic/alt. Hwy. 98., right on Fairhope Ave., left on Church St.
Near: Gulf of Mexico beaches, 16 golf courses
Building: Early 1900s Spanish-style
Grounds: Garden, courtyard
Public Space: LR, porch, courtyard w/ fountain
Food & Drink: Cont'l breakfast
Recreation: Bicycling, walking, swimming, golf
Amenities & Services: Restaurant guides, maps, newspapers

ACCOMMODATIONS

Units: 3 guest rooms
All Rooms: Antiques
Some Rooms: Claw-foot tub
Bed & Bath: King, queen, or twin; private baths
Favorites: Choose upstairs for quiet, privacy
Comfort & Decor: Many antiques

RATES, RESERVATIONS, & RESTRICTIONS

Deposit: Credit card; 72-hour cancellation, 2 weeks for special events
Discounts: Certain months, singles
Credit Cards: AE, MC, V
Check-in/Out: 3 p.m./11 a.m.
Smoking: No
Pets: "Very, very, very" limited
Kids: "Very, very" limited
Minimum Stay: April–Sept. 2 nights on weekends
Open: All year
Hosts: Bill & Becky Jones
51 South Church St.
Fairhope, AL 36533
(334) 928-8976
Fax: (334) 928-0360
www.bbonline.com/al/churchstreet

TOWLE HOUSE, Mobile

Overall: ★★★★ Room Quality: B Value: A Price: $85–$70

Towle House is located in the Dauphin Way District, an area with an eclectic mixture of homes and ancient live oak trees. The house was built in 1874 as a school for boys. A small two-bedroom cottage is available across the street and is rented only to a single set of visitors—families or couples traveling together. The host serves wine and cheese in the evening, a good time to ask for dinner recommendations. We particularly enjoyed the garden view through the windows.

Setting & Facilities

Location: Mobile Historic District, corner of Hallet St. & Montauk
Near: Mobile Convention Center, Civic Center & Auditorium, historic homes, antiques shopping, *USS Alabama* battleship
Building: 1874 Italianate design
Grounds: Large lot w/ azaleas, dogwoods, seasonal flowers
Public Space: Breakfast room, parlor
Food & Drink: Full breakfast w/ fruit compote, egg dish, meat, sweet rolls; afternoon wine or beverages
Recreation: Walking, sight-seeing, antiques shopping
Amenities & Services: Nightly turn-down w/ chocolate mints, local restaurant menus, daily newspaper

Accommodations

Units: 3 guest rooms plus 2-BR cottage
All Rooms: Garden view, TV, phone
Some Rooms: Sitting area
Bed & Bath: Antique double, queen reproduction rice beds; private baths
Favorites: Magnolia Room is largest; Azalea Room is smaller but provides the greatest degree of privacy
Comfort & Decor: Many turn-of-the-century antiques

Rates, Reservations, & Restrictions

Deposit: Credit card or 1 night
Discounts: Corp., longer stays
Credit Cards: AE, V, MC, D
Check-in/Out: 2 p.m./noon
Smoking: No, ashtrays provided on porch outside
Pets: No
Kids: W/ prior approval only
No-Nos: Kitchen privileges, loud music
Minimum Stay: None
Open: All year
Hosts: Felix & Carolyn Vereen
1104 Montauk Ave.
Mobile, AL 36604
(334) 432-6440 or (800) 938-6953
Fax: (334) 433-4381
jfvereen@aol.com
www.towle-house.com

ORIGINAL ROMAR HOUSE, Orange Beach

Overall: ★★★★ Room Quality: B Value: B Price: $79–$139

Forget all your impressions of mildewed, slightly seedy beach cottages that you may have retained from too many late-night Caribbean movies with Humphrey Bogart or Alec Baldwin. The Original Romar House is outright luxury inside with numerous Art Deco touches, mahogany furniture, beautiful stained-glass windows, and a wraparound deck that was made for early morning coffee and Gulf watching. There are no phones or TVs (hooray! who needs 'em?) in the rooms, but both are available for business or Dan Rather addicts in the Parrot Bar. After a day on the beach, bike to shops or visit the nearby historic site of Fort Morgan. The Spanish explorers called this area the "Lost Bay." Get "lost" here. You'll love it.

Setting & Facilities

Location: On Beach Hwy. 182 (Perdido Beach Blvd.), 25 mi. east of Pensacola, FL
Near: Gulf Shores, Gulf of Mexico, 7 golf courses
Building: 1920s Art Deco beach house
Grounds: Tropical landscaping w/ palm & banana trees

Public Space: Purple Parrot Honor Bar room w/ TV & VCR, covered sun deck
Food & Drink: Full Southern breakfast featuring "Better than Sex" peach pancakes; wine & cheese at sunset
Recreation: Swimming, shelling, tennis, golf
Amenities & Services: private beach on Gulf of Mexico, morning newspaper, guest bikes, hot tub

ACCOMMODATIONS

Units: 5 guest rooms, 1 suite, 1 cottage
All Rooms: 1920s Art Deco furniture
Bed & Bath: Queens; private baths
Favorites: Internat'l Song Writer's Festival Room w/ blond Art Deco furniture, stained & beveled windows
Comfort & Decor: All rooms feature original paintings by local Gulf Coast artists.

RATES, RESERVATIONS, & RESTRICTIONS

Deposit: 1 night
Discounts: Extended stays
Credit Cards: AE, V, MC
Check-in/Out: 4 p.m./11 a.m.
Smoking: Only in bar & outside deck
Pets: No
Kids: 12 & older, but arrangements must be made w/ manager
Minimum Stay: 2 nights on weekends, 3 nights Memorial Day, Fourth of July, Labor Day, Shrimp Festival weekends
Open: All year
Host: Darrell Finley
23500 Perdido Beach Blvd.
Orange Beach, AL 36561
(334) 974-1625 or (800) 487-6627
Fax: (334) 974-1163
original@gulftel.com
www.bbonline.com./al/romarhouse

GRACE HALL BED & BREAKFAST, Selma

Overall: ★★★★½ Room Quality: A Value: A Price: $79–$135

If you are looking for the "Old South," you'll find it at Grace Hall. Built in 1857, the house was occupied by Union officers after the Battle of Selma. There are many Greek Revival and Georgian homes in Selma, but Grace Hall is the finest. In addition to the architectural beauty of the house, every room is filled with stunning antiques. At bedtime guests who have not been working out in health clubs may find a new meaning for the term "climbing into bed"—eighteenth-century beds are very high. Allergy-prone guests need to be aware there are feather pillows. Grace Hall comes complete with its own ghost, Miz Eliza, a beautiful lady in a white gown—reportedly captured in a photograph. Other ghosts appear from time to time. Small wonder the ghosts may be a little restless, since this gorgeous bed-and-breakfast is for sale (at press time), so you may encounter new hosts. We only hope that the new owners maintain the high standards and elegance of this lovely home.

SETTING & FACILITIES

Location: I-80 from Montgomery to Selma
Near: Civil War battle reenactments (in April, one of largest in the South), historic homes, Nat'l Voting Rights Museum, Old Depot Museum
Building: Italianate Antebellum
Grounds: Enclosed garden
Public Space: Parlors
Food & Drink: Full Southern breakfast
Recreation: Sight-seeing
Amenities & Services: Newspapers, local restaurant list

ACCOMMODATIONS

Units: 6 guest rooms
All Rooms: 12-foot ceilings, phone, TV, VCR
Some Rooms: Fireplace, canopy bed
Bed & Bath: 5 queens, 1 king; private baths
Favorites: Mauve Room w/ great view of walled garden & fountain
Comfort & Decor: 1850s to early 1900s antiques

RATES, RESERVATIONS, & RESTRICTIONS

Deposit: Credit card
Discounts: None
Credit Cards: AE, V, MC
Check-in/Out: 2 p.m./11 a.m.
Smoking: No
Pets: W/ approval
Kids: 5 & older
Minimum Stay: None
Open: All year
Hosts: Unknown at press time
506 Lauderdale St.
Selma, AL 36701
(334) 875-5744
Fax: (334) 875-9967

GOVERNORS HOUSE B&B, Talladega

Overall: ★★★½ Room Quality: B Value: C Price: $75–$150

Early morning mist rolls off the lake, cattle munch hay, and calves bound through the fields. Sounds like the beginning of a bad novel, but it is also the real-life setting of the Governors House B&B. Alabama Governor

Lewis Parsons built a comfortable three-bedroom bungalow in 1850 for himself. But 140 years later, the house stood in the way of the extension of a hospital and had to be moved to its present location. To complete the restoration, the current owners used lumber from a tobacco barn to build an adjacent barn/guest house (our favorite here). This is a comfortable laid-back place. You can even play gentlemen and gentlewomen farmers. During the calving season, the strong of stomach can watch calves being birthed (yechh!). Or they can feed the chickens, gather eggs, and participate in other farm-life activities. Others prefer to sit by the pond, pole in water, and contemplate Thoreau and possibly a freshly caught bass. There is a lit tennis court on the farm. On the negative side: Privacy is hard to come by if there are many other guests. The window shades are inadequate, and locks between some bedrooms are missing.

Setting & Facilities

Location: Exit 165 off I-65 & south 2 mi.
Near: Talladega Motor Sports Hall of Fame, Super Speedway, Desoto Caverns, Cheaha Park (highest point in AL)
Building: 1850s Federal style
Grounds: 169-acre farm overlooking lake; pear orchard, blueberry patch, boat launch, stocked bass pond
Public Space: Family room
Food & Drink: Full breakfast; specialties: French toast stuffed w/ jelly & cream cheese, sesame & blueberry breads; breakfast served in room or on porch on request; coffee & cold drinks avail. all day
Recreation: Boating, fishing, golfing, tennis
Amenities & Services: Newspapers, local restaurant menus

Accommodations

Units: 4 guest rooms
All Rooms: Comfortable antiques, sitting areas
Bed & Bath: Four-poster, queen, twin, or double; 2 rooms w/ private baths, 2 share bath
Favorites: Adel Room—2 double beds & porch w/ wonderful views of lake at sunset
Comfort & Decor: Antiques are family pieces; framed newspaper and magazine articles describe how entire house was moved from another location.

Rates, Reservations, & Restrictions

Deposit: 1 night; 5-day cancellation
Discounts: 65 & older
Credit Cards: None
Check-in/Out: 3–7 p.m./11 a.m.
Smoking: No
Pets: No, but "son-in-law is a vet & can board animals"; horses can be boarded in stables
Kids: 12 & older
No-Nos: No cooking privileges, but guests can store wine in fridge
Minimum Stay: None
Open: All year
Hosts: Ralph & Mary Sue Gaines
500 Meadow Ln.
Talladega, AL 35160
(205) 763-2186
Fax: (256) 362-2391
aineslaw@aol.com
www.bedandbreakfast.com

Zone 14
Northern Alabama

Birmingham sits in a valley at the beginning of the Appalachian foothills. Travelers come here for such attractions as the Alabama Sports Hall of Fame Museum (Hank Aaron and Willie Mays memories); the Birmingham Museum of Art, with the largest collection of Chinese paintings in the Americas; and for sophisticated shopping in super-modern malls, such as the soaring, glass-walled Riverchase Galleria.

As you drive north from Birmingham, the foothills grow in elevation and character. The "character" comes from caves, lakes, and noncommercialized small towns. In October the white stuff arrives on many landscapes; not snow, cotton balls. In the highlands you can stop for a country dinner, throw a line in a lake or swim, find a covered bridge, or photograph a waterfall.

Huntsville is a good family destination. Everybody can enjoy the U.S. Space Camp where they will see NASA shuttle test sites and participate in hands-on rocketry exhibits.

For More Information

Alabama Mountain Lakes Tourist Assn.
(800) 648-5381
www.walmtlakes.org

SECRET BED & BREAKFAST LODGE, Leesburg

Overall: ★★★★ Room Quality: B Value: B Price: $95–$135

Drive up the winding road to a stunning view of Weiss Lake in a valley surrounded by the Appalachian Mountains. The Secret, built by an Alabama business executive for secluded living and elaborate entertaining, perches on a sheer cliff and could be the Great Gatsby's mountaintop retreat. A large rooftop swimming pool adds to the party atmosphere. Inside, the two-story great room comprises half of the 5,800-square-foot house and offers sections of seating areas and a huge fireplace. This room also displays the host's antique baby bottle collection. A full breakfast, simple but good, is served on a ten-foot-diameter table with a large lazy Susan for passing those pancakes and eggs. Think of your stay here as a party in a quiet, secluded place.

Setting & Facilities

Location: 9 mi. along I-59 (about 1 hour, 15 min. from Birmingham)
Near: Little River Canyon Nat'l Preserve, Little River Falls, Cherokee Rock Village, Silver Lakes & Robert Trent Jones Golf Trail, Alabama Band Fan Club & Museum, Gadsden Cultural Arts Center
Building: 1965 ranch-style home made w/ Crab Orchard stone
Grounds: Atop mountain (rock outcroppings become seats to view 2 states!)
Public Space: Large common area w/ TV, entertainment center, patio
Food & Drink: Full breakfast: specialties: pecan pancakes, French toast, eggs, sausage; call for special dietary needs
Recreation: Walking, golf, fishing, water-skiing, sailing, mountain biking, swimming
Amenities & Services: Selection of 200 movie videos, sample menus from local restaurants, dinner reservations made, petting zoo on premises w/ deer & pet peacock, rooftop swimming pool

Accommodations

Units: 4 guest rooms in main house plus 2 cottages
All Rooms: Great mountain views, TV, VCR, private balcony
Some Rooms: Whirlpool, fireplace, kitchen, washer/dryer
Bed & Bath: King or queen; private baths
Favorites: The Sugar Shack w/ dbl. whirlpool tub, king bed, fireplace; Jailhouse, designed like an old jail w/ comforts of home
Comfort & Decor: Antiques and porcelain doll and baby bottle collections

Rates, Reservations, & Restrictions

Deposit: Credit card; 7-day cancellation
Discounts: 7th night free
Credit Cards: V, MC
Check-in/Out: 2–5 p.m./11 a.m.
Smoking: No
Pets: No
Kids: No
No-Nos: No kitchen privileges in main house; guests needing a kitchen should ask for the Cottage
Minimum Stay: 2 nights on New Year's Eve, Valentines Day, Talladega Car Race weekend, Fourth of July, Thanksgiving
Open: All year
Hosts: Carl & Diann Cruickshank
2356 Hwy. 68 West
Leesburg, AL 35983
(256) 523-3825
Fax: (256) 523-6477
secret@peop.tds.net
www.bbonline.com/al/thesecret

MOUNTAIN LAUREL INN, Mentone

Overall: ★★★ Room Quality: C Value: A Price: $65–$130

Follow Baxter, he knows the way to great views of the Little River Gorge and the great DeSoto Falls with its 80-foot cascade. Don't expect much conversation along the way—Baxter is the host's golden retriever. The inn itself is comfortably divided among three cabins. The main cabin is home to the hostess and site of an elegant breakfast. The guest house has four professionally decorated bedrooms. The Gathering Place is a community cabin with sitting areas, snacks, drinks, TV and VCR, and a refrigerator. Do what you like—build a bonfire and roast marshmallows, ride horses at the adjoining ranch, or just take a hike along the river. Baxter is ready whenever you are.

Setting & Facilities

Location: Exit 231 from I-59; take Hwy. 117 S., right on East River Rd.
Near: DeSoto Falls, DeSoto State Park, Little River Canyon, Sequoyah Caverns, Cloudmont Ski & Golf Resort, Alabama Fan Club & Museum
Building: Country house mountain batten board, 3 buildings

Grounds: 7 acres on a bluff, raised herb beds, native wildflowers
Public Space: The Gathering Place, sitting area & library
Food & Drink: Full breakfast; specialties: decadent French toast, eggs rancheros, chili cheese eggs, cinnamon bread, baked fruit
Recreation: Hiking, horseback riding, swimming, golf, skiing, tennis, rappelling, fishing, bird-watching
Amenities & Services: Will make dinner reservations, maps & hiking information, fridge & outdoor grill for guest use

Accommodations

Units: 5 guest rooms
All Rooms: Private entrance, TV
Some Rooms: Outside porch w/ rockers, efficiency kitchen
Bed & Bath: King, queen, twin, trundle beds; private baths
Favorites: Deer Room—very private w/ king bed
Comfort & Decor: Mountain house theme with rustic pieces

Rates, Reservations, & Restrictions

Deposit: 1 night; 72-hour cancellation
Discounts: Vary by season, but offered to singles, business travelers, for long stays
Credit Cards: V, MC, D
Check-in/Out: 3–7 p.m./11 a.m.
Smoking: No
Pets: No; resident pet, Baxter
Kids: Welcome
No-Nos: Kitchen privileges, unsupervised children
Minimum Stay: 2 nights on holidays, Oct. & May weekends, special occasions
Open: All year except Christmas
Host: Sarah Wilcox
624 Road 948
Mentone, AL 35984
(256) 634-4673 or (800) 889-4244
Fax: Same as local phone; call first
sawilcox@mindspring.com
www.bbonline.com/al/mli

CAPPS COVE BED AND BREAKFAST, Oneonta

Overall: ★★★★ Room Quality: B Value: B Price: $80–$150

It's nine miles up the mountain from the little village of Springville, then another quarter-mile drive into the mountain estate of Capps Cove. And it is worth the drive. This bed-and-breakfast sits on a small knoll above a creek filled with bass, bream, and catfish. The home is filled with antique furniture, linens, dishes, and even old Victrolas. There are two rustic sleeping cabs and a barn for receptions or community gatherings, plus a chapel for quiet reflection or a wedding. Everything is new, but the estate has the ambience of an attractive country village. Breakfast is served on antique dishes with pearl-handled cutlery.

Setting & Facilities

Location: 30 mi. north of Birmingham, 10 mi. west of I-59 from Exit 154
Near: Talladega Race Track, Sister Angelica's $23 million Monastery, Space & Rocket Center in Huntsville, new Limestone Springs Golf Course
Building: Colonial Home w/ rustic cabins & outbuildings
Grounds: 20 acres w/ creek, wildflower trails
Public Space: Parlor, den
Food & Drink: Full breakfast; specialties: baked German pancakes, smoked ham, stone-ground grits
Recreation: Fishing, golf, rock repelling, hiking, white-water rafting, antiquing
Amenities & Services: Scented soaps, fluffy bathrobes

Accommodations

Units: 2 main house guest rooms, 2 cabins
All Rooms: Antiques
Some Rooms: Cabins have wood-burning fireplace, small fridge, coffeemaker, microwave
Bed & Bath: Full; private baths
Favorites: Cabin by the Creek is particularly liked by honeymooners
Comfort & Decor: Antiques are used throughout the main house.

Rates, Reservations, & Restrictions

Deposit: Credit card or check; 72-hour cancellation
Discounts: None
Credit Cards: V, MC
Check-in/Out: 2 p.m./noon
Smoking: No
Pets: No
Kids: 12 & older
Minimum Stay: 2 nights during Talladega race
Open: All year
Hosts: Carson & Sybil Capps
4126 County Hwy. 27
Oneonta, AL 35121
(205) 625-3039 or (800) 583-4750
Fax: (205) 625-3039
cappscov@otelco.net
www.cappscove.com

IVY CREEK INN, Scottsboro

Overall: ★★★★½ Room Quality: B Value: C Price: $79–$125

Ivy Creek was born for nature lovers. This rambling two-story house is nestled in the mountains beside a clear, flowing creek. Follow the stream to a spectacular waterfall. Beavers work the stream and the wildlife refuge supports migratory birds, black bears, and panthers. Guests can choose a special breakfast in bed or dinner by candlelight. Kids have a ball here. They are encouraged to hike to the bamboo grove on the property and cut a cane pole for fishing. Breakfast is very satisfying and can include eggs Benedict, sausage, muffins, and homemade preserves.

SETTING & FACILITIES

Location: Take Hwy. 79 from Gunterville to Scottsboro, left on Carlton Rd.
Near: 4 golf courses, including Robert Trent Jones Golf Trail course (Hampton Cove), Guntersville State Park, Little River Canyon
Building: Colonial
Grounds: Formal yard, nature park, flower & herb gardens
Public Space: Den, reading/conversation room, country store stocked w/ local artists' crafts & works, long front porch filled w/ white wicker rockers
Food & Drink: Full breakfast
Recreation: Walking, hiking, golf, fishing, boating, eagle watching (winter)
Amenities & Services: Local restaurant list, professional guide service avail. (extra fee) w/ all equipment furnished

ACCOMMODATIONS

Units: 4 guest rooms plus apt. w/ full kitchen & private entrance
All Rooms: Walk-in closets, mountain views, TV, VCR, coffee pot
Some Rooms: Fireplace
Bed & Bath: Queens; private baths
Favorites: Fisherman Room w/ fireplace
Comfort & Decor: Rooms display simple elegance.

RATES, RESERVATIONS, & RESTRICTIONS

Deposit: Credit card; 72-hour cancellation
Discounts: None
Credit Cards: V, MC
Check-in/Out: 3 p.m./11 a.m.
Smoking: No
Pets: No
Kids: By arrangement
Minimum Stay: None
Open: All year
Hosts: Hess & Kathy Fridley
985 Carlton Rd.
Scottsboro, AL 35769
(256) 505-0722 or (800) 379-4711
ivycreekn@aol.com
www.bbonline.com/al/ivycreek

Mississippi

In 1540 Hernando De Soto was the first European to see the huge muddy waterway now known as the Mississippi River. Frenchman Robert La Salle turned the tables on the Spanish about a hundred years later when he came down the river from Illinois to its mouth on the Gulf of Mexico. Naturally, following this back-door feat, he claimed the whole region for France. Then Spain reclaimed it during the American Revolution and lost it to the United States a few years later, in an early version of Realpolitik.

The land was hotly contested during the Civil War. The Union army destroyed Jackson and laid siege to Vicksburg. The scars, physical and mental, remain to this day.

Mississippi is a land of legends, famous writers and musicians, great battlefields, Antebellum homes and plantations, and quiet little hamlets. You can catch some of the spirit of the state in William Faulker's novels and Eudora Welty's short stories; both authors are natives of the state. And people still pay homage to Elvis at his birthplace in Tupelo.

Summers in semi-tropical Mississippi are predictably warm to hot. But fall and winter temperatures can surprise visitors with sudden cold snaps.

Must-see sights in Mississippi include the many Antebellum plantation homes, the historic sites included in many annual "pilgrimages" (annual tours) in more than two dozen small and large towns, Indian mounds, the Vicksburg National Military Park, and other Civil War sites. The Shrimp Festival and Mardi Gras in Biloxi are annual events worth planning for.

Interstate 20 serves as our zone marker; it runs across the lower third of the state from near Meridian on the Alabama border on the east to Vicksburg on the Mississippi River to the west. Head north from I-20 and you are in our Northern Zone; head south and you're in the Southern Zone.

For More Information

Division of Tourism Development
(800) WARMFEST (927-6378)
www.mississippi.org

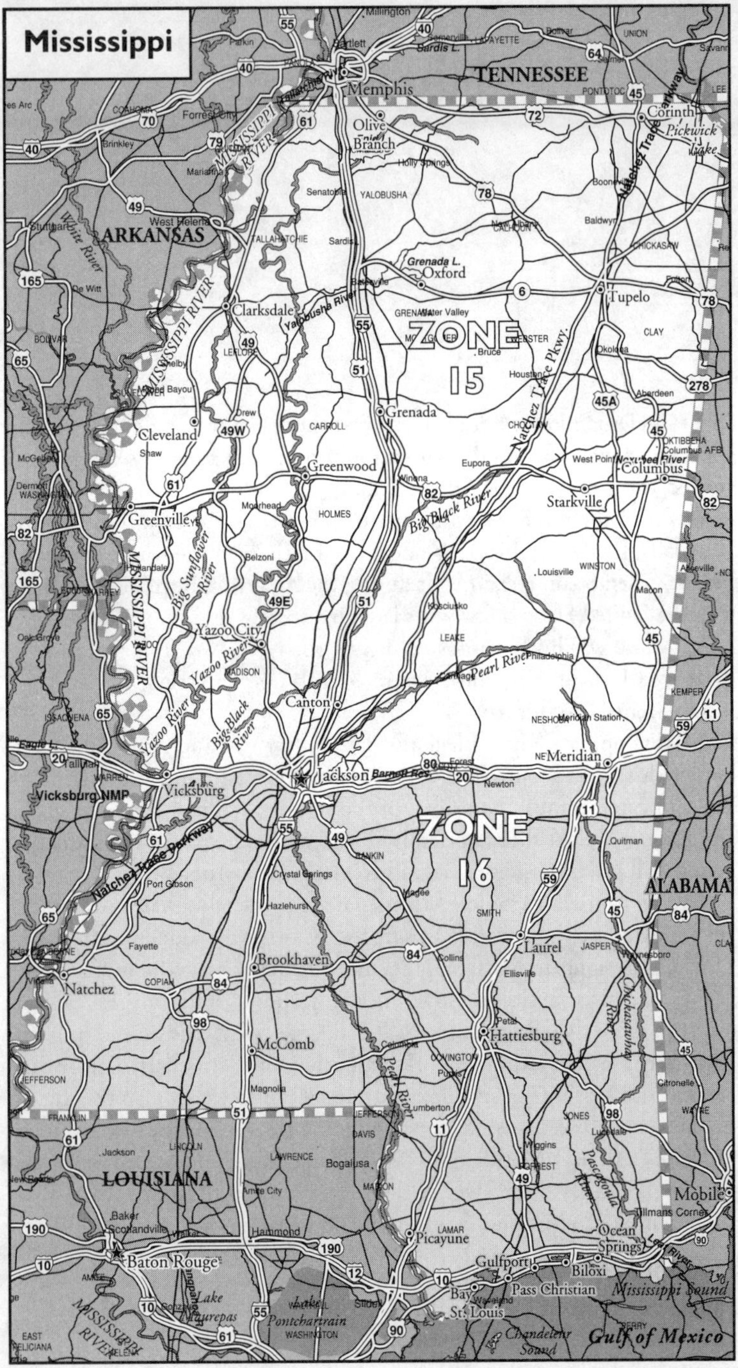
Mississippi
TENNESSEE
ARKANSAS
LOUISIANA
ALABAMA
ZONE 15
ZONE 16
Memphis
Olive Branch
Corinth
Pickwick Lake
Tupelo
Oxford
Clarksdale
Grenada
Cleveland
Greenwood
Greenville
Starkville
Columbus
Yazoo City
Canton
Jackson
Vicksburg
Vicksburg NMP
Meridian
Laurel
Brookhaven
Natchez
McComb
Hattiesburg
Picayune
Gulfport
Biloxi
Ocean Springs
Pass Christian
Bay St. Louis
Mobile
Baton Rouge
Mississippi Sound
Gulf of Mexico
Lake Pontchartrain
Lake Maurepas
Chandeleur Sound
MISSISSIPPI RIVER
Yazoo River
Big Black River
Pearl River
Big Sunflower River
Yalobusha River
White River
Pascagoula River
Chickasawhay River
Natchez Trace Pkwy.
Natchez Trace Parkway

Bay St. Louis
Bay Town Inn, p. 279
Heritage House, p. 280
Trust Bed & Breakfast, p. 281

Biloxi
Father Ryan House Inn, p. 282
Green Oaks, p. 283

Hattiesburg
Sunny Grove Bed & Breakfast, p. 284

Jackson
Fairview Inn, p. 269
Millsaps Buie House, p. 270
Old Capitol Inn, p. 271
Poindexter Park, p. 272

Natchez
Burn, p. 285
Cedar Grove Mansion Inn, p. 286
Dunleith, p. 286
Governor Holmes House Bed & Breakfast, p. 287
Linden, p. 288
Magnolia's Bed & Breakfast, p. 289
Monmouth Plantation, p. 290
Wensel House B&B, p. 291
Weymouth Hall, p. 292

Nesbit
Bonne Terre Country Inn & Cafe, p. 273

Ocean Springs
Shadowlawn Bed & Breakfast, p. 293

Olive Branch
Brigadoon Farm and Conference Center, p. 274

Pass Christian
Harbour Oaks Inn, p. 294

Starkville
Caragen House, p. 275

Tupelo
Mockingbird Inn, p. 276

Vicksburg
Annabelle Bed & Breakfast, p. 295
Balfour House Bed & Breakfast, p. 296
Belle of the Bends, p. 297
Cedar Grove Mansion Inn, p. 298

Zone 15
Northern Mississippi

Jackson is the state capital (named after Andrew Jackson), and the Old Capital Building (now the State Historical Museum) is a good place to get a sense of Mississippi's colorful past. The Greek Revival City Hall on S. President Street was one of the few Jackson buildings to escape the torches of Sherman's troops during the Civil War.

In Vicksburg, the "Gibraltar of the Confederacy" (so called because it once kept Union gunboats from navigating the Mississippi), you can tour many of the most famous battle sites using a self-guided tour map from the Vicksburg National Military Park.

Tupelo is the state's largest city and is also the site of another major Civil War battlefield, where Confederate Gen. Nathan Bedford Forrest's army clashed with the Union army commanded by Gen. William T. Sherman. Of more contemporary interest to music buffs is the birthplace of the "King," Elvis Presley. Fans can visit his house, a museum, memorial chapel, and, of course, a gift shop.

Oxford is the hometown of William Faulkner. He wrote about the town in some of his novels but renamed it "Jefferson." Oxford is also the home of the University of Mississippi. The Center for the Study of Southern Culture at the university may also give you some insights into the continuing civil war between the states over barbecue—which state has the best?

The Natchez Trace Parkway, following early Indian trails, is a scenic road that wanders through Tishomingo State Park to Tupelo and continues on through the state (313 miles in all). Trucks are prohibited and picnics along the way are encouraged.

For More Information

Jackson Tourism Office
(800) 354-7695

Vicksburg Convention and Visitors Bureau
(800) 221-3536

FAIRVIEW INN, Jackson

Overall: ★★★★½ Room Quality: A Value: B Price: $115–$165

Wedding night couples, honeymoon couples, and those in love are drawn to Fairview Inn. "We even have businesspeople who wish they weren't traveling alone," adds Bill. Flanked by towering magnolias and pink crepe myrtles, this Corinthian column home exudes aristocratic and romantic charm. A groom would be proud to carry his bride across the threshold into the grand foyer, with Venetian marble floors reflected in the golden hues of a massive chandelier. We were torn between the room with a hand-carved Greek bed, sleeping under an angel in the muslin-draped king bed backed by a Palladian window, or the inviting executive suite with a separate library/sitting room.

Setting & Facilities

Location: Exit 98A off I-55 on Woodrow Wilson, left on North State, left on Fairview St.
Near: Old Capitol Museum, Governor's Mansion, State Capitol, Agriculture & Forestry Museum, Sports Hall of Fame, Natural Science Museum Arts Museum, Davis Plantetarium, New State Theatre
Building: Colonial Revival mansion
Grounds: Lawns bordered by magnolias & crepe myrtles, formal garden w/ marble statue (*La Baigneuse* by Allegrain)
Public Space: Library, foyer, garden room
Food & Drink: Full breakfast w/ eggs, quiche, pancakes, banana bread
Recreation: Walking, sight-seeing, golf
Amenities & Services: Library well stocked w/ military history & Civil War books

Accommodations

Units: 8 guest rooms & suites
All Rooms: TV, cordless phone, data port, coffeemaker, clock radio, terry robes, individually controlled heat/AC, iron & ironing board, extra pillows, bottled water, take-home sack of potpourri, Godiva chocolates
Some Rooms: Fireplace
Bed & Bath: King or queen w/ down pillows; private baths
Favorites: None
Comfort & Decor: Attractive wall coverings and window treatments, prairie school–style moldings, comfortable furnishings

Rates, Reservations, & Restrictions

Deposit: Credit card; 72-hour cancellation
Discounts: 10% AAA
Credit Cards: AE, V, MC, D, DC
Check-in/Out: 4 p.m./11 a.m.
Smoking: No
Pets: No
Kids: Welcome

No-Nos: "Don't try to sneak a smoke in the bathroom," says host
Minimum Stay: None
Open: All year except Christmas Day & New Year's Eve
Hosts: Carol & William Simmons, Claudia Berry

734 Fairview St.
Jackson, MS 39202
(601) 948-3429 or (888) 948-1908
Fax: (601) 948-1203
fairview@fairviewinn.com
www.fairviewinn.com

MILLSAPS BUIE HOUSE, Jackson

Overall: ★★★★ Room Quality: B Value: C Price: $90–$175

The elegant facade complements the interior with striking stained-glass windows and a beautifully appointed parlor with a piano, drawing room, and library for guests. Guests are pampered, and many cite this as the reason they return. The fresh flowers, fruit bowls, and bottled water in the rooms add an intimate touch. Joan Rivers, Art Linkletter, and cast members from *A Time to Kill* were well taken care of at this stately home.

SETTING & FACILITIES

Location: Corner of High & North State Sts.
Near: State Capitol, Old State Capitol
Building: 1888 Greek Revival
Grounds: Gardens
Public Space: Parlor, library, 4 porches
Food & Drink: Full Southern breakfast
Recreation: Sight-seeing, shopping
Amenities & Services: Newspapers, turn-down, access to nearby fitness center, disabled access

ACCOMMODATIONS

Units: 11 guest rooms
All Rooms: Cable TV, phone w/ data port, antiques, 14-foot ceiling, phone in bathroom
Bed & Bath: Beds vary; 10 rooms w/ private baths
Favorites: Room 4 Buie—large
Comfort & Decor: Period antiques and high ceilings

RATES, RESERVATIONS, & RESTRICTIONS

Deposit: Ask
Discounts: 10% AAA
Credit Cards: AE, V, MC, DC, D
Check-in/Out: 2 p.m./11 a.m.
Smoking: No
Pets: No
Kids: 12 & older
Minimum Stay: None
Open: All year
Host: Joe Morris

628 North State St.
Jackson, MS 39202
(601) 352-0221
Fax: Same as phone
www.millsapsbuiehouse.com

OLD CAPITOL INN, Jackson

Overall: ★★★½ | Room Quality: B | Value: C | Price: $85–$155

Three-room designer suites have transformed this former YWCA for Southern women. Don't let the large room-count fool you; the staff is friendly and likes to know something about guests' tastes to match them with the perfect room. Little extras include evening wine and cheese, early morning coffee stations on all floors, daily newspapers, irons, hair dryers, whirlpool tubs, and a data port. A rooftop garden has private space for sunning and a hot tub. Other public areas include a sprawling lobby and patio with swimming pool, a nicely landscaped goldfish pond, and outdoor tables.

Setting & Facilities

Location: Pearl St. exit off I-55, right on State St.
Near: Eudora Welty Library, Old Capitol Museum, Mississippi Museum of Art, State Capitol
Building: Traditional red brick building w/ black wrought iron balconies
Grounds: Enclosed courtyard
Public Space: Courtyard, rooftop garden w/ hot tub, sun room, den
Food & Drink: Full Southern breakfast; evening wine & cheese
Recreation: Sight-seeing
Amenities & Services: Newspaper, list of local restaurants

Accommodations

Units: 2 guest rooms, 22 suites
All Rooms: Phone w/ data port, hair dryer
Some Rooms: Garden view
Bed & Bath: King or queen; private baths
Favorites: 2-story suites w/ whirlpool tubs
Comfort & Decor: Distinctive suites, created by Mississippi designers, reflect Mississippi themes—from the popular Faulkner's Flat with larger-than-life six-foot-high book covers for a headboard to the Walter Anderson room with an old crab trap filled with magazines, animal prints, and seashore furnishings.

Rates, Reservations, & Restrictions

Deposit: Ask
Discounts: AAA
Credit Cards: AE, V, MC
Check-in/Out: 3 p.m./noon
Smoking: No
Pets: No
Kids: 12 & older
Minimum Stay: None
Open: All year
Host: Mende Malouf
226 North State St.
Jackson, MS 39211
(601) 359-9000 or (888) 359-9000
Fax: (601) 353-5587
inn@misnet.com
www.oldcapitolinn.com

POINDEXTER PARK, Jackson

Overall: ★★ Room Quality: D Value: C Price: $59–$69

This sunny yellow home in one of Jackson's oldest neighborhoods is a good choice for students on a budget, guests looking for legendary blues connections, and bicyclists on the Natchez Trace. Poindexter has a boarding house feel—tiny rooms, spartan furnishings with clever twists like upturned suitcases for end tables and herbal bath balms for soaking in the claw-foot tub. There are no phones or TVs in the rooms, just antique radios tuned to the blues. Marcia, the first woman council member in Jackson, now promotes legendary blues singer Dorothy Moore, known for her 1970s hit "Misty Blue." Marcia has the inside track on juke joints and hideaway blues bars and offers a self-guided blues tour of theaters, record shops, and favorite haunts. Because the Natchez Trace doesn't run through Jackson, Marcia will pick up cyclists with their bikes and drop them on the other side the next day.

SETTING & FACILITIES

Location: Exit 96A off I-55, right on Pearl St., left on Amite St., left on Lemon St.
Near: Old Capitol, Jackson Zoo, Dizzy Dean Museum, Davis Planetarium
Building: 1907 Victorian, Greek Revival front
Grounds: Small yard
Public Space: Veranda
Food & Drink: All-you-can-eat cont'l w/ cereal, muffins, fresh fruit, seasonable edible flowers such as pansies & day lilies; snacks, tea, coffee (24 hours)
Recreation: Walking, bird-watching
Amenities & Services: Restaurant recommendations; can even help guests locate graves of distant relatives in Jackson's oldest cemetery

ACCOMMODATIONS

Units: 5 guest rooms
All Rooms: Phone, ceiling fan
Some Rooms: Claw-foot tub
Bed & Bath: 5 queens, 1 twin; private baths
Favorites: Large room overlooking veranda w/ antique claw-foot tub
Comfort & Decor: Photographs, paintings, and musical artifacts are used throughout.

RATES, RESERVATIONS, & RESTRICTIONS

Deposit: Ask
Discounts: Extended stays
Credit Cards: AE, V, MC
Check-in/Out: 3–5 p.m./noon
Smoking: No
Pets: Yes, w/ limitations; ask
Kids: Welcome
Minimum Stay: None
Open: All year
Host: Marcia Weaver
803 Deer Park St.
Jackson, MS 39203
(601) 944-1392
ppinn@yahoo.com
www.bbchannel.com

BONNE TERRE COUNTRY INN & CAFE, Nesbit

Overall: ★★★½ Room Quality: Unknown Value: D Price: $150–$475

We couldn't rate the quality of rooms here because the hostess on duty said they all were occupied. We understand and applaud her concern for the privacy of her guests, but she was a little curt. She finally said, "Just look around." And what we saw was wonderful. The setting on a lake is beautiful, framed by azaleas and dogwoods. Guests we talked with were very enthusiastic about the inn. Our only concerns were the gravel road leading to the inn and the soaring cost of weekend rates for the two-bedroom suite ($475 versus $300 on weekdays). The rate is a bit much, even for this bit of Southern heaven. Go on the reasonably priced weekdays, and let us know about the quality of the rooms since we couldn't see them ourselves.

Setting & Facilities

Location: 4.4 mi. west of I-55 & Church Rd. interchange
Near: Mississippi Highlands, Memphis
Building: Greek Revival
Grounds: 100 acres, 5-acre lake
Public Space: Lake area, gardens
Food & Drink: Full breakfast; specialties: Belgian waffles, omelets; served in the resident cafe that also serves dinner
Recreation: Swimming, walking, fly-fishing
Amenities & Services: Catered picnics in garden, pool, massages avail.

Accommodations

Units: 12 guest rooms
All Rooms: Balcony or porch w/ lake or garden view, fireplace
Some Rooms: Jacuzzi tub; new 2-BR suite has LR & kitchenette
Bed & Bath: Beds vary; private baths
Favorites: None
Comfort & Decor: Open, pleasant surroundings feature beautiful art and English and French antiques.

Rates, Reservations, & Restrictions

Deposit: Ask
Discounts: None
Credit Cards: AE, V, MC, D
Check-in/Out: 4 p.m./11 a.m.
Smoking: No
Pets: No
Kids: No
Minimum Stay: None
Open: All year except major holidays
Hosts: Max & June Bonnin
4715 Church Rd. West
Nesbitt, MS 38651
(601) 781-5100
Fax: (601) 781-5466
www.bonneterre.com

BRIGADOON FARM AND CONFERENCE CENTER, Olive Branch

Overall: ★★★½ | Room Quality: C | Value: B | Price: $89–$135

Brigadoon Farm was originally built for groups and retreats, but accommodations have also been added for couples and families. The rooms in the "Country Goose Inn" are designed specifically for people traveling in groups. They are small and spartan with shared bathrooms. Families traveling with children would probably like this retreat. Kids can stay in the Honeymoon Cottage, which can accommodate up to ten people. There are many family facilities available—ample picnic tables, paddle-boats, volley ball areas, even a miniature train. This may be a good place for kids to burn off excess energy after long car rides.

SETTING & FACILITIES

Location: Hwy. 305 intersects Hwy. 78 at Olive Branch, 6 mi. south on 305
Near: Memphis, Graceland, Beale St.
Building: Rustic log lodge, house
Grounds: Lake & gazebo
Public Space: Family room
Food & Drink: Full breakfast; lunch & dinner by reservation
Recreation: Walking, swimming, pedal boating, fishing
Amenities & Services: Hot tub, swimming pool (seasonal), meeting facil.

ACCOMMODATIONS

Units: 11 guest rooms at Country Goose Inn plus cottage, bunk house
Some Rooms: Lake view, kitchen
Bed & Bath: Beds vary; groups share bathrooms; private baths for individual travelers
Favorites: Honeymoon cottage
Comfort & Decor: Rustic, art prints, antiques

Rates, Reservations, & Restrictions

Deposit: Credit card
Discounts: Seasonal specials
Credit Cards: AE, V, MC, D
Check-in/Out: 3 p.m./noon
Smoking: No
Pets: No
Kids: Welcome in some rooms
No-Nos: No kitchen privileges
Minimum Stay: None
Open: Feb.–Dec. (closed Jan.)
Host: Jeanette Martin
350 Hwy. 305
Olive Branch, MS 38654
(601) 895-3098 or (800) 895-3098
www.brigadoonfarms.com

CARAGEN HOUSE, Starkville

Overall: ★★★★ Room Quality: B Value: A Price: $95–$107

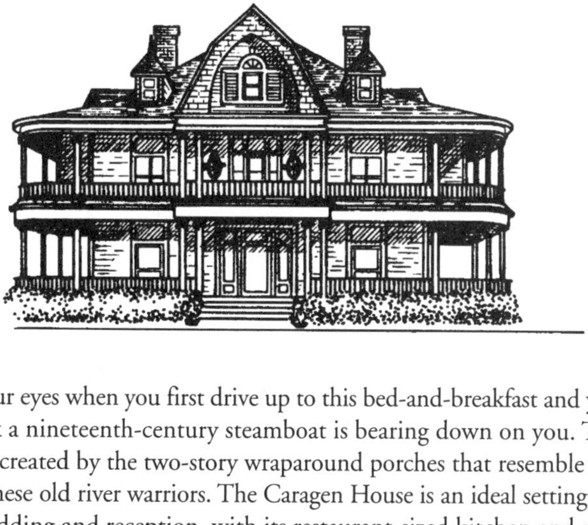

Squint your eyes when you first drive up to this bed-and-breakfast and you may think a nineteenth-century steamboat is bearing down on you. The illusion is created by the two-story wraparound porches that resemble the decks of these old river warriors. The Caragen House is an ideal setting for a large wedding and reception, with its restaurant-sized kitchen and spacious rooms. Guest rooms are unusually large and have modern facilities. We believe at $100 per night this bed-and-breakfast represents an elegant bargain. All aboard!

Setting & Facilities

Location: On Hwy. 82 near Stark Rd.
Near: Mississippi State University, shopping, entertainment
Building: 1890 Steamboat Gothic design
Grounds: 22 acres
Public Space: Library, formal sitting room
Food & Drink: Full breakfast
Recreation: Nature walks, shopping
Amenities & Services: Spa, VCR

Accommodations

Units: 5 guest rooms
All Rooms: TV, wet bar, individually decorated
Bed & Bath: Kings; private baths
Favorites: None
Comfort & Decor: Nineteenth-century elegance with antique reproductions

Rates, Reservations, & Restrictions

Deposit: $25
Discounts: None
Credit Cards: V, MC, D
Check-in/Out: Noon/noon
Smoking: No
Pets: No
Kids: Welcome
Minimum Stay: 2 nights on football weekends
Open: All year
Host: Kay Shurden
1108 Hwy. 82 W.
Starkville, MS 39759
(662) 323-0340

MOCKINGBIRD INN, Tupelo

Overall: ★★★½ Room Quality: B Value: B Price: $69–$129

Here are some verbatim comments from recent guests. "Each room has a unique look, for example, Venice, Bavaria, Africa—and each is furnished with appropriate artifacts and paintings." "The hostess will prepare special meals for guests with health problems." "Our host's baked apple pancake is a delicious breakfast treat." "Interesting things to look at, like a wedding-canopy bed." Sounds like a very satisfied quorum.

Setting & Facilities

Location: Corner of Gloster & Jefferson (enter from Jefferson)
Near: Milam School (one of Elvis's grade schools), Elvis's birthplace, Natchez Trace, Tupelo Coliseum
Building: Colonial
Grounds: Garden & patio
Public Space: Sun porch, LR w/ fireplace, TV, CD player
Food & Drink: Full breakfast w/ fresh fruit, hot entrees; afternoon snack
Recreation: Hiking, biking
Amenities & Services: Local newspaper, carriage rides, massage therapy can be scheduled

Accommodations

Units: 7 guest rooms
All Rooms: Cable TV, phone
Some Rooms: Corner fireplace, whirlpool tub, porch swing, feather mattress
Bed & Bath: Beds vary; private baths
Favorites: Athens Room w/ dbl. whirlpool, Greek columns
Comfort & Decor: International themes are used throughout the house.

RATES, RESERVATIONS, & RESTRICTIONS

Deposit: Credit card or 50% deposit check; 72-hour cancellation
Discounts: 10% seniors (over 65—ask), AAA
Credit Cards: AE, V, MC, D
Check-in/Out: 3–8 p.m./noon
Smoking: No
Pets: No
Kids: 12 & older
Minimum Stay: None
Open: All year
Host: Sharon Robertson
305 North Gloster St.
Tupelo, MA 38804
(662) 841-0286
Fax: (662) 840-4158
sandbird@netdoor.com
www.bbonline.com/ms/mockingbird

Zone 16
Southern Mississippi

Natchez is a great place to relive the wild, wild West legacy of the Mississippi River. Card sharks once plied the riverboats, interrupted perhaps by occasional bandit raids. Ruffians mingled and fought with land- and fortune-seekers. It was a grand Mississippi stew of people, ideas, and ideals. The gambling action is still here but is now heavily regulated by state laws, on permanently docked casino riverboats.

In Hattiesburg you can smell the roses of 750 patented bushes, blooming spring and summer at the campus of the University of Southern Mississippi. The Hattiesburg Zoo may really surprise the kids. They can ride a small railroad train right to the animals.

Highway 90 takes you all along the state's Gulf Coast. It's called the "Hospitality Highway" (an advertising euphemism that really means this road is jammed burger-to-burger with fast food eateries, souvenir shops, casino boats, and neon signs). To save your sanity, explore some of the moss-draped trails behind this strip and the beautiful Gulf Island National Seashore that includes Ship, Horn, and Petit Bois Islands.

For More Information

Natchez Convention and Visitors Bureau
(800) 647-6724
www.natchez.ms.us

Gulf Coast Convention and Visitors Bureau
(800) 237-9493
www.gulfcoast.org

Gulf Islands National Seashore Headquarters
(601) 875-9057

BAY TOWN INN, Bay St. Louis

Overall: ★★★★	Room Quality: B	Value: C	Price: $90–$105

When Delta Burke of *Designing Women* and her mother come to town they like to stay in Martha's Room. This ocean-view suite with lace-draped bay windows features a claw-foot tub with herbal bath oils, Battenburg lace towel holders, a hand-crocheted ruffle on the king bed, and a day bed for beauty naps. On the other hand, singer/songwriter Jimmy Buffett prefers the de Montluzin Room, decorated in masculine burgundies and deep greens, facing the bay where he can dream of sailing away. The white-sand beaches and ocean views are awesome, especially from the front porch at sunset.

SETTING & FACILITIES

Location: North Beach Blvd. in Old Town Bay St. Louis, across street from beach
Near: Historic Old Town, art galleries, antiques shops, restaurants
Building: Turn-of-the-century planter's house
Grounds: Large yard w/ 300-year-old live oak & huge magnolia tree
Public Space: Parlor, DR, porches
Food & Drink: Full breakfast; complimentary bottled water, soda
Recreation: Beaches, shopping, golf, fishing, bicycling
Amenities & Services: Daily papers

ACCOMMODATIONS

Units: 7 guest rooms
All Rooms: Ceiling fan
Some Rooms: King & twin beds, separate vanity/closet area, writing desk
Bed & Bath: King or queen; private baths
Favorites: de Montluzin Room, which faces the bay; claw-foot tub/shower & antique sink
Comfort & Decor: This typical turn-of-the-century planter's home showcases high ceilings, crystal chandeliers, and a variety of interesting antiques.

RATES, RESERVATIONS, & RESTRICTIONS

Deposit: Credit card; 48-hour cancellation
Discounts: None
Credit Cards: AE, D, MC, V
Check-in/Out: 3 p.m./11 a.m.
Smoking: No
Pets: No
Kids: 14 & older
Minimum Stay: 2 nights on 3-day holiday weekends
Open: All year
Hosts: Ann Tidwell, owner; Kevan Guillory, manager
208 N. Beach Blvd.
Bay St. Louis, MS 39520
(228) 466-5870 or (800) 533-0407
Fax: (228) 466-5668
info@baytowninn.com
www.baytowninn.com

HERITAGE HOUSE, Bay St. Louis

Overall: ★★★★ Room Quality: B Value: C Price: $95–$125

After a stint in the army, Paul returned to his hometown and found a laid-back life managing his brothers' bed-and-breakfast. It could be the little extras that keep guests returning, like the use of the washer and dryer or a free separate room for children. Friends traveling together or older couples who prefer separate beds will enjoy Grammy's Victorian Room, while honeymooners are drawn to the sleigh bed, skylight, and magnolia tree view in the French Room. A full tantalizing breakfast, run on an eight-day menu (so extended-stay guests don't get the same thing twice), runs from eggs Benedict to crêpes, but it is the recipe for the secret Japanese fruit sauce that is most often requested. Surrounded in camellias, magnolias, and azaleas, draped in sprawling live oaks, the gardens offer a tranquil escape.

Setting & Facilities

Location: 2 blocks from historic Old Town Bay St. Louis
Near: Bay of St. Louis, white-sand beaches, casino, golf course
Building: 1900 Colonial
Grounds: Yard w/ 200-year-old live oak tree
Public Space: Music room, LR, sitting room w/ large-screen TV
Food & Drink: Full breakfast; specialties: marinated pork chops w/ braised new potatoes in maple-butter sauce; complimentary soft drinks, bottled water
Recreation: Beach activities, gambling, canoeing, golfing
Amenities & Services: Daily paper

Accommodations

Units: 3 guest rooms
All Rooms: Extra large
Some Rooms: Hearts-of-pine floors
Bed & Bath: Queen sleigh bed, four-poster queen, Victorian twins; 1 w/ private bath, 2 rooms share bath
Favorites: Magnolia Room
Comfort & Decor: Art prints are used extensively.

Rates, Reservations, & Restrictions

Deposit: Credit card; 7-day cancellation
Discounts: Military, gov't., corp., long stays
Credit Cards: AE, V, MC
Check-in/Out: 1 p.m./noon
Smoking: No
Pets: No
Kids: 14 & older
Minimum Stay: 2 nights on holiday weekends
Open: All year
Hosts: Winston & Alma Levy; Paul Larsen, manager
118 Ulman Ave.
Bay St. Louis, MS 39520
(228) 467-1649 or (888) 702-2686
Fax: (228) 467-7210
heritage@goldinc.com

TRUST BED & BREAKFAST, Bay St. Louis

Overall: ★★★★	Room Quality: B	Value: A	Price: $85–$150

Every furnishing and renovation in this home has a story, and if you'll lend an ear to Hilton, your gregarious Cajun host, he'll bend it for sure. He'll show you a step for the high Mallard canopy bed with a secret potty chamber inside and military discharge papers signed by William Cody, dated years after he was already dead. A showcase from years of gathering unusual and tasteful antique furnishings, coats of arms, a King Louis XV table, Queen Elizabeth coronation door knockers, a grand piano, and chandeliers grace the guest and public rooms. Breakfasts are served on crystal, china, and sterling silver under yet another chandelier around a 20-foot dining table. "The queen of England has almost as much silverware as I do," boasts Hilton, "but I still have to do the dishes since most of it's in the bank."

SETTING & FACILITIES

Location: Hwy. 90 to Bay St. Louis, south on South Beach Blvd., right on Bookter St.
Near: St. Stanislaus College, Historic Train Depot, 5 blocks from Old Town
Building: Colonial Revival
Grounds: Yard w/ gardens; historic oak tree w/ swing
Public Space: Library, LR, sitting room
Food & Drink: Full Southern breakfast; complimentary beverages
Recreation: Beach activities, sightseeing, casino gambling
Amenities & Services: Lists of local restaurants, attractions

ACCOMMODATIONS

Units: 6 guest rooms
All Rooms: Hardwood floors, period antiques
Some Rooms: Antique area rugs
Bed & Bath: Doubles; 3 rooms w/ private baths, 1 w/ bath down hall, 2 rooms share bath
Favorites: None
Comfort & Decor: Antique furniture

RATES, RESERVATIONS, & RESTRICTIONS

Deposit: 1 night
Discounts: None
Credit Cards: AE, V, MC
Check-in/Out: 3 p.m./11 a.m.
Smoking: No
Pets: No
Kids: Welcome
Minimum Stay: None
Open: All year
Host: Hilton J. Eymard
204 Bookter St.
Bay St. Louis, MS 39520
(228) 467-5715 or (800) 467-5715
Fax: (228) 467-5690

FATHER RYAN HOUSE INN, Biloxi

Overall: ★★★★ Room Quality: B Value: C Price: $100–$175

Built in 1841, this former home of the poet laureate of the Confederacy, Father Abrams Ryan, has been lovingly restored and furnished in period antiques by Rosanne McKenney, a nurse from Italy, and her physician husband. It was here that Father Ryan wrote some of his best-known poems, and all rooms and suites are named after his works. Many rooms have fireplaces, balconies, and whirlpools with Gulf and garden views. A full gourmet breakfast and tea time savory and sweet delights are included. The spirit of sharing is with the McKenneys, as proceeds from catering are donated toward the completion of a hospital in Honduras.

Setting & Facilities

Location: On Hwy. 90 6 blocks from I-110 exit
Near: Jefferson Davis home, Ft. Massachusetts on Ship Island, Walter Anderson Museum, beach
Building: 1841 classic beach home
Grounds: Beach across from inn
Public Space: Pool
Food & Drink: Full breakfast; specialty: fruit Clafoutis (fruit custard)
Recreation: Swimming
Amenities & Services: Swimming pool, conf. facil. (50)

Accommodations

Units: 15 guest rooms
All Rooms: Cable TV, phone w/ data port, Gulf of Mexico views
Some Rooms: Hand-crafted beds
Bed & Bath: Beds vary; private baths
Favorites: Jefferson Room w/ whirlpool tub & great Gulf view
Comfort & Decor: Early nineteenth-century furnishings, Swiss linens, mosquito-netted canopy beds, down pillows, and duvet comforters whisper amour.

Rates, Reservations, & Restrictions

Deposit: Credit card 1 night
Discounts: None
Credit Cards: AE, V, MC
Check-in/Out: 3 p.m./11 a.m.
Smoking: No
Pets: No
Kids: Welcome
Minimum Stay: 2 nights during holiday weekends
Open: All year
Hosts: The McKenneys
1196 Beach Blvd.
Biloxi, MS 39530
(228) 435-1189 or (800) 295-1189
Fax: (228) 436-3063
www.innbook.com/ryan

GREEN OAKS, Biloxi

Overall: ★★★★ Room Quality: B Value: C Price: $140–$155

Two sets of stairs lead to the double front porch, one side for the ladies and the other for gents. In the 1800s, when this home was built, it was considered improper that men should catch a glimpse of a lady's ankle while mounting the steps. The front rooms of this home feature French doors leading to the gallery (porch), with views of the Gulf. Besides gourmet breakfast in the sunny, bricked breakfast nook, afternoon tea, evening muffins, or snacks and turned-down beds, there are courtesy beach supplies, towels, chairs, mats, and coolers. The beach is right across the street. Thoughtful amenities like aloe gel to relieve a day of too much sun, tropical robes, and modern conveniences such as cable TV and phones with voice mail and data ports for computers, are mixed with period antique decor. Lydia has a special treat for honeymooners and anniversary guests, just ask. She is also happy to help with dinner reservations and boating, fishing, golf, and sight-seeing arrangements.

Setting & Facilities

Location: From I-10 S. exit Hwy. 90 E. toward Ocean Springs
Near: Beauvoir (last home of Jefferson Davis), Beau Rivage (newest casino on Mississippi's Gulf Coast), Ship Island, Gulf Islands Nat'l Park
Building: Antebellum Creole cottage
Grounds: 2 acres w/ live oaks
Public Space: Veranda, porch, breakfast room, center hall
Food & Drink: Full breakfast w/ eggs Diaz, eggs Pontalba, Belgian waffles w/ buttery bananas, ham crêpes, & smoked salmon potato pancakes (wow!—never even heard of that)
Recreation: Biking, walking, beachcombing, sailing, fishing, historic tours
Amenities & Services: Restaurant menus, entertainment guides, concierge service

Accommodations

Units: 8 guest rooms
All Rooms: Cable TV, phone w/ data port
Some Rooms: Canopy bed, fireplace, Gulf views, access to porch or veranda
Bed & Bath: Queen or double; private baths
Favorites: Carquot room—French doors open on veranda & wide view of Gulf, fireplace
Comfort & Decor: Furnished with rugs and Antebellum fixtures

Rates, Reservations, & Restrictions

Deposit: Credit card; 72-hour cancellation
Discounts: Singles—$15 off per night, 10% AAA, AARP Sun.–Thur., guests staying 5 or more nights, 15%
Credit Cards: AE, V, MC, D
Check-in/Out: 3 p.m./11 a.m.
Smoking: No
Pets: No

Kids: Ask before you bring children; recommended for 12 & older
Minimum Stay: 3 nights on holidays, 2 nights on some weekends; ask
Open: All year
Hosts: Oliver & Jennifer Diaz, owners; Lydia Pena, manager
580 Beach Blvd.
Biloxi, MS 39530
(228) 436-6257 or (888) 436-6257
Fax: (228) 43-6225
greenoaks@aol.com
www.gcww.com/greenoaks

SUNNY GROVE BED & BREAKFAST, Hattiesburg

Overall: ★★★ Room Quality: C Value: B Price: $80–$90

We copied (with permission) notes from a recent guest: "Mountain bikes available for use on Rails to Trails path . . . full, delicious homemade breakfast with grits . . . delightfully soft water for bathing." This bed-and-breakfast is a romantic hideaway at bargain prices. It is also a very quiet place where you can sit on the wraparound porch with a good book or walk through a grove of pecan trees.

SETTING & FACILITIES

Location: West on Hwy 98, north on Cole Rd.
Near: Golf courses; convention centers in New Orleans, Mobile, Gulf Coast; rails to trails hiking path
Building: Colonial farmhouse
Grounds: Rural w/ ponds, pecan orchard
Public Space: DR, porch
Food & Drink: Full breakfast
Recreation: Fishing, bird-watching, wildlife viewing: deer, raccoons
Amenities & Services: Bikes

ACCOMMODATIONS

Units: 3 suites
Some Rooms: Fireplace
Bed & Bath: Beds vary; private baths
Favorites: None
Comfort & Decor: Bird prints and original floral paintings

RATES, RESERVATIONS, & RESTRICTIONS

Deposit: None
Discounts: 10% w/o breakfast
Credit Cards: None
Check-in/Out: Very flexible; ask
Smoking: No
Pets: No
Kids: Welcome
Minimum Stay: None
Open: All year
Hosts: Sunny Ewell & Randy Davis
627 Cole Rd.
Hattiesburg, MS 39402
(601) 296-0309

BURN, Natchez

Overall: ★★★★ Room Quality: B Value: C Price: $120–$200

Live oaks and gardens, a hideaway pool, and tree frogs serenading you to sleep, it's hard to imagine you're downtown. Catherine, a very spoiled 12-year-old cat, is the official host. "She's a hussy and walks guests to their rooms, wanting to spend the night," explains owner Layne. "She has competition now from Shammy, the new blond (cat) in town." The cats may be the official greeters, but Layne pampers his guests with complimentary cocktails, courtesy wine in their rooms, and a fun tour of the house with its unusual free-flying staircase. Suites with state-of-the-art bathrooms and original period antiques are comfortable and old world–like. The romantic Sarah Suite has a 14-foot ceiling, Rosewood queen tester, chandeliers, and a fireplace. We think the paisley-pink full drapes with matching canopy bed and chairs are a bit much, but it's the most photographed bedroom in Natchez and very popular with honeymooners. Maybe it has something to do with the special champagne Layne pulls from the cellar for celebrating couples.

Setting & Facilities

Location: Downtown Natchez
Near: Mississippi River (3 blocks), Jefferson St. antiques shops, Antebellum homes & plantations
Building: 1832 Greek Revival Mansion
Grounds: 5 acres of terraced gardens, ancient fountain & goldfish pond
Public Space: None
Food & Drink: Full Southern plantation breakfast
Recreation: Swimming, bird-watching, carriage rides
Amenities & Services: Guest privileges at local health club, newspapers, suggestions for local tours, make appointments for baby-sitters, manicures, pedicures, massage

Accommodations

Units: 7 guest rooms
All Rooms: Color cable TV, antique furnishings
Some Rooms: Fireplace, garden & fountain views
Bed & Bath: Queen, tester, four-poster; private baths
Favorites: Sarah Room
Comfort & Decor: Many period antiques

Rates, Reservations, & Restrictions

Deposit: Credit card 1 night
Discounts: None
Credit Cards: Major credit cards
Check-in/Out: 2–6 p.m./11 a.m.
Smoking: No
Pets: No
Kids: 12 & older
Minimum Stay: None
Open: All year
Host: Layne Taylor
712 North Union St.
Natchez, MS 39120
(601) 442-1334
Fax: (601) 445-0606

CEDAR GROVE MANSION INN, Natchez

Overall: ★★★★ Room Quality: B Value: A Price: $65–$145

Once a prosperous cotton plantation, today it's a 150-acre country retreat nestled in rolling hills and farmland, a half-hour's drive from Natchez. Hailing from Pittsburgh and retired from the steel industry, Donnie uncovered a well-kept family secret while researching family genealogy—his ancestors owned a cotton plantation with over 100 slaves. Generations later, the plantation is back in the family.

Setting & Facilities

Location: Half-hour drive from Natchez
Near: Antebellum homes, casinos, golf courses
Building: 1830 Greek Revival
Grounds: 150 rural acres
Public Space: Library, study, LR, 2 porches
Food & Drink: Full Southern breakfast w/ pancakes, waffles, grits, bacon, sausage, eggs
Recreation: Walking trails, horseshoes, fishing, biking, swimming
Amenities & Services: Swimming pool, newspapers

Accommodations

Units: 7 guest rooms
All Rooms: Pool or grounds view
Some Rooms: Cypress floor, fireplace, 12-foot ceiling
Bed & Bath: 6 queens, 1 king; private baths
Favorites: Clarissa Room w/ king bed, walk-in closet, 2 fainting couches
Comfort & Decor: Furnished with rare antiques and Persian rugs

Rates, Reservations, & Restrictions

Deposit: Credit card; 7-day cancellation
Discounts: None
Credit Cards: AE, V, MC, CB, DC
Check-in/Out: 2 p.m./11 a.m.
Smoking: No
Pets: Not in house; kennels on site
Kids: 12 & older
Minimum Stay: None
Open: All year
Host: John Holyoak
617 Kingston Rd.
Natchez, MS 39120
(601) 445-0585
Fax: (601) 442-9586; call first
holysmok@bkbank.com

DUNLEITH, Natchez

Overall: ★★★★ Room Quality: B Value: C Price: $110–$225

One look at this majestic Greek Revival mansion flanked with 26 Tuscan columns and it's hard to believe you can actually spend the night here. Hike on many trails through wooded bayous and green pastures in the

40-acre park surrounding the home. There is lemonade on arrival, snack baskets in the rooms, and a tour of the house. The new owner has recently renovated all the rooms and added Jacuzzi tubs to already modern bathrooms with antique sideboards and touches. We like the wraparound porch overlooking beautifully lit gardens for reflective evenings. All rooms have gas-log fireplaces, adding warmth and charm.

Setting & Facilities

Location: Close to heart of Natchez
Near: Mississippi River, Antebellum homes & churches, antiques shopping, Natchez Trace
Building: Greek Revival
Grounds: 40 acres of pastures & woods
Public Space: Gallery, grounds
Food & Drink: Southern breakfast; complimentary refreshments
Recreation: Sight-seeing, carriage rides, hot-air balloon races (Oct.)
Amenities & Services: House tour

Accommodations

Units: 8 guest rooms main house, 10 in courtyard wing
All Rooms: TV, individual heat & AC, fireplace, phone
Bed & Bath: Four-poster, canopy; private baths
Favorites: Master BR
Comfort & Decor: Beautiful antiques; the dining room is dazzling with gorgeous French Zuber wallpaper depicting forest scenes.

Rates, Reservations, & Restrictions

Deposit: 1 night; 72-hour cancellation
Discounts: None
Credit Cards: V, MC, D
Check-in/Out: 1–9 p.m./11 a.m.
Smoking: No
Pets: No
Kids: 14 & older
Minimum Stay: None
Open: All year
Host: John Holyoak
84 Homochitto St.
Natchez, MS 39120
(601) 446-8500 or (800) 433-2445
dunleith@bkbank.com
www.natchez-dunleith.com

GOVERNOR HOLMES HOUSE BED & BREAKFAST, Natchez

Overall: ★★★★ | Room Quality: B | Value: B | Price: $110

If there were a prize for the most eccentric ambassador of Natchez, it would definitely go to Robert Pully. The big draw here is the innkeeper himself. At 70-something, Robert's life has been far from ordinary. From his early days studying dance with Shirley MacLaine, to managing New York's legendary Algonquin Hotel where he hobnobbed with, among 0others, William Faulkner, Angela Lansbury, Laurence Olivier, and Peter

Ustinov, his tales could fill a best-seller. After retiring, he fell in love with Natchez, bought homes (including the Governor Holmes House), became Natchez's King of Mardi Gras, and continues to welcome and entertain his guests in grand style. They are welcomed to his 200-year-old home with open arms, greeted by the fragrance of fresh flowers and chocolates in their rooms and surrounded in decadent luxuries. The house is reportedly the oldest in Natchez. According to some reports, it was owned at one time by Jefferson Davis, president of the Confederacy.

SETTING & FACILITIES

Location: From New Orleans, I-10 N to I-110 N to US 61 N
Near: Many Antebellum homes, Mississippi Balloon Race, Opera Festival
Building: 1794 Federal
Grounds: Courtyard w/ 200 grapevines & a magnolia tree; lion-head fountain
Public Space: Drawing room, keeping room
Food & Drink: Full breakfast w/ regional surprises such as "pig-in-a-poke," a type of Yorkshire pudding w/ warm maple syrup
Recreation: Golf, swimming, walking, tennis
Amenities & Services: Local restaurant recommendations

ACCOMMODATIONS

Units: 4 guest rooms
All Rooms: Canopy beds
Bed & Bath: Beds vary; private baths
Favorites: Governors Suite
Comfort & Decor: Rooms have an intimate feeling and are decorated in Federal period style.

RATES, RESERVATIONS, & RESTRICTIONS

Deposit: Credit card; 7-day cancellation
Discounts: 10% AAA, AARP
Credit Cards: AE, V, MC, D
Check-in/Out: 1 p.m./11 a.m.
Smoking: No
Pets: No
Kids: 12 & older
Minimum Stay: None
Open: All year
Host: Robert Pully
207 South Wall St.
Natchez, MS 39120
(601) 442-2366 or (888) 442-0166
Fax: (601) 442-0166

LINDEN, Natchez

Overall: ★★★ Room Quality: B Value: C Price: $90–$120

This Federal plantation has been in Jeanette's family since 1849, and following in the footsteps of descendants to reside here, her children are the sixth generation carrying on the tradition. Bedrooms are furnished with antiques and canopy beds, and most open on to the gallery where guests relax on old-fashioned rocking chairs. Jeanette, a retired schoolteacher and interior designer, takes guests on a private tour of the home. Early morning coffee, a full Southern breakfast (one seating time only) in the formal dining room under a cypress punkah fan or on the back gallery, and a house tour are included.

SETTING & FACILITIES

Location: On Melrose Ave. off US 61 South
Near: Duncan Park, golf courses, casinos, antiques shops
Building: 1800 Federal House
Grounds: 7 acres w/ live oaks
Public Space: Back gallery w/ rocking chairs
Food & Drink: Full Southern breakfast, lighter cereals on request; early morning coffee
Recreation: Sight-seeing, golf
Amenities & Services: Local restaurant menus

ACCOMMODATIONS

Units: 7 guest rooms
All Rooms: Canopy bed, courtyard or grounds view
Bed & Bath: King, queen, double plus ¾ day beds; private baths
Favorites: Upstairs room offers more privacy, large bath
Comfort & Decor: Furnished with 1800 Federal antiques

RATES, RESERVATIONS, & RESTRICTIONS

Deposit: Credit card
Discounts: None; $30 add'l person
Credit Cards: Taken for reservations only, not for payment
Check-in/Out: 1 p.m./11 a.m.
Smoking: No
Pets: No
Kids: 10 & older
Minimum Stay: 2 nights during major holidays
Open: All year
Host: Jeanette Feltus
1 Linden Pl.
Natchez, MS 39120
(601) 445-5472 or (800) 254-6336
Fax: (601) 442-7548
www.natchezms.com/linden

MAGNOLIA'S BED & BREAKFAST, Natchez

Overall: ★★★★½ Room Quality: A Value: B Price: $85–$140

Where do harried TV network executives go to escape the Hollywood madness? Well, for Mary, it was back home to Natchez to open her bed-and-breakfast. Minutes from downtown, this Bellum home (built during the Civil War), with its picket-fenced front yard filled by a rainbow of flowers, paints a timeless facade. Chicory cafe and beignets are served in your suite as a wake-up call. A signature breakfast in the formal dining room starts with fresh fruit served on Waterford crystal. Through French doors is an enchanting courtyard fringed in broad-leaf banana trees with fountains, goldfish, lily pads, and an aviary of cooing pigeons.

SETTING & FACILITIES

Location: Corner of Madison & Pearl Sts.
Near: Riverboat casino, many Antebellum homes
Building: 1860 Greek Revival style
Grounds: Gardens w/ patio & fountain
Public Space: Porch, patio
Food & Drink: Full Southern breakfast; cafe au lait & beignets served in room prior to breakfast
Recreation: Bird-watching, sightseeing
Amenities & Services: Newspapers, tour guides; restaurant reservations made

ACCOMMODATIONS

Units: 3 guest rooms
All Rooms: Fireplace, TV, VCR, phone
Bed & Bath: Queen or full; private baths
Favorites: None
Comfort & Decor: The tastefully elegant parlor glows under a Baccarat crystal chandelier and is accented with gold gilded mirrors, breathtaking Tiffany lamps, exquisite antiques, and tropical greenery. The Master suite features a private porch, fireplace, and an oversized Jacuzzi surrounded by candles and marble statues of Muses.

RATES, RESERVATIONS, & RESTRICTIONS

Deposit: Credit card
Discounts: None
Credit Cards: V, MC
Check-in/Out: 2 p.m./11 a.m.
Smoking: No
Pets: No
Kids: 10 & older
Minimum Stay: 2 nights
Open: Closed Christmas holidays
Host: Mary Ann Henderson
501 Madison St.
Natchez, MS 39120
(601) 442-4161
Fax: (601) 445-8895
marymag1@aol.com

MONMOUTH PLANTATION, Natchez

Overall: ★★★★★ Room Quality: A Value: C Price: $145–$375

If you've seen *Gone with the Wind* ten times like most of us, you've already had a preview of the exterior of Monmouth Plantation. Scarlett is just about ready to burst out of the front door through the white columns. Rhett Butler may be striding purposefully over the white garden bridge. A number of publications, including *Glamour* and *USA Today*, have rated Monmouth Plantation as one of the most romantic inns in America. It also has won four diamonds from AAA. "We've had famous people stay here (President and Mrs. Clinton, Alec Baldwin, Rob Reiner, and Michael Eisner, to name a few), but it's more important to us that our guests who make a special effort to be with us leave with a wonderful memory of their stay here," host Ron explained.

SETTING & FACILITIES

Location: 1.5 mi. from downtown Natchez
Near: Mississippi Riverfront (2 mi.), Antebellum homes, public golf course, 1 hour from Vicksburg & Civil War battlefield
Building: 1818 Greek Revival Mansion plus guest houses
Grounds: 26 garden acres, pebble paths
Public Space: Study, courtyard
Food & Drink: Full Southern breakfast w/ eggs (scrambled, fried, or omelet), bacon, sausage, biscuits, and—of course—grits
Recreation: Golf, bicycling, hiking, picnics
Amenities & Services: Daily papers, local maps

ACCOMMODATIONS

Units: 31 guest rooms & suites (7 rooms & suites in main house, 24 rooms & suites in other buildings
All Rooms: Phone, terry robes; access to porch, balcony, or courtyard
Some Rooms: Gas-log fireplace
Bed & Bath: King, queen, or twins; private baths (13 w/ whirlpool tubs)
Favorites: Riches Suite w/ Mallard queen bed, separate parlor, & 2 baths
Comfort & Decor: Antiques and reproductions from 1800s; fine art in every room

RATES, RESERVATIONS, & RESTRICTIONS

Deposit: Credit card; 7-day cancellation
Discounts: Group rates (10 or more rooms)
Credit Cards: AE, V, MC, D, CB
Check-in/Out: 3 p.m./11 a.m.
Smoking: No
Pets: No
Kids: 14 & older
Minimum Stay: None
Open: All year
Hosts: Ron & Lani Riches, owners; Keith MacGregor, host
36 Melrose Ave.
Natchez, MS 39120
(601) 442-5852 or (800) 828-4531
Fax: (601) 442-5852
luxury@monmouthplantation.com
www.monmouthplantation.com

WENSEL HOUSE BED & BREAKFAST, Natchez

Overall: ★★★★ Room Quality: B Value: A Price: $85–100

Staying at the Wensel House is like staying at the home of a good friend. It has that casual and relaxed feel. A refreshing change from the drab, funeral parlor decor of most Natchez homes, it's sunny and free of clutter. Ron and Mimi keep a busy schedule working at the Historic Natchez Foundation. Mimi is happy to help with dinner reservations, boating, fishing, golf, and sight-seeing. Ron is an excellent source of local information. You may have seen him talking about Natchez on

A&E's *American Castles* and Bob Vila's *Historic Homes of America*. Breakfast is a great time for asking them about preservation, history, art, and architecture in the area. A premier central location, off-street parking, and the town's lowest bed-and-breakfast rates set this home apart.

SETTING & FACILITIES

Location: Heart of Historic District, across street from Pilgrimage Tour Headquarters
Near: Antiques shopping, casino, Mississippi River
Building: 1888 Victorian—Queen Anne/Italianate styles, plus cottage
Grounds: Small town front yard w/ sidewalk
Public Space: Parlor, DR
Food & Drink: Full Southern breakfast served at set time each morning w/ eggs, bacon, fresh biscuits; cont'l served all morning
Recreation: Golf, fishing nearby lakes, tennis
Amenities & Services: Newspapers (local, state, nat'l); restaurant menus; hosts avail. to give recommendations on tours, dining, etc.

ACCOMMODATIONS

Units: 3 guest rooms in main house, 2-br cottage
All Rooms: Phone, cable TV, iron & ironing board, hair dryer, VCR (on request)
Some Rooms: Cottage w/ LR, DR
Bed & Bath: Main house guest rooms have double & single bed & private bath; 2 BRs in cottage, double beds, share 1 bath
Favorites: Front Room—very bright in the morning
Comfort & Decor: Ultra-clean spacious rooms have rich hardwood floors, crisp white linens and towels, and practical antique furnishings that don't overwhelm the senses. The emphasis is on natural light and comfort; nineteenth-century American antiques and reproductions.

RATES, RESERVATIONS, & RESTRICTIONS

Deposit: Ask
Discounts: Long stays in low season
Credit Cards: AE, V, MC
Check-in/Out: 2 p.m./noon
Smoking: No
Pets: No
Kids: Sometimes; ask
Minimum Stay: None
Open: All year
Hosts: Ron & Mimi Miller
206 Washington St.
Natchez, MS 39120
(601) 445-8577 or (888) 775-8577
Fax: (601) 442-2525
wensellHouse@natchez.org
www.bedandbreakfast.com

WEYMOUTH HALL, Natchez

Overall: ★★★★ Room Quality: B Value: B Price: $95–$135

This Greek Revival mansion, set on a bluff, has hands-down the most awesome view of the mighty Mississippi River in all of Natchez. Sit back on the veranda or patio and enjoy the parade of barges, tugboats, and river traffic. Charles, the resident host, has been a mainstay of the house through two owners. He's an excellent source for sight-seeing tips, maps, historic house brochures, and arranging special requests. Ring that outside bell, just like in the old days, to announce your arrival, and Charles will be there to greet you.

SETTING & FACILITIES

Location: 1.1 mi. from Main & Canal
Near: Little Theatre, Nat'l Cemetery
Building: Greek Revival
Grounds: On bluff overlooking Mississippi River
Public Space: Glassed entry w/ seating & TV
Food & Drink: Full Southern breakfast w/ eggs, grits, biscuits, bacon, fruit, or crêpes
Recreation: Bird-watching, golf
Amenities & Services: Phone & fax avail.; restaurant reviews, dinner reservations made on request

ACCOMMODATIONS

Units: 3 guest rooms
All Rooms: On Lower floor, cable TV, private entrance
Bed & Bath: Full canopy bed, queen; private baths
Favorites: River View room
Comfort & Decor: Furnished in period antiques

RATES, RESERVATIONS, & RESTRICTIONS

Deposit: Credit card; 10-day cancellation
Discounts: None
Credit Cards: AE, V, MC
Check-in/Out: 2–4 p.m./11 a.m.
Smoking: No
Pets: No
Kids: Welcome, w/ some age limits; ask
No-Nos: No kitchen or laundry privileges
Minimum Stay: None
Open: All year
Hosts: Troyce & Lynda Guice, owners; Charles Combs, host
1 Cemetery Rd.
Natchez, MS 39120
(601) 445-2304
Fax: (601) 445-0602

SHADOWLAWN BED & BREAKFAST, Ocean Springs

Overall: ★★★★½ Room Quality: B Value: C Price: $100–$125

Bill is looking for binoculars for a couple taking breakfast on the porch who've spotted a red-headed woodpecker. Nancy is holding court in the dining room with four Europeans helping to plan their day, amidst a bountiful table of quiche, pineapple-carrot muffins, and all the fixins. One guest says he feels like he's in another world, a haven of tranquility. Down the driveway, lined in majestic oaks, the Wilson's dogs greet arriving guests with tails-a-waggin'. It's casual and relaxed, like a visit to a family summer home. Catch morning breezes off the Mississippi Sound, play croquet, wander to the water's edge, or explore acres of peaceful grounds, but come back in time for afternoon tea. Extras here include a wake-up tea or coffee tray brought to your room, a jar of homemade cookies to raid, and cold drinks and sodas for guests.

Setting & Facilities

Location: Exit 50 off I-10 (Ocean Springs/Washington), Washington to left on Government St., right on Pine Dr. to Shearwater Dr.
Near: Mississippi River, Shearwater Pottery, Walter Anderson Museum, Biloxi casinos, Gulf Nat'l Seashores
Building: 1907 Prairie Renaissance
Grounds: 5 acres of lawns, gardens, water garden w/ waterfall
Public Space: LR, DR, sun porch, screened front porch overlooking Mississippi River
Food & Drink: Full breakfast, afternoon tea
Recreation: Bird-watching, canoeing, kayaking, bicycling
Amenities & Services: Kayak, canoe avail.

Accommodations

Units: 4 guest rooms
All Rooms: Ceiling fan, easy chair, TV/VCR
Some Rooms: Views of Mississippi River
Bed & Bath: Queens; private baths
Favorites: Old Master BR w/ private entrance, wonderful water view
Comfort & Decor: Comfortable antiques are meant to be used.

Rates, Reservations, & Restrictions

Deposit: Credit card; 72-hour cancellation
Discounts: 10% AAA, AARP, stays of 4 or more days
Credit Cards: V, MC
Check-in/Out: 2 p.m./11 a.m.
Smoking: No
Pets: No
Kids: 14 & older; younger children accepted if family occupies all 4 rooms
Minimum Stay: None
Open: All year
Hosts: Bill & Nancy Wilson
112A Shearwater Dr.
Ocean Springs, MS 39564
(228) 875-6945
Fax: (228) 875-6595
shadowos@ametro.net

HARBOUR OAKS INN, Pass Christian

Overall: ★★★½ Room Quality: B Value: B Price: $83–$118

Call it Midwest charm in the Deep South. From the Heartland, Tony and Diane were drawn to this three-story 1850s former legendary hotel, and it became home. Two sunny front rooms have a commanding view of Pass Christian yacht harbor, and the inviting porch is a great place to relax, inhale salty ocean breezes, and watch sailboats rock with the tides. Guests can play a round of pool, chess, or help themselves to soft drinks, wine, and carrots in the kitchen. Carrots, we wondered? They're for Bucky, the horse corralled out back, and guests are encouraged to feed him healthy treats. Historic notes: This is the last remaining nineteenth-century inn on the Gulf Coast. John L. Sullivan trained here for the last (official) bare-fisted fight in America.

SETTING & FACILITIES

Location: On Scenic Drive just off US 90 in downtown Pass Christian
Near: Pass Christian harbor & beaches, Gulf Shores Nat'l Park, casinos, Jefferson Davis home, Confederate cemetery
Building: 1860 coastal cottage
Grounds: 1 acre w/ flower gardens overlooking water
Public Space: 2 sitting parlors, billiards room, guest kitchen, porches
Food & Drink: Full breakfast (cont'l on Tuesdays); complimentary wine, soft drinks, snacks
Recreation: Beaches, 20 golf courses, horseback riding, canoeing, kayaking, jet-skiing
Amenities & Services: Billiards table, piano for guests to play

ACCOMMODATIONS

Units: 5 guest rooms
All Rooms: On first floor, ceiling fan, phone, cable TV
Some Rooms: 3 w/ harbor views
Bed & Bath: Double, queen, or king; spacious private baths, 1 w/ whirlpool tub
Favorites: Front Room—best view of the harbor
Comfort & Decor: Rooms are accented in family Colonial pieces, heirlooms, and handmade quilts.

RATES, RESERVATIONS, & RESTRICTIONS

Deposit: Holidays, special event weeks, extended stays require non-refundable deposit; other reservations held w/ credit card
Discounts: 15% for 5 days or more, corp., military on weekdays
Credit Cards: AE, V, MC
Check-in/Out: 3–9 p.m./10:30 a.m.
Smoking: In billiards room
Pets: No
Kids: 10 & older
Minimum Stay: Certain weekends & holidays; ask
Open: All year
Hosts: Tony & Diane Brugger
126 West Scenic Dr.
Pass Christian, MS 39571
(228) 452-9399 or (800) 452-9399
Fax: (228) 452-9321
harbour@global.net
www.harbouroaks.com

ANNABELLE BED & BREAKFAST, Vicksburg

Overall: ★★★½ | Room Quality: B | Value: C | Price: $93–$115

Southern graciousness and European hospitality merge at Annabelle to create a special ambience in this home. George was born in the Czech

Republic and speaks fluent German, Spanish, and Portuguese, making overseas guests feel very much at home. Carolyn, raised on a farm near New Orleans, has tastefully yet comfortably furnished rooms with family treasures and antiques. Classical music can be heard throughout the home, adding to the peaceful mood. Guests enjoy relaxing by the pool or in a hammock in the terra-cotta–walled Italian-style courtyard. The couple presents a special gift to honeymoon and anniversary couples, so be sure to let them know if you're celebrating. George and Carolyn meet their guests at breakfast and take them on a tour of the home.

SETTING & FACILITIES

Location: Exit 1-A off I-20, 2.2 mi. on Washington to left on Speed
Near: Civil War battlefield, *USS Cairo* (salvaged Union ironclad gunboat), Old Court House Museum, Natchez Trace
Building: 1868 Italianate Victorian
Grounds: Courtyard, swimming pool
Public Space: Parlor, LR, DR
Food & Drink: Full Southern breakfast; brandy in parlor
Recreation: Sight-seeing
Amenities & Services: Off-street parking, swimming pool

ACCOMMODATIONS

Units: 3 guest rooms main house, 3 in guest house, 1 suite
All Rooms: Color TV, phone, AC
Some Rooms: Chandeliers, high ceilings, four-poster bed, whirlpool tub
Bed & Bath: King or queen; private baths
Favorites: None
Comfort & Decor: Beautiful chandeliers and Oriental rugs

RATES, RESERVATIONS, & RESTRICTIONS

Deposit: Credit card
Discounts: AAA
Credit Cards: AE, V, MC, D
Check-in/Out: 2 p.m./11 a.m.
Smoking: No
Pets: No
Kids: "Babies" & "school age" accepted—no in-between toddlers
Minimum Stay: None
Open: All year
Hosts: George & Carolyn Mayer
501 Speed St.
Vicksburg, MS 39180
(601) 638-2000 or (800) 791-2000
Fax: (601) 636-5054
annabelle@vicksburg.com
www.missbab.com/annabelle

BALFOUR HOUSE BED & BREAKFAST, Vicksburg

Overall: ★★★½ Room Quality: B Value: C Price: $85–$150

Steeped in history, this intimate inn is meticulously restored right down to the foyer inlaid floors, interior and exterior columns, and original wall colors in the bedrooms. You may want to accept that welcome drink to steady yourself to climb the unusual three-story elliptical spiral staircase to your room. Home of siege diarist Emma Balfour, history comes alive when guests take the free house tour and learn about the gala ball interrupted at the start of the siege and how this house later became the headquarters of Union General James McPherson. You will enjoy beautifully appointed public areas and large antiques-filled rooms with gas-log fireplaces, in-room beverages, and evening turn-down service. The host says, "Many guests coming here are particularly interested in history." Then she adds, "We were under siege for 47 days by the Union Army." Something many locals don't forget.

Setting & Facilities

Location: On Crawford St. at Hall's Ferry Rd.
Near: Joining of Yazoo & Mississippi Rivers, Old Court House, Vicksburg Nat'l Military Park
Building: 1835 Greek Revival
Grounds: Gardens
Public Space: 2 parlors, DR, veranda
Food & Drink: Full breakfast; specialty: quiche lorraine; wine or soft drinks on arrival
Recreation: Golf, tennis, sight-seeing
Amenities & Services: Newspaper, good local guidebook w/ maps

Accommodations

Units: 3 guest rooms
All Rooms: Antiques
Some Rooms: Fireplace
Bed & Bath: King, queen, twins; private baths
Favorites: Balfour Room w/ fireplace
Comfort & Decor: Period antiques

Rates, Reservations, & Restrictions

Deposit: Credit card
Discounts: Seniors (60 & older)
Credit Cards: AE, V, MC, D
Check-in/Out: 2 p.m./11 a.m.
Smoking: No
Pets: Yes
Kids: Welcome
Minimum Stay: 2 nights during holiday weekends
Open: All year
Host: Sharon Humble
1002 Crawford St.
Vicksburg, MS 39181
(601) 638-7113 or (800) 294-7113
shumble@vicksburg.com
www.balfourhouse.com

BELLE OF THE BENDS, Vicksburg

Overall: ★★★★ Room Quality: B Value: C Price: $85–$150

Known as the home with river connections, this classic Victorian Italianate mansion overlooks the mighty Mississippi and has an interesting display of steamship memorabilia from the late 1800s. Victorian-era rooms, two with river views, are sunny and pleasant, furnished by Jo, the granddaughter of Captain Tom Morrissey, with family heirlooms. A tour of the home, a history of the steamboats of the Morrissey line, and afternoon tea are included. Some guests take the free shuttle to the casinos while others enjoy a relaxing evening in their Jacuzzi and save a few bucks, selecting historic videos and movies from the library to watch in bed.

SETTING & FACILITIES

Location: Take Washington St. exit off I-20, north 1.5 mi. to left on Klein St.
Near: Riverboat casino (4 blocks), antiques shops, historic military park, Old Court House museum
Building: 1876 Victorian brick
Grounds: Extensive gardens; brick walkways wend through arbors, rose gardens, fishponds w/ fountains
Public Space: Garden, kitchen, parlor, DR
Food & Drink: Full Southern breakfast; afternoon tea
Recreation: Sight-seeing
Amenities & Services: Complimentary historic tour, historic movies

ACCOMMODATIONS

Units: 4 guest rooms
All Rooms: TV/VCR, individual temperature control
Some Rooms: 13.5-foot ceiling, Oriental rug, early-nineteenth-century antiques
Bed & Bath: Unusual beds (four-poster, Renaissance Revival half-tester); private baths
Favorites: Captain Tom's Room—great view of the Mississippi & Yazoo Rivers
Comfort & Decor: Antiques everywhere include Eastlake night tables, an Empire dressing table, and a Victorian armoire.

RATES, RESERVATIONS, & RESTRICTIONS

Deposit: Credit card; 72-hour cancellation
Discounts: AAA, on Internet site; $20 add'l person
Credit Cards: AE, V, MC, D
Check-in/Out: 2 p.m./11 a.m.
Smoking: No
Pets: Yes, if definitely house-broken
Kids: Welcome
Minimum Stay: None
Open: All year except Christmas
Host: Jo Pratt
508 Klein St.
Vicksburg, MS 39180
(601) 634-0737 or (800) 844-2308
Fax: (601) 638-0544
www.belleofthebends.com

CEDAR GROVE MANSION INN, Vicksburg

Overall: ★★★★ Room Quality: B Value: C Price: $95–$185

Talk about keeping memories of the Civil War alive—a Union cannonball is still embedded in the parlor wall, and you can still see the hole where one went through the floor. Lavish is a good way to describe many antique suites and rooms inside this 50-room mansion. You can sleep in

General Grant's bed, retrieve yourself on a swooning couch in Scarlett's Penthouse, or feel like you're on the front lines where you can find yet another cannonball hole in Rhett's Penthouse. Private courtyards and spa tubs are notable on main-floor suites in the Tara Carriage House. The atmosphere is friendly, gracious, and inviting. Enjoy courtyards; five acres of gardens with water fountains, statues, and a romantic gazebo; and a rooftop garden with a view. For fun there is lawn croquet, a Victorian tennis court, and a swimming pool.

Setting & Facilities

Location: Exit 1-A (Mississippi River) off I-20, north 2 mi. to 2300 block of Washington St.
Near: Vicksburg Nat'l Military Park, Civil War Museum, Mississippi River Adventure Tours, riverboat casinos, Great Animal Adventure Children's Museum, Antebellum homes
Building: 1840 Greek Revival mansion
Grounds: Formal gardens w/ gazebos, fountains, courtyards, Victorian tennis court, swimming pool, lawn croquet court
Public Space: Double parlors, ballroom, Wicker Room, verandas, gardens
Food & Drink: Full Southern breakfast; afternoon tea; full-service restaurant on site (Andre's)
Recreation: Swimming, tennis, croquet, walking trails
Amenities & Services: Local papers, sherry & chocolates (on request) at turn-down

Accommodations

Units: 30 guest rooms
All Rooms: Cable TV, phone
Some Rooms: Fireplace, private courtyard, deck, water views, wet bar, kitchen
Bed & Bath: King, queen, double, twins; private baths
Favorites: Klien's Grand Suite—extra-large room w/ parlor, wet bar, private porch, 2 TVs, stereo
Comfort & Decor: On the Antebellum tour, this B&B showcases wonderful antiques and paintings.

Rates, Reservations, & Restrictions

Deposit: Credit card; 3-day cancellation
Discounts: 10% AAA, AARP
Credit Cards: All major cards
Check-in/Out: Noon/noon
Smoking: Only in room 8 & bar
Pets: No; boarding avail. nearby
Kids: Welcome
Minimum Stay: None
Open: All year
Hosts: Ted & Estelle Mackey; Pamela Wetterville
2200 Washington St.
Vicksburg, MS 39180
(601) 636-1000 or (800) 862-1300
Fax: (601) 634-6126
info@cedargroveinn.com
www.CedarGroveInn.com

Louisiana

Much of subtropical Louisiana consists mainly of lowlands, marshes, and flood plains. The average elevation is only 100 feet, and hurricanes and heavy rainstorms pose serious threats of flooding to major population centers, such as New Orleans. Fortunately New Orleans (below sea level) has dodged the bullet many times in recent stormy years. Perhaps that is why the Mardi Gras festival is so intense and parties last until the last beads have been thrown from floats.

Like most of the Southern states, Louisiana was fought over by the Spanish and French. But finally the pen replaced the sword, and the United States and France signed the Louisiana Purchase agreement, effectively selling the future state to America as part of the deal. Louisiana became a state in 1815. Another part of the area's history was enacted when the British evicted a large segment of the French population (4,000 people) from Nova Scotia and transported them to Louisiana. Today their descendants are known as Cajuns.

For too many travelers, New Orleans is the first and sometimes last place they think of when they hear the word *Louisiana*. That's unfortunate because as fascinating, silly, beautiful, headstrong, and famous as New Orleans is today, it is only one facet of this state. There is also a whole region known as French Louisiana that includes Lafayette, Breaux Bridge, New Iberia, and Martinville. Thanks to the growing nationwide craze for Cajun food, working in a local restaurant could be the key to future cookbook authorship or chef positions in New York, Chicago, and San Francisco.

There is also plantation country and a line of fabulous Antebellum homes that begin north of Baton Rouge and run all the way to New Orleans. In the northern zone you will find the Louisiana Purchase Gardens and Zoo (Monroe), and fascinating old plantation homes along the

Cane River and elsewhere. And, if you're like most travelers, you will eventually come back to New Orleans for all of the fun and hoopla.

Make a long list of sights to see in Louisiana: the French Quarter, Mardi Gras (if you can stand the incredible crowds, including, as we delicately put it, some inebriates), the Longfellow-Evangeline Memorial Park, Hodges Gardens, riverboat casinos, Cajun restaurants, and much more.

For More Information

Louisiana Office of Tourism
(800) 633-6970

Louisiana State Parks
(888) 677-1400

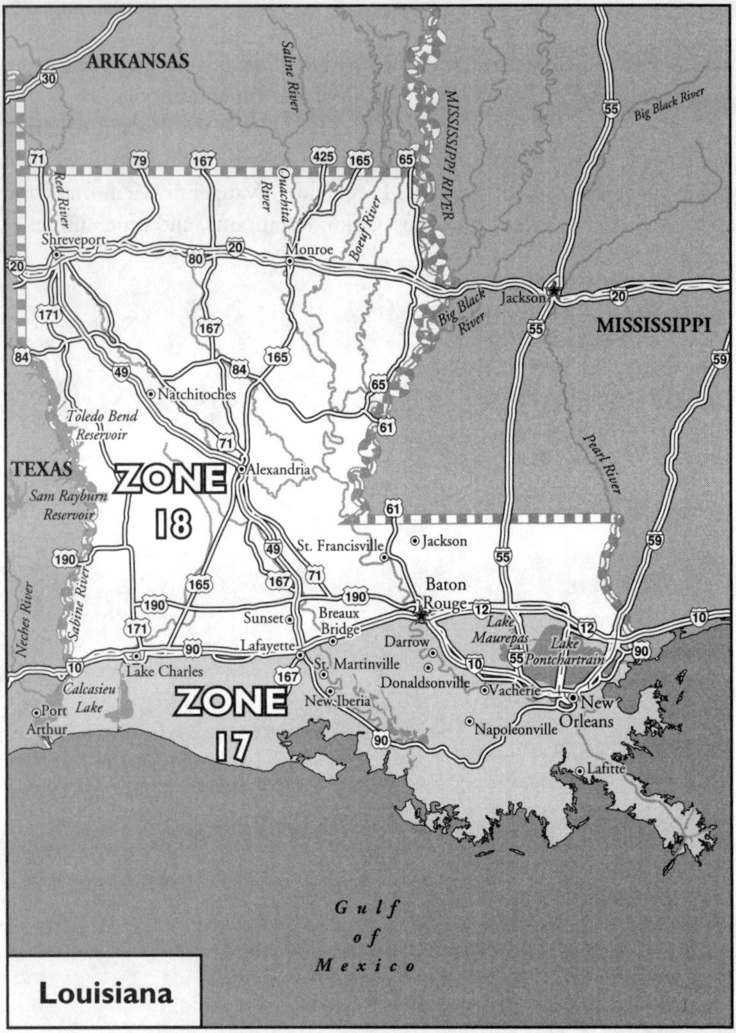
ARKANSAS
TEXAS
MISSISSIPPI
ZONE 18
ZONE 17
Louisiana
Saline River
MISSISSIPPI RIVER
Big Black River
Red River
Ouachita River
Boeuf River
Big Black River
Toledo Bend Reservoir
Sam Rayburn Reservoir
Neches River
Sabine River
Pearl River
Calcasieu Lake
Lake Maurepas
Lake Pontchartrain
Gulf of Mexico
Shreveport
Monroe
Jackson
Natchitoches
Alexandria
St. Francisville
Jackson
Baton Rouge
Sunset
Breaux Bridge
Lafayette
Lake Charles
Port Arthur
St. Martinville
New Iberia
Darrow
Donaldsonville
Vacherie
Napoleonville
New Orleans
Lafitte
30
71
79
167
425
165
65
20
80
171
84
49
84
165
65
61
71
61
55
59
190
49
167
71
190
165
190
171
90
10
167
12
10
55
12
90
10
90
20
55
59
55

Zone 17
Southern Coastal Louisiana

We have used Interstate 10 as our north/south zone divider. New Orleans, of course, is the belle of the ball in this zone. Everyone who has been here has a favorite memory—street performers in Jackson Square, an incredible French dinner, a wild throng on Bourbon Street in the Latin Quarter, the Voodoo Museum, the elegant homes of the Garden District, and . . . but there's the rub, there is so much to see and do. It is absolutely essential that you create a sight-seeing and activities plan if you want to get the most out of a visit to New Orleans. Crime can be a problem, especially at night in areas several blocks from the most crowded tourist areas. One of the things we do when visiting a strange city—talk to a policeman. Ask him or her what areas to avoid. Most are happy to oblige.

Outside New Orleans you can take narrated swamp tours by boat, past quiet bayous lined with cypress trees and dark still waters occasionally broken by the head of an alligator. There are numerous plantation mansions in this southern area. One famous one is Shadow-on-the-Teche on a lush bayou in New Iberia. The Greek Revival mansion is surrounded by azalea gardens with moss-draped live oak.

Casinos, bayous, great fishing, and sailing trips are just some of the recreational opportunities awaiting you in southern Louisiana. One bit of advice you may not get from tourist offices is about "lovebugs." No, we're not talking about that cuddly couple in the room next to you at the bed-and-breakfast, but tiny little bugs that swarm in the spring and fall. These little acidic guys, mashed on your car finish, can quickly start corroding your paint. Get to a car wash quickly if you see suspicious spots.

For More Information

New Orleans Welcome Center
(504) 566-5068

CHEZ DES AMIS, Breaux Bridge

Overall: ★★★ Room Quality: B Value: C Price: $95–$120

On a quiet residential street in the crawfish capital of the world, this recently restored 1890s Cajun cottage has been transformed into a showcase for talented Louisiana sculptors and artists. It's like sleeping in an art gallery, surrounded by inspirational and unique art. One room features a sculptured flaming bed, stained-glass windows, and a fish armoire. Guests share a sunroom and kitchen area with a refrigerator stocked with sodas and water and a coffeemaker. Tucked away behind a picket fence, the landscaped cottage has meditative gardens under an ancient oak tree in the backyard. The breakfast, while definitely Cajun gourmet, is not served in the house—a little inconvenient when you are in a hurry. You must walk or drive to Cafe des Amis, 0.7 mile away.

SETTING & FACILITIES

Location: Exit 109 off I-10, Rees St. to Bridge St.
Near: Atchafalaya Basin (fishing, boat tours), Lake Martin nature trails, Rip Van Winkle Gardens
Building: 1890 Cajun cottage
Grounds: Gardens
Public Space: Sunroom/kitchen w/ fridge, front & side porches, side deck
Food & Drink: Cajun breakfast: crawfish etouffée omelets, grilled boudin patties, beignets, juices, coffee
Recreation: Boating, fishing, bird-watching, Cajun dance & music
Amenities & Services: Can arrange swamp boat tours

ACCOMMODATIONS

Units: 2 guest rooms
All Rooms: Hardwood floors, restaurant & activity recommendation book
Some Rooms: Stained-glass windows
Bed & Bath: Kings; private baths w/ claw-foot tubs
Favorites: Room w/ "flaming bed" (lit by stained-glass window)
Comfort & Decor: Original oils and furniture made by famous Louisiana sculptors are the highlights here.

RATES, RESERVATIONS, & RESTRICTIONS

Deposit: Credit card
Discounts: Singles, long stays, weekdays
Credit Cards: AE, MC, V, D
Check-in/Out: 2 p.m./noon
Smoking: No
Pets: No
Kids: No
Minimum Stay: None
Open: All year
Hosts: Janice & Dickie Breaux
912 S. Main St.
Breaux Bridge, LA 70517
(337) 332-5273
Fax: (337) 332-2227

COUNTRY OAKS CAJUN COTTAGES, Breaux Bridge

Overall: ★★ Room Quality: D Value: C Price: $75–$150

Past fields of grazing horses and cattle, on an unpaved road, are peaceful country cottages nestled around a tranquil fishing lake. Guests can fish in the stocked lake or launch a pirogue (canoe) and paddle past gaggles of geese and ducks. The goat, practical for yard maintenance, says Jim, is the most amusing resident. Guests join the Allens and over 200 teddy bears for a country breakfast in their 1830 Acadian farmhouse. The four-acre lake on the grounds has received high praise from some guests. "A fisherman's dream," reported one who reeled in an eight-pound bass, or so he said.

Setting & Facilities

Location: Exit 109 off I-10, 4 mi. north, watch for "Cajun Country Cottages" signs
Near: Vermilionville, Acadian Village, Live Oak Gardens, many antiques stores
Building: Main house, cottages restored typical early-1800s Acadian architecture
Grounds: 14 wooded acres w/ private fishing lake
Public Space: Cottages have LRs, dining areas, porches; parlor, garden area of main house
Food & Drink: Country breakfast; specialties: Cajun scrambled eggs w/ crawfish au gratin sauce, stuffed French toast w/ strawberries & toasted pecans
Recreation: Boating, canoeing, fishing, bird-watching, swamp tours
Amenities & Services: Boat, canoes, barbecue pits

Accommodations

Units: 5 individual cottages
All Rooms: Lake views
Bed & Bath: Beds vary; private baths
Favorites: None
Comfort & Decor: Themed cottages include Noah's Place, Farm House (featuring an all-cow accented kitchen and pig and bunny themes in the bedrooms), and Little Cypress (an original schoolhouse with busy eclectic Americana fare and primitive antiques).

RATES, RESERVATIONS, & RESTRICTIONS

Deposit: $25 per night
Discounts: None
Credit Cards: No; cash or check only
Check-in/Out: 3–5 p.m./11 a.m.
Smoking: No
Pets: No
Kids: Welcome
Minimum Stay: 2 nights
Open: All year
Hosts: Jim & Judy Allen
1138 Lawless Tauzin Rd.
Breaux Bridge, LA 70517
(337) 332-3093 or (800) 318-2423
countryoaks@email.msn.com

MAISON DES AMIS, Breaux Bridge

Overall: ★★★½ Room Quality: B Value: B Price: $80–$149

Maison Des Amis is the older sister to the newer Chez Des Amis nearby, started by the same family. In the heart of the quaint artist community of Breaux Bridge, this restored Caribbean Creole Boudier house is a tropical oasis. Out back, past landscaped gardens with fountains and gazebos, on the banks of Bayou Teche, guests gather to meet, feed flocks of mallard ducks, and watch dragonflies flirt over lily pads. The Breauxs live off-property, but follow your nose to the trendy laid-back celebrity haunt Cafe Des Amis for an anything-off-the-menu breakfast, and chat with the couple over breakfast. Don't miss Saturday's Zydeco breakfast with the captivating rhythms of local musicians. We believe it's more convenient to have breakfast in the house, but some people may prefer going out to a famous local restaurant.

SETTING & FACILITIES

Location: Exit 109 off I-10, take Rees St. downtown, right on Bridge St., cross bridge, turn left
Near: Atchafalaya Basin (fishing, boat tours), Lake Martin nature trails, Rip Van Winkle Gardens

Building: Caribbean Creole-style building, 1880
Grounds: Tropical, native Louisiana landscaping
Public Space: Glassed-in porch w/ fridge, coffee, phone, games; gazebo on bayou
Food & Drink: Full Cajun breakfast served at Cafe Des Amis, 1 block away; complimentary beverages
Recreation: Boating, fishing, bird-watching, walking trails, Cajun dancing & music
Amenities & Services: Can arrange swamp tours

Accommodations

Units: 3 guest rooms
All Rooms: Antique furnishings, hardwood floors, restaurant & activity recommendation book
Bed & Bath: Queen, four-poster plantation bed; private baths w/ claw-foot tubs
Favorites: Mini Suite—spacious w/ plantation bed
Comfort & Decor: Spacious, private quarters with canopied plantation beds, fine linens, tapestry drapes, fireplaces, distinctive period antiques, and folk art are chic and inviting; original oils and Old Louisiana–style decor.

Rates, Reservations, & Restrictions

Deposit: Credit card
Discounts: Singles, 3rd/4th person, long stays, weekdays
Credit Cards: AE, MC, V, D
Check-in/Out: 2 p.m./noon
Smoking: No; on porches only
Pets: No
Kids: Sometimes; ask
Minimum Stay: None
Open: All year
Hosts: Cynthia & Dickie Breaux
111 Washington St.
Breaux Bridge, LA 70517
(318) 332-5273
Fax: (318) 332-2227

TEXCUCO PLANTATION HOME, Darrow

Overall: ★★ Room Quality: C Value: C Price: $65–$145

On the sprawling grounds of Texcuco, an Antebellum Greek Revival home built in 1855, are country cottages for overnight guests. Cottages are furnished in antiques, artifacts, and oriental rugs with modern bathrooms, fully equipped kitchens, and fireplaces. Guests enjoy sitting on rocking chairs on the front porch, taking a complimentary tour of the main house with a hoop-skirted guide, or exploring the chapel, blacksmith shop, a Civil War museum, or the life-size doll house on the grounds. Guests will find a welcome bottle of wine chilling in their cottage.

Setting & Facilities

Location: 1 mi. north of Sunshine Bridge on LA 44
Near: Numerous plantation buildings
Building: 1855 Antebellum plantation house (Greek Revival style) plus country-style cottages

Grounds: 25 acres
Public Space: None
Food & Drink: Full country breakfast w/ eggs, sausage, grits, fresh homemade biscuits; wine on arrival
Recreation: Golf, gambling (on boats), swamp tours
Amenities & Services: Civil War museum on site, complimentary tour of main house

Accommodations

Units: 3 guest rooms in main house & 20 1–3 BR suites in cottages
Some Rooms: Fireplace, kitchenette
Bed & Bath: King, queen, or twins—some antiques; private baths
Favorites: Master BR in main house w/ lady's parlor
Comfort & Decor: Victorian, late-nineteenth-century ambience

Rates, Reservations, & Restrictions

Deposit: Credit card, 1 night
Discounts: AAA
Credit Cards: AE, V, MC, D
Check-in/Out: 2–9 p.m./noon
Smoking: Not in main house; yes, in cottages
Pets: Yes, w/ $25 deposit (refundable if no damage)
Kids: Welcome
Minimum Stay: None
Open: All year except Thanksgiving, Christmas, & New Year's Day
Host: Anette Harland
3138 Highway 44
Darrow, LA 70725
(225) 562-3929
Fax: (225) 562-3923

BITTERSWEET PLANTATION, Donaldsonville

Overall: ★★★★½ Room Quality: B Value: D Price: $250–$295

Savoring a personally prepared three-course breakfast as an honored guest in Chef John's home is the ultimate food experience. Internationally acclaimed for his Louisiana indigenous cuisine, Chef John Folse has received culinary distinction from Rome to Moscow. With a passion for great bed-and-breakfasts, he opened his home to guests, stirring it up with his favorite bed-and-breakfast traits. Besides the unparalleled cuisine, comfort and exposure to local culture are top priorities here, with historic towns, museums, forts, and great plantations nearby. Priority reservations for dinner at Lafitte's Landing, the chef's premier restaurant, is assured. Tip: Check this bed-and-breakfast's Web site for everything from recipes to tips on other bed-and-breakfasts.

Setting & Facilities

Location: Hwy. 70 to LA 3089, then north to Donaldsville
Near: Plantation & bayou country
Building: 1859 plantation house
Grounds: Patio, gardens
Public Space: Patio, gardens

Food & Drink: Choice of 3-course "Planters breakfast" w/ Louisiana specialties or cont'l breakfast

Recreation: Hunting, fishing, golfing

Amenities & Services: Praline truffles on pillow, local & nat'l newspapers

Accommodations

Units: 2 guest rooms (2 more expected in 2000)

All Rooms: Art prints, robes, fluffy embossed towels, fresh flowers, candles, CDs, movies, snacks, stocked fridge w/ choice of beverages, coffee service

Some Rooms: Bitter Suite has antique sleigh bed, fireplace, Jacuzzi tub, office w/ phone, fax, computer, & treadmill

Bed & Bath: Beds vary; private baths

Favorites: Bitter Suite

Comfort & Decor: Located above the restaurant, rooms are extra large and feature attractive decor.

Rates, Reservations, & Restrictions

Deposit: Ask

Discounts: None

Credit Cards: AE, V, MC

Check-in/Out: 3–5 p.m./11 a.m.

Smoking: Only in Bar Room area

Pets: No

Kids: Ask

Minimum Stay: None

Open: All year

Hosts: John Folse or Kim Capone
404 Claiborne Ave.
Donaldsonville, LA 70346
(225) 473-1232
Fax: (225) 473-1161
folse@jfolse.com
www.jfolse.com

AHHH! T' FRERE'S HOUSE, Lafayette

Overall: ★★★ Room Quality: C Value: B Price: $85–$100

We initially found the "Ahhh! T' Frere's" name as vaguely annoying as "Toys 'R Us," but all semantic snobbery was forgotten when we actually visited this bed-and-breakfast. You'll feel like family after a night at T' Frere's. Guests are blown away when innkeeper and gourmet Cajun chef Maugie sweeps into the formal dining room in red-silk pajamas serving a breakfast fit for a cotton king. "I'm an innkeeper, not a chef anymore. I'm comfortable in my house and want my guests to feel that way, too," says Maugie. Breakfast banter is often centered around the ghost of Amilee Comeaux, a young widow who drowned in the backyard well, who is frequently seen drifting through the house by guests. Ladies traveling with a manly man should avoid the 1890s room, a charming overdose of flowers and frills. The "Garconniere" rooms (where Cajun men could leave early without disturbing the household) offer privacy and lighter decor.

SETTING & FACILITIES

Location: Hwy. 90 to Verot School Rd.
Near: Vermillionville, Acadian Cultural Center, Avery Island, Rip Van Winkle Gardens, Lake Martin
Building: 1880 2-story Early Acadian Colonial
Grounds: Acre of land w/ 100-year-old Catableau tree, gardens
Public Space: Parlor, DR, glass-enclosed porch, gazebo
Food & Drink: Full breakfast w/ Cajun cuisine; welcome drink (T'Juleps) & Cajun canapés
Recreation: Swamp tours, airboat rides, bird-watching
Amenities & Services: Brochures of local attractions

ACCOMMODATIONS

Units: 6 guest rooms
All Rooms: Antiques, TV, phone
Some Rooms: Mary Room has 1800 Mallard bed
Bed & Bath: Beds vary; private baths
Favorites: None
Comfort & Decor: Old-style plantation decor, sparkling hardwood floors, and cozy, flowery wallpaper grace the rooms.

RATES, RESERVATIONS, & RESTRICTIONS

Deposit: Credit card; 7-day cancellation
Discounts: Long stays
Credit Cards: AE, V, MC, D, DC
Check-in/Out: 4:30 p.m./10 a.m.
Smoking: On glass-enclosed porch
Pets: No
Kids: Welcome
Minimum Stay: None
Open: All year
Hosts: Pat & Maugie Pastor
1905 Verot School Rd.
Lafayette, LA 70508
(337) 984-9347 or (800) 984-9347
Fax: (337) 984-9347
tfreres@mindspring.com
www.tfreres.com

BOIS DES CHENES BED & BREAKFAST, Lafayette

Overall: ★★★½ Room Quality: B Value: C Price: $95–$150

This historic 1820 plantation is nestled under a canopy of live oaks on a quiet residential corner. Simple yet elegant and furnished with period furniture and treasured antiques, all suites have full poster canopy beds, and some have fireplaces. Inside the plantation home are two spacious suites with a sitting room. The Carriage house features Louisiana country, Victorian, and Acadia style suites. All guests get to tour the home with its interesting displays of antique weapons, pottery, and glass. Innkeeper Coerte and son Kim run daily boat tours to the Atchafalaya swamp to view marsh birds, alligators, cypress wilderness, Cajun crawfish fishermen, and swamp critters. Deep-sea fishing in the Gulf can also be arranged.

Setting & Facilities

Location: Mudd Ave., 1.5 mi. from I-10
Near: Vermilionville, plantation homes
Building: 1820 Creole French Colonial
Grounds: 1.9 acres w/ live oaks
Public Space: None
Food & Drink: Full breakfast w/ French toast, French omelet w/ bacon & sausage
Recreation: Hunting, salt-water fishing
Amenities & Services: Recommendations for local restaurants, attractions

Accommodations

Units: 5 guest rooms plus 1 attached Main Suite
All Rooms: Period antiques, Audubon bird prints, garden views, cable TV, small fridge
Some Rooms: Wood-burning fireplace
Bed & Bath: Double or queen; private baths
Favorites: Zouave Suite w/ fireplace, parlor
Comfort & Decor: Plantation-style antiques

Rates, Reservations, & Restrictions

Deposit: Major credit card
Discounts: "Negotiable"
Credit Cards: AE, V, MC
Check-in/Out: 2 p.m./11 a.m.
Smoking: No
Pets: Yes, "if their owners are well behaved"
Kids: Welcome
Minimum Stay: None
Open: All year except Christmas Eve & Day
Hosts: Coerte & Marjorie Voorhies
338 N. Sterling
Lafayette, LA 70501
(337) 233-7816
Fax: (337) 233-7816
boisdchene@aol.com
ivillage.bbchannel.com or
members.aol.com/boisdchene/bois.htm

COUNTRY FRENCH BED & BREAKFAST, Lafayette

Overall: ★★★★ Room Quality: B Value: B Price: $115–$125

French antiques enthusiasts who adore old world European charm will feel like they're in seventh heaven at this elegant country French home on top of an antiques shop. Discreet private entrances through a jasmine-and-gardenia-scented courtyard lead to cozy suites adorned with authentic French antiques. Enjoy a European continental breakfast en suite at your leisure, but be sure to meet innkeeper and French antiques aficionado Jane Fleniken for a chat over evening hors d' oeuvres and her signature gumbo in the antiques shop.

Setting & Facilities

Location: I-40 to Evangeline Thruway to Taft St., right on General Mouton
Near: Acadian Village, Tabasco factory, Vermilionville
Building: Country French
Grounds: None
Public Space: None
Food & Drink: Cont'l plus w/ French pastries
Recreation: Walking trails, birdwatching
Amenities & Services: Lists of area attractions, restaurants

Accommodations

Units: 3 guest rooms
All Rooms: Furnished w/ antiques
Bed & Bath: Beds vary; private baths
Favorites: Downstairs room for couples
Comfort & Decor: European linens, tapestries, French paintings, and exquisite armoires are notable among the many treasures here.

Rates, Reservations, & Restrictions

Deposit: $50 check/money order
Discounts: None
Credit Cards: None
Check-in/Out: 3 p.m./11 a.m.
Smoking: No
Pets: No
Kids: 12 & older
Minimum Stay: None
Open: All year
Host: Jane Fleniken
616 General Mouton
Lafayette, LA 70501
(337) 234-2866

LA MAISON DE REPOS, Lafayette

Overall: ★★½	Room Quality: C	Value: B	Price: $65–$85

Mildred and Roland, a salt-of-the-earth farming couple, speak with a lilting Cajun French accent and capture the spirit of true Cajun hospitality and what bed-and-breakfasts are all about. The Doucet's six children grew up, left home, and emptied rooms. This warm couple shares fascinating life stories of growing up Cajun over cups of community coffee with fresh put-up preserves in the kitchen. Three spotlessly clean rooms, an off-the-main-studio with private entrance and patio, and two nicely decorated rooms are inside. Guests feel right at home staying with this delightful and friendly couple.

Setting & Facilities

Location: Exit 100 off I-10, south on Ambassador Caffery, right on Vincent Rd.
Near: Cajundome, Acadiana Mall, golf course
Building: Acadian style

Grounds: Large backyard
Public Space: Patio deck, family room w/ fireplace, bar
Food & Drink: Happy hour w/ mint juleps, Cajun hors d'oeuvres; Southern breakfast w/ Cajun specialties: spicy egg omelet in a croissant, jalapeño cornbread
Recreation: Walking, jogging
Amenities & Services: Disabled access, recommendations of area attractions, restaurants

Accommodations

Units: 3 guest rooms
All Rooms: Cable TV, dinette
Some Rooms: Private entrance, patio
Bed & Bath: Beds vary; 1 private bath, 2 share bath
Favorites: Damon's Room w/ private bath, entrance through carport, & patio
Comfort & Decor: Country French

Rates, Reservations, & Restrictions

Deposit: Credit card
Discounts: 3rd night free, 10% senior
Credit Cards: AE, V, MC, others
Check-in/Out: Noon/11 a.m.
Smoking: Yes; in restricted areas
Pets: No
Kids: Welcome
Minimum Stay: None
Open: All year
Hosts: Mildred & Roland Doucet
218 Vincent Rd.
Lafayette, LA 70508
(337) 856-6958
Fax: (337) 857-8113
mddoucet@aol.com

VICTORIA INN AND GARDENS, Lafitte

Overall: ★★★★ Room Quality: B Value: B Price: $89–$189

Playful Dalmatians greet guests at Dale and Roy's country home. Relax in a hammock, stroll the Shakespeare and rose gardens, or grab a tape from the VCR library. Head to the private dock for a charter fishing trip, hand trawl for shrimp on an authentic skiff, enjoy high tea in the gardens, get a massage, binge on fresh local seafood, or indulge in the in-suite Jacuzzi. Complimentary pedal boats and pirogues (canoes) are available for exploring. Meet Lafitte's locals and dance to the rhythms of accordions and washboards at the nightly Cajun Fais Do Do. However, don't miss breakfast. Dale creates an awesome Southern spread, set on fine china and linens.

Setting & Facilities

Location: 23 miles south of New Orleans, take Business 90 west from New Orleans to Exit 4B (Hwy. 45)
Near: Jean Lafitte Nat'l Park, New Orleans
Building: West Indies Plantation
Grounds: 9 acres of formal gardens, woodland, large lake
Public Space: DR w/ bar, double parlor

Food & Drink: Full breakfast; complimentary drink at check-in
Recreation: Walking trails, lake swimming, bird-watching, swamp tours, sea-plane tours, airboat tours, Cajun dancing
Amenities & Services: Robes, full concierge, newspaper, toiletries, paddle boats, pirogues

ACCOMMODATIONS

Units: 13 guest rooms
All Rooms: Garden view, ceiling fan, individual AC & temperature controls, cable TV
Some Rooms: Antiques, coffeemaker, private entrance, Jacuzzi, hair dryer, VCR
Bed & Bath: Single, double, or queen; private baths
Favorites: Suite w/ full LR, antiques, double Jacuzzi
Comfort & Decor: Cajun country antiques and a coastal Louisiana atmosphere

RATES, RESERVATIONS, & RESTRICTIONS

Deposit: Credit card; 14-day cancellation
Discounts: Summer packages
Credit Cards: V, MC, AE, D
Check-in/Out: 2–6 p.m./11 a.m.
Smoking: Outside only
Pets: No
Kids: Welcome
Minimum Stay: None, except during major events
Open: All year
Hosts: Roy & Dale Ross
Hwy 45, Box 0545
Lafitte, LA 70067
(800) 689-4797
Fax: (504) 689-3399
daler13@aol.com

MADEWOOD PLANTATION HOUSE, Napoleonville

Overall: ★★★★½ Room Quality: A Value: C Price: $225

This majestic Antebellum plantation offers elegant accommodations in a homey, relaxed atmosphere. Christine, who manages the inn, is originally from France and believes in highly personalized service, recommending swamp tours, restaurants, and Cajun attractions. Guests gather for a wine and cheese social in the evening, morning wakeup coffee is presented en suite on a silver tray and Wedgwood plates, and crystal glasses and candelabra grace the table at plantation breakfast. The house rule is that everything is to be used and that guests feel comfortable. Brad Pitt felt right at home here. So did Jennifer Jason Leigh and Cicely Tyson when they were being filmed in movies at Madewood. All fine linens from napkins to bed sheets are ironed. The atmosphere in the Charlet House is more informal than in the main house.

Setting & Facilities

Location: On Hwy. 308 off Spur 70 (45 mi. from Baton Rouge)
Near: Plantation homes, Donaldsonville
Building: 1846 21-room mansion
Grounds: 21 acres w/ brick patio
Public Space: Parlor, music room, library, ballroom
Food & Drink: Full breakfast; specialties: egg puff & baked cheese grits; candlelight dinner; breakfast & dinner included in rate; wine & cheese in library
Recreation: Golf, swamp tours, antiques shops
Amenities & Services: Conference facil. (100), French spoken

Accommodations

Units: 5 guest rooms in main house, 3 suites in Charlet House (1830 raised Greek Revival cottage)
All Rooms: Hardwood floors
Some Rooms: Fireplace
Bed & Bath: Queen or double; private baths
Favorites: Master BR w/ access to front balcony
Comfort & Decor: Garden-fresh flowers perfume the spacious chambers with elegant antiques, canopy beds, fireplaces, and balconies.

Rates, Reservations, & Restrictions

Deposit: Credit card
Discounts: None
Credit Cards: AE, V, MC, D
Check-in/Out: 3 p.m./10 a.m.
Smoking: No
Pets: No
Kids: Welcome
Minimum Stay: None
Open: All year except Thanksgiving, & Christmas & New Year's eves & days
Host: Christine Gauder
4250 Highway 308
Napoleonville, LA 70390
(504) 369-7151 or (800) 375-7151
Fax: (504) 369-9848
www.madewood.com

LA MAISON DU TECHE, New Iberia

Overall: ★★★ Room Quality: C Value: C Price: $85

This 100-year-old restored Victorian home is the only bed-and-breakfast overlooking the Bayou Teche. It is a short walk up the canopied live oak street to nearby historic homes, plantations, and restaurants. Guests can relax on the galley on swings and rocking chairs or watch television in the parlor. The informal rooms sport spacious hardwood floors, Victorian antiques, claw-foot tubs, and views of the bayou. Breakfast is served boarding house style, so guests can eat as little or as much as they want. New Iberia is as different from New Orleans as night and day, with the feeling of drifting back into another time. While it is usually not safe to generalize, the people here—guests and innkeepers—seem very friendly. Meeting a couple at dinner might lead to an invitation to visit their home.

Setting & Facilities

Location: Historic District of New Iberia
Near: Bayou Teche, Avery Island, Acadian Village
Building: 1892 Victorian Home
Grounds: Half-acre right on bayou
Public Space: Parlor
Food & Drink: Full breakfast; specialties: Cajun French toast w/ home-grown cane syrup or praline sauce, toasted apples, fresh Cajun sausage
Recreation: Sight-seeing, walking tours
Amenities & Services: Menus of local restaurants (3 Cajun restaurants w/in walking distance)

Accommodations

Units: 2 guest rooms, 1 suite (suite can be divided into 2 private rooms, each w/ bath)
All Rooms: Hardwood floors, Victorian furniture
Bed & Bath: Beds vary; private baths
Favorites: None
Comfort & Decor: House is like a fine piece of cypress furniture with handsome woodwork, including a hand-carved cypress staircase.

Rates, Reservations, & Restrictions

Deposit: 1 night
Discounts: None
Credit Cards: V, MC
Check-in/Out: 3 p.m./11 a.m.
Smoking: No
Pets: No
Kids: Welcome
Minimum Stay: None
Open: All year
Host: Mary Livandis
417 East Main St.
New Iberia, LA 70560
(318) 367-9456 or (800) 667-9456

LEROSIER COUNTRY INN, New Iberia

Overall: ★★★★ Room Quality: B Value: B Price: $95–$115

If you want to wake up to the smell of rose gardens and no traces of tobacco, you will appreciate this totally smoke-free property. Tucked behind perfumed rose gardens blooming in the spring and fall, tropical trees and baskets of flowers surround the raised Acadian cottage with subtle and stylish guest quarters. Rooms are accented in the English country style with modern bathrooms and amenities. Congenial innkeepers Mary Beth and Hallman—excuse us, that's Chef Hallman, one of the Discovery Channel's Great Chefs of the South, who creates rave-about Creole dishes in the restaurant—send happy guests off with a gourmet country breakfast. The inn faces the Shadow-on-the-Teche Plantation on what James Lee Burke describes as "one of the most beautiful streets in the old south." Avery Island, about nine miles away, is an interesting stop coming or going to LeRosier. That's the birthplace of Tabasco sauce and the home to Jungle Gardens and Bird City. You will find the tour interesting and even come home with some Tabasco sauce samples.

Setting & Facilities

Location: Historic downtown New Iberia
Near: Shadow-on-the-Teche (the South's best-known plantation home), city park w/ tennis courts, barbecue shelters
Building: 1870 inn
Grounds: Tropical vegetation
Public Space: Ginger-shaded patio, porches, 2 parlors
Food & Drink: Full country breakfast
Recreation: Tennis, sight-seeing, fishing
Amenities & Services: None

Accommodations

Units: 6 guest rooms
All Rooms: Color TV, phone, fridge
Some Rooms: Whirlpool tub, private outside sitting area
Bed & Bath: Kings; private baths
Favorites: None
Comfort & Decor: Many antiques

Rates, Reservations, & Restrictions

Deposit: 1 night
Discounts: None
Credit Cards: MC, AE
Check-in/Out: 3 p.m./11 a.m.
Smoking: No
Pets: No
Kids: 13 & older
Minimum Stay: None
Open: All year
Hosts: Hallman & Mary Beth Woods
314 E Main St.
New Iberia, LA 70560
(888) 804-7673
Fax: (337) 365-1216
www.lerosier.com

RIP VAN WINKLE GARDENS BED & BREAKFAST, New Iberia

Overall: ★★★★ Room Quality: B Value: C Price: $135–$175

Three cottages are nestled in 25 acres of semitropical paradise at the gardens of Rip Van Winkle. Imagine exploring romantic garden paths through a fragrant parade of magnolias, camellias, roses, and hibiscus; past formal fountains; aviaries of doves and love birds, peacocks, lily ponds; and Spanish moss–weeping oaks that line the banks of the enchanted lake. Absolute privacy. Rejuvenate, relax—the fridge is stocked with liqueurs, mint juleps, and continental morning treats. One may be inclined to hibernate like old Rip, but this hideaway also stirs many romantic thoughts—an ideal place for couples to celebrate a special occasion or the pleasures of doing nothing at all.

Setting & Facilities

Location: I-10 to Lafayette, Exit 103-A, Hwy. 167/90 to exit Hwy. 90 at Hwy. 675 (Jefferson Island Rd.), then south 6 mi.
Near: Joseph Jefferson Home, Shadows-on-the-Teche Plantation, Konriko Rice Mill, Tabasco factory
Building: Acadian-style Cook's cottage (1930), Servant's Quarters (1870)
Grounds: 25-acre garden
Public Space: None
Food & Drink: Cont'l w/ Danishes, croissants, yogurt
Recreation: Walking trails, bird-watching, nearby Cajun music
Amenities & Services: Access to lake & gardens

Accommodations

Units: 3 cottages
All Rooms: Garden & lake views, CD player, fresh flowers, hair dryer, phone, TV
Some Rooms: Whirlpool tub in Cook's Cottage
Bed & Bath: Beds vary; private baths
Favorites: None
Comfort & Decor: Suites are luxuriously appointed with French beds, fine sheets, down pillows, with a selection of sultry CDs and invigorating orange-scented aromatherapy products.

Rates, Reservations, & Restrictions

Deposit: 1st night; 48-hour cancellation
Discounts: None
Credit Cards: AE, V, MC, D
Check-in/Out: 3 p.m./11 a.m.
Smoking: No
Pets: No
Kids: Welcome
Minimum Stay: None
Open: All year
Host: Shereen Minvielle
5505 Rip Van Winkle Rd.
New Iberia, LA 70560
(337) 365-3332 or (800) 375-3332
Fax: (337) 365-3354
rvw@ripvanwinkle.com
www.ripvanwinkle.com

B&W COURTYARDS, New Orleans

Overall: ★★★½ Room Quality: B Value: C Price: $125–$235

It's quintessentially French Quarter. If you've ever wondered what is hidden beyond those French Quarter iron-gated courtyards, you'll experience it here. Behind the nondescript facade is a showcase of gurgling porcelain fountains, a jungle of tropical greenery, sculptures, lily pad ponds, and Balinese and Zen meditation spots. Beds draped in mosquito nets with sculptured headboards, exotic chandeliers, tapestry pillows, and hand-painted walls are tastefully incorporated into the small bedrooms in traditional carriage house quarters. With a flair for intriguing interiors, Rob and Kevin are the ultimate "Nawlins" hosts, sharing tips and secrets for exploring the quarter with guests at breakfast in the formal dining room.

Setting & Facilities

Location: 4 blocks from French Market in Faubourg Marigny
Near: Bourbon St., French Quarter, convention center, aquarium
Building: 1854 Creole compound w/ carriage house, main house, dependency
Grounds: Walled courtyards w/ fountains, hot tub
Public Space: Courtyard
Food & Drink: Cont'l plus w/ pastries, granola; complimentary sherry
Recreation: Sight-seeing, shopping
Amenities & Services: Personal guide by hosts: "Fun Things We Like to Do," avail. in each room, hot tub

Accommodations

Units: 4 guest rooms, 2 suites
All Rooms: Entrance onto courtyard, phone, cable TV, AC
Bed & Bath: Beds vary; private baths
Favorites: Back Carriage House near fountains
Comfort & Decor: Original artwork and 1850s architectural details

Rates, Reservations, & Restrictions

Deposit: 1st night
Discounts: 7 days or more
Credit Cards: AE, V, MC, D
Check-in/Out: By arrangement/ noon
Smoking: No
Pets: No
Kids: 12 & older
Minimum Stay: 3 nights on weekends
Open: All year
Hosts: Rob Boyd & Kevin Wu
2425 Chartes St.
New Orleans, LA 70117
(504) 945-9418 or (800) 585-5731
Fax: (504) 949-3483
faubourg@aol.com
www.bandwcourtyards.com

DEGAS HOUSE, New Orleans

Overall: ★★★½ Room Quality: B Value: C Price: $125–$200

Degas slept here. This unique bed-and-breakfast is the only place in the world where guests can stay at the family home of a renowned artist. Built in the early 1850s and owned by the Degas-Musson families, French Impressionist Edgar Degas lived and worked in-studio here, producing 22 works of art during his Louisiana period. Inspired by his surroundings, areas of the home are immortalized in paintings like "Portrait of a Woman Sitting on a Balcony." Guests staying in the spacious Estelle's Suite have exclusive access to the famous balcony. Four garret rooms, a French term for small low-rent attic rooms, popular with artists and musicians, are furnished with drawing easels, paper, and pastel chalks, where guests are often inspired to create their own artistic impressions.

Setting & Facilities

Location: I-10 to downtown New Orleans, exit City Park, left on City Park, left on Wisner Ave., right on Esplanade Ave.
Near: French Quarter
Building: 1854 Greek Revival
Grounds: Large courtyard w/ gardens
Public Space: Double parlors, breakfast room, art gallery, porch
Food & Drink: Cont'l plus weekdays; Creole breakfast weekends; sherry in room
Recreation: Sight-seeing, guided tours of house & neighborhood
Amenities & Services: Daily newspaper, guides to local restaurants & activities

Accommodations

Units: 5 guest rooms, 2 suites, 4 studios
All Rooms: Cable TV, phone w/ data port & voice mail, individual temperature control
Some Rooms: Private balcony, whirlpool tub, artist easels
Bed & Bath: Beds vary; private baths
Favorites: Main suite w/ private balcony
Comfort & Decor: More than 60 framed prints of Edgar Degas's paintings along with antiques

Rates, Reservations, & Restrictions

Deposit: 1st night at time of reservation, balance 21 days prior to arrival; less than 21 days, full payment due
Discounts: Seasonal, military, corp., airline
Credit Cards: V, MC
Check-in/Out: 3 p.m./noon
Smoking: No
Pets: No
Kids: Welcome, but space is limited
Minimum Stay: 2 nights on weekends, 4 nights during special events
Open: All year
Host: David Villarrubia
2306 Esplanade Ave.
New Orleans, LA 70119
(504) 821-5009 or (800) 755-6730
Fax: (504) 821-0870
degas@bellsouth.net

GRAND VICTORIAN BED & BREAKFAST, New Orleans

Overall: ★★★★½ Room Quality: A Value: C Price: $150–$300

In New Orleans, location is everything. On the St. Charles streetcar line, this 1897 Queen Anne Victorian fits right in with the famous mansions along the avenue of live oaks in the Garden District. Under the glow of a Strauss crystal chandelier, the parlor offers a warm welcome. Innkeeper Bonnie, a New Orleans local, fulfilled a lifelong dream to own a bed-and-breakfast and loves sharing her hometown with guests. And what a vision this place is—colorful stained-glass windows with transoms and unique beds (a Shadows rolling pin bed, half and full testers, and mahogany high-back burled woods) are the centerpieces of every room. It's not pretentious but intriguing and charming.

SETTING & FACILITIES

Location: I-10 to Exit 234, then exit to St. Charles Ave., right at St. Charles Ave.; in historic Garden District
Near: French Quarter, Superdome, convention center, Audubon Park, zoo, Tulane & Loyola Universities
Building: Queen Anne Victorian, circa 1893
Grounds: Residential
Public Space: Parlor, dining & serving rooms, port cochere balcony on second floor
Food & Drink: Cont'l breakfast
Recreation: Shopping, sight-seeing
Amenities & Services: Daily paper, many maps & brochures

ACCOMMODATIONS

Units: 6 guest rooms, 2 suites
All Rooms: Cable TV, toiletries, individual temperature control, armoire, hardwood floors, phone w/ data port & voice mail
Some Rooms: Suites have private balcony, Jacuzzi
Bed & Bath: 1 king, 1 queen, 6 plantation-size beds (between queen & full); private baths
Favorites: Greenwood Suite w/ balcony overlooking St. Charles Ave., large Jacuzzi, Mardi Gras stained-glass window, & king-size four-poster bed is spacious
Comfort & Decor: Comfortable period furnishings adorn all rooms.

RATES, RESERVATIONS, & RESTRICTIONS

Deposit: $150–$300, 1 night (balance due at check-in); cancellation refund info on request
Discounts: Limited corp. rates
Credit Cards: V, MC, AE, D
Check-in/Out: 3–6 p.m./11 a.m.
Smoking: Outside only
Pets: No
Kids: Children under 12 discouraged
Minimum Stay: 2 nights on weekends; various minimums for special events
Open: All year
Host: Bonnie Rabe
2727 St. Charles Ave.
New Orleans, LA 70130
(504) 895-1104
Fax: (504) 896-8688
brabe2727@aol.com

THE HOUSE ON BAYOU ROAD INN, New Orleans

Overall: ★★★★ Room Quality: B Value: C Price: $120–$295

Dan Ayckroyd loves this petite Creole indigo plantation, staying in the secluded cottages out back whenever he's in town on House of Blues business. Maybe it's those rubber ducks, which come with every bathtub. Delightful and enchanting, this inn has the feeling of the country in the city, just blocks from the French Quarter. It's the thoughtful touches—soft lighting, hand-painted tiles, fresh flowers, a decanter of sherry, tropical robes and slippers for wandering to the pool, hot tub, or porch—that stand out here. The pond, surrounded by tropical gardens, provokes a relaxing Caribbean-Creole ambience. The full plantation breakfast (Cynthia also runs a cooking school) is top-notch.

Setting & Facilities

Location: I-10 to Metairie Rd. exit, left on North Carrollton, right on Esplanade Ave., left on North Tonti, left on Bayou Rd.
Near: French Quarter, Garden District, New Orleans Museum of Art, aquarium, IMAX, riverboats, city park
Building: 1798 West Indies–style plantation home
Grounds: 2 acres, pool, patios, gazebo w/ Jacuzzi, tropical gardens
Public Space: DR, parlors, porches, deck, pool, Jacuzzi
Food & Drink: Full plantation-style breakfast w/ eggs Benedict; brunch on weekends; complimentary sherry
Recreation: Golf, tennis, canoeing, jogging
Amenities & Services: Robes, slippers, newspaper, local guidebooks, honor bar

Accommodations

Units: 8 guest rooms including 2 suites, private cottage
All Rooms: Toiletries
Some Rooms: Fireplace, Jacuzzi, private porch, sitting room, hardwood floors
Bed & Bath: 2 kings, 6 queens; private baths
Favorites: Private cottage w/ porch & rocking chairs, fireplace, Jacuzzi, wet bar, walk-in closet
Comfort & Decor: Antiques-filled rooms, cozy fireplaces

Rates, Reservations, & Restrictions

Deposit: 1 night; 10-day cancellation
Discounts: Week or longer
Credit Cards: V, MC, AE
Check-in/Out: Varies
Smoking: Outdoors only
Pets: No
Kids: 12 & older
Minimum Stay: 2 days
Open: All year
Host: Cynthia Reeves
2275 Bayou Rd.
New Orleans, LA 70119
(800) 882-2968
Fax: (504) 945-0993
hobr@aol.com

MANDEVILLA BED & BREAKFAST, New Orleans

Overall: ★★★★ Room Quality: B Value: B Price: $75–$350

Breakfast conversation here is often fascinating, as visiting professors or zoologists are repeat guests here, working at and visiting the two colleges and Audubon Zoo nearby. You may have seen the Mandevilla before. It's one of the most photographed houses on St. Charles Avenue, and the streetcar runs by the front door for guests headed to the French Quarter. Marnie and Allen are well-traveled, captivating conversationalists, and Allen's passion for historic restoration is showcased in every corner of the home. Porcelain sinks in antique sideboards, whirlpool tubs, an inviting parlor, and a library with an Italian marble fireplace create elegant yet comfortable surroundings. Balcony and patio rooms surround a courtyard lit by flickering, gas-burning lights accented by the rejuvenating sounds of trickling fountains. A pretty setting for a wedding, and they are held here frequently.

Setting & Facilities

Location: I-10 exit at St. Charles St.
Near: St. Charles St. Car, Audubon Park, zoo, Tulane & Loyola Universities
Building: 1850 Southern plantation
Grounds: Many gardens, croquet lawn, brick courtyard w/ antique fountain, stone patio w/ pond & waterfall
Public Space: LR, DR, library, den, porches
Food & Drink: Cont'l plus breakfast; complimentary evening cocktails; beverages throughout day
Recreation: Sight-seeing, golf, tennis, bike paths, sailing, canoeing, horseback riding
Amenities & Services: Business center

Accommodations

Units: 6 guest rooms
All Rooms: Spacious, period antiques, radio alarm clock, phone, cable TV
Some Rooms: Dbl. Jacuzzi, private porch
Bed & Bath: 1 extra-long king plus queen, doubles, 2 singles; private baths
Favorites: None
Comfort & Decor: Period antiques, crystal chandeliers, Italian marble mantles, Oriental rugs, and tiger stripe oak floors create an elegant atmosphere.

Rates, Reservations, & Restrictions

Deposit: Call
Discounts: AAA, AARP, VFW, weekly, corp.
Credit Cards: V, MC
Check-in/Out: Flexible
Smoking: Outdoors only
Pets: No
Kids: Welcome
Minimum Stay: None
Open: All year
Hosts: Marnie & Allen Borne
7716 St. Charles Ave.
New Orleans, LA 70118
(800) 288-0484
Fax: (504) 866-4104
mandevilla.bellsouth.net

MCKENDRICK-BREAUX HOUSE, New Orleans

Overall: ★★½ Room Quality: C Value: C Price: $110–$195

Paintings by local artists, fresh flowers, and antiques adorn the comfortable and unpretentious quarters in this home. Several rooms have been renovated with new paint, duvets, and curtains. Exceptional plaster moldings and medallions grace the parlor and dining area. Galleries overlook the courtyard, and a patio rich in tropical trees and plants give the place an authentic New Orleans feel. Into the local music scene? Host Eddie Breaux updates a board filled with events, knows where to find great musical talent in the city, and has a good library on local culture and attractions.

SETTING & FACILITIES

Location: Lower Garden District
Near: Convention center, Arts & Warehouse Districts, French Quarter
Building: 1865 Greek Revival
Grounds: Patio
Public Space: Parlor, DR, courtyard
Food & Drink: Cont'l plus breakfast; honor fridge w/ soda, juice, wine, beer
Recreation: Magazine St. shopping, sight-seeing, historic cemeteries
Amenities & Services: Limited off-street parking, daily newspaper

ACCOMMODATIONS

Units: 9 guest rooms
All Rooms: Antiques, family collectibles, artwork, phone w/ data port & voice mail, cable TV, ice, fresh flowers, AC & heat
Some Rooms: Door to courtyard, balcony
Bed & Bath: Beds vary; private baths
Favorites: None
Comfort & Decor: Light and open throughout the house

RATES, RESERVATIONS, & RESTRICTIONS

Deposit: 1 night
Discounts: None
Credit Cards: AE, V, MC
Check-in/Out: 2–6 p.m./11:30 a.m.
Smoking: No
Pets: No
Kids: Welcome
Minimum Stay: 2 nights on weekends
Open: All year
Host: Eddie Breaux
1474 Magazine St.
New Orleans, LA 70130
(504) 586-1700 or (888) 570-1700
Fax: (504) 522-7138
mckenbro@cmq.com
mckendrick-breaux.com

MELROSE MANSION, New Orleans

Overall: ★★★★½ Room Quality: A Value: C Price: $225–$425

If your tastes are similar to former guests like Lady Bird Johnson or perhaps the sultry jazz crooner Harry Connick Jr., this Victorian Gothic mansion offers the ultimate in decadent luxury and pampering. The concierge can arrange an evening jaunt by horse and buggy through the French Quarter or guests can walk, as it's just across the street. Indulge with a massage and aromatherapy treatments or treat yourself to a bottle of Chateau Lafitte Rothschild from the wine cellar before retiring to your ivory whirlpool tub or private balcony. The attention to every detail is on par with a stay at a grand hotel, but guests feel special here. Fresh flowers, fine linens, and elegant decor set a romantic mood. Cocktail hour features wine and hors d'oeuvres with your host. The host offers this suggestion to guests coming for New Year's Eve or Mardi Gras: "When you're traveling with a family or small group, always try to arrange for a central meeting place before you go out. It is so easy to get lost in the huge crowds in the French Quarter."

Setting & Facilities

Location: On Esplanade at Burgundy
Near: French Quarter
Building: 1884 Victorian Gothic mansion
Grounds: Patio
Public Space: Parlor w/ honor bar, heated pool in patio
Food & Drink: Cont'l breakfast; complimentary evening wine; mimosas on arrival
Recreation: Sight-seeing, jazz
Amenities & Services: Spa services avail. from manicures to massages, heated pool

Accommodations

Units: 9 guest rooms; 16 add'l rooms avail. at nearby B&Bs owned by same company
All Rooms: Terry robes, fresh flowers
Some Rooms: Marble whirlpool tub, private patio, wet bar, balcony overlooking French Quarter
Bed & Bath: Queen, twin, or king; private baths
Favorites: Donecio Suite w/ fabulous whirlpool tub
Comfort & Decor: Extremely elegant in the fashion of a grand European hotel.

Rates, Reservations, & Restrictions

Deposit: 50%; 30-day cancellation; full prepayment for Mardi Gras, Jazz Festival, & New Year's Eve periods
Discounts: None
Credit Cards: AE, V, MC
Check-in/Out: 3 p.m./noon
Smoking: No
Pets: "Prefer not to," which means they may, sometimes
Kids: Welcome
Minimum Stay: 3 nights on weekends, 5 nights during special events, e.g., Mardi Gras
Open: All year
Host: Sidney Torres
937 Esplanade Ave.
New Orleans, LA 70116
(504) 944-2255 or (800) 650-3323
Fax: (504) 945-1794
melrosemansion@worldnet.att.net
www.melrosemansion.com

BIENVENUE HOUSE BED & BREAKFAST, St. Martinville

Overall: ★★★★½ Room Quality: A Value: B Price: $90–$115

At Leslie's home, guests get a warm and friendly Cajun welcome. This Antebellum abode is a showcase of the cultures of Bayou country with artistic and elegant theme rooms. In the Evangeline room, the rustic decor depicts the lifestyles of Acadians exiled from Nova Scotia who settled along the banks of the Bayou Teche. Echoes of Tara and Southern grandeur are embodied in Scarlett's Room, while Josephine's Room is accented in the flamboyant style of the aristocratic French. Leslie will draw maps for a boudin (the famous Cajun sausage) tasting tour. She knows all the little grocery stores in the area that carry these local treats for about a dollar. She also offers Civil War mystery weekends where guests dress in costumes, ride in carriages, and play out a mystery written for the house. Lagniappe, Cajun for a little something extra, includes wake-up coffee and newspapers, a basket of take-home goodies, and a Cajun gourmet breakfast.

SETTING & FACILITIES

Location: From I-10 at Breaux Bridge, south on Rees St. to Bridge St., right on Hwy. 31, 12 mi. on left
Near: Evangeline Oak, Bayou Teche, Cajun Country, Le Petit Paris Museum
Building: Greek Revival
Grounds: Yard & garden w/ swings
Public Space: Parlor, DR, porches
Food & Drink: Full gourmet breakfast w/ 9 menus; specialty: Bienvenue eggs Benedict w/ tasso
Recreation: Swamp tours, biking, hiking, canoeing, backpacking, walking track, dancing
Amenities & Services: Newspaper, local maps of attractions for any taste

Accommodations

Units: 5 guest rooms
All Rooms: AC, spacious
Some Rooms: Balcony, canopy bed, fireplace
Bed & Bath: 3 queens, 2 fulls; private baths
Favorites: Room w/ private balcony
Comfort & Decor: Interesting mixture of classic and Acadian styles; each room has a unique ambience.

Rates, Reservations, & Restrictions

Deposit: Credit card; 7-day cancellation
Discounts: Senior, extended stay, corp.
Credit Cards: V, MC, AE
Check-in/Out: 4:30 p.m./11 a.m.
Smoking: Outside only
Pets: No
Kids: 15 & older
Minimum Stay: None
Open: All Year
Host: Leslie Leonpacher
421 N. Main St.
St. Martinville, Louisiana 70582
(888) 394-9100
Fax: (337) 394-9100
bienvenue@mindspring.com
www.bienvenuehouse.com

OAK ALLEY PLANTATION, Vacherie

Overall: ★★★½ Room Quality: B Value: C Price: $95–$125

On the grounds of the Antebellum Oak Alley Plantation, with its impressive avenue of 350-year-old live oaks, are five turn-of-the-century Creole cottages for guests. The cottages are private and comfortably furnished, but it's the grounds that are most impressive here. Stroll through the live oak promenade to watch barges and traffic on Old Man River. When the plantation bell tolls, guests may want to get tickets to tour the mansion with an Antebellum-dressed guide. Day-trip to nearby plantations like Laura Plantation, where folk tales of West African slaves were published as the *Tales of Brer Rabbit and Brer Fox.* There are no telephones or televisions in the cottages, but an emergency pay phone is available at the gift shop. The attendants leave at 10 p.m., so try to arrive before nightfall and get directions for area restaurants or you're on your own.

Setting & Facilities

Location: I-10 to Gramery Exit 194 across river, left on Hwy. 18 (River Rd.)
Near: Other plantation homes, swamp tours, Cajun restaurants
Building: Turn-of-the-century Creole cottages

Grounds: Plantation
Public Space: Restaurant/patio area
Food & Drink: Full Southern breakfast (served in on-site restaurant)
Recreation: Touring, shopping
Amenities & Services: Weddings (250) w/ bridal consultant, gift shop, masion tours

Accommodations

Units: 3 individual cottages, 2 units in 1 cottage w/ shared porch
All Rooms: Coffeemaker, microwave, sitting area
Some Rooms: Antique brass bed, full kitchen
Bed & Bath: Beds vary; private baths
Favorites: Cottage #6 w/ enclosed sun porch
Comfort & Decor: Country ambience

Rates, Reservations, & Restrictions

Deposit: Amount of full reservation
Discounts: None
Credit Cards: AE, V, MC
Check-in/Out: 2 p.m./11 a.m.
Smoking: No
Pets: No
Kids: Welcome
Minimum Stay: None
Open: All year; restaurant closed for breakfast during Mardi Gras, Christmas, Thanksgiving, New Year's
Hosts: Staff

3645 Highway 18
Vacherie, LA 70090
(800) 442-5539
Fax: (225) 265-2626
oakalleyplantation@att.net
www.oakalleyplantation.com

Zone 18
Northern Louisiana

The American Indians used a red stick as a boundary marker between two tribes. When the literal French arrived in the area, they immediately dubbed it Baton Rouge. Not having any sticks handy, we have arbitrarily assigned Baton Rouge, the state capital, to the northern zone, because our Interstate 20 marker divides the city in half. One of the best places for kids in town is the Old Arsenal Museum. What kid wouldn't like to play inside a powder keg!

Do you remember the movie *Steel Magnolias* with Julia Roberts, Sally Fields, and Dolly Parton? Some of it was shot in Natchitoches (a jaw-breaker that is pronounced NAK-a-tish). There are many large lakes and national and state forests in the northern part of Louisiana, affording many opportunities for outdoor recreation including fishing and boating. Black Lake near Shreveport is reportedly filled with hungry bass. You will also find some of the largest wildlife sanctuaries in the world in the north. It is also a bird-watcher's paradise, home to millions of migratory birds switching between northern and southern climes with the seasons.

For More Information

Baton Rouge Convention and Visitors Bureau
(800) 527-6843

National Forest Information
(318) 473-7160

OLD CENTENARY INN, Jackson

Overall: ★★★½ Room Quality: B Value: B Price: $55–$150

Two elegant fantasy suites with unbelievable beds are the highlights of this romantic property. In the Rhett Butler room, guests sleep on an old surrey transformed into a step-up bed, complete with fringe on top. Not to be outdone, the Harvey Couch suite features a stunning oak sleigh bed on train wheels placed on standard gauge tracks. Step back in time in this charming white-column home with an antique elevator, mirrored bar with a stained-glass canopy, and a colonial fountain courtyard. Enjoy wine from the local winery, homemade pâté, cheeses, fresh baked cookies, mint juleps, and a full country breakfast. Pat can arrange a private candlelight dinner on the balcony or in the courtyard on request. Tour the winery, visit antiques shops, ride a train through the rolling countryside, or play golf at the nearby Arnold Palmer golf course. Note to lead-footers: If you're on Louisiana 10 coming into town, watch those speed signs. The speed limit drops precipitously from 55 and, according to a local resident, the police in this area love to give tickets.

SETTING & FACILITIES

Location: US 61 North toward St. Francisville, then east on Hwy. 68, left on Hwy. 10
Near: Pelicans Cellar Winery, plantations, antiques shops
Building: Colonial
Grounds: Courtyard w/ fountain, patio
Public Space: Lobby, bar, balconies w/ rockers
Food & Drink: Full breakfast; wine & cheese or mint julep in afternoon
Recreation: Arnold Palmer golf course, hiking/walking tours
Amenities & Services: Candlelight dinners arranged for guests

ACCOMMODATIONS

Units: 8 guest rooms
All Rooms: VCR, TV, Jacuzzi
Some Rooms: Suites have private balcony
Bed & Bath: King, queen, or twins; private baths
Favorites: Rhett Butler Room
Comfort & Decor: Period antiques and decor

RATES, RESERVATIONS, & RESTRICTIONS

Deposit: Credit card, 1 night
Discounts: None
Credit Cards: AE, V, MC
Check-in/Out: 3 p.m./11 a.m.
Smoking: No
Pets: No
Kids: Ask
Minimum Stay: None
Open: All year
Host: Pat Tolle
1740 Charter
Jackson, LA 70748
(225) 634-5050
Fax: (225) 634-5151

LEVY-EAST HOUSE BED & BREAKFAST INN, Natchitoches

Overall: ★★★★½ Room Quality: B Value: C Price: $85–$200

Guests are sipping coffee on the second-floor iron-lace balcony overlooking the Cane River Lake as wonderful smells waft up from the kitchen. Silver candelabra, fresh flowers, and Royal Albert china grace the dining room table as heart-shaped eggs, scones, sweetbreads, and cheese grits arrive from the kitchen. Elegant Victorian period antiques and heirlooms accent the queen-bed rooms with whirlpool tub. Guest rooms are on the second floor with a private entrance. The home is in the heart of downtown Natchitoches with its many historic homes and antiques and craft shops.

SETTING & FACILITIES

Location: I-49 to Exit 138, left on Jefferson St.
Near: Cane River Lake & plantation, Kisatchie Nat'l Forest, Bayou Pierre Gator Park & Show
Building: Greek Revival, circa 1838
Grounds: Yard & garden area bordering bayou amulet
Public Space: Parlor, DR, sitting area, balcony, front & back porches
Food & Drink: Full gourmet breakfast; wine on arrival
Recreation: Riverboat & trolley tours, golf, tennis, *Steel Magnolias* walking tour
Amenities & Services: Guidebooks to local attractions & restaurants, complimentary bottle of champagne for honeymooners and anniversary couples, turn-down w/ chocolates

ACCOMMODATIONS

Units: 4 guest rooms
All Rooms: TV w/VCR, carpet, ceiling fan, piped-in music, AC & heat, phone
Some Rooms: Antiques & wicker furniture
Bed & Bath: Queens; private baths

Favorites: Honeymoon Suite w/ wedding dress on a dress form & other wedding memorabilia
Comfort & Decor: Designer fabrics, heirlooms, exquisite window treatments, and antiques that have been in the house for over 100 years

Rates, Reservations, & Restrictions

Deposit: Credit card; 7-day cancellation
Discounts: Call for details
Credit Cards: V, MC, AE
Check-in/Out: 4 p.m./10 a.m.
Smoking: Outdoors only
Pets: No
Kids: No
Minimum Stay: Varies by season
Open: All year except Christmas week
Hosts: Judy & Avery East
358 Jefferson St.
Natchitoches, LA 71457
(800) 840-0662
Fax: (318) 356-5582
levy/cast@wnonline.com

BUTLER GREENWOOD PLANTATION, St. Francisville

Overall: ★★★★ Room Quality: B Value: B Price: $110–$160

Six unique and distinctive cottages grace the grounds of the Butler Plantation. The Dovecote is a romantic, three-story cottage resembling a windmill with a mahogany king bed, designer linens, double Jacuzzi, and a wood-burning fireplace. The nine-foot stained-glass church windows make the Gazebo cottage something special. Multitalented innkeeper Ann Butler is the author of ten books, including the Little Chase storybooks for children. She includes a tour of her home, which has been in her family since the 1790s. Ann can make reservations for a guided nature walk or ballooning, or guests can explore the extensive grounds of live oak trees and Antebellum gardens or bird-watch on their own. This bird-rich region was the inspiration for many of artist John James Audubon's famous bird and habitat portraits. On request, a resident family member who is a local historian-author will take you on a personal tour of the main house—worth asking for!

Setting & Facilities

Location: 2.5 mi. north of St. Francisville on Great River Rd.
Near: English plantation country w/ 7 historic plantations
Building: 1790 Antebellum home w/ Victorian trim added
Grounds: 2,200-acre plantation w/ 45 acres forming lawns & gardens
Public Space: Pool pavilion, decks, porches
Food & Drink: Cont'l plus breakfast in each individual kitchen
Recreation: Swimming, bird-watching, guided nature walks, hot-air ballooning by reservation, horseback riding
Amenities & Services: Swimming pool & pool pavilion w/ TV & rest rooms; tour of plantation

ACCOMMODATIONS

Units: 6 cottages
All Rooms: Partial or full kitchen, porch, ceiling fan
Some Rooms: Fireplace, pond or wooded ravine views
Bed & Bath: Beds vary; private baths
Favorites: Dovecote cottage w/ 2-level deck, working fireplace, barbecue grill on deck
Comfort & Decor: Mixture of antiques and comfortable furniture; antique stained-glass windows

RATES, RESERVATIONS, & RESTRICTIONS

Deposit: Credit card
Discounts: Stays of 1 month or longer, 10%
Credit Cards: AE, V, MC
Check-in/Out: 2 p.m./10:30 a.m.
Smoking: Limited; ask
Pets: Yes, "if not disturbing to other guests"
Kids: Welcome
Minimum Stay: None
Open: All year
Host: Ann Butler
8345 US 61
St. Francisville, LA 70775
(225) 635-6312
Fax: (225) 635-6370
ButlerGree@aol.com
www.butlergreenwood.com

GREEN SPRINGS BED & BREAKFAST, St. Francisville

Overall: ★★★ Room Quality: B Value: C Price: $110–$175

Nestled in the scenic area of the rolling Tunica Hills, this country inn overlooks cattle pastures and an ancient Indian mound. The plantation-style home, built in 1991, has over 150 forested acres of dogwoods, oaks, and magnolias, with plant trails and places to hike and ride bicycles or do a little bird-watching. Several restored Louisiana shotgun houses, some pastel-colored cottages with wonderful front porches and others with rustic cabin exteriors, are surrounded by nature. King beds, whirlpool tubs and heart-shaped Jacuzzis, fireplaces, quaint kitchenettes, and antiques grace the spacious interiors. There are three bedrooms in the main house, one with a suite for families. Save some time for a hike over the hillside trails with views of an ancient Indian Mound, Big Bayou Sara Creek, or to a natural spring in the valley. If you don't feel like walking, there's a golf cart to ride.

SETTING & FACILITIES

Location: LA 66, 3 mi. north of St. Francisville
Near: Plantation country, Tunica Hills Nature Area, Cat Island swamp preserve, Mississippi River ferry, Louisiana State University campus, Port Hudson Civil War battlefield
Building: Louisiana bluffland style
Grounds: 150 hillside acres
Public Space: Gathering room, porches

Food & Drink: Hot country breakfast w/ scrambled eggs, homemade biscuits, pear preserves
Recreation: Tours of historic homes & churches, hiking & biking trails, birdwatching
Amenities & Services: Maps, local restaurant menus

Accommodations

Units: 3 guest rooms, 6 cottages
All Rooms: Antiques, forest views
Some Rooms: Fireplace, hardwood floors, daybed for extra guests
Bed & Bath: Beds vary; private baths; all cottages w/ whirlpool tubs
Favorites: Woodrose, Honeysuckle, Persimmon Cottages w/ decks overlooking woods
Comfort & Decor: Antique furnishings and museum prints of Audubon and Georgia O'Keeffe on walls

Rates, Reservations, & Restrictions

Deposit: Credit card; 48-hour cancellation
Discounts: Long stays, singles
Credit Cards: AE, V, MC
Check-in/Out: 3–5 p.m./11 a.m.
Smoking: No
Pets: Small pets w/ advance notice
Kids: Welcome w/ advance notice
Minimum Stay: None
Open: All year
Host: Madeline Nevill
7463 Tunica Trace
St. Francisville, LA 77057
(225) 635-4232 or (800) 457-4978
Fax: (225) 635-3355

HEMINGBROUGH, St. Francisville

Overall: ★★★★ Room Quality: B Value: C Price: $90–$110

This secluded hideaway isn't the typical bed-and-breakfast experience, but more of a private and romantic retreat. The guesthouse is discreetly tucked into a wooded area surrounded by ponds and fountains, manicured lawns with roving albino peacocks, rose gardens, Greek statues, and a gazebo. Hemingbough is a conference and convention center and holds summer symphonies, opera, and popular entertainment events in a Roman amphitheater overlooking Audubon Lake. Although the guesthouse is away from the events, if you want privacy it's best to check the events schedule before booking and avoid big gatherings. One surprise in relatively flat Louisiana: The parklike acres are on rolling hills with ravines. Don't miss the gardens and statuary.

Setting & Facilities

Location: US 61, left on Hwy. 965
Near: Plantation homes, Baton Rouge
Building: Replica of a famous plantation that was destroyed to build a levee in 1955
Grounds: 235 acres filled w/ statues, gardens, new museum (under construction)

Public Space: All parklike facilities
Food & Drink: Cont'l breakfast
Recreation: Walking, hiking, plantation sight-seeing
Amenities & Services: Guide to local restaurants, attractions

ACCOMMODATIONS

Units: 8 guest rooms in main house, 2 suites in guest house
All Rooms: TV, phone, VCR, coffee pot
Some Rooms: Private entrance
Bed & Bath: Beds vary; private baths
Favorites: None
Comfort & Decor: Rooms are charmingly furnished with gilded mirrors, canopy beds, and antiques; turn-of-the-century ambience.

RATES, RESERVATIONS, & RESTRICTIONS

Deposit: Credit card; 1 night; 7-day cancellation
Discounts: AAA, AARP weeknights
Credit Cards: AE, V, MC
Check-in/Out: 2 p.m./11 a.m.
Smoking: No
Pets: Sometimes; ask
Kids: Welcome
Minimum Stay: None
Open: All year
Host: Johnny Rhea Bennet
P.O. Box 1640
St. Francisville, LA 70775
(225) 635-6617
Fax: (225) 635-3800

LAKE ROSEMOUND INN, St. Francisville

Overall: ★★★ Room Quality: B Value: C Price: $75–$125

Surrounded by picturesque Lake Rosemound, this is a relaxing stopover north of St. Francisville on the way to historic Natchez, Mississippi. In the clubhouse parlor guests help themselves to complimentary sundaes and heaping cones at the old-fashioned ice cream bar and enjoy games of Ping-Pong, darts, or pool. In the great outdoors, Jeanne keeps her guests busy with canoes, a paddleboat, fishing gear, horseshoes, and croquet. Good for families with road-weary kids and ideal for reunions with the use of the clubhouse's full kitchen and gas grill. The modern Felicianna Suite has a huge bathroom, Jacuzzi, and adjoining room for children with its own TV. A home-cooked, country breakfast is served upstairs in Jeanne's quarters.

SETTING & FACILITIES

Location: 13 mi. north of St. Francisville
Near: Many plantation homes, Lake Rosemound, Rosemont Plantation (Jefferson Davis's home)
Building: Greek Revival
Grounds: 190-acre private lake
Public Space: Clubhouse parlor, lake
Food & Drink: Full country breakfast
Recreation: Fishing, canoeing, croquet, paddleboats
Amenities & Services: TV, stereo, dart boards, pool table, help-yourself ice cream bar

Accommodations

Units: 4 guest rooms
All Rooms: Lake view, TV, AC
Some Rooms: Fireplace
Bed & Bath: King or queen; private baths
Favorites: Rosemound Suite w/ king bed, fireplace, dbl. whirlpool tub
Comfort & Decor: Very comfortable furnishings

Rates, Reservations, & Restrictions

Deposit: Credit card
Discounts: None
Credit Cards: AE, V, MC, D
Check-in/Out: 3 p.m./noon
Smoking: No
Pets: Yes
Kids: Welcome
Minimum Stay: None
Open: All year
Hosts: Jeanne Peters & Jon Peters (her son)
10473 Lindsey Lane
St. Francisville, LA 70775
(225) 635-3176
Fax: (225) 635-2224
www.virtualcities.com/ons

MYRTLES PLANTATION, St. Francisville

Overall: ★★★½ Room Quality: B Value: C Price: $99–$195

Many guests stay at the Myrtles because it's supposedly the most haunted house in the South. Judging from a drawer full of photographs taken by guests with strange apparitions and ghostly images and letters of eyewitness accounts, it could be true. After purchasing the house in 1990, John and Teeta have recently moved off-property. Could it be confessions of frightened guests who've been shaken awake in their beds and enveloped in a claustrophobic mist or heavy beds and furniture mysteriously rearranged, which caused them to move from the main house? The gift shop girls, Hester and Fern, take care of all the guests' needs.

Setting & Facilities

Location: US 61 in St. Fransville
Near: Baton Rouge, Natchez, nature preserves, historic plantations
Building: Plantation home on Nat'l Historical Register
Grounds: Spacious w/ live oak trees, crepe myrtles, camellias
Public Space: 3,000-sq.-ft. old brick courtyard, veranda
Food & Drink: Cont'l breakfast w/ biscuits, sweet rolls
Recreation: Golf, biking, hiking, ghost hunting (really!)
Amenities & Services: Maps, guides, restaurant menus, local magazines

Accommodations

Units: 11 guest rooms
All Rooms: Period furnishings
Some Rooms: Hand-hewn four-poster bed, disabled access
Bed & Bath: Beds vary; private baths

Favorites: None
Comfort & Decor: Chandeliers, tester and four-poster beds, claw-foot tubs, and period antiques grace the rooms of the main house and give it an old plantation ambience. Additional rooms in the carriage house have modern, motel-like furnishings.

Rates, Reservations, & Restrictions

Deposit: Credit card; 2-week cancellation
Discounts: 4 days or more
Credit Cards: V, AE, MC
Check-in/Out: 2 p.m./11 a.m.
Smoking: No, in courtyard only
Pets: No; local vets offer boarding
Kids: Welcome
Minimum Stay: None
Open: All year
Hosts: John, Teeta, Hester, or Fern Marsh
7747 US 61
St. Francisville, LA 70775
(225) 635-6277 or (800) 809-0565
Fax: (225) 635-5837

SHADETREE INN, St. Francisville

Overall: ★★★★½ Room Quality: B Value: C Price: $99–$195

The smell of freshly baked pecan cookies wafts in from the kitchen. The Shadetree cat, everyone's new best friend, sleeps on the porch despite the tolling church bells. A silver filigree martini shaker, a fifth of gin and vermouth, pecan cheese spread under glass, and warm cookies await arriving guests. "Guests request favorite cocktails when booking and everyone is greeted by their first names," Gloria explains. Purely magical . . . a bathroom is washed in thousands of tiny rainbows when the sun strikes a crystal hanging from the skylight. An oversized Jacuzzi surrounded in scented candles and enticing bath salts, stained-glass windows, and cathedral ceilings breathe romance. Swing on a rope like a kid, borrow a bike to explore historic St. Francisville, or watch butterflies. It's addictive, and most guests return to recapture the magic.

Setting & Facilities

Location: US 61, left on Hwy. 10
Near: Bluff's Golf Course, Port Hudson State Park, historical homes
Building: Rustic pre–Civil War cottage
Grounds: 3-acre hilltop (half wooded)
Public Space: None
Food & Drink: Cont'l plus breakfast
Recreation: Bird-watching, walking, biking, shopping
Amenities & Services: Guest-recommended restaurant & activities guide, books, magazines, toiletries, bikes avail.

Accommodations

Units: 3 guest rooms
All Rooms: Private outdoor area, fridge, toaster, coffeemaker, microwave, phone, cable TV, candles, fresh flowers
Some Rooms: Jacuzzi
Bed & Bath: Kings; private baths
Favorites: Gardener's Cottage w/ Jacuzzi for 2, VCR w/ selection of movies
Comfort & Decor: Rustic twig furniture, rough-heart cypress walls and ceilings, skylights, and stained-glass windows are highlights.

Rates, Reservations, & Restrictions

Deposit: Credit card; 14-day cancellation
Discounts: Corp., weekdays
Credit Cards: V, MC, D
Check-in/Out: 3 p.m./noon
Smoking: No
Pets: By special permission
Kids: No small children
Minimum Stay: None
Open: All year
Host: K. W. Kennon
9407 Royal (P.O. Box 1818)
St. Francisville, LA 70775
(225) 635-6116
Fax: (225) 635-0072
shadetreein@bsf.net

ST. FRANCISVILLE INN, St. Francisville

Overall: ★★ | Room Quality: D | Value: A | Price: $55–$75

In the center of downtown, this 1880 Victorian gingerbread-trimmed Gothic home rests under 100-year-old moss-draped live oak trees. Patrick and Laurie are hands-on innkeepers who run the gift shop, coffee house, and meet their overnight guests. The extensive buffet breakfast, with everything from crêpes and quiche to French specialties, is the best in St. Francisville, as are the room rates. Some furnishings are worn, but renovations are ongoing. Champagne is arranged for honeymooners, who love the new whirlpool tub suite. The historic district features a wealth of interesting old homes.

Setting & Facilities

Location: Left off US 61 to Commerce St.
Near: Walking distance of historic district, plantation homes
Building: 1880 Victorian Gothic
Grounds: Courtyard
Public Space: TV room, front porch
Food & Drink: Buffet breakfast w/ egg crêpes, alligator sausage, quiche, bananas Foster, Caribbean potatoes
Recreation: Sight-seeing
Amenities & Services: Swimming pool, local newspaper, maps, restaurant menus

Accommodations

Units: 10 guest rooms
All Rooms: Antiques, country-style furnishings
Some Rooms: Whirlpool tub
Bed & Bath: Beds vary; private baths
Favorites: None
Comfort & Decor: Each of the spacious rooms with four-poster beds overlooks the New Orleans–style courtyard and swimming pool.

Rates, Reservations, & Restrictions

Deposit: Credit card
Discounts: None
Credit Cards: AE, MC, V, D, DC
Check-in/Out: Noon/11 a.m.
Smoking: No
Pets: No
Kids: Welcome; 6 & under stay free in parent's room
Minimum Stay: None
Open: All year except Christmas Eve & Day
Hosts: Patrick & Laurie Walsh
5720 Commerce St.
St. Francisville, LA 70775
(225) 635-6502 or (800) 488-6502
Fax: (225) 635-6421
wolfsinn@aol.com

CHRETIEN POINT PLANTATION, Sunset

Overall: ★★★★½ Room Quality: B Value: B Price: $110–$225

Unlike some plantation-on-tour homes, there is no early check-out or hiding of belongings when the public comes calling. Always the pampered guest, you can enjoy an afternoon nap and keep your room off the tour. After 5 p.m., the 20-acre oak-covered grounds and mansion are exclusively for overnight guests, as the on-site host plies you with frosty mint juleps on the porch rockers. During the Civil War, this plantation was spared by the Yankees because of the exchange of a Masonic Order sign between the owner and a Yankee officer, as 20,000 troops fought on the grounds. The first lady of the house, an eccentric belle, was friends with the notorious pirate Lafite, smoked cigars, and hosted parlor poker games—she even shot a Yankee intruder on the steps, just like Scarlett.

Setting & Facilities

Location: 15 mi. north of Lafayette
Near: Lafayette, Opelousas, Grand Coteau
Building: 1831 French Colonial
Grounds: 20 acres of lawns, gardens, woods
Public Space: Upstairs & downstairs porches, parlor, family room, formal DR
Food & Drink: Full breakfast w/ fresh cheese & garlic grits, fritatta, Anna Maria pancakes, sausages, scones, homemade biscuits (menu varies)
Recreation: Swimming, tennis, walking
Amenities & Services: Guides for attractions, restaurant menus, free phone

Accommodations

Units: 5 guest rooms
All Rooms: Beautiful antiques, some original to the 1830s
Some Rooms: Fireplace, private entrance from downstairs, view of pool & garden, Jacuzzi
Bed & Bath: 1 king, 2 queens, 2 fulls; private baths
Favorites: Prime Minister's suite—huge bath w/ Jacuzzi, largest room, fireplace, & four-poster canopy queen bed
Comfort & Decor: Beautiful antiques throughout the house

Rates, Reservations, & Restrictions

Deposit: Credit card
Discounts: Subject to manager's approval
Credit Cards: AE, MC, V, D
Check-in/Out: 2 p.m./noon
Smoking: On porches only
Pets: No
Kids: Very welcome
Minimum Stay: 2 days during festivals
Open: All year
Hosts: Yogi Bahm & others
665 Chretien Point Rd.
Sunset, LA 70584
(800) 880-7050
Fax: (318) 662-5876
chretienpt@aol.com
www.bbchannel.com

LA CABOOSE BED & BREAKFAST, Sunset

Overall: ★★ Room Quality: D Value: B Price: $75–$95

Railroad buffs are in for a treat at this unique bed-and-breakfast. All the comforts of home—a kitchen, intimate breakfast nook, and bedroom—are integrated into the original facades of a red caboose, an 1800s mail/passenger car, a 1904 train depot, and a railroad ticket office. Wild herb patches, fairy gardens, flowering flora, and fruit orchards attract cardinals, Louisiana ibis, entertaining raccoons, wild rabbits, and special fairies to the idyllic surroundings. The fruits and herbs are for innkeeper Margaret's organic jams and preserves, sold at the gift shop.

Setting & Facilities

Location: Take LA 93, right on LA 18, left on Budd St.
Near: Within 30 minutes of 2 historic towns
Building: Railroad theme
Grounds: None
Public Space: None
Food & Drink: Home-baked bread, midnight snack of buttermilk cake & milk
Recreation: Cajun music, swamp tour, nature preserves
Amenities & Services: Gift shop

Accommodations

Units: 4 guest rooms
All Rooms: Kitchen, sitting area
Some Rooms: Private garage, clawfoot tub
Bed & Bath: Beds vary; private baths
Favorites: Mail Passenger Car, spacious w/ gardens & pond
Comfort & Decor: Oil paintings and railroad theme

Rates, Reservations, & Restrictions

Deposit: Credit card
Discounts: Singles
Credit Cards: MC, D
Check-in/Out: Noon/11 a.m.
Smoking: On porches only
Pets: No
Kids: No
Minimum Stay: 2 nights (preferred)
Open: All year
Hosts: Margaret & Armand Brinkhaus
145 S. Budd St.
Sunset, LA 70584
(318) 662-5401
Fax: (318) 662-5813
www.bbchannel.com

Tennessee

Tennessee touches a surprisingly large number of states—Kentucky, Virginia, North Carolina, Georgia, Alabama, Mississippi, Arkansas, and Missouri—and shares some of the geographic features and climate of them all. On the eastern side the Great Smoky Mountains soar into the sky, star attractions of the most visited national park in America. The largest portion of the state is a low plateau with rolling hills, and there is a swamp and flood plain on the extreme western part. All of this creates a kaleidoscope weather map with changes that range from subtropical Mississippi weather to frigid Kentucky winter weather.

Nashville is the capital of the state and of country music, with the Grand Ole Opry, Music Row, and, more recently, new sports teams. There is a wide variety of large and small cities throughout the state.

Those ubiquitous Spanish explorers were again the first Europeans to see this part of the New World in 1541. Much later English settlers became fascinated with the Smoky Mountains. France also sent explorers, edging the territory along the Mississippi River. But it was the Virginians who claimed the prize with the first permanent settlement on the Watauga River. Tennessee left the Union in 1861, but its population was deeply divided between sentiments for the North and South and sent soldiers to both sides.

Here's our must-see (and do) list for Tennessee: a Grand Ole Opry performance, the Hermitage (Andrew Jackson's home), country music theaters in Pigeon Forge, the Parthenon, Graceland (Elvis Presley's home in Memphis), the Tennessee Aquarium in Chattanooga, and the Casey Jones Home & Museum in Jackson. And this will only get you started.

For More Information

Tennessee Department of Tourist Information
(800) 836-6200

Bureau of State Parks
(888) 867-2757

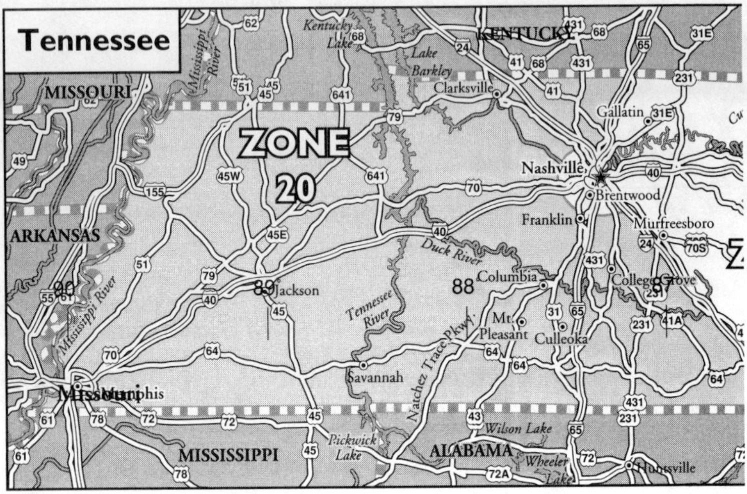
Tennessee
ZONE 20
MISSOURI
KENTUCKY
ARKANSAS
MISSISSIPPI
ALABAMA
Mississippi River
Kentucky Lake
Lake Barkley
Clarksville
Gallatin
Nashville
Brentwood
Franklin
Murfreesboro
Duck River
Columbia
College Grove
Jackson
Tennessee River
Mt. Pleasant
Culleoka
Savannah
Natchez Trace Pkwy.
Memphis
Wilson Lake
Pickwick Lake
Wheeler Lake
Huntsville
88
89
90

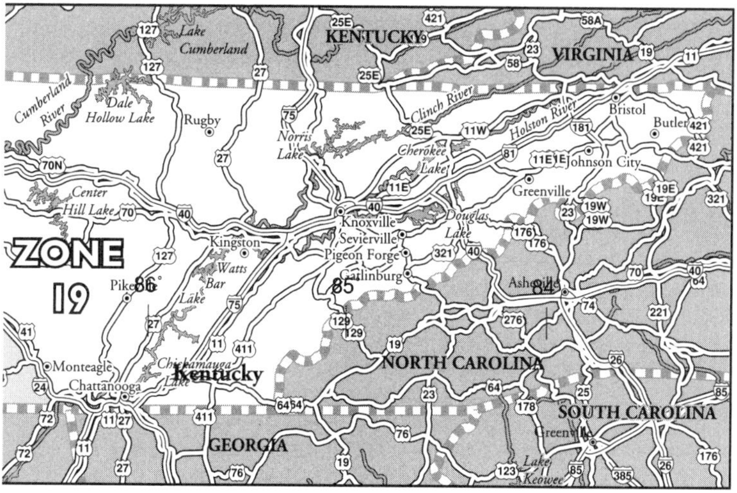

Kingston
Whitestone Country Inn, p. 356

Knoxville
Maple Grove Inn, p. 357
Maplehurst Inn Bed & Breakfast, p. 358
Masters Manor Inn, p. 359

Monteagle
Adams Edgeworth Inn, p. 360

Mt. Pleasant
Academy Place Bed & Breakfast, p. 377

Murfreesboro
Simply Southern, p. 361

Nashville
Linden Manor, p. 363
Rose Garden, p. 364

Pigeon Forge
Hilton's Bluff B&B Inn, p. 365

Pikeville
Fall Creek Falls Bed & Breakfast, p. 366

Rugby
Gray Gables B&B, p. 367

Savannah
White Elephant B&B Inn, p. 379

Sevierville
Blue Mountain Mist Country Inn & Cottages, p. 368
Calico Inn, p. 369

Zone 19
Eastern Tennessee

Many travelers begin their vacation by flying or driving to Nashville, close to the center of the state. Some are country music fans on their way to listen to their favorite stars at the Grand Ole Opry or Printer's Alley or Ryeman Auditorium (original home of the Opry). Or they head for the Bluebird Cafe where fledgling songwriters try out their latest "She left me for good this time" country music ballads. Another attraction is the Tennessee State Museum, which uses artifacts and a real log cabin to bring the early days of life in Tennessee back to life.

There are interesting stops all through this eastern zone. Murfreesboro is the self-proclaimed "Antiques Center of the South." Knoxville is a modern, clean city with several excellent bed-and-breakfasts. Chattanooga now boasts one of the largest freshwater homes for fish ever built. But the greatest attraction in this eastern area is the Great Smoky Mountains National Park (500,000 acres), shared with neighboring North Carolina. Spring (wildflowers) and fall (foliage) are definitely the times to come. *Hint:* When you drive through the Smoky Mountains, look for knots of people and cars stopped along the road. That usually means black bears or other wildlife have been spotted. We saw a bear and her cub scrambling up a tree at an unbelievable speed.

Country music shows in Pigeon Forge attract a big following, and Dollywood is the most popular amusement park, founded by Dolly Parton, who was raised in this area. You can pose for pictures by a brass statue of her at the courthouse in Sevierville right down the road, and then walk across the street and be married in a feed store in about twenty minutes. (We are not kidding you; we were witnesses to one of these quickie nuptials.)

For More Information

Nashville Convention and Visitors Bureau
(615) 259-4747

ENGLISH MANOR BED & BREAKFAST INN, Brentwood

Overall: ★★ Room Quality: D Value: D Price: $75–$125

We give this bed-and-breakfast a mixed report card: An "A" for the full breakfast, the den with a fireplace and large-screen TV, and the country setting. A "C" for some of the decor, which seems a little dated, and some of the small bathrooms. While the management does say "no" to pets, exceptions can be made if the dog or cat is relatively small, and may be allowed to stay inside with the owner. But a deposit may be required or payment due if any damage is done. To sum up, we liked some of the other bed-and-breakfasts in the Nashville area a little better than this one.

Setting & Facilities

Location: 15 mi. from downtown Nashville
Near: Historic Franklin, Cool Springs Galleria, Vanderbilt University
Building: 2-story Colonial
Grounds: 5 hillside acres w/ horses
Public Space: Lounging area, breakfast room, patio
Food & Drink: Full breakfast
Recreation: Sight-seeing, golf, bird-watching
Amenities & Services: Washer & dryer avail., robes, hair dryers, iron & ironing boards

Accommodations

Units: 4 guest rooms, 3 suites
All Rooms: 2-line phone, ceiling fan, TV
Some Rooms: Fireplace
Bed & Bath: Beds vary; private baths
Favorites: Room #2 w/ fireplace, bar, & stereo
Comfort & Decor: Antiques and traditional furniture

Rates, Reservations, & Restrictions

Deposit: Credit card
Discounts: AAA, 10% senior, long stays
Credit Cards: AE, V, MC, D, DC
Check-in/Out: 2 p.m./11 a.m.
Smoking: No
Pets: No, but kennel nearby
Kids: Welcome
Minimum Stay: None
Open: All year
Host: Willia Dean English
6304 Murray Lane
Brentwood, TN 37027
(615) 373-4627 or (888) 264-4690
Fax: (615) 221-9666
www.EnglishManor.com

BRISTOL'S NEW HOPE BED & BREAKFAST, Bristol

Overall: ★★★★ Room Quality: B Value: C Price: $95–$155

This is a turn-of-the-century middle-class home in a historic middle-class neighborhood. It's big and comfortable but not opulent. The host, Tonda, is an interior designer, and she has furnished the home with antiques and reproductions suitable to the period. The garage has been converted into a recreation room with a pool table. Special weekend packages include a murder mystery and an all-female weekend.

SETTING & FACILITIES

Location: Off I-81 take Exit 1 to downtown Bristol
Near: Downtown Bristol, Bristol Caverns
Building: 1892 Victorian
Grounds: Small lawn
Public Space: LR, DR, porch, game room
Food & Drink: Full breakfast may include biscuits & gravy, bread pudding
Recreation: Fishing, hiking
Amenities & Services: Robes, hair dryers

ACCOMMODATIONS

Units: 4 guest rooms
All Rooms: Phone, TV, high ceiling, hardwood floors
Some Rooms: Claw-foot or whirlpool tub
Bed & Bath: Beds vary; private baths
Favorites: Andes Room w/ whirlpool tub, fireplace, private entrance
Comfort & Decor: Victorian furnishings, "but comfort comes first"

RATES, RESERVATIONS, & RESTRICTIONS

Deposit: 1 night; 3-day cancellation
Discounts: 10% seniors, AAA, 15% corp.
Credit Cards: AE, V, MC
Check-in/Out: 2–10 p.m. (call to advise of expected arrival time)/noon
Smoking: No
Pets: No
Kids: 6 & older
Minimum Stay: Sometimes during special weekends; ask
Open: All year
Hosts: Tom & Tonda Fluke
822 Georgia Ave.
Bristol, TN 37620
(423) 989-3343 or (888) 989-3343
Fax: (423) 989-3422
newhope@preferred.com
www.bbonline.com/tn/newhope

IRON MOUNTAIN INN, Butler

Overall: ★★★ Room Quality: C Value: C Price: $130–$250

There is a discouraging steep, curved, gravel and semi-paved drive about a mile up the mountain to this inn. But stay with it! The inn and view are worth the climb. First, that view. From the porch you look out over an almost endless vista of mountains while you sip a cup of steaming hot chocolate. The decks have wrought-iron tables, chairs, rockers, and hammocks. Outside the building looks a little rustic, but the interior is attractive and comfortable with Egyptian sheets and handmade quilts on the beds. When the weather is good, guests breakfast on the deck. During afternoons and evenings there are always refreshments, including wine. Dinner is available at an extra fee by request, and complimentary wine is served or you can bring your own (this is a dry county). In winter you may want to plan on the in-house dinner. It can be a long drive to restaurants other than the grilled-hamburger variety. Throughout the year you have a choice of special weekends that include a Sweetheart Special with champagne, Watercolor Workshops with instructions to bring out the Van Gogh in guests, and even a Storytelling Festival. Current special weekends are listed on this inn's Internet site. Ahhh, but the mountain views. Those are unforgettable.

Setting & Facilities

Location: Close to Mountain City, off Hwy. 67
Near: Watauga Lake, Roan Mountain, Appalachian Trail
Building: 1998 modern log lodge
Grounds: 140 forested acres w/ mountain range in background
Public Space: Porch, parlor w/ fireplace, library nook
Food & Drink: Full breakfast
Recreation: Hiking, golf, horseback riding, skiing, white-water rafting, fly-fishing
Amenities & Services: Extras (avail. for a fee) include in-room massage, candles for the bath, & fresh floral arrangements

Accommodations

Units: 4 guest rooms
All Rooms: Theme
Some Rooms: 3 w/ private balcony, sitting area, four-poster bed
Bed & Bath: King, queen, or twins; private baths; whirlpool tub in all rooms, steam shower in 2 rooms
Favorites: Green Room w/ private balcony, best view of the mountains
Comfort & Decor: Comfortable "feet up" kind of furniture; family antiques, heirlooms

Rates, Reservations, & Restrictions

Deposit: Credit card, 1 night
Discounts: 10% AAA, AARP (must advise of membership at time of reservation), 4th night free
Credit Cards: AE, V, MC, D
Check-in/Out: 1 p.m./1 p.m.
Smoking: No
Pets: Small; $25 per night fee
Kids: 12 & older
Minimum Stay: 2 nights on weekends
Open: All year
Host: Vicki Woods
138 Moreland Dr.
Butler, TN 37640
(423) 768-2446 or (888) 781-2399
innkeeper@ironmountaininn.com
www.ironmountaininn.com

HANCOCK HOUSE, Gallatin

Overall: ★★★ Room Quality: C Value: B Price: $90–$200

In 1875 after a bumpy, dust-filled drive over Tennessee country roads, stagecoach passengers were delighted to file into the large log building, a stagecoach stop known as Avondale Station. Today travelers are equally delighted to arrive at the Hancock House, the revived station, restored to life as a bed-and-breakfast. The guest rooms are extra spacious, but being a log house some are a little dark. The separate Honeymoon Cabin has a sitting area downstairs, kitchenette, and large bath with a whirlpool tub for two. Stairs (rather narrow) lead to an upstairs bedroom. The hosts are very accommodating. Want breakfast at 10 a.m.? Okay. In your room? No problem. And special dietary requests are accommodated. This inn makes a great headquarters for enjoying all the music and fun of nearby Nashville.

Setting & Facilities

Location: 20-min. drive from downtown Nashville
Near: Grand Ole Opry, Hermitage (home of Andrew Jackson), Nashville's Music Row, Parthenon, General Jackson Showboat
Building: Colonial Revival long inn (pre-1878)
Grounds: Rural setting
Public Space: Large DR
Food & Drink: Full country or cont'l breakfast
Recreation: Sight-seeing, country music shows, swimming, golf, tennis, horseback riding
Amenities & Services: TV, fax, VCR avail., access to fridge, airport pickup, picnic baskets avail.

Accommodations

Units: 5 guest rooms plus Honeymoon Cabin
All Rooms: Spacious, fireplace (gas log), sitting area, coffeemaker, phone
Some Rooms: Jacuzzi, antique tester
Bed & Bath: Beds vary; private baths, 4 w/ whirlpool tubs
Favorites: Cabin w/ den, fireplace
Comfort & Decor: Nicely furnished with antiques

Rates, Reservations, & Restrictions

Deposit: Credit card
Discounts: 10% AAA, AARP
Credit Cards: AE, V, MC, D
Check-in/Out: 3 p.m./11 a.m.
Smoking: No
Pets: No, but there is a "pet resort" .25 mi. away
Kids: Welcome
Minimum Stay: None
Open: All year
Hosts: Carl & Roberta Hancock
2144 Nashville Pike
Gallatin, TN 37066
(615) 452-8431
www.bbonline.com/hancock

BUCKHORN INN, Gatlinburg

Overall: ★★★ Room Quality: C Value: D Price: $115–$260

A labyrinth is a series of concentric circular paths that lead to a center core. One of the most famous labyrinths is at Chartres Cathedral in France. People walk these circles and meditate. Some labyrinths are built in hospitals to promote relaxed walking by patients. We're going on about this obscure bit of medieval lore because there is a labyrinth built behind the Buckhorn Inn, almost an exact copy of the one in Chartres. The mountain views surrounding the inn are wonderful. Guests love to sit outside and watch the changing vistas of light and clouds. Actually, we liked the scenery a little better than the inn, which is clean, simple, and attractive but somewhat overpriced. This whole area is part of a colony of writers, artists, and craftspeople. Popular tours are held through this area every year. The labyrinth is actually a metaphor for Gatlinburg, a city choking on mountain boundaries, where finding a place to park in the summer and fall is a task for someone not bothered by endless driving, a person in deep meditation.

SETTING & FACILITIES

Location: From Gatlinburg take Hwy. 321 North to Buckhorn Rd.
Near: Great Smoky Arts & Crafts Community, Great Smoky Mountains, Dollywood
Building: English country
Grounds: 25 acres w/ walking trails, labyrinth, duck pond
Public Space: Large lobby area
Food & Drink: Full breakfast w/ eggs Benedict, peach-almond French toast, banana-walnut whole wheat pancakes; dinner also served
Recreation: Hiking the Smoky Mountains
Amenities & Services: Meeting facil. (25)

ACCOMMODATIONS

Units: 6 guest rooms in the main inn, 14 individual cottages
Some Rooms: Mountain view, fireplace, fridge, cable TV
Bed & Bath: Beds vary; private baths
Favorites: Rooms on second floor of inn w/ mountain views
Comfort & Decor: Comfortably but modestly furnished; check out the cottages with a fireplace and picture window.

RATES, RESERVATIONS, & RESTRICTIONS

Deposit: 1st night
Discounts: Winter
Credit Cards: MC, V, D
Check-in/Out: 3 p.m./11 a.m.
Smoking: No
Pets: No
Kids: 6 & older in cottages
Minimum Stay: 2 nights

Open: All year
Hosts: Staff
2140 Tudor Mountain Rd.
Gatlinburg, TN 37738
(865) 436-4668
buckhorninn@msn.com
www.buckhorninn.com

EIGHT GABLES INN, Gatlinburg

Overall: ★★★★ Room Quality: B Value: C Price: $79–$189

Eight Gables Inn may remind you of a Colorado ski lodge with its huge main room flanked by two wood-burning fireplaces. It really does have eight gables that, combined with skylights, provide the second floor rooms with wonderful light. This is a good thing, since rooms on the first floor, while beautifully appointed, are a little dark during the day. Despite that minor flaw, we were really impressed by the Master Suite in hunter green and burgundy colors on the first floor; it has a king bed, a whirlpool tub for two, and a private porch. Another room ideal for couples is Hearts of Love, also with a whirlpool tub for two and a CD player. There the darkened room might be just right for honeymooners.

Setting & Facilities

Location: Right off main road between Pigeon Forge & Gatlinburg
Near: Smoky Mountains, Dollywood, golf courses
Building: Modern 1991 octagonal building
Grounds: At foothill of Smoky Mountains
Public Space: Huge double lobby
Food & Drink: Full breakfast; specialty: French toast w/ cream cheese & strawberry jam; for $15 will prepare gourmet luncheon picnic basket for 2; lunch served at inn Tue.–Fri.
Recreation: Sight-seeing mountains, hiking, shopping outlet malls, theaters
Amenities & Services: Menus of local restaurants

Accommodations

Units: 12 guest rooms
All Rooms: Antiques
Some Rooms: Vaulted ceiling, skylights
Bed & Bath: Beds vary; private baths
Favorites: Rooms on second floor are brighter
Comfort & Decor: Rustic modern

Rates, Reservations, & Restrictions

Deposit: Credit card
Discounts: Corp., 10% (a business card will get you the discount)
Credit Cards: All major cards
Check-in/Out: 3–6 p.m./11 a.m.
Smoking: No
Pets: No
Kids: Welcome
Minimum Stay: 2 nights on weekends, 3 nights during holidays

Open: All year
Hosts: Don & Kim Cason
219 North Mountain Trail
Gatlinburg, TN 37738
(865) 430-3344 or (800) 279-5716
Fax: (865) 430-3344 (dial, then hit *51)
www.virtualcities.com/ons/tn/g/tngh601.htm

HIPPENSTEAL'S MOUNTAIN VIEW INN, Gatlinburg

Overall: ★★★★½ Room Quality: A Value: B Price: $95–$125

There are two great views. The first is of three mountains from the front porches of the rooms and in front of the inn. The second is from inside the inn of dozens of mountains, a waterfall, and woodlands—all captured in watercolors by one of the area's most prolific artists, Vern Hippensteal. The inn itself is a reproduction of the Gatlinburg inn that was the first home of Vern's wife, Lisa. As a wedding present, he built the same type of inn near the mountain where he proposed to her. Women seem to love this romantic story when one of the inn's hosts tells it; men less so. A great pleasure is sitting on one of the rocking chairs, and a second enjoyable activity is buying one of Hippensteal's paintings right off the wall; they are in every room and line every hallway. This is a handsome inn and a real retreat from all the sounds and hubbub of the nearby mountain towns.

Setting & Facilities

Location: Entrance off Birds Creek Rd., east into downtown Gatlinburg
Near: Smoky Mountains, Gatlinburg, Dollywood, Pigeon Forge, Seveirville
Building: 3-story stone/wood Appalachian-style retreat
Grounds: Wooded mountainous area
Public Space: Large lobby area, DR, board room/library
Food & Drink: Full breakfast; specialties: cheese soufflé, sausage pinwheels, apple-raisin breads; afternoon tea
Recreation: Sight-seeing, show-going, shopping at nearby Smoky Mountain towns
Amenities & Services: None

Accommodations

Units: 11 guest rooms
All Rooms: Walls covered w/ artwork, porch w/ mountain views
Some Rooms: Whirlpool tub
Bed & Bath: Beds vary; private baths
Favorites: None
Comfort & Decor: Very relaxing furniture built for comfort

Rates, Reservations, & Restrictions

Deposit: Credit card
Discounts: 6 nights or more
Credit Cards: AE, MC, V
Check-in/Out: 3 p.m./11 a.m.
Smoking: No
Pets: No
Kids: Welcome
Minimum Stay: None

Open: All year
Hosts: Vern & Lisa Hippensteal
P.O. Box 37736
Gatlinburg, TN 37738
(865) 436-5761 or (800) 527-8110
Fax: (865) 436-8617
vernhippen@aol.com
www.hippensteal.com

HILLTOP HOUSE BED & BREAKFAST, Greenville

Overall: ★★ Room Quality: C Value: B Price: $75

The Hilltop House is more like a home than a bed-and-breakfast business. There is some clutter scattered about, so you definitely won't feel intimidated as you do in some of the museum-quality bed-and-breakfasts. And there are some nice homelike touches, such as muffins and coffee delivered to your room before the full breakfast is served in the dining room. The hostess can tailor a complete vacation for you, including golf, hiking the Appalachian Trail, a honeymoon package, or many other options, including dinner by reservation at the Hilltop House.

Setting & Facilities

Location: Near Greenville off Hwy. 70 South
Near: Gatlinburg, Nolichuckey River, Great Smoky Mountain Nat'l Park, Andrew Johnson Nat'l Historic Site
Building: 1920s farm homestead
Grounds: Bluff above Nolichuckey River Valley
Public Space: Porch, common room
Food & Drink: Full breakfast; afternoon tea
Recreation: Hiking, golf, white-water rafting, horseback riding
Amenities & Services: Swing & rockers on porch, small guest fridge on second floor, airport pickup w/ advance notice at Knoxville McGree-Tyson Airport

Accommodations

Units: 3 guest rooms
All Rooms: Mountain views, many windows
Some Rooms: Veranda
Bed & Bath: King, queen, full, brass beds; private baths
Favorites: None
Comfort & Decor: Rooms are larger than in many other B&Bs and feature English antiques.

Rates, Reservations, & Restrictions

Deposit: Credit card or 50%; 7-day cancellation
Discounts: 10% corp., 20% 5 or more nights
Credit Cards: AE, V, MC
Check-in/Out: 3 p.m./11 a.m.
Smoking: No
Pets: No
Kids: 3 & older
Minimum Stay: None
Open: All year
Host: Denise Ashworth
6 Sanford Circle
Greenville, TN 37743
(423) 639-8202
ashworth@greene.xtn.net
www.tennesseeinns.com

JAM N JELLY INN, Johnson City

Overall: ★★ Room Quality: D Value: C Price: $65–$85

The Jam n Jelly name for this inn suggests a very informal place, and it lives up to the name with family-style breakfasts around two large tables and pleasant gathering places on the first and second floors. In fact, many guests can slip into the hot tub on the back porch at the same time; it holds 8–10 people, depending on guest girth, of course. We'd rate the rooms as Holiday Inn quality, pleasant but certainly not super-elegant. The inn is centrally located, close to a strip of fast-food places but also convenient for business travelers, with many major corporations in town. One advantage of building a bed-and-breakfast from scratch is that more modern conveniences and safety features can be built in that may not be possible when older Victorian homes are converted to bed-and-breakfasts at a later date. For example, the Jam n Jelly Inn offers disabled access and has sprinkler systems throughout the building.

SETTING & FACILITIES

Location: : 2.5 blocks off West Market St. on Indian St. Rd.
Near: Johnson City Medical Center, East Tennessee State University, Blue Ridge Parkway, Great Smoky Mountains National Park
Building: 1990s 2-story log inn
Grounds: Grassy knoll
Public Space: Common areas on 1st & 2nd floors (1 w/ fireplace, other w/ big-screen TV & videos), large back porch
Food & Drink: Full breakfast w/ homemade muffins &—of course—jams & jellies; specialty: baked French toast; complimentary evening snacks & beverages
Recreation: Sight-seeing, fall foliage, skiing, running, bicycling
Amenities & Services: Hot tub, volleyball court, airport pickup, business equip. avail.: computer, copier, fax

ACCOMMODATIONS

Units: 6 guest rooms
All Rooms: Antique reproductions, TV
Bed & Bath: Queens, sofa beds; private ceramic-tiled baths
Favorites: None
Comfort & Decor: Comfortable overstuffed furniture in the great room; homey, country casual furnishings

RATES, RESERVATIONS, & RESTRICTIONS

Deposit: Credit card; 7-day cancellation for special event weekends; otherwise before 6 p.m. on day of reservation
Discounts: 10% AAA, AARP, corp., groups, long stays
Credit Cards: AE, V, MC, D
Check-in/Out: 4 p.m./10 a.m.
Smoking: No
Pets: No

Kids: Welcome; crib avail. on request
Minimum Stay: None
Open: All year
Hosts: Bud & Carol Kidner
1310 Indian Ridge Rd.
Johnson City, TN 37604
(423) 929-0039
Fax: (423) 929-9026
jjkidner@preferred.com
www.jamnjellyinn.com

WHITESTONE COUNTRY INN, Kingston

Overall: ★★★★★ Room Quality: A Value: A Price: $115–$225

There's no way around it. This is going to sound like one of those gushy, rose-colored-glasses travel brochures, but the Whitestone Inn is beautiful! Here's a guest's description of his accommodations: "Our room was located in the turret called Eagles' Landing. We had a stocked refrigerator, coffee pot with tea, and a jar of cookies. There were bay windows all around the room and the view was wonderful. Breakfast the next morning was delicious with baked apples, eggs, and bacon." And the guest didn't even mention the fireplace that turns on with a wall switch, the eight miles of walking trails, the canoes, kayaks, paddleboats, and so on. This is a soup-to–wedding reception kind of inn, with just about everything available for a couple in love—a wedding chapel, a gazebo for the de rigueur outdoor wedding photos, and wonderful honeymoon rooms a minute's walk away. This is the most interesting bed-and-breakfast we found in Tennessee.

SETTING & FACILITIES

Location: I-75 South to Exit 72, Hwy. 72 West, 8.5 mi. to right on Point Rock Rd.
Near: Great Smoky Mountains Nat'l Park, Gatlinburg, Chattanooga, Knoxville
Building: Federal style, New England–like village of 5 separate buildings
Grounds: 360-acre estate w/ 800-foot frontage on Watts Bar Lake, plus pasture & woodlands
Public Space: Recreation room, 3 DRs, library, great room, chapel, decks, porches
Food & Drink: Full breakfast; lunch & dinner also served
Recreation: Fishing, tennis, hiking trails, bird-watching
Amenities & Services: Canoes, kayaks, & paddleboats avail.; croquet; pool table; gift shop

ACCOMMODATIONS

Units: 20 guest rooms & suites
All Rooms: Very large, fireplace, TV & VCR, phone
Bed & Bath: 19 kings, 1 queen; private baths w/ spa tubs

Favorites: Ask for one of 5 rooms w/ "spa showers"—an 85 gal./min. waterfall & body spa! These rooms also have private decks w/ lake views.

Comfort & Decor: Many rooms are named after birds, with themes tastefully executed.

RATES, RESERVATIONS, & RESTRICTIONS

Deposit: Credit card, 1 night; 7-day cancellation
Discounts: 50% off for ministers, free to missionaries
Credit Cards: AE, V, MC, D
Check-in/Out: 3 p.m./11 a.m.
Smoking: No
Pets: No
Kids: 6 & older
Minimum Stay: None
Open: All year
Hosts: Paul & Jean Cowell
1200 Paint Rock Rd.
Kingston, TN 37763
(865) 376-0113 or (888) 247-2464
www.whitestones.com

MAPLE GROVE INN, Knoxville

Overall: ★★★★★ Room Quality: A Value: C Price: $125–$200

Plato believed that a perfect model for a chair or virtually any object existed in heaven. And the closer we came to that perfect model, the more beautiful we would perceive that subject. The Maple Grove Inn must come very close to that Platonic ideal of an inn. You enter the grounds through a long tunnel of trees. The mansion ahead is Knoxville's oldest residence, but it's still looking as grand as ever. The suites in this inn are magnificently decorated. Everything seems larger than life, from the high ceilings to the period antiques and the wood-burning fireplaces. This inn's only fault is that it may be almost too grandiose for a couple seeking a remote weekend getaway. *Intimate* is not a word that comes to mind here. But it's almost perfect for an executive retreat or board meeting, or a posh getaway for Nashville country stars. Somehow we kept imagining Thomas Jefferson coming here to sign something important. Or maybe even Plato himself.

SETTING & FACILITIES

Location: I-40 to West Hill exit, left at light, right on Morrell Rd., right on Westland Dr.
Near: World's Fair Park, University of Tennessee, Knoxville Zoo
Building: 1799 Georgian mansion
Grounds: 16 acres
Public Space: Large parlor, library, sunroom
Food & Drink: Full breakfast; specialties: eggs Benedict, blueberry muffins, omelets, crêpes; complimentary beverages
Recreation: Swimming, tennis, sightseeing
Amenities & Services: Swimming pool, tennis court, robes

Accommodations

Units: 6 guest rooms, 2 suites
All Rooms: Cable TV, large closet, garden views
Some Rooms: Four-poster rice bed, fireplace, screened veranda, disabled access
Bed & Bath: Beds vary; private baths
Favorites: Oak Suite w/ sitting room, fireplace, whirlpool tub
Comfort & Decor: Ultra-elegant antiques and furnishings are throughout. Everything here is done in extraordinarily good taste.

Rates, Reservations, & Restrictions

Deposit: Ask
Discounts: None
Credit Cards: AE, V, MC
Check-in/Out: 3 p.m./11 a.m.
Smoking: No
Pets: No
Kids: 12 & older
Minimum Stay: 2 nights on weekends
Open: All year except Dec. 27–Jan. 5
Hosts: Staff
8800 Westland Dr.
Knoxville, TN 37923
(865) 690-9565 or (800) 645-0713
Fax: (865) 690-9385
www.maplegroveinn.com

MAPLEHURST INN BED & BREAKFAST, Knoxville

Overall: ★★★ Room Quality: B Value: D Price: $89–$149

There's a lot to like at Maplehurst Inn and a few things to dislike. Its number one attraction is its location right at the beginning of downtown Knoxville, and number two is the friendliness and enthusiasm of the host, Sonny Harben. This is a good place to stay for business travelers, with its off-street parking and proximity to local businesses. But we are concerned about the sunken tubs in some of the bathrooms, almost at floor level—a possible hazard for sleepy guests at night. The winding stairwell to the dining room below is hard to navigate, especially for elderly travelers. Still, there are unusual perks, and views of the Tennessee River behind the inn are beautiful. Just watch your step on those winding stairs to the dining room.

Setting & Facilities

Location: From I-40 East take Exit 388 (Hwy. 441), follow Henley St. signs through tunnel, right on West Hill Ave.
Near: World's Fair Park, 18 golf courses, Ladies' Basketball Hall of Fame, convention center
Building: 1917 mansion
Grounds: None
Public Space: Parlor, DR
Food & Drink: Full breakfast; specialty: egg/cheese/sausage casserole; complimentary soft drinks, cookies, nuts

Recreation: Downtown attractions, local champion sports teams
Amenities & Services: Free membership and "two-fer" dining offer at an exclusive private Knoxville club

Accommodations

Units: 11 guest rooms
All Rooms: Cable TV, AC/heating system
Some Rooms: Whirlpool tub
Bed & Bath: Beds vary; private baths
Favorites: Penthouse Suite w/ deck overlooking Tennessee River
Comfort & Decor: Pleasant and homelike

Rates, Reservations, & Restrictions

Deposit: 1st night
Discounts: None
Credit Cards: Ask
Check-in/Out: 3 p.m./11 a.m.
Smoking: No
Pets: No
Kids: Welcome
Minimum Stay: None
Open: All year
Hosts: Sonny & Becky Harben
800 West Hill Ave.
Knoxville, TN 37902
(865) 523-7733 or (800) 451-1562
www.maplehurstinn.com

MASTERS MANOR INN, Knoxville

Overall: ★★★★ Room Quality: B Value: C Price: $95–$200

Our host, Rhonda, strikes us as somewhat of a character, but a "nice" character. She juts out her jaw and says, "I can judge people by whether or not they like dogs. Dog lovers are good people." As if in appreciation of her sentiment, two resident dogs appear behind her and wag on cue. But she obviously likes a lot of people, because she is soon chatting about the early history of the house. "Most of our guests during the week are businesspeople," she says. "On weekends we get couples who come to see

Knoxville." She is particularly proud of the antique classic wallpaper in the house. She and her husband also have made one room on the first floor fully accessible to disabled travelers. We chose the Elm Room as our favorite (each guest room is named for the tree right outside its window). Its king bed is surrounded by seven-foot-tall posts, and the antique Victorian tile of the fireplace reminded us of another era. Although the room gave a visual feeling of seclusion and privacy, the double connecting doors (locked) to the next room didn't prevent sounds from a next-door TV and alarm clock from being a little disturbing.

SETTING & FACILITIES

Location: From I-75 exit at Merchants Dr. (which becomes Cedar Ln.)
Near: University of Tennessee, World's Fair Park, Knoxville Museum of Art
Building: 1896 Victorian
Grounds: 2 landscaped acres
Public Space: LR, DR
Food & Drink: Full breakfast; specialties:quiche, country ham, cheese grits
Recreation: Sight-seeing, Smoky Mountains
Amenities & Services: Sight-seeing tips

ACCOMMODATIONS

Units: 6 guest rooms
All Rooms: 12-foot ceiling, antiques, phone w/ data port
Some Rooms: Fireplace
Bed & Bath: Beds vary; private baths
Favorites: Elm Room
Comfort & Decor: Homelike environment

RATES, RESERVATIONS, & RESTRICTIONS

Deposit: Credit card
Discounts: 10% AAA, AARP, corp.
Credit Cards: AE, V, MC
Check-in/Out: 4 p.m./noon
Smoking: Designated areas
Pets: Yes
Kids: Welcome; stay free in parents' room
Minimum Stay: None
Open: All year
Hosts: Dana & Rhonda Hallet
1909 Cedar Lane
Knoxville, TN 37918
(865) 219-9888
Fax: (865) 219-9811
rbhallet@nss.net
www.mastersmanor.com

ADAMS EDGEWORTH INN, Monteagle

Overall: ★★★★ Room Quality: B Value: C Price: $75–$295

This 1896 inn is located in the 96-acre Monteagle Sunday School Assembly, a turn-of-the-century summer community of Victorian homes and recreational facilities. The School Assembly provides a Chautauqua series beginning on Father's Day weekend and lasting six weeks, with 11 different programs. The neighborhood has more than 170 historic buildings. And it's only a short walk to tennis courts, a gymnasium, park, and a waterfall. The inn itself is very romantic. At night you sit at separate tables with candles, the only light in the room besides the art lights over paintings. Some extra fees can be annoying. The Monteagle Sunday School Assembly requires you to pay a guest membership fee at the front gate. And rooms with fireplaces are charged an extra fee in winter. However, the inn itself and the School Assembly activities are fascinating. Said one couple on departing: "We didn't want to leave."

Setting & Facilities

Location: Top of Monteagle Mountain
Near: University of the South, Chautauqua Village, Tennessee Williams Theatre, Jack Daniels Distillery, Arnold Air Force Base, Sewanee & Arnold Engineering Center
Building: 1896 historic inn
Grounds: Limited; inside historic village
Public Space: Wraparound porch, large common area w/ books
Food & Drink: Full breakfast; dinner avail. by reservation
Recreation: Fishing, swimming, hiking, tennis, bicycling, bird-watching
Amenities & Services: Computer, data port, fax, copier

Accommodations

Units: 12 guest rooms
All Rooms: AC, phone, robes, high ceiling
Some Rooms: Color TV, fireplace
Bed & Bath: Beds vary; private baths
Favorites: Third floor penthouse w/ galley kitchen, fitness area
Comfort & Decor: Inlaid floors and decorative wood moldings contribute to an English country manor ambience.

Rates, Reservations, & Restrictions

Deposit: Only on special occasions
Discounts: None during high season; other times: seniors, group, gov't., corp.
Credit Cards: AE, V, MC
Check-in/Out: 4 p.m./11 a.m.
Smoking: No
Pets: Small only, for $25 daily fee
Kids: Welcome by prior arrangement
Minimum Stay: 2 nights on weekends
Open: All year
Hosts: David & Wendy Adams
Monteagle Assembly
Monteagle, TN 37356
(615) 924-4000 or 87-RELAXINN
Fax: (615) 924-3236
www.bbhost.com

SIMPLY SOUTHERN, Murfreesboro

Overall: ★★★★½ Room Quality: A Value: A Price: $89–$149

Host/owners Carl and Ann really have the hang of this bed-and-breakfast business. They live upstairs and leave all the other rooms to the guests. These include two parlors, a beautifully decorated dining room, and a great recreation room with the works—TV, VCR, pool table, player piano, karaoke machine, and a dime Coke machine (not a misprint—a dime). Unusual touches: kaleidoscopes in every room, and teddy bears to sleep with for the childhood-disadvantaged. Breakfast is served by candlelight, and if you like what you're having as much as we did, you'll buy the cookbook, with many of the hosts' recipes.

Setting & Facilities

Location: 1 mi. from East Main courthouse, north on Tennessee Blvd.
Near: Jack Daniels Distillery, Nashville, Walking Horses Nat'l Celebration, Shelbyville, Middle Tennessee State University (right across the st.)
Building: Turn-of-the–(20th!) century American Four-Square
Grounds: Courtyard garden
Public Space: LR, parlor, sitting area, recreation room
Food & Drink: Full breakfast at guest's requested time; specialties: wine & cheese casserole, eggs in a nest, French banana crêpes, pineapple casserole
Recreation: Nashville music scene, river walks, fishing, boating, golf (3 public courses)
Amenities & Services: Newspapers delivered to rooms, local restaurant menus, surprises for special occasion guests

Accommodations

Units: 4 guest rooms, 1 suite
All Rooms: TV, VCR, phone w/ data port, 2 chairs, down pillows & comforters, coffeemakers
Some Rooms: Fireplace
Bed & Bath: King, queen, or twins; private baths
Favorites: None
Comfort & Decor: Original artwork and scenes of Tennessee adorn the walls.

Rates, Reservations, & Restrictions

Deposit: Credit card or 50% of reservation; 7-day cancellation
Discounts: Not advertised; ask
Credit Cards: AE, V, MC, D
Check-in/Out: 4 p.m./11 a.m.
Smoking: No
Pets: No
Kids: 12 & older by arrangement
Minimum Stay: 2 nights during certain holidays
Open: All year
Hosts: Carl & Georgia Buckner
211 North Tennessee Blvd.
Murfreesboro, TN 37130
(615) 896-4988 or (888) 723-1199
info@simplysouthern.net
www.simplysouthern.net

LINDEN MANOR, Nashville

Overall: ★★★	Room Quality: B	Value: B	Price: $95–$135

The two words we'd use to describe Linden Manor are *homey* and *clean*. The owners' quarters are on the lower level of the house, and your hosts are very cordial and great sources of information about Nashville and the surrounding area. They have also created special packages, such as a spa vacation with a licensed massage therapist and a romantic weekend with flowers in the room, dinner at Zola's in Nashville, and stuffed French toast by candlelight in the morning. As this book goes to press, the interior has been completely remodeled, with exterior renovations to be finished shortly.

SETTING & FACILITIES

Location: 2 blocks from Vanderbilt University
Near: Belmont University, Nashville's Music Row
Building: 1893 Victorian
Grounds: Half acre
Public Space: LR, parlor, DR
Food & Drink: Full breakfast; specialty: stuffed French toast w/ apricot sauce; afternoon homemade cookies; champagne on request
Recreation: Sight-seeing, massage, Grand Ole Opry
Amenities & Services: TV on request, fax avail.

ACCOMMODATIONS

Units: 3 guest rooms
All Rooms: Beautiful antiques (many Oriental items collected by owner while overseas)
Some Rooms: Rare rice bed from China
Bed & Bath: Beds vary; private baths
Favorites: Linden Room w/ king bed & whirlpool tub
Comfort & Decor: It's furnished with many collectible items, including Japanese dollars, a beautiful room divider from Bali, carved Micronesian "storyboards" that tell folk stories with pictures.

Rates, Reservations, & Restrictions

Deposit: Credit card
Discounts: Corp., military
Credit Cards: AE,V, MC
Check-in/Out: 4 p.m./11 a.m.
Smoking: No
Pets: No
Kids: 12 & older
Minimum Stay: 2 nights on weekends
Open: All year
Hosts: Tom & Catherine Favreau
1501 Linden
Nashville, TN 37212
(615) 298-2701
lindenbb@aol.com
www.bbonlin.com/tn/linden

ROSE GARDEN, Nashville

Overall: ★★★½ Room Quality: B Value: B Price: $105–$150

So you like bed-and-breakfasts but don't feel like talking to new people in the morning or really want to spend time with a significant other. As the ads say, have we got a place for you. The Rose Garden accommodates only one party at a time in one completely private 1,000-square-foot suite with its own private entrance. It's ideal for business travelers, lovers, or families. There is a small kitchen area with a washer and dryer. The entertainment center is stocked with movies and books. Put on the furnished robe and step outside on the patio to your own hot tub, which is spotlessly clean (unlike some hot tubs in other bed-and-breakfasts that seem covered with layers of grime). There is turn-down service at night with GooGoo clusters on the pillow (a Nashville tradition).

Setting & Facilities

Location: 0.3 mi. west of junction of Hwy. 70 South & Hwy. 100 (on Hwy. 70)
Near: Percy Warner Park (Iroquois Steeplechase), Belle Meade Mansion, Natchez Trace, Vanderbilt University
Building: 30-year-plus traditional home
Grounds: Rose garden
Public Space: None
Food & Drink: Cont'l breakfast
Recreation: Antiques shopping, sight-seeing, tennis, mountain hiking
Amenities & Services: Fax & modem access, health club nearby w/ pool & tennis for $3.50 guest pass

Accommodations

Units: 1 suite
All Rooms: TV, VCR, fireplace, patio, grill, 5-person hot tub, office area
Bed & Bath: Queen & trundle beds; private bath
Favorites: N/A
Comfort & Decor: Cozy and relaxing

Rates, Reservations, & Restrictions

Deposit: Full payment for 1 night; 50% for 2 nights or more by check
Discounts: Week-long stays
Credit Cards: None
Check-in/Out: 4–6 p.m./11 a.m.
Smoking: No
Pets: No
Kids: No
Minimum Stay: 2 nights on weekends
Open: All year
Hosts: Jim & Shirley Ruppert
6213 Harding Rd.
Nashville, TN 37205
(615) 356-8003
Fax: (615) 352-7661
www.bbonline.com/tn/rosegarden

HILTON'S BLUFF B&B INN, Pigeon Forge

Overall: ★★	Room Quality: D	Value: D	Price: $79–$109

This ten-year-old building is not particularly attractive, more closely resembling a motel than a bed-and-breakfast. But there are some beauty marks on this rustic face—an impressive stone fireplace in the great room and a wonderful full-length porch. The view from the back rooms is not great unless you're into parking lots. Breakfasts are served family-style, which can be pleasant for single travelers who want to meet others. This bed-and-breakfast seems a little overpriced to us, but much of the area can get costly in season. If you're using it primarily as a place for eight hours of sleep so you can spend your days shopping and hiking the Great Smoky Mountains, okay. But if you want more luxurious surroundings at night, check out some of the other bed-and-breakfasts we reviewed in nearby Gatlinburg. And check out the night scene. Pigeon Forge is really starting to pick up the ball Nashville is dropping by becoming a real center of country music. Dollywood, the Louise Mandrell Theater, and the Governor's Palace are just a few of the country music theaters that line Highway 441. The Nascar Cafe in next-door Sevierville seems to be a crowd-pleaser with good food, but the overpowering roar of replayed races on big screens could fill ear doctors' offices for years to come.

Setting & Facilities

Location: In Pigeon Forge travel south on Hwy. 321, 0.5 mi. to Valley Heights Dr., then go uphill
Near: Great Smoky Mountains Nat'l Park, Dollywood, Pigeon Forge shops & theaters
Building: 2-story cedar lodge
Grounds: Rural
Public Space: 2 LRs, DR, 2 covered decks
Food & Drink: Full breakfast may include fried apples, egg casserole, bacon, yogurt pancakes
Recreation: Hiking, swimming, miniature golf, country music theaters
Amenities & Services: Newspaper, cable TV, menus for local restaurants

Accommodations

Units: 10 guest rooms
All Rooms: Balcony or deck, mountain views
Some Rooms: Whirlpool tub
Bed & Bath: King or queen; private baths
Favorites: Wild Rose Room w/ red heart-shaped whirlpool tub
Comfort & Decor: Modest—nothing stands out.

Rates, Reservations, & Restrictions

Deposit: Credit card; 10-day cancellation
Discounts: Negotiable; ask
Credit Cards: AE, V, MC
Check-in/Out: 3 p.m./11 a.m.
Smoking: No
Pets: No
Kids: 9 & older
Minimum Stay: 2 nights
Open: All year
Hosts: Bob & JoAnn Quandt
2654 Valley Heights Dr.
Pigeon Forge, TN 37863
(865) 428-9765 or (800) 441-4188
www.bbonline.com/tn/hiltonsbluff

FALL CREEK FALLS BED & BREAKFAST, Pikeville

Overall: ★★★ Room Quality: C Value: B Price: $69–$140

Country music stars such as Tanya Tucker have wandered down the "Elvis Presley Boulevard" here, a long hallway with an Elvis street sign and pictures and articles about the King. The rooms are smallish but decorated nicely with four-poster beds and other antique furnishings. Tanya picked the Sweetheart Room, which has a brass bed and heart-shaped whirlpool tub. Our favorite is the separate cabin with living room, dining area, kitchen, and a large porch with picnic table and grill. It is much more contemporary than rooms in the main house. The hosts are very friendly and will talk your arm off if you let them.

Setting & Facilities

Location: 15 mi. from Pikeville
Near: Falls Creek Falls State Park & spectacular waterfall
Building: 1981 1.5-story country manor & separate cabin
Grounds: Rural, 40-acre horse & hay farm
Public Space: Sun porch, 2 sitting rooms, yard (5 acres!) w/ picnic tables
Food & Drink: Full breakfast; specialty: stuffed French toast strata w/ apple cider syrup
Recreation: Horseback riding, hiking, canoeing, fishing, golf
Amenities & Services: Access to fax & copy machine, ice machine

Accommodations

Units: 7 guest rooms, 2-room suite
All Rooms: Phone, clock radio
Some Rooms: Dbl. whirlpool tub, gas-log fireplace
Bed & Bath: Beds vary; private baths
Favorites: Cabin
Comfort & Decor: A mix of Victorian and country antiques

Rates, Reservations, & Restrictions

Deposit: Credit card; 7-day cancellation
Discounts: 10% AAA, corp., gov't., $10 less for singles
Credit Cards: AE, V, MC, D
Check-in/Out: Weekdays 3–6 p.m.; Sun. 3–5 p.m./11 a.m.
Smoking: No
Pets: No
Kids: Welcome one at a time, 8 & older

GRAY GABLES B&B, Rugby

Overall: ★★★★ Room Quality: A Value: B Price: $80–$115

This homey bed-and-breakfast is situated along a ridge of the rugged Cumberland Plateau one mile from historic Rugby, a late-nineteenth-century English trial utopian community. Perfectly located for outdoor recreation, this bed-and-breakfast is within spitting distance of some of the best hiking, canoeing, fishing, and mountain biking in Tennessee. Although the guest rooms are both elegant and creative in their appointments, this establishment's real strength lies in the friendliness of its hosts and in the extraordinary product of their kitchen. As a former restaurateur and author of a successful cookbook, Bill and Linda Jones offer a gourmet dining experience that is scarcely believable in a rural bed-and-breakfast.

Setting & Facilities

Location: 90 min. NW of Knoxville on TN 52 between Rugby & Jamestown
Near: Dale Hollow Lake, Obed/ Emory River, Big South Fork Gorge Recreation Area, Pickett State Park
Building: 2-story frame Victorian inn w/ 80-foot covered front & back porch
Grounds: 32 acres w/ woods, horse pasture, & lawn
Public Space: Great room, upstairs sitting room, formal DR, front & back porches
Food & Drink: Full country breakfast; "plateau gourmet" dinner served on antique china
Recreation: Horseshoes, croquet, & badminton on property; hiking, horseback riding, fishing, river running, mountain biking, road biking, sightseeing nearby
Amenities & Services: TV in great room, games, piano

Accommodations

Units: 8 guest rooms
All Rooms: Country & Victorian antiques, ceiling fan, windows
Some Rooms: Private bath
Bed & Bath: 7 queens, 1 room with twins; 4 w/ private baths, 4 share bath w/ 1 other room

Heritage, Tiffany, ... ecor: Great room ... stered seating around a ... d a TV. Styling of the great ... dining room, and upstairs sit- ... room is a blend of early American ... nd Victorian accented with antiques, historic artifacts, and rural memorabilia. The 80-foot covered front porch features wicker furniture, while the equally long back porch has casual furniture and tables for outdoor dining. Guest rooms are ornate with sashed drapes and valence window treatments and antique furnishings.

Rates, Reservations, & Restrictions

Deposit: 1 night; 72-hour cancellation, $30 fee
Discounts: None
Credit Cards: V, MC, AE
Check-in/Out: 4–8 p.m. or by arrangement/11 a.m.
Smoking: Outside only
Pets: Outside kennel avail.
Kids: Welcome
No-No's: Smoking indoors; more than 2 adults per room
Minimum Stay: None
Open: All year
Hosts: Linda & Bill Jones
P.O. Box 52, TN 52
Rugby, TN 37733
(423) 628-5252
Fax: (423) 628-5252
greygablestn@highland.net
www.RugbyTN.com

BLUE MOUNTAIN MIST COUNTRY INN AND COTTAGES, Sevierville

Overall: ★★½ | Room Quality: C | Value: B | Price: $90–$140

This inn is a great rural retreat after fighting some of the tourist traffic in Sevierville and Pigeon Forge, and its rates are a great bargain, too, for a bed-and-breakfast of this quality in mountain tourist land. Though all the rooms are pleasant, the cottages behind the inn may be the best choice for honeymooners and families. They all have fireplaces, whirlpool tubs for two, a kitchenette, and an outdoor grill and picnic table. Guests can reduce their food costs by preparing some meals in their cottage (restaurant prices in this tourist area are not cheap). People staying in the cottages can elect to have a breakfast basket delivered to their door or join the rest of the guests for a country meal at the inn.

Setting & Facilities

Location: Right outside Sevierville
Near: Dollywood, country music theaters, Gatlinburg Arts & Crafts Community, Great Smoky Mountain Nat'l Park
Building: 1982 Victorian
Grounds: 60-acre farm w/ pond
Public Space: TV & conf. room
Food & Drink: Full country breakfast w/ eggs, grits, sausage
Recreation: Sight-seeing, miniature golf, hiking
Amenities & Services: Books about the area, videos

ACCOMMODATIONS

Units: 12 guest rooms, 5 cottages
All Rooms: Antiques, family heirlooms
Some Rooms: Kitchenette, TV, VCR, grill (cottages)
Bed & Bath: Beds vary; private baths
Favorites: None
Comfort & Decor: Country casual

RATES, RESERVATIONS, & RESTRICTIONS

Deposit: Ask
Discounts: None
Credit Cards: MC, V
Check-in/Out: 3–9 p.m./11 a.m.
Smoking: No
Pets: No
Kids: Welcome
Minimum Stay: None
Open: All year
Hosts: Norman & Sarah Ball
1811 Pullen Rd.
Sevierville, TN 37862
(865) 428-2335 or (800) 497-2335
Fax: (865) 453-1720
bluemtnmist@aol.com
www.bbonline.com/tn/bluemtnmist

CALICO INN, Sevierville

Overall: ★★★ Room Quality: C Value: C Price: $89–$99

In 1998, readers of Pamela Lanier's well-regarded bed-and-breakfast book named Calico "Inn of the Year," so we felt it was worth a close look. This is a genuine log cabin chinked and daubed as in Abe Lincoln's days. The guest rooms are small and a little dark because of the small windows. There are two large trailers on the farm next door, which detracts a little from the mountain view. But that view (of five ranges) is awesome. And the warmth of the hosts can make you quickly forget minor flaws. They decorate the inn for each season. When guests want to go hiking or head for nearby Great Smoky Mountain National Park, the hosts can prepare a picnic basket and cooler. When guests leave, Jim and Lillian photograph them for a growing inn scrapbook and mail prints to the guests.

SETTING & FACILITIES

Location: 2 mi. off Hwy. 441 between Pigeon Forge & Sevierville
Near: Pigeon Forge, country music theaters, Great Smoky Mountain Nat'l Park
Building: Large log cabin
Grounds: 25 rural acres
Public Space: Great Room, kitchen, DR, back deck
Food & Drink: Full breakfast; refreshments on arrival
Recreation: Hiking, theater-going, shopping
Amenities & Services: Picnic basket on request, gift certificates

Accommodations

Units: 3 guest rooms
All Rooms: Mountain & forest views
Some Rooms: Double sink
Bed & Bath: Beds vary; private baths
Favorites: Wildflower Room
Comfort & Decor: Country casual

Rates, Reservations, & Restrictions

Deposit: Credit card
Discounts: None
Credit Cards: V, MC
Check-in/Out: 3 p.m./11 a.m.
Smoking: No
Pets: No
Kids: 6 & older
Minimum Stay: None
Open: All year
Hosts: Jim & Lillian Katzbeck
757 Ranch Way
Sevierville, TN 37862
(865) 428-3833 or (800) 235-1054
www.bbonline.com/tn/calico

Zone 20
Western Tennessee

Standing on Beale Street in Memphis, you can almost see a young Elvis getting ready to perform. Although born in Tupelo, Mississippi, Elvis will always be associated with Memphis, where he recorded his first hits and built his home, the famous Graceland. Graceland continues to be a mecca for his legion of fans who come to tour his house and car museum and quietly visit the Meditation Garden where he is buried.

The most famous battlefield in Tennessee is located at Shiloh National Military Park, scene of one of the bloodiest battles in the Civil War. The cannons still point over these now silent fields. The Davy Crockett Cabin in Rutherford is an interesting picture stop. For a look at how the Tennessee River was formed and the role of this riverway in steamboat and Civil War days, stop at the Tennessee River Museum in Savannah. There's a spectacular view of that river from the nearby Pickwick Landing Dam.

For More Information

Memphis Convention and Visitors Bureau
(800) 447-8278

PEACOCK HILL COUNTRY INN, College Grove

Overall: ★★★★½ Room Quality: A Value: A Price: $125–$225

This is a beautiful country inn—warm, inviting, spotlessly clean, decorated in a wonderful way by a professional decorator from Atlanta (the owner's niece). A little log house and grainery on the property house suites that offer maximum privacy. The McCall House is also part of the inn, located about a mile down the road. It has a suite with a log living and dining room, a large bedroom and bath, full kitchen facilities, and two additional guest rooms. It would be perfect for a small family reunion. What impressed us most was the quality of the bedrooms, with soft blankets, great new baths, and even an extra L.L. Bean wool blanket to snuggle under while watching some of the inn's large selection of movies on the VCR.

Setting & Facilities

Location: From I-65 South take Franklin exit, left on Hwy. 96, right on Arno Rd. to right on Giles Hill Rd.
Near: Franklin, Murfreesboro, Nashville
Building: Restored 1850s farmhouse plus rustic log cabin, grainery, add'l house
Grounds: 700 acres w/ cattle, deer, wild turkey, peacocks
Public Space: Foyer, parlor, den, DR, sun porch
Food & Drink: Full country breakfast; box lunches & candlelight dinners w/ 48 hours' notice; soft drinks avail. all day in mud room
Recreation: Sight-seeing
Amenities & Services: Selection of movie videos

Accommodations

Units: 10 guest rooms
All Rooms: TV, VCR, individually decorated, robes, ironing board & iron, piped-in music, individually controlled heat & AC

Some Rooms: Fireplace
Bed & Bath: Kings; private baths
Favorites: McCall House suite
Comfort & Decor: This is one of the most beautifully decorated inns we saw in Tennessee; comfortable seating & two stone fireplaces create a cozy feeling.

Rates, Reservations, & Restrictions

Deposit: Credit card
Discounts: Weekly, 10% corp. Sun.–Thurs.
Credit Cards: AE, V, MC, D
Check-in/Out: 4 p.m./1 p.m.
Smoking: No
Pets: In barn only
Kids: Not in farmhouse; ask about other accommodations here
Minimum Stay: 2 nights during Oct. weekends
Open: All year except Christmas Eve & Christmas Day
Hosts: Walter & Anita Ogilvie
6994 Giles Hill Rd.
College Grove, TN 37046
(615) 368-7727 or (800) 327-6663
www.peacockhill.com

LOCUST HILL BED & BREAKFAST, Columbia

Overall: ★★★½ Room Quality: B Value: B Price: $95–$124

The two-level Smokehouse is our favorite spot here. Built in 1840, the original beams are still on display. The downstairs has a small but comfortable sitting area with a fireplace and rockers. The bedroom upstairs has a low ceiling, which those with claustrophobia might call "close," and romantics would say was "cozy." The ceiling is painted with clouds. The highlight of the morning is definitely breakfast. The Southern-style biscuits are wonderful, as is the homemade coffeecake, all served in a homelike atmosphere. "Many women like to stay here," said hostess/owner Beverly. "That's why we have several rooms with two beds, a queen and a twin, so women can share a room without sharing a bed. Many like that."

Setting & Facilities

Location: Exit 37 off I-65 to Moorseville Pike
Near: James Polk home, Saturn manufacturing (assembly line tours avail.), horse ranches
Building: 1840 Antebellum home
Grounds: 8.5 acres w/ 2 acres of lawn & flower beds (marigolds, asters, chrysanthemums) & pond
Public Space: LR, DR, parlors w/ fireplaces
Food & Drink: Full breakfast w/ scrambled eggs w/ cheese & chives, cheese grits casserole, coffee cake; other specialties: blueberry or orange French toast; morning coffee delivered to room
Recreation: Bicycling, hiking, golf, visiting nearby Tennessee Walking Horse stables
Amenities & Services: Discount coupons for local restaurants

Accommodations

Units: 4 guest rooms
All Rooms: 20 x 20 feet in size
Some Rooms: Upholstered rocking chairs, window seat
Bed & Bath: Queen, double, twin; private baths
Favorites: Smokehouse
Comfort & Decor: Family antiques and items hosts have collected are displayed throughout; quilts, lace curtains, and rockers give the home a comfortable feeling.

Rates, Reservations, & Restrictions

Deposit: Credit card; 7-day cancellation
Discounts: AAA, seniors ("We don't 'card' seniors," says the hostess w/ smile." All guests have to do is say they're seniors to get the discount.")
Credit Cards: AE, V, MC, D
Check-in/Out: 4 p.m./11 a.m.
Smoking: No
Pets: No
Kids: No
Minimum Stay: During "Mule Day" Festival (we're not making this up)
Open: All year
Hosts: Bill & Beverly Beard
1185 Moorseville Pike
Columbia, TN 38401
(931) 388-8531 or (800) 577-8264
Fax: (931) 540-8719
www.bbonline.com/tn/locust

SWEETWATER INN BED & BREAKFAST, Culleoka

Overall: ★★★★ Room Quality: B Value: B Price: $90–$125

The Sweetwater Inn is a beautifully restored home with wraparound porches with direct private access to each of the guest rooms. There are rockers by each of the doors and tables covered with white linen tablecloths. The outdoor area is attractive and has easily handled wedding receptions for up to 200 people. On request the host will prepare picnic baskets. Dinners are also available by reservation, but bring your own wine; the bed-and-breakfast has no liquor license.

Setting & Facilities

Location: Exit 32 off I-65, west on Hwy. 373 6.2 mi., left on Campbell Station Rd.
Near: Antebellum homes, James Polk home, The Athenaeum, Rattle & Snap Plantation, Historic Elm Springs
Building: 1900 Gothic Steamboat–style home
Grounds: 10 rural acres
Public Space: Porch, deck, music room, sunroom
Food & Drink: Full breakfast served by candlelight; specialties: Southern fried garlic potatoes, pineapple casserole, stuffed French toast; call for special dietary needs
Recreation: Hiking, horseshoes, antiques auctions, bicycling, canoeing, fishing, skeet shooting, cave spelunking, tennis
Amenities & Services: TV on request

Accommodations

Units: 4 guest rooms & suites
All Rooms: Private door to upstairs porch
Bed & Bath: Queens; private baths
Favorites: Captain Campell's Room w/ attractive late-Victorian decor
Comfort & Decor: Rooms have various themes, including late Victorian, country farmhouse, and European country.

Rates, Reservations, & Restrictions

Deposit: 1 night
Discounts: AAA
Credit Cards: V, MC
Check-in/Out: 4 p.m./11 a.m.
Smoking: No
Pets: No
Kids: No
Minimum Stay: None
Open: All year except Easter, Christmas–New Year's Day
Hosts: Melissa McEwen & Thommy Young
2436 Campbells Station Rd.
Culleoka, TN 38451
(931) 987-3077
Fax: (931) 987-0730
sweetwaterinn@att.net

INN AT WALKING HORSE FARM, Franklin

Overall: ★★★★ Room Quality: B Value: B Price: $80–$100

You can stay in a scenic rural area with great access to historic Franklin and lively Nashville. The inn has a very casual country decor on the traditional side and a casual feel to the hospitality. Rooms were very clean and nicely decorated with a variety of antiques and reproductions. One of the rooms has an adjoining guest room with a walk-through bathroom between them, suitable for family use. You can hike the 40 acres, watch the walking horses practice their famous gait, and even pitch horseshoes—possibly with funny sidelong glances from the horses. Or retreat indoors to the paneled den upstairs with TV and billiards. The inn is now developing its corporate meeting and reception business with a big commercial kitchen that can serve up to 125 people for dinner.

Setting & Facilities

Location: I-65 South to Exit 61, right 0.9 mi. to Hwy. 431,left 0.9 mi
Near: Franklin, Nashville, Civil War sites
Building: Colonial
Grounds: 40-acre rural walking horse farm
Public Space: Rec. room, DR, porches
Food & Drink: Full country breakfast w/ omelets, sausage, biscuits
Recreation: Touring Civil War sites
Amenities & Services: Dining/meeting facil. (200), horse boarding

Accommodations

Units: 3 guest rooms
All Rooms: Large
Some Rooms: Antique furnishings, countryside views
Bed & Bath: Queens; private baths
Favorites: None
Comfort & Decor: The traditional country atmosphere is enhanced with warm yellow and red hues.

Rates, Reservations, & Restrictions

Deposit: Credit card
Discounts: None
Credit Cards: V, MC
Check-in/Out: 3 p.m./11 a.m.
Smoking: No
Pets: No
Kids: No
No-Nos: Some restrictions on use of alcohol; ask
Minimum Stay: None
Open: All year
Hosts: Dwight & Sherry Stacey
1409 Lewisburg Pike
Franklin, TN 37064
(615) 790-2022
www.bbonline.com/tn/walkinghorse

HIGHLAND PLACE BED & BREAKFAST, Jackson

Overall: ★★★★½ Room Quality: B Value: A Price: $80–$135

You'll find wonderful hospitality here, with cookies and Cokes in every room and popcorn waiting by a hall microwave. We liked all the rooms. Our only minor complaint was the bath in the Louis Room. It's private but down the stairs from the bedroom, and that always means put-on-your-robe inconvenience, especially during the night. But the mansion, located in the North Highland Historical District, is truly beautiful. The cherry-paneled den is particularly attractive. On request (and for an extra fee), a host in an authentic Civil War tuxedo will serve guests dinner by the fire. Hand me the robe, Mildred, we're staying no matter where the bathroom is!

Setting & Facilities

Location: 3.3 mi. off I-40 (Exit 82-A)
Near: Casey Jones Village, Davey Crockett log cabin & museum, Cypress Grove Nature Area, Graceland (Memphis home of Elvis Presley), Shiloh Battlefield
Building: 1911 Modified Colonial
Grounds: Half-acre yard
Public Space: Main floor all public space (living/music room, library, DR, breakfast room, porch)
Food & Drink: Full breakfast w/ fruit, granola, egg casseroles; 24-hour access to soft drinks & ice cream
Recreation: Golf, horseback riding, tennis, fishing, hiking
Amenities & Services: Large video library, local restaurant menus, complimentary tickets to local sporting events, symphony performances

Accommodations

Units: 4 guest rooms
All Rooms: TV/VCR, desk & sitting space
Some Rooms: Working fireplace, feather mattress, skylight, canopy four-poster bed
Bed & Bath: King, queen, or twins; private baths, including claw-foot tub & waterfall shower
Favorites: In summer choose the suite w/ full-length skylight for a super bright room; in winter, take the room w/ the wood-burning fireplace & tub for 2
Comfort & Decor: The entire house was redecorated in 1995 by 28 interior designers for the West Tennessee Designer Showhouse; antiques & reproductions, original oil paintings, antique prints, and lithographs are highlights.

Rates, Reservations, & Restrictions

Deposit: Credit card; 72-hour cancellation
Discounts: 10% seniors, military, corp.
Credit Cards: AE, V, MC
Check-in/Out: 3 p.m./11 a.m. (Sunday check-out 2 p.m.)
Smoking: No
Pets: No
Kids: 12 & older
Minimum Stay: Holiday weekends
Open: All year
Hosts: Glenn & Janice Wall, owners; Don & Maria, "relief" innkeepers
519 N. Highland Ave.
Jackson, TN 38301
(901) 427-1472
Fax: (901) 422-7994
www.highlandplace.com

ACADEMY PLACE BED & BREAKFAST, Mt. Pleasant

Overall: ★★★½ Room Quality: B Value: C Price: $85–$135

This very Victorian bed-and-breakfast is built on the foundation of a school constructed in 1835. Two of the rooms are adjoining, share a bath, and are reserved for families. This suite also has a kitchenette. Another room does have a private bath, but you have to come out of the room and step down into the bath, an arrangement we don't like at night, especially for senior travelers. The spa room with hot tub located on a glassed-in porch is a treat. Your hosts like to talk about the local attractions, including Civil War battlefields and Antebellum homes. Ask for directions to Lumpy's, a great little 1950s-style soda shop and restaurant.

SETTING & FACILITIES

Location: 10 mi. from Columbia, TN; take Rt. 243 to Mt. Pleasant
Near: Tattle & Snap plantation, James Polk Home, Amish community, Natchez Trace
Building: 1904 Queen Anne Victorian
Grounds: 2.5 parklike acres
Public Space: Parlor, DR, study, hot spa room, porches
Food & Drink: Full breakfast w/ baked apple French toast; homemade bedtime dessert
Recreation: Bicycling, canoeing, fishing, golf, hiking, horseback riding, cave spelunking
Amenities & Services: Brochures on dining, local attractions; computer, fax, copier avail.

ACCOMMODATIONS

Units: 4 guest rooms
All Rooms: Views of grounds, desk
Some Rooms: Attractive (but non-working) fireplaces
Bed & Bath: Queen or double; 3 rooms w/ private baths, 2-BR suite shares bath
Favorites: Laura's Room—extra bright & cheerful
Comfort & Decor: Family antiques include antique mirrors, and soothing colors such as peach tones, roses, and yellows provide a restful atmosphere.

RATES, RESERVATIONS, & RESTRICTIONS

Deposit: 1 night
Discounts: Long stays
Credit Cards: None
Check-in/Out: 3 p.m./10:30 a.m.
Smoking: No
Pets: No
Kids: Welcome
Minimum Stay: None
Open: All year
Hosts: Randall & Faye Wyatt
301 Goodloe St.
Mt. Pleasant, TN
(931) 379-3198 or (888) 252-1892
Fax: (931) 379-3198
apbb@usit.met

WHITE ELEPHANT BED & BREAKFAST INN, Savannah

Overall: ★★★½ Room Quality: B Value: C Price: $85–$105

History and Civil War buffs will particularly enjoy Savannah and touring nearby Shiloh National Military Park (your host offers tour guide services of Shiloh). You can easily walk to the Tennessee River and downtown shops and restaurants. Breakfast is served with beautiful antique silverware and depression glass. The birds on the feeder seen through the bay windows provide a morning show. The hosts seem a little more reserved than other bed-and-breakfast owners, but ask them a few questions about the area and they'll soon open up with information. Bluegrass festivals and Christmas celebrations with carriage rides are great times to be in Savannah.

SETTING & FACILITIES

Location: Just off Hwy. 64 (Savannah's Main St.); driveway behind B&B is a little complicated to find; call for directions
Near: Tennessee River Museum, Tennessee River, Shiloh Nat'l Military Park, Pickwick Lane & Dam, Natchez Trace
Building: 1901 Queen Anne–style Victorian
Grounds: 1.5 acres w/ high sugar maples
Public Space: 2 parlors w/ original fireplaces, central hallway w/ bookcases, large DR
Food & Drink: Full breakfast; specialties: German apple pancakes, Southern pecan waffles, Scottish scones; chocolate chip cookies
Recreation: Canoeing, boating, fishing, bird-watching, golf (5 courses w/in 15 mi.)
Amenities & Services: Terry robes, numerous books & magazines in public rooms, local restaurant menus

Accommodations

Units: 3 guest rooms
All Rooms: On 2nd floor, ceiling fan, chairs, reading lamp
Some Rooms: Unique carved-oak century bed, antique iron bed frame, 1900 claw-foot tub
Bed & Bath: Queens; private baths
Favorites: Poppy Room—largest guest room, largest bathroom
Comfort & Decor: 1901 late-Victorian decor and nineteenth-century themes are featured (nature, flowers, fauna).

Rates, Reservations, & Restrictions

Deposit: 1 night; 10-day cancellation
Discounts: Singles, $10 off; long stays
Credit Cards: None
Check-in/Out: 3–6 p.m./11 a.m.
Smoking: No; "smokers are not welcome," says host; so there!
Pets: No
Kids: Older children welcome; ask
Minimum Stay: During some special events, holidays
Open: All year
Hosts: Ken & Sharon Hansgen
304 Church St.
Savannah, TN 38372
(901) 925-6410
www.bbonline.com/tn/elephant

Kentucky

Kentucky is known as the Bluegrass State, and the grass in much of the central horse country around Lexington really does look blue and green. The state presents a high mountain face to the east that moderates to more rolling terrain in the heartland and rocky hills to the west, culminating in large man-made lakes in the western portion.

For once, American explorers got to the area that became Kentucky before the Spanish, creating the first permanent settlement at Harrodsburg in 1744. Daniel Boone, star of stage, screen, and history, hacked out the Wilderness Trail through the Cumberland Gap. The town he founded became Boonesborough. Kentucky was admitted to the Union as the fifteenth state. Like Tennessee, Kentucky residents were of two minds about the Civil War, and brothers fought brothers in blue or gray uniforms. There is some intriguing speculation that Abraham Lincoln and Jefferson Davis, who were born a year apart in western Kentucky, may even have passed each other as boys on some of the country roads, perhaps exchanging waves with no premonition of the fateful days ahead for both of them.

Louisville is Kentucky's largest city. Lexington is in the heart of the state, its presence on the interstate is signaled by long white fences, stately mansions, and horses at pasture. Many of Kentucky's smaller city's Main streets have been going through extensive restoration in recent years. Shelbyville has a Victorian downtown that people from the nineteenth century would have felt right at home in. Springfield's Washington County courthouse is the oldest still in use in Kentucky. Its most unusual document is the marriage certificate of Captain Thomas Lincoln and Nancy Hanks, Abe Lincoln's parents.

We suggest planning your bed-and-breakfast vacation with a good map and a guidebook to the state. Here are some recommended stops: Louisville for the Kentucky Derby, Lexington Shaker Village, Land Between the Lakes National Recreation Area (highly recommended

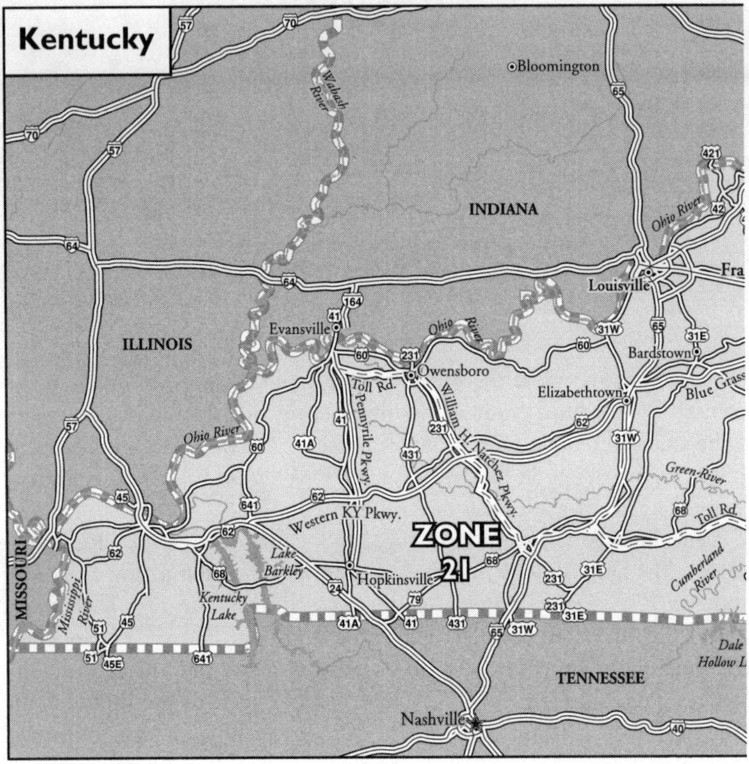

restoration of early rural life with farmers and laborers working as they might have in another era), Hodgenville (Lincoln's birthplace), My Old Kentucky Home State Park, and the Kentucky Horse Park.

Incidentally, the name Kentucky is a corruption of an Iroquois Indian phrase that means "Land of Tomorrow."

For More Information

Kentucky Department of Travel
(800) 225-8747

Kentucky Department of Parks
(800) 255-7275

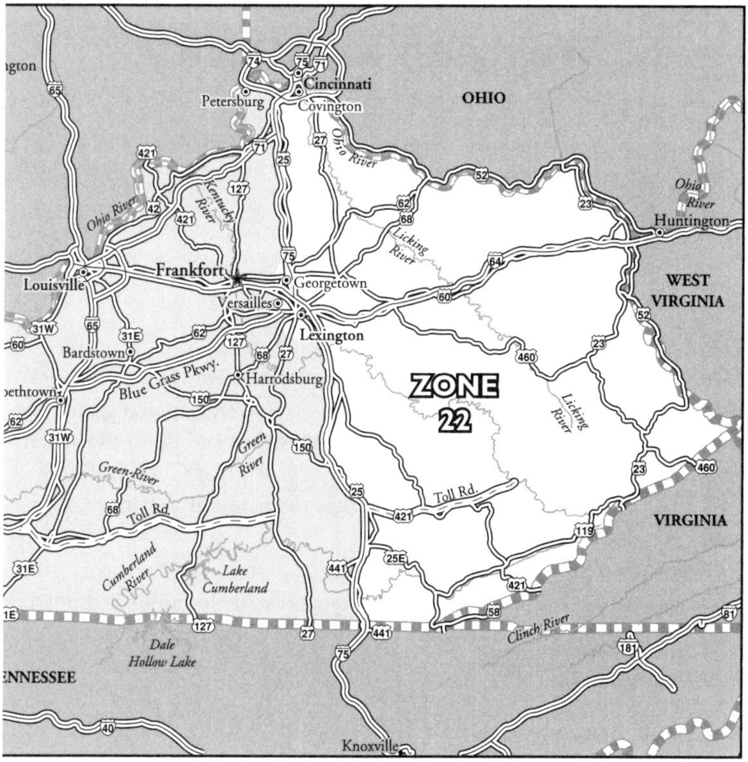

Bardstown
Beautiful Dreamer, p. 385
Jailer's Inn, p. 386

Covington
Amos Shinkle Bed & Breakfast Townhouse, p. 397

Georgetown
Blackridge Hall Bed & Breakfast, p. 387
Pineapple Inn Bed & Breakfast, p. 388

Harrodsburg
Canaan Land Farm Bed & Breakfast, p. 389

Lexington
Silver Springs Farm, p. 398
Swann's Nest at Cygnet Farm, p. 399

Louisville
Inn at Woodhaven, p. 390
Old Louisville Inn, p. 391

Petersburg
First Farm Inn, p. 392

Versailles
1823 Historic Rose Hill Inn, p. 394

Zone 21
Western Kentucky

Those fortunate enough to have (or to have inherited!) tickets come each spring to Louisville for the most famous two minutes in racing, the Kentucky Derby. But there is considerably more to see and do in town, starting with the interesting Kentucky Derby Museum at Churchill Downs, and the Louisville Slugger Museum, where the bats and memories of baseball's greatest hitters are preserved.

Kentucky Lake and Lake Barkley in the extreme western part of the state offer some 2,300 miles of shore line and virtually unlimited boating and fishing opportunities (with bass, bluegill, walleye, and other fish). Families enjoy a ride on a steam or diesel train at the Kentucky Railway Museum at Bardstown. Another favorite family spot is Mammoth Cave, the world's longest underground system of caves. Other museums worth an afternoon are the National Corvette Museum in Bowling Green and the Civil War Museum in Bardstown.

For More Information

Louisville and Jefferson County Convention and Visitors Bureau
(800) 792-5595

Tennessee Wildlife Resources Agency
(hunting and fishing regulations)
(615) 781-6500

BEAUTIFUL DREAMER, Bardstown

Overall: ★★★★½ Room Quality: B Value: A Price: $99–$129

"Beautiful dreamer . . . waken to me." You may find yourself humming this famous American classic when you sit on one of the upper or lower verandas of this bed-and-breakfast, with a romantic view of the real *My Old Kentucky Home* immortalized by Stephen Foster. The spacious interior of Beautiful Dreamer is beautifully decorated with exquisite antiques and reproductions. A cheery wood fire greeted us in the dining room and a gas log fire in the bedroom. Our host clearly loves her home and loves to cook. Calorie alert! Cookies and home-baked pies are served in the afternoon. Our host asked about our dietary needs (too late after that pie!) and always tried to anticipate what we wanted before we asked. If you're going to this part of Kentucky, plan on some beautiful dreams here.

SETTING & FACILITIES

Location: Exit 25 off Bluegrass Parkway (Rt. 150), west 1.75 mi.
Near: My Old Kentucky Home State Park (right across street), Stephen Foster's home
Building: Federal w/ dbl. front porches
Grounds: 1-acre yard
Public Space: LR, DR, porches
Food & Drink: 5-course breakfast w/ baked French toast w/ strawberry syrup, stone-ground grits, hash browns w/ Vidalia onions
Recreation: Sight-seeing Civil War sites, carriage rides, antiques shops
Amenities & Services: Local restaurant menus

ACCOMMODATIONS

Units: 4 guest rooms
All Rooms: Color TV, hair dryer
Some Rooms: Park views, canopy bed, whirlpool tub
Bed & Bath: Queens; private baths
Favorites: Beautiful Dreamer Room w/ its cherry canopy bed, TV w/ VCR, & dbl. whirlpool tub
Comfort & Decor: Antiques, wood-burning fireplace in DR

RATES, RESERVATIONS, & RESTRICTIONS

Deposit: Credit card; 14-day cancellation
Discounts: 10% AAA, seniors (must ask for discount at time of reservation)
Credit Cards: AE, V, MC
Check-in/Out: 4 p.m./11:30 a.m.
Smoking: No
Pets: No
Kids: No
Minimum Stay: 2 nights during special events (e.g., Kentucky Derby)
Open: All year
Hosts: Daniel & Lynell Ginter
440 E. Stephen Foster Ave.
Bardstown, KY 40004
(502) 348-4004 or (800) 811-8312
www.geocities.com/bdreamerbb

JAILER'S INN, Bardstown

Overall: ★★★½ Room Quality: B Value: B Price: $65–$115

We like the host's own description of his bed-and-breakfast: "Iron bars on windows, 30-inch-thick limestone walls, and a heavy steel door slamming behind you" may not sound like the typical tourist accommodation. However . . . Jailer's Inn offers a unique and luxurious way to "do time." The rooms are surprisingly attractive (for a former jail!), furnished with Colonial and Victorian antiques. We stayed in a room with an unpainted, rough-timbered ceiling and three walls hand-painted with stencils. Kids seem to love the converted women's cell with two of the original jail bunks and a security door. This place is certainly not your typical bed-and-breakfast, but it is fun and really different. Don't miss the opportunity to take the free jail tour.

Setting & Facilities

Location: Center of Bardstown, right off court square
Near: My Old Kentucky Home, Makers Mark Distillery, Civil War Museum, Bernheim Forest
Building: Federal brick building
Grounds: Courtyard surrounded by 10-foot-high stone wall
Public Space: Common area, courtyard, porch
Food & Drink: Full breakfast; specialties: cheese-stuffed toast, peach French toast
Recreation: Golf, swimming, antiquing, walking
Amenities & Services: List of local restaurants, tour of old jail

Accommodations

Units: 6 guest rooms
All Rooms: Large
Some Rooms: Fireplace, canopy bed, heirloom furnishings
Bed & Bath: Beds vary; private baths
Favorites: 1819 Room (Colonial)
Comfort & Decor: All rooms are individually decorated.

Rates, Reservations, & Restrictions

Deposit: Full deposit; 5-day cancellation
Discounts: None
Credit Cards: AE, V, MC, D
Check-in/Out: 2 p.m./11 a.m.
Smoking: In designated areas
Pets: No
Kids: Welcome
Minimum Stay: None
Open: Feb. 1–Dec. 31 (closed Jan.)
Hosts: C. Paul McCoy
111 W. Stephen Foster Ave.
Bardstown, KY 40004
(502) 348-5551 or (800) 948-5551
Fax: (502) 349-5551
Cpaul@jailersinn.com
www.jailersinn.com

BLACKRIDGE HALL BED & BREAKFAST, Georgetown

Overall: ★★★★★ Room Quality: A Value: A Price: $89–$179

Guests enter this handsome bed-and-breakfast to the sound of music and host Jim Black announcing, "This is the finest bed-and-breakfast in Kentucky." That's hard to dispute as you walk through the beautifully decorated house and guest rooms. Breakfast is served in the formal dining room or breakfast room. In good weather, ask to have breakfast on the brick veranda with great views of the bluegrass countryside. Guests can also visit a nearby farm to view miniature show horses.

SETTING & FACILITIES

Location: 2.7 mi. from Georgetown on Hwy. 460 East
Near: Georgetown College, University of Kentucky, Keeneland Race Track, Kentucky Horse Park
Building: Southern Georgian-style mansion
Grounds: Rolling bluegrass landscape
Public Space: DR, guest kitchen
Food & Drink: Full breakfast; specialty: unique baked grapefruit dish & French oven bread
Recreation: Tours of Toyota Motor Corp., antiques shopping, factory outlet stores
Amenities & Services: Use of kitchenette

ACCOMMODATIONS

Units: 3 guest rooms, 3 suites
All Rooms: TV, intercom w/ music, games
Some Rooms: Rice-carved four-poster bed, marble whirlpool tub, sitting area, private entrance
Bed & Bath: Beds vary; private baths
Favorites: Old Kentucky Home Master Suite
Comfort & Decor: Eighteenth- and nineteenth-century antiques; master suites are particularly attractive with luxurious touches such as a marble whirlpool tub, fireplace, love seat, and live plants.

RATES, RESERVATIONS, & RESTRICTIONS

Deposit: Credit card; 7-day cancellation
Discounts: None
Credit Cards: All major cards
Check-in/Out: 4–10 p.m./noon
Smoking: No
Pets: No
Kids: Not encouraged
Minimum Stay: 2 nights during special events
Open: All year
Hosts: Jim Black
4055 Paris Pike
Georgetown, KY 40324
(502) 863-2069 or (800) 768-9308

PINEAPPLE INN BED & BREAKFAST, Georgetown

Overall: ★★★ Room Quality: C Value: B Price: $70–$90

Rooms are large with many antique family heirlooms. There's no TV, but games and books are available. There was excellent lighting in the rooms. However, one room's detached bath was a couple steps down and a possible hazard at night. Ask for another one if you get it. Finding a restaurant is another small problem. Scott County is dry, so there are two restaurants in town, which close at 5 p.m. Fava's restaurant is open Friday and Saturday. Fortunately, there is a wide selection of restaurants in nearby Lexington. You will see a Ginkgo tree in the yard. Ask your hostess about this tree; it's a fascinating story.

SETTING & FACILITIES

Location: On Hwy. 25 about 2 mi., Exits 125–126 on I-75
Near: Kentucky Horse Park, Toyota Motor manufacturing facil. (tours avail.), local horse farms
Building: 1886 Victorian
Grounds: Landscaped lawn
Public Space: LR, DR, family room, porch
Food & Drink: Full breakfast; specialties: eggs Benedict, apple cinnamon French toast
Recreation: Hiking, biking
Amenities & Services: Restaurant guides, local newspapers

ACCOMMODATIONS

Units: 4 guest rooms
All Rooms: Antiques
Some Rooms: Queen canopy bed, antique tub
Bed & Bath: Beds vary; private baths
Favorites: None
Comfort & Decor: Furnished with many antiques

RATES, RESERVATIONS, & RESTRICTIONS

Deposit: Credit card; 48-hour cancellation
Discounts: For stays over 4 days
Credit Cards: V, MC
Check-in/Out: 3–4 p.m./11 a.m.
Smoking: In designated areas
Pets: No
Kids: Welcome

Minimum Stay: None
Open: All year
Hosts: Muriel & Les Olsen
645 S. Broadway
Georgetown, KY 40324
(502) 868-5453
Fax: (502) 868-5453
www.georgetownky.com

CANAAN LAND FARM BED & BREAKFAST, Harrodsburg

Overall: ★★★ Room Quality: C Value: C Price: $75–$125

Want to visit a real farm? Here it is! In the spring you can watch a special "lambing" time when new baby lambs arrive almost daily from March through April. There are multiple births of triplets and quads (but no clones that we know of). This is a wonderful place for kids, who can go meet the resident goats and miniature donkeys. For an old-time treat, choose the reconstructed log house with two stone chimneys on the Canaan Land Farm. It has three individual guest rooms and a large great room with a fireplace. The house was built originally by Philemon Waters in 1815, who frequently took to the woods with Daniel Boone. Standing in the doorway you have a real sense of life in frontier days. Don't expect anything fancy at this bed-and-breakfast—furnishings are comfortable but rustic. Come here for peace and quiet and perhaps some strolls to the nearby Kentucky River.

SETTING & FACILITIES

Location: From Shakertown take Hwy. 68 & turn left on Canaan Land Rd.
Near: Shakertown, Old Fort Harrod State Park
Building: 1795 brick farmhouse
Grounds: 189-acre farm
Public Space: Large deck area
Food & Drink: Full breakfast w/ Kentucky bourbon French toast, sausage, biscuits
Recreation: Horseback riding, boat rentals
Amenities & Services: Swimming pool

ACCOMMODATIONS

Units: 6 guest rooms including 3 in restored cabin
All Rooms: Hardwood floors
Some Rooms: Fireplace
Bed & Bath: Beds vary; private baths
Favorites: None
Comfort & Decor: Period furniture and family heirlooms

RATES, RESERVATIONS, & RESTRICTIONS

Deposit: $25 for each night reserved
Discounts: Reduced winter rates
Credit Cards: None
Check-in/Out: 3 p.m./11 a.m.
Smoking: No
Pets: No

Kids: 12 & older
Minimum Stay: 2 nights Oct. weekends (fall foliage & festival time)
Open: All year

Hosts: Fred & Theo Bee
700 Canaan Land Rd.
Harrodsburg, KY 40330
(859) 734-3984 or (888) 734-3984
www.bbonline.com/ky/canaan

INN AT WOODHAVEN, Louisville

Overall: ★★★½ Room Quality: B Value: B Price: $65–$75

One very good sign: 75 percent of this inn's business is repeat business. The location is ideal for business travelers who can come in late, serve themselves a hot chocolate or cappuccino in the room, nibble on biscotti, and then transmit their report to the home office via their laptop computers hooked up to their private phones with computer connections. The Rose Cottage is very attractive, a separate octagon-shaped building with a sitting area with fireplace, a double whirlpool tub, and really high ceilings (25 feet!). This is a long-established area and considered one of the safer residential neighborhoods in the city.

Setting & Facilities

Location: From I-264, exit for Breckenridge Ln. North, right on Kresge, left on Hubbards Ln.
Near: Kentucky Derby, Louisville Slugger museum, Louisville Antique Mall
Building: 1850s Greek Revival home plus carriage house & cottage
Grounds: Landscaped lawn w/ gardens
Public Space: 3 common areas

Food & Drink: Full breakfast; specialties: breakfast pie w/ mushrooms, swiss cheese, sherry; caramel French toast; warm chocolate cookies at check-in
Recreation: Kentucky Derby, sightseeing, St. James Art Festival, tennis, golf
Amenities & Services: Passes to nearby fitness center

Accommodations

Units: 8 guest rooms (4 in main house, 3 in carriage house, 1 Rose Cottage)
All Rooms: Coffee, tea, hot chocolate w/ peanut butter crackers for late-night snacking, iron & ironing board, phone w/ data port, TV
Some Rooms: 12-foot ceiling, sitting area, dbl. whirlpool tub, loft
Bed & Bath: Beds vary; private baths
Favorites: Rose Cottage
Comfort & Decor: Antiques and diamond-paned windows create an elegant atmosphere.

Rates, Reservations, & Restrictions

Deposit: Credit card
Discounts: None
Credit Cards: AE, V, MC, D
Check-in/Out: 3 p.m./11 a.m.
Smoking: No
Pets: Dogs welcome in Rose Cottage, but ask about precautions needed
Kids: Welcome
Minimum Stay: None
Open: All year
Host: Marsha Burton
401 South Hubbards Ln.
Louisville, KY 40207
(502) 895-1011 or (888) 895-1011
info@woodhaven.com
www. bbonline.com/ky/woodhaven

OLD LOUISVILLE INN, Louisville

Overall: ★★★ | Room Quality: C | Value: B | Price: $95–$195

The man who owned this massive Victorian mansion in 1901 was the president of the Louisville Home Telephone Company, and he obviously loved to entertain. The entrance is not exactly bright and cheery, but the original red mahogany paneling throughout the inn and the ceiling frescoes in the lobby give you the feeling that you are walking through history. If you want to impress a companion, you can give the meanings of each of the frescoes. They are illustrations of Franklin Roosevelt's four freedoms: freedom from want, of speech, from fear, and of religion. At breakfast, we overindulged in an omelet layered with portobello mushrooms, cheese, and sausage. Breakfast is served until the civilized hour of 10:30 a.m.

Setting & Facilities

Location: St. Catherine exit off I-65, left on Third St.
Near: Churchill Downs (Kentucky Derby), antiques shopping on Bardstown Rd. & Frankfort Ave., *Belle of Louisville* sternwheeler, Louisville Slugger Museum (a "must" for baseball fans)
Building: 1901 10,000-square-foot mansion
Grounds: Small lawn
Public Space: Parlor, breakfast room, game room

Food & Drink: Full breakfast; specialties: popovers & peach French toast, homemade granola, muffins, juice, fresh fruit, yogurt; cookies & tea on arrival

Recreation: Sight-seeing, antiques shopping

Amenities & Services: Local restaurant menus, games & puzzles

Accommodations

Units: 11 guest rooms
All Rooms: Antique quilt
Some Rooms: Original Italian marble bath, working fireplace
Bed & Bath: Beds vary; private baths
Favorites: Room 11, romantic Celebration Suite; often used by honeymooners
Comfort & Decor: Filled with numerous antiques and heirlooms.

Rates, Reservations, & Restrictions

Deposit: 1 night full amount, multi-nights 50%; 48-hour cancellation
Discounts: None
Credit Cards: AE, MC, V, D
Check-in/Out: 3 p.m./10 a.m.
Smoking: In restricted areas
Pets: W/ host's approval
Kids: Welcome; 12 & under stay free in parents' room
Minimum Stay: No, except during Kentucky Derby, other major events
Open: All year
Host: Marianne Lesher
1359 South Third St.
Louisville, KY 40208
(502) 635-1574
Fax: (502) 637-5892
info@oldlouinn.com
www.oldlouinn.com

FIRST FARM INN, Petersburg

Overall: ★★★½ Room Quality: B Value: B Price: $90–$99

After a warm greeting from our host, her daughter, and their dog, we went to the barn to make friends with the horses by brushing them. The horses, as well as riding lessons, are available for guests for an extra fee. After a wonderful ride through the woods and around the fishing pond, we found an outside hot tub a welcome relief for some stiffening muscles. This place is really bucolic, but there are some unwelcome interruptions. Sounds from the interstate highway distracted us from the bird calls and other natural sounds. The separation of family and guests is not as much as we would prefer. We were welcome in the family room, but a four-year-old was watching cartoons there. When we went to bed, we were still conscious of the host family in the next room. We would certainly go back for the horse rides and the well-stocked fishing pond. We'd just prefer that the bed-and-breakfast be a little less stocked with family members, friendly though they all are.

Setting & Facilities

Location: Across Ohio River in a corner of KY that meets IN & OH, several exits west of greater Cincinnati airport (which is in Kentucky); it's a little difficult to find, so get clear directions when you call
Near: Historic Burlington merchants (quilts, herbs, antiques), Dinsmore Homestead, Big Bone Lick State Park, Cincinnati & Covington riverfronts
Building: 1870 farmhouse
Grounds: 21 acres w/ pond, pasture, barn, outdoor spa
Public Space: DR, LR, family room w/ fireplace
Food & Drink: Full breakfast w/ creative specialties: whole wheat biscuits, banana–chocolate chip or peanut butter–banana pancakes; call for special dietary needs (vegetarian, low fat, low sodium)
Recreation: Boating, hiking, birdwatching, fishing
Amenities & Services: Travel recommendations, local restaurant menus, riding lessons avail., massage therapy, board games

Accommodations

Units: 2 guest rooms
All Rooms: Hillside views, antique oak furniture
Some Rooms: Stained-glass window, daybed & trundle
Bed & Bath: Queens; private baths
Favorites: None
Comfort & Decor: Original art and stained-glass windows are the highlights here.

Rates, Reservations, & Restrictions

Deposit: Credit card
Discounts: Multiday, midweek (check Web site)
Credit Cards: V, MC
Check-in/Out: 3 p.m./noon
Smoking: No
Pets: Ask; resident dog, cats
Kids: Welcome
Minimum Stay: None
Open: All year
Hosts: Jennifer Warner, Dana Kisor
2510 Stevens Rd.
Petersburg, KY 41080
(859) 586-0299 or (800) 277-9527
Fax: (859) 586-0199
firstfarm@goodnews.net
www.bbonline.com/ky/firstfarm

1823 HISTORIC ROSE HILL INN, Versailles

Overall: ★★★★½ Room Quality: A Value: B Price: $85–$125

Rose Hill Inn was once surrounded by hundreds of acres of farmland. Today it is in the midst of a bevy of restaurants and antiques shops in small, picturesque Versailles (pronounced Versales, not the French way, Versigh). This house is a living history book, with antique chandeliers and stained-glass windows. Families with children and pets may prefer the guest cottage; couples who want privacy and romantic Victorian surroundings should stay in the main house. One thing we particularly liked—the hosts' quarters were completely hidden. We enjoyed talking with them but felt no sense of intrusion. Guests can choose their own breakfast time and tell the host of any dietary restrictions. A lovely bed-and-breakfast experience.

SETTING & FACILITIES

Location: I-64 to 60 South to Versailles, right on Bus. 60 to downtown area (Main St.), right on Rose Hill
Near: Keeneland, Kentucky Horse Park, Shaker Village at Pleasant Hill, Irish Acres Antiques Gallery, Red Mile Harness Race Track
Building: 1832 Federal-style home
Grounds: 3 acres w/ water, rose gardens
Public Space: Library, parlor, upstairs sitting room
Food & Drink: Full breakfast; specialties: banana-filled French toast, spinach egg puff, apple pannekoeken
Recreation: Walking trail (next door), bird-watching
Amenities & Services: Newspapers in parlor, local restaurant menus, fridge w/ sodas

Accommodations

Units: 6 guest rooms
All Rooms: Hardwood floors w/ area rugs, TV, phone
Some Rooms: Dbl. whirlpool, full kitchen
Bed & Bath: Beds vary; private baths
Favorites: Miss Lucie's Room w/ four-poster bed
Comfort & Decor: Antiques, traditional furnishings; 14-foot ceilings downstairs

Rates, Reservations, & Restrictions

Deposit: Credit card
Discounts: Corp.
Credit Cards: AE, V, MC, D
Check-in/Out: 3 p.m./noon
Smoking: No
Pets: Yes, w/ some restrictions; ask
Kids: Welcome
Minimum Stay: 2 nights on racing season weekends (Apr., Oct.)
Open: All year
Hosts: Sharon & Marianne Amberg
233 Rose Hill
Versailles, KY 40383
(606) 873-5957 or (800) 307-0460
Fax: (606) 873-1813
Innkeepers@rosehillinn.com
www/ rosehillin.com

Zone 22
Eastern Kentucky

Lexington is the state's second largest city, surrounded by many of the nation's top thoroughbred horse farms. Some of these horses test their mettle at the Keeneland Race Course in April and October. Guided tours of the horse farms are available, and at some, children can pet and pose with the horses. Ashland is one of the beautiful mansions in this area, an 18-room home built for U.S. Senator Henry Clay in the nineteenth century.

Cumberland Gap has been called the "doorway" to the American West. It was used as a natural passageway for animals through the mountains, a path later followed by many pioneers, including Daniel Boone. It is now part of 20,000-acre Cumberland Gap National Historical Park. Hike some of the trails to views of three states—Kentucky, Tennessee, and Virginia.

Another fascinating stop is the National Geological Area in the Daniel Boone National Forest. At the Red River Gorge here you can pass more than 150 sandstone arches. If the kids are lagging behind, you can speed them up with the same nickname the Indians gave to Daniel Boone, "the great turtle." At Breaks Interstate Park, shared by Virginia and Kentucky, you can see a spectacular gorge known as the "Grand Canyon of the South."

The Kentucky Highlands Museum in Ashland on the extreme eastern edge of the state has special displays of the area's cultural and industrial history. Afterward, take a self-guided walking tour of early houses and businesses.

For More Information

Lexington Convention and Visitors Bureau
(800) 845-3959
www.visitlex.com

AMOS SHINKLE BED & BREAKFAST TOWNHOUSE, Covington

Overall: ★★★★½ Room Quality: B Value: A Price: $89–$150

What happens when you give 14 designers carte blanche to each work on a different section of a townhouse? The result could be something like the splendid Amos Shinkle Townhouse. Bernie and Don, two retired scientists, own and operate this historic mansion with its high ceiling, elaborate architectural details, and combined eclectic ideas of all those designers. The hosts respect the privacy of their guests but enjoy sharing ideas about their favorite restaurants (such as the five-star Misonette in Cincinnati, or Coco, with Southwestern cuisine, just a block away from the Townhouse). Suggestion: Don't take your car into downtown Cincinnati, even though its shops and attractions are so temptingly close. As in most major cities, parking is tight. On good days you can walk across the bridge. Or take the TANK (Transit Authority Northern Kentucky) shuttle for a quarter.

Setting & Facilities

Location: Across the river from Cincinnati, follow Fifth St. in Covington, left on Garrard St.
Near: Cincinnati attractions, restaurants, 10-min. walk across Shinkle/Roebling Bridge to Cinery Field (Cincinnati Reds, Cincinnati Bengals), Cincinnati Music Hall
Building: 1854 Greco-Italianate 2-story brick townhouse & carriage house w/ guest rooms
Grounds: Garden yard planted w/ perennials, lilac bushes, dogwood trees
Public Space: 2 parlors main building, porches, patio, DR
Food & Drink: Full breakfast; specialties: coffee cake w/ walnuts & apples, pancakes, scrambled eggs w/ cream cheese & herbs
Recreation: Walking, sight-seeing, golf, strolling nearby Riverside Drive w/ Cincinnati skyline view
Amenities & Services: Local restaurant menus & recommendations from hosts

Accommodations

Units: 3 guest rooms in main house, 4 in Carriage House
All Rooms: TV, phone, AC
Some Rooms: Oversized whirlpool tub, crystal chandelier, 16-foot ceiling
Bed & Bath: Queen or full; private baths
Favorites: Amos Shinkle Room
Comfort & Decor: This designer's showcase (literally!) is truly elegant.

RATES, RESERVATIONS, & RESTRICTIONS

Deposit: Credit card, 1 night
Discounts: 10% over 60, AARP, AAA, 7 continuous stays; $15 add'l person
Credit Cards: AE, V, MC, D
Check-in/Out: 1–10 p.m./noon
Smoking: No
Pets: No; hosts generously recommend other B&Bs that accept pets
Kids: Welcome in carriage house
No-Nos: Kitchen privileges
Minimum Stay: None
Open: All year except Dec. 24–25
Hosts: Dan Nash, Bernie Moorman
215 Garrard St.
Covington, KY 41011
(859) 431-2118 or (800) 972-7012
Fax: (859) 491-4551
amosshinkle@yahoo.com
www.amosshinkle.net

SILVER SPRINGS FARM, Lexington

Overall: ★★★★ Room Quality: B Value: C Price: $99–$199

This is a spacious old farmhouse with enormous guest rooms that are big enough for sitting areas and desks. Unfortunately, bathrooms are shared by three rooms in the main house. Even though robes are provided, it can still be an inconvenience to wait for shower time. This may not be a problem for some leisure travelers, but it could be more so for business travelers with appointments. Silver Springs Farm is very informal. Guests frequently gather in the kitchen for early morning coffee before breakfast. Host Cindy is very convivial and is interested in talking with all of the guests. Ask her about the best places to eat and what to see. Cindy prides herself in being sort of an ambassador for the Lexington area, and she's good at it. If you're traveling across the state with your horse (don't laugh, this is horse country), overnight stabling is proved, although ironically, there is no horseback riding possible here.

SETTING & FACILITIES

Location: 5 mi. from downtown Lexington
Near: Kentucky Horse Park
Building: Federal home plus 2-BR cottage
Grounds: 21 acres
Public Space: LR w/ fireplace, brick patio, kitchen
Food & Drink: Full breakfast; call for special dietary needs
Recreation: Sight-seeing
Amenities & Services: Turnout paddocks for guests traveling w/ horses, fax machine avail.

ACCOMMODATIONS

Units: 2 guest rooms plus cottage
All Rooms: TV, high ceilings, ceiling fan
Some Rooms: Full kitchen, covered front porch, phone, stereo
Bed & Bath: King or queen; cottage w/ private bath; 3 guest rooms in main house share bath
Favorites: The Cottage—1,200-foot space w/ 2 BRs
Comfort & Decor: Oak and maple floors

RATES, RESERVATIONS, & RESTRICTIONS

Deposit: Credit card; 14-day cancellation
Discounts: None
Credit Cards: V, MC
Check-in/Out: 4–6 p.m./11 a.m.
Smoking: No; $75 service fee if you smoke in room!
Pets: Yes (cottage)
Kids: Yes (cottage)
Minimum Stay: None
Open: All year
Host: Cindy Loving
3710 Leestown Park
Lexington, KY 40511
(859) 255-1784 or (877) 255-1784
innkeeper@bbsilverspringsfarm.com
www.bbsilverspringsfarm.com

SWANN'S NEST AT CYGNET FARM, Lexington

Overall: ★★½	Room Quality: C	Value: D	Price: $75–$150

Many guests come here for the nearby races at Keeneland Race Course. Others come for horse sales. But some come because they love horses. And, boy, that's what they get at Swann's Nest, set in the midst of a thoroughbred horse farm. Virtually every room looks out on a paddock. Early risers can walk the mile to Keeneland Race Course and watch the thoroughbreds run the track, every morning of the year from 5 to 8 a.m. While the house and gated drive seem opulent from the outside, inside you'll find everything plain, simple, and very comfortable—the kind of place where you can put up your feet without worrying about kicking over a priceless Chinese glass sculpture. Your host, Rosalie, was raised with horses and can tell you everything you might want to know about thoroughbreds, paints, and quarter horses (our interest waned after paints). She's a friendly lady. We just wish she'd serve something besides cold cereal and toast-your-own bagels, hardly a sumptuous breakfast for a full vacation day. You can go just a few feet out the door and pet the horses, but as the sign warns, "horses can bite." Of course, if you gave them a cold bagel . . .

Setting & Facilities

Location: Off Versailles Rd.
Near: Lexington, Bluegrass Airport, Keeneland Racecourse, antiques shops
Building: Main home of thoroughbred horse farm
Grounds: 3 acres
Public Space: LR w/ fireplace, screened porch, bricked courtyard
Food & Drink: Cont'l breakfast
Recreation: Antiques shopping, going to races
Amenities & Services: For extra fee: horse farm tours, spa services, box lunches for picnics, fax & copy machines

Accommodations

Units: 3 guest rooms, 2 suites
All Rooms: Cable TV, sitting area
Bed & Bath: Beds vary; shared baths for guest rooms, private baths for suites
Favorites: None
Comfort & Decor: Plain and comfortable

Rates, Reservations, & Restrictions

Deposit: 1 night; 7-day cancellation
Discounts: None
Credit Cards: AE, V, MC
Check-in/Out: 4:30 p.m./11 a.m.
Smoking: Yes
Pets: No
Kids: 16 & older
Minimum Stay: 3 nights during special events (e.g., Kentucky Derby, NCAA tournaments)
Open: All year except Dec. holiday week
Host: Rosalie Swann
3463 Rosalie Ln.
Lexington, KY 40510
(859) 226-0095
Fax: (859) 252-4499
rswann.home.mindspring.com

Appendix

Additional Bed-and-Breakfasts and Small Inns

While our profiles give you a fine range of bed-and-breakfasts and small inns, some may be fully booked when you want to visit, or you may want to stay in areas where we have not included a property. So we have included this listing of more than 300 additional bed-and-breakfasts and small inns, spread geographically throughout the Southeast. All properties meet our basic criteria for this guide: They usually have about 3–25 guest rooms, a distinct personality and individually decorated guest rooms, are open regularly, and include breakfast in the price (with a few exceptions). Prices are a range from low to high season. Unlike the previous profiles, we have not visited all of these properties so we cannot recommend them across the board. We suggest you get a brochure, look on the Internet, or call and ask about some of the categories that are on the profile format to find out more. While some of these supplementals are famed and excellent, others may not be up to the level of the profiled properties.

North Carolina

Zone 1: Coastal North Carolina

Carolina Beach

The Beacon House Inn Bed and Breakfast
$60–$105
(910) 458-6244 or (910) 458-7322
lhuhn@ix.netcom.com

Duck

Advice 5¢, a Bed and Breakfast
$95-$175
(252) 255-1050 or (800) ADVICE 5
advice5@theouterbanks.com
www.theouterbanks.com/advice5

Zone 2: Central North Carolina

Aberdeen

Inn at Bryant House
$60–$95
(800) 453-4019
lsteele@eclipsetel.com

Page Manor House
$100–$165
(910) 944-5970

Charlotte

The Carmel Bed and Breakfast
$89–$99
(704) 542-9450 or (800) 229-5860
lmoag@carolina.rr.com

Chez Arlaine
$125–$135
(704) 331-9808
ChezArlaine@aol.com

Chez Francine Bed and Breakfast
$75–$90
(704) 965-4242
francine@chezfrancine.com
www.chezfrancine.com

The Inn Uptown Bed and Breakfast
$79–$159
(704) 342-2800 or (800) 959-1990

Dunn
Simply Divine, Inc. Bed and Breakfast
$69
(910) 891-1103 or (800) 357-9336
SimplyDivine@ibm.net
www.bbonline.com/nc/simplydivine

Durham
Morehead Manor Bed and Breakfast
$100–$165
(919) 687-4366 or (888) 437-6333
moheadmanr@aol.com
www.citysearch.com/rdu/moreheadmanor

Old North Durham Inn
$100–$165
(919) 683-1885
dvick1885@aol.com
www.bbonline.com/nc/oldnorth

Zone 3: Western North Carolina

Andrews
The Cover House Bed and Breakfast and Cottage
$60–$120
(828) 321-5302 or (800) 354-7642
www.vit.com/nc/236nc

The Hawkesdene House Bed and Breakfast Inn
$70–$95
(800) 447-9549 or (828) 321-6027
hawke@dnet.net www.hawkbb.com

Rail's End Bed and Breakfast
$80–$100
(828) 321-4486 or (800) 551-3961
www.bbonline.com/nc/railsend

Banner Elk
Azalea Inn Bed and Breakfast
from $99
(828) 898-8195 or (888) 898-2743
azaleainn@skybest.com
www.azalea-inn.com

Deer Brook Inn Bed and Breakfast
$105–$150
(828) 898-5934
deerbrook@skybest.com

The Old-Turnpike House Bed and Breakfast
from $65
(828) 898-5611 or (888) 802-4487
otph@skybest.com
www.oldturnpikehouse.com

Blowing Rock
Maple Lodge Bed and Breakfast
$85–$140
(828) 295-3331
innkeeper@maplelodge.net
www.maplelodge.net

The Inn at Ragged Gardens
$140–$245
(828) 295-9703
Innkeeper@ragged-gardens.com
www.ragged-gardens.com

Rocksberry Inn Bed and Breakfast
$120–$130
(828) 295-3311
innkeeper@rocksberry.com
www.rocksberry.com

Stone Pillar Bed and Breakfast
$65–$110
(828) 295-4141 or (800) 962-9955
stonepillar@appstate.campuscwix.net
www.stonepillarbb.com

Brevard
Clayton Bed and Breakfast
$75–$125
(828) 884-4718 or (800) 673-3514
claytonbb@citcom.net
www.bbonline.com/nc/clayton

The Red House Inn
$59–$99
(828) 884-9349

Bryson City
Charleston Inn
$89–$145
(828) 488-4644 or (888) 285-1555
chasinn@dnet.net
www.charlestoninn.com

Folkestone Inn
$69–$108
(828) 488-2730 or (888) 812-3385
innkeeper@folkestone.com
www.folkestone.com

Chimney Rock
Dogwood Inn Bed and Breakfast
$84–$129
(828) 625-4403 or (800) 992-5557
dogwoodinn@blueridge.net

Esmeralda Inn and Restaurant
$129
(828) 625-9105
info@esmeraldainn.com
www.esmeraldainn.com

The Wicklow Inn Bed and Breakfast
$75–$105
(828) 625-4038 or (877) 625-4038
wicklowinn@blueridge.net

Lake Toxaway
Earthshine Mountain Lodge
$130–$170
(828) 862-4207
info@earthshinemtnlodge.com

South Carolina

Zone 4: Coastal South Carolina

Beaufort
The Beaufort Inn
$125–$300
(843) 521-9000
bftinn@hargray.com
www.beaufortinn.com

The Cuthbert House Inn Bed and Breakfast
$145–$210
(843) 521-1315 or (800) 327-9275
cuthbert@hargray.com

Craven Street Inn
$115–$225
(843) 522-1668 or (888) 522-0250
rditty@islc.net
www.bbhost.com/cravenstreetinn

Old Point Inn
$65–$95
(803) 524-3177

Charleston
16 Fulton Street Bed and Breakfast
$85–$115
(843) 723-3294
JohnHBennett@juno.com

139 Church Street
$175–$200
(704) 375-3884 or (888) 724-9805
BtheD@aol.com
www.bbhost.com/139churchstreet

Ansonborough Inn
$129–$199
(843) 723-1655 or (800) 522-2073
AnsonboroughInn@aesir.com

Ashley Inn Bed and Breakfast
$79–$185
(843) 723-1848 or (800) 581-6658
ashley@cchat.com

Bed, No, Breakfast
$60–$90
(843) 723-4450
knottgreely@worldnet.att.net

Cannonboro Inn Bed and Breakfast
$79–$185
(843) 723-8572 or (800) 235-8039
cannon@cchat.com

Charleston's Vendue Inn
$120–$275
(843) 577-7970 or (800) 845-7900
www.bbchannel.com/bbc/p206618.asp

Charlotte Street Cottage
$225–$275
(843) 577-3944

Country Victorian Bed and Breakfast
$75–$115
(843) 577-0682
www.bbchannel.com/bbc/p206601.asp

East Bay Bed and Breakfast
$140–$185
(843) 722-4186
ebaybb@bellsouth.net

Fulton Lane Inn
$90–$265
(843) 720-2600 or (800) 720-2688

The Hayne House Bed and Breakfast
$120–$295
(843) 577-2633

Indigo Inn
$110–$185
(843) 577-5900 or (800) 845-7639
IndigoInn@aesir.com
www.aesir.com/IndigoInn/Welcome.html

The Jasmine House
$135–$250
(800) 845-7639
JasmineHouse@aesir.com

King's Courtyard Inn
$95–$240
(843) 723-7000 or (800) 845-6119

King George IV Inn
$85–$169
(843) 723-9339 or (888) 723-1667
www.bbonline.com/sc/kinggeorge

Lodge Alley Inn
from $139
(843) 722-1611 or (800) 845-1004
info@lodgealleyinn.com

Long Point Inn
$89–$175
(843) 849-1884
info@charleston-longptinn.com

Palmer Home Bed and Breakfast
$120–$165
(843) 853-1574 or (888) 723-1574
palmerbnb@aol.com

Rutledge Victorian Inn
$69–$280
(843) 722-7551 or (888) 722-7553
normlynn@prodigy.net

Thomas Lamboll House B&B
$115–$155
(843) 723-3212 or (888) 874-0793
lamboll@aol.com

Timothy Ford's "Kitchen House"
$150–$250
(843) 577-4432
HPruitt182@aol.com
www.bbonline.com/sc/kitchen

Victoria House Inn
$110–$235
(843) 720-2944 or (800) 933-5464

Wentworth Mansion
$275–$625
(843) 853-1886 or (888) INN-1886

Zero Water Street Bed and Breakfast
$110–$250
(843) 723-2841; bettygeer@aol.com

Conway

Cypress Inn
$95–$140
(843) 248-8199 or (800) 575-5307
acypress@sccoast.net
www.acypressinn.com

Dillon

Magnolia Inn Bed and Breakfast
$75–$95
(843) 774-0679
innmagnoli@aol.com

Georgetown

1790 House Bed and Breakfast
$85–$135
(843) 546-4821 or (800) 890-7432

Alexandra's Inn Bed and Breakfast
$95–$135
(843) 527-0233 or (888) 557-0233
alexinn@sccoast.net

Ashfield Manor Bed and Breakfast
$45–$65
(843) 546-0464 or (800) 483-5002

DuPre House Bed and Breakfast
$75–$115
(843) 546-0298 or (800) 921-DUPRE
dupre@sccoast.net

King's Inn at Georgetown Bed and Breakfast
$89–$139
(843) 527-6937 or (800) 251-8805
kingsinres@aol.com

Mansfield Plantation Bed and Breakfast Country Inn
$95–$115
(843) 546-6961 or (800) 355-3223

The Shaw House Bed and Breakfast
$55–$75
(843) 546-9663

Greenville
Creekside Plantation Bed and Breakfast
$150
(864) 297-3293

Pettigru Place Bed and Breakfast
$90–$180
(864) 242-4529

Marion
Montgomery's Grove Bed and Breakfast
$80–$100
(843) 423-5220 or (877) 646-7721

Moncks Corner
Rice Hope Plantation
$80–$165
(843) 761-4832
doris@ricehope.com

Mt. Pleasant
Sunny Meadows Bed and Breakfast
$85–$95
(843) 884-7062

Myrtle Beach
Brustman House Bed and Breakfast
$75–$190
(843) 448-7699 or (800) 448-7699
wcbrustman@worldnet.att.net

Pawleys Island
Litchfield Plantation
$140–$450
(843) 237-9322 or (800) 869-1410
vacation@litchfieldplantation.com

Summerville
Flowertown Bed and Breakfast
$85–$100
(843) 851-1058
innkeeper@flowertownbandb.com

Linwood Bed and Breakfast
$75–$125
(843) 871-2620
www.bbonline.com/sc/linwood

Price House Cottage Bed and Breakfast
$125
(843) 871-1877
phcbb@aol.com
www.bbonline.com/sc/pricehouse

Zone 5: Central South Carolina

Aiken
The Briar Patch
$50
(803) 649-2010

The Sandhurst Estate
$75–$200; (803) 642-9259
sandhurst@scescape.net

Town & Country Inn Bed-Breakfast-Barn
$60–$95
(803) 642-0270
tcinn@duesouth.net
www.bbonline.com/sc/sandhurst

Blythewood
The Candlelight Inn
$65–$83
(803) 714-1960

Camden
Candlelight Inn
$65
(803) 424-1057

Clio
The Henry Bennett House
$55
(843) 586-9290
info@bennetthouse.com
www.bennetthouse.com

Ehrhardt
Ehrhardt Hall
$65–$85
(803) 267-2020

Saint Matthews
Two Lora's Guest House
$50–$75
(803) 682-6077 or (800) 913-3131
lfogle9424@aol.com
www.bbonline.com/sc/twoloras

Sumter
The Bed and Breakfast of Sumter
$70–$80
(803) 773-2903

Zone 6: Western South Carolina

Anderson
Evergreen Inn and 1109 Restaurant
$56–$75
(864) 225-1109 or (800) 241-0034
newfeel@carol.net
www.traveldata.com/inns/data/1109.thml

Calhoun Falls
Latimer Inn
$29–$39
(864) 391-2747

Campobello
The Bell Tower Inn
$75–$95
(864) 468-4266 or (877) BELL-TOWER
belltowr@greenville.infi.net
www.bbonline.com/sc/belltower

Gaffney
Jolly Place
$59–$99
(864) 489-4638

Landrum
Country Mouse Inn
$60–$90
(864) 457-4061
www.bbonline.com/sc/countrymouse

The Red Horse Inn
$110–$125
(864) 895-4968
www.bbonline.com/sc/redhorse

Newberry
Barklin House
$55–$75
(803) 321-9155 or (877) 422-7554
barklin@barklinhouse.com

Rock Hill
The Book and the Spindle
$50–$65
(803) 328-1913

East Main Guest House Bed and Breakfast Inn
$59–$79
(803) 366-1161

Harmony House Bed and Breakfast
$65–$75
(803) 329-5886 or (888) 737-0016

Park Avenue Inn
$55–$75
(803) 325-1764

Taylors
Besserrae Bed and Breakfast
$70–$90
(864) 268-5596

Union
Juxa Plantation
from $85
(864) 427-8688; nolasjuxa@aol.com

Winnsboro
Songbird Manor Bed and Breakfast
$65–$110
(803) 635-6963 or (888) 636-7698
susan.yenner@gte.net

Woodruff
The Nicholls-Crook Plantation House Bed and Breakfast
$75–$150
(864) 476-8820

Georgia

Zone 7: Coastal Georgia

Brunswick
McKinnon House B&B
$85–$125
(912) 261-9100
www.stay-in-ga.com/inns/mckinnonhouse

Savannah

Joan-on Jones
$115–$130
(912) 234-1455 or (800) 407-3863

Pulaski Square Inn
$48–$125
(912) 232-8055

St. Simons Island

Wisteria Cottage
$135–$275
(912) 638 1482 or (800) 441-2027

Zone 8: Northern Georgia

Athens

Nicholson House Inn
$75–$85
(706) 353-2200
sjkelley@bellsouth.net
www.virtualcities.com/ons/ga/h/gahc701

Atlanta

Abbett Inn
$79–$149
(404) 767-3708 abbettinn@bellsouth.net
www.abbettinn.com

Ansley Inn
$109–$159
(404) 872-9000 or (800) 446-5416
reservations@ansleyinn.com
www.ansleyinn.com

Beverly Hills Inn
$90–$160
(404) 233-8520 or (800) 331-8520
www.beverlyhillsinn.com

The Bonaventure B&B
$90–$145
(404) 817-7024
innkeeper@thebonaventure.com
www.thebonaventure.com

The Gaslight Inn
$85–$195
(404) 875-1001
innkeeper@gaslightinn.com
www.gaslightinn.com

King-Keith House
$75–$175
(404) 688-7330 or (800) 728-3879
kingkeith@mindspring.com
www.kingkeith.com

Shellmont B&B
$95–$200
(404) 872-9290
innkeeper@shellmont.com
www.shellmont.com

Stonehurst B&B
$80–$95
(404) 881-0722
stonehurst@mindspring.com
www.stonehurstbandb.com

The University Inn at Emory
$58–$124
(404) 634-7327 or (800) 654-8591
info@univinn.com, www.univinn.com

Augusta

The Partridge Inn
$65–$150
(706) 737-8888 or (800) 476-6888
www.virtualcities.com/ons/ga/z/gaza801

Blairsville

Misty Mountain Inn and Cottages
$55–85
(912) 956-2498 or (888) 647-8966
www.JWWW.COM/misty

Souther Country Inn
$75–$150
(706) 379-1603 or (800) 297-1603
alecitrin@pol.net
www.souther-country-inn.com

Clarkesville

The Burns-Sutton Inn
$75–$125
www.georgiamagazine.com/burns-sutton

Clayton

Old Clayton Inn
$45–$125
(706) 782-7722 or (800) 454-3498
claytoninn@oldclaytoninn.com
www.oldclaytoninn.com

Beechwood Inn
$85–$135
(706) 782-5485
www.stay-in-ga.com/inns/beechwood.htm

Dahlonega
The Blueberry Inn
$75–$105
(706) 219-4024 or (877) 219-4024
bluberrybb@aol.com
www.blueberryinnandgardens.com

Royal Guard Inn B&B
$75–$90
(706) 864-1713
www.virtualcities.com/ons/ga/d/gad8703

Worley Homestead Inn B&B
$85–$125
(706) 864-7002
www.virtualcities.com/ons/ga/d/gad7701

Hiawasse
Henson Cove Place B&B and Cabin
$70
(706) 896-6195 or (800) 714-5542
www.bbonline.com/ga/hensoncove

Newnan
The Old Garden Inn
$89–$119
(800) 731-5011 or (770) 304–0594
oldgarden@webtv.net
www.virtualcities.com/ons/ga/a/gaa6701

Palmetto
Serenbe B&B
$140–$175
(770) 463-2610
steve@serenbe.com; www.serenbe.com

Stone Mountain
The Village Inn
$115–$189
(770) 469-3459 or (800) 214-8385
www.villageinnbb.com

Zone 9: Southern Georgia

Byron
Memories Inn
$75–$95
(912) 956-2498 or (800) 671-8111
www.hom.net/~memories

Concord
Inn Scarlett's Footsteps
$79–$125
(770) 884-9012
gwtw@gwtw.com
www.virtualcities.com/ons/ga/p/gap6701

Greenville
The Georgian Inn
$100–$125
(706) 672-1600
georgianinn@hotmail.com
www.virtualcities.com/ons/ga/p/gapa701

The Samples Plantation Inn
$145
(706) 672-4765
www.virtualcities.com/ons/ga/p/gap4801

Thomasville
Melhana Plantation
$250–$650
(912) 226-2290 or (888) 920-3030
info@melhana.com www.melhana.com

Florida

Zone 10: East Coast

Amelia Island
Florida House Inn
$70–$140
(800) 258-3301
innkeepers@floridahouseinn.com
www.virtualcities.com/ons/fl/a/fla9801

Cocoa
Indian River House
$75–$195
(407) 631-5660
www.virtualcities.com/ons/fl/d/fld9701

Flagler Beach
The White Orchid, an Oceanfront Inn
$90–$165
(904) 439-4944
www.virtualcities.com/ons/fl/d/fld39010

Ft. Lauderdale
Caribbean Quarters
$100–$200
(888) 414-3226
bigbedsbnb@juno.com
www.virtualcities.com/ons/fl/l/fl1301

The Homeplace B&B
$85–$110
(800) 251-5473
www.virtualcities.com.ons/fl/s/fls4701

Jacksonville Beach
Pelican Path B&B
$80–$175
(888) 749-1177
ppbandb@aol.com

Key West
Heron House
$99–$329
(800) 294-1644
heronkyw@aol.com
www.virtualcities.com/ons/fl/k/flk8702

Lake Worth
Mango Inn Bed and Breakfast
$65–$145
(888) 626-4619
info@mangoinn.com
www.virtualcities.com/ons/fl/s/fls6901

New Smyrna Beach
Night Swan Intracoastal B&B
$80–$150
(800) 465-4261
nightswanb@aol.com
www.virtualcities.com/ons/fl/d/fldb5010

North Hutchinson Island
Mellon Patch Inn
$80–$130
(800) 656-7824
www.virtualcities.com/ons/fl/v/flv5501

St. Augustine
Casa de La Paz Bayfront
$95–$195
(800) 929-2915
delapaz@aug.com
www.virtualcities.com/ons/fl/d/fldc801

Zone 11: Central Florida

Eustis
Dreamspinner B&B
$95–$150
(888) 474-1229
dreamspinner@cde.com
www.virtualcities.com/ons/fl/o/flo7702

Lady Lake
Shamrock Thistle & Crown Bed and Breakfast
$69–$139
(800) 425-2763
shamrock@atlantic.net
www.virtualcities.com/ons/fl/m/flma801

Lake Wales
Chalet Suzanne
$159–$219
(800) 433-6011
info@chalet suzanne.com
www.virtualcities.com/ons/fl/o/flo5901

Orlando
Things Worth Remembering
$65–$70
(800) 484-3585
www.virtualcities.com/ons/fl/o/flo2601

Winter Garden
Briar Patch Bed and Breakfast
$99–$119
(407) 465-0394
briarpatch@netzero.net
www.virtualcities.com/ons/fl/m/flmb801

Zone 12: Gulf Coast

Apalachicola
Coombs House Inn
$79–$139
(850) 653-9199
www.virtualcities.com/ons/fl/p/flp/6601

Destin
Henderson Park Inn
$94–$279
(800) 837-4853
www.virtualcities.com/ons/fl/p/flp/7801

Holmes Beach
Harrington House Beachfront Bed & Breakfast
$129–$229
(941) 778-5444
harhousebb@mail.pcsonline.com
www.virtualcities.com/ons/fl/x/flx6602

Naples
Lemon Tree Inn
$50–$160
(888) 800-5366
lt@aol.com
www.virtualcities.com/ons/fl/w/flw4801

St. Marks
The Sweet Magnolia Bed and Breakfast
$75–$125
(850) 925-7670

St. Petersburg
Bayboro House on Old Tampa Bay B& B
$85–$145
(813) 823-4955
bayborohouse@juno.com
www.virtualcities.com/ons/fl/x/flx6601

Siesta Key
Turtle Beach Resort
$125–$285
(941) 349-4554
TurtleBch1@aol.com
www.virtualcities.com/ons/fl/x/flxa601

Tallahassee
Calhoun Street Inn B&B
$65–$95
(850) 425-5095
gailrei@juno.com
www.virtualcities.com/ons/fl/p/flp8701

Tampa
Gram's Place Bed & Breakfast
$65–$95
(813) 221-0596 gramspl@aol.com
www.virtualcities.com/ons/fl/p/flp8701

Venice
Banyan House Bed and Breakfast
$69–$119
(941) 484-1385
vnc@gte.net
www.virtualcities.com/ons/fl/w/flwb801

Alabama

Zone 13: Southern Alabama

Auburn
The Crenshaw Guest House
$48–$75
(334) 826-8123 or (800) 950-1131
www.bedandbreakfast.com/bbc/p207427

Alexander City
Mistletoe Bough Bed and Breakfast
$85–$125
(256) 329-3717 or (877) 330-3707
www.bbonline.com/al/mistletoe

Daphne
Southern Oaks Plantation
$69–$99
(334) 621-9274
www.bbonline.com/al/southernoaks

Fairhope
The Blue House on Magnolia
$475 (3 days)
(616) 469-1416
www.bbonline.com/al/bluehouse

A Touch of Class Bed and Breakfast
$70–$85
(334) 928-7499 or (334) 928-3729
www.bbonline.com/al/atouchof class

Foley
Katy's Gourmet INN-Spirations B&B
$50
(334) 970-1529 katysinn@datasync.com

Greensboro
Blue Shadows Guest House
$55–$75
(334) 624-3637
www.bedandbreakfast.com/bbc/p217657

Gulf Shores
The Beach House
$120–$231
(334) 540-7039 or (800) 659-6004
carol@gulftel.com
www.bigbeachhouse.com

Jemison
The Jemison Inn B&B and Gardens
$75
(205) 688-2055
theinn@scott.net
www.bbonline.com/al/jemison

Magnolia Springs
Magnolia Springs Bed and Breakfast
$94–$104
(334) 965-7321 or (800) 965-7321
msbbdw@gulftel.com
www.bbonline.com/al/magnolia

Mobile
Riverhouse Bed and Breakfast
$90–$130
(334) 973-2233 or (800) 552-9791
riverhsbb@aol.com
www.bbonline.com/al/riverhouse

Montgomery
Colonel's Rest Bed and Breakfast
$60 and up
(334) 215-0380
www.bbonline.com/al/colonel

Red Bluff Cottage Bed and Breakfast
$65–$75
(334) 264-0056 or (888) 551-CLAY
RedblufBnB@aol.com,
www.bbonline.com/al/redbluff

New Brockton
The Brock House Bed and Breakfast
$45–$50
(334) 894-6788
www.bbonline.com/al/brockhouse

Prattville

Rocky Mount Bed and Breakfast
$85 and up
(334) 285-0490 or (800) 646-3831
www.bbonline.com/al/rockymount

Sylacauga
Towassa—A Bed and Breakfast
$69–$109
(256) 249-3450
towassa@aol.com
www.bbonline.com/al/towassa

Talladega
Historic Oakwood Bed and Breakfast
$49–$89
(256) 362-0662
www.bbonline.com/al/oakwood

Theodore
Riverhouse Bed and Breakfast
$90
(334) 973-2233 or (800) 552-9791
riverhsbb@aol.com
www.bbonline.com/al/riverhouse

Zone 14: Northern Alabama

Albertville
Twin House Bed and Breakfast
$70–$90
(256) 878-7499
twinhouse@mindspring.com
www.bbonline.com/al/twinhouse

Aliceville
Myrtlewood Historic Bed and Breakfast
$50
(205) 373-8153 or (800) 367-7891
www.bbonline.com/al/myrtlewood

Anniston
The Victoria Country Inn
$69–$219
(256) 236-0503 or (800) 260-8781
thevic@mindspring.com
www.bbonline.com/al/victoria

Decatur
Hearts and Treasures Bed and Breakfast
$60–$75
(256) 353-9562
www.bbonline.com/al/hearts

Elmore
Sweetnin' House Bed and Breakfast
$75–$95
(334) 285-0938 or (800) 250-3337
leescottl@aol.com
www.bbonline.com/alSweetnin

Fayette
Rose House Inn
$55–$90
(205) 932-ROSE or (800) 925-7673
Treasure@Fayette.net

Florence
Limestone Manor Bed and Breakfast
$72–$95
(256) 765-0314 or (888) 709-6700
ellisons@HiWAAY.net
www.bbonline.com/al/limestone

Wood Avenue Inn
$64–$97
(256) 766-8441
WoodAveInn@aol.com
www.bbonline.com/al/limestone

Guntersville
Lake Guntersville Bed and Breakfast
$55–$125
(256) 505-0133
www.bbonline.com/al/lakeguntersville

Hartselle
The Oden House Bed and Breakfast
$85
(256) 751-2933

Wisteria Inn Bed and Breakfast
$50–$75
(256) 773-9703 wisteriabb@aol.com

Lacey's Spring
Apple Jack's Inn
$65–$85
(256) 778-7734
AppleJ123@aol.com
www.bbonline.com/al/applejacks

Lincoln
Bonniemoore Inn Bed and Breakfast
$85
(205) 763-9341
Bonniemoore@dotcomnow.com

Madison
Bibb House Bed and Breakfast
$75–$100
(256) 772-0586
philwhatley@msn.com

Mentone
Mentone Springs Hotel Bed and Breakfast
$54–$79
(256) 634-4040 or (800) 404-0100
www.virtualcities.com/ons/al/n/n/aln981

Raven Haven Bed and Breakfast
$80–$95
(256) 634-4310
www.virtualcities.com/ons/al/n/alnc502

ToneyThe Church House Inn Bed and Breakfast
$75
(256) 828-5192
jwrider@aol.com

Valley Head
Winston Place
$125–$200
(256) 635-6381 or (888) 4-WINSTON
www.virtualcities.com/ons/al/n/aln1602

MISSISSIPPI

Zone 15: Northern Mississippi

Aberdeen
Huckleberry Inn
$65–$95
(800) 565-7294
www.bbonline.com/ms/huckleberry

Canton
Cummins Cottage
$85
(800) 377-2770
www.bbonline.com/natcheztrace/south1

Columbus
Amzi Love Bed & Breakfast
$85–$125
(662) 328-5413
www.bedandbreakfast.com/bbc/p207770.asp

Backstrom's Country Bed & Breakfast
$75
(662) 328-7213
www:bedandbreakfast.com/bbc/p207778.asp

Churchill
Jim's Cottage
$100–$125
(800) 377-2770
www.bbonline.com/natcheztrace/south1

Corinth
Bed & Breakfast at Robbins Nest
$75–$95
(662) 286-3109
twhyte@tsixroads.com
www.RobbinsNestCorinth.com

The General's Quarters Bed & Breakfast Inn
$75–$100
(601) 286-3325
genqtrs@tsixroads.com
www.tsixroads.com~genqtrs

Samuel D. Bramlitt House
$75
(601) 286-5370

Greenwood
Bridgewater Inn
$65–$85
(877) 793-7473
bridgewater@microsped.com
www.microsped.com//bridgewater

Iuka
Eastport Inn Bed & Breakfast
$40–$50
(601) 423-2511

New Albany
Heritage House
$65–$75
(800) 363-4903
heritagehse@aol.com
bedandbreakfast.com/bbc/p603811.asp

Senatobia
Spahn House Bed & Breakfast
$65–$150
(800) 400-9853
spahn@gmi.net
www.spahnhouse.com

Starkville
Carpenter Place
$75–$95
(662) 323-4669
www.bbchannel.com/bbc/p207787.asp

West
The Alexander House
$65–$110
(800) 350-8034
alexbnb@netdoor.com
www.alexander-house.com

Zone 16: Southern Mississippi

Hattiesburg
Dunhopen Inn Bed & Breakfast
$85–$175
(888) 543-0707
reservations@dunhopen.com
www.dunhopeninn.com

Tally House Historic B&B
$65–$80
(601) 582-3467
www.virtualcities.com

Laurel
The Laurel Inn
$85
(800) 290-5474 (pin 42)
kevpegoc@aol.com
www.laurelinn.com

The Morning Dove
$101–$133
(800) 863-DOVE

Long Beach
Red Creek Inn, Vineyard & Racing Stables
$53–$98
(800) 729-9670
info@redcreekinn.com
www.RedCreekInn.com

Port Gibson
Oak Square Plantation
$85–$125
(800) 729-0240
Kajunmade@aol.com
www.bedandbreakfast.com/bbc/p207731.asp

Vicksburg
Cedar Grove Mansion Inn
$95–$185
(800) 862-1300
info@cedargroveinn.com
www.cedargroveinn.com

Louisiana

Zone 17: Southern Coastal Louisiana

Broussard
Maison d' André Billeaud B&B
$95–$130
(800) 960-7378; maison1@bellsouth.net
www.bbonline.com/la/maison

Lake Charles
The Eddy House Bed & Breakfast
$80
(318) 436-3980
www.bbchannel.com/bbc/p602212.asp

Walter's Attic Bed & Breakfast
$65–$110
(337) 439-3210 waltersatt@aol.com
www.travelguides.com

New Orleans
Fleur-de-Lis B&B
$60–$80
(318) 352-6621
www.virtualcities.com/ons/la/z/laz/4501

Rayne
Maison D' Memorie
$75–$140
(318) 334-2477 memorie@iamerica.net
www.maisondmemorie.com

St. Martinville
Old Castillo Bed & Breakfast
$50–$80
(800) 621-3017
phulin@worldnet.att.net

Slidell
Garden Guest House
$90–$135
(888) 255-0335
bonnie@gardenbb.com
www.gardenbb.com

Zone 18: Northern Louisiana

Alexandria
Matt's Cabin/Inglewood Plantation
$100–$125
(888) 575-6288
susan@inglewoodplantation.com
www.bbchannel.com/bbc/p240900.asp

Cheneyville
Loyd Hall Plantation
$95–$145
(800) 240-8135 loydhallpltn@aol.com
www.louisianatravel.com

Natchitoches
Breazeale House Bed & Breakfast
$65–$100
(800) 352-5631
wfreeman@cp-tel.net
www.bbchannel.com/bbc/p211360.asp

Queen Anne Bed & Breakfast
$85–$100
(888) 685-1585
lhowell@cp-tel.net
www.natchitoches.net/queenanne

New Roads
Garden Gate Manor
$80–$140
(800) 487-3890
www.bbchannel.com/bbc/p211311.asp

Mon Reve B & B
$75–$95
(800) 324-2738 monreve@eatel.net
www.monreve-mydream.com

Opelousas
The Estorge House Bed & Breakfast
$95–$125
(888) 655-9539
www.bbonline.com/la/estorge

Shreveport
Columns on Jordan Bed & Breakfast
$125
(800) 801-4950
BnB615@aol.com
www.bbonline.com/la/columns

Fairfield Place
$135–$250
(318) 222-0048
fairfldpl@aol.com
www.fairfieldbandb.com

2439 Fairview, A Bed & Breakfast
$135–$200
(318) 424-2424 2439
fair@bellsouth.net
www.bbonline.com/la/fairfield

TENNESSEE

Zone 19: Eastern Tennessee

Allardt
Old Allardt School House
$65–$150
(931) 879-8056
www.bbonline.com/tn/schoolhouse

Turner House
$65
(931) 879-6560
www.bbonline.com/turnerhouse

Gatlinburg
Colonel's Lady Inn
$95–$115
(800) 515-5432
www.colonelsladyinn.com

Cornerstone Inn
$75
(865) 430-5064
www.bbonline.com/tn/cornerstone

Olde English Tudor Inn
$79–$109
(800) 541-3798

Hendersonville
Morning Star Bed and Breakfast
$90–$175
(615) 264-2614
www.bbonline.com/tn/morningstar

Spring Haven Bed and Breakfast Inn
$95–$125
(615) 826-1825
www.bbonline.com/tn/springhaven

Monteagle
North Gate Inn
$80–$110
(931) 924-2799
www.bbonline.com/tn/northgate

Monterey
Garden Inn at Bee Rock
$125
(888) 293-1444

New Market
Barrington Inn
$85–$125
(888) 205-8482
www.bbonline.com/tn/barrington

New Port
Christopher Place
$150–$300
(800) 595-9441
thebestinn@aol.com
www.christopherplace.com

Nashville
Carole's Yellow Cottage
$85–$105
(615) 226-2952

Hillsboro House
$100–$110
(800) 228-7851
hillsboro@acelink.net
www.bbonline.com/tn/hillsboro

Ocoee
Chestnut Inn
$65–$70
(800) 993-7873
www.bbonline.com/tn/chestnut

Rugby
Clear Fork Farm Bed and Breakfast
$70–$85
(423) 628-2967
tablank@highland.net
www.bbonline.com/tn/clearfork

Sevierville
Bonny Brook B&B
$120–$130
(865) 908-4745

Camelot Bed and Breakfast
$100–$125
(865) 429-2070
www.bbonline.com/tn/camelot

Little Greenbrier Lodge
$75–$95
(865) 429-2500

Persephone's Farm Retreat
$75–$95
(865) 428-3904
bgonia@smokeymtnmall.com

River Piece Inn
$81–$125
(888) 265-3097

Victorian Dreams Bed and Breakfast
$89–$145
(865) 428-6085
www.victoriandreamsbnb.com

Von-Bryan Inn
$100–$220
(800) 633-1459

Townsend
Abode and Beyond Bed and Breakfast
$70–$95
(888) TN-ABODE
abode@planetc.com

Richmond Inn
$115–$135
(931) 455-2546
www.bbonline.com/tn/twinvalley

Watertown
Watertown Bed and Breakfast
$50–$125
(615) 237-9999
www.bbonline.com/tn/watertown

Zone 20: Western Tennessee

Fayetville
Bagley House Bed and Breakfast
$80
(931) 433-3799
bagley@vallnet.com
www.bbonline.com/tn/bagleyhouse

Frankewing
Hollow Pond Farm Bed and Breakfast
$85–$130
(800) 463-0154
www.bbonline.com/tn/hollowpond

Franklin
Blueberry Hill B&B
$70–$80
(615) 791-9947

Namaste Acres Country Ranch Inn
$75–$85
(615) 791-0333 namastebb@aol.com
www.bbonline.com/tn/namaste

Summit by the Trace
$85–$115
(800) 807-9335
www.bbonline.com/tn/thesummit

Sweeney Hollow Bed & Breakfast
$95
(615) 591-0498

Lynchburg
Goose Branch Farm Bed and Breakfast
$65
(931) 759-5919
gbfarmbb@aol.com

Lynchburg Bed and Breakfast
$60
(931) 759-7158

Tucker Inn
$75
(931) 759-5922
tuckerinn@witty.com
www.bbonline.com/tn/tuckerinn

Memphis
Bridgewater House
$110
(800) 466-1001

King's Cottage Bed & Breakfast Inn
$85–$125
(901) 722-8686
thekingscottage@aol.com
www.thkingscottage.com

Sassafras Inn
$75–$125
(662) 429-5864
sassyinn@memphis.to

Mulberry

Mulberry House Bed and Breakfast
$55
(931) 433-8461

Nolensville
Sumner's View B&B
$100–$150
(888) 326-4334
sumnersvu@aol.com
www.bbonline.com/tn/sumnersview

Normandy
Parish Patch Farm and Inn
$68–$185
(800) 876-3017
parish.patch@mindspring.com
www.bbonline.com/tn/parishpatch

Paris
Sunset View Bed and Breakfast
$45–$95
(888) 642-4778

Shelbyville
Cinnamon Ridge Bed and Breakfast
$55–$65
(877) 685-9200

Gore House
$50–$75
(931) 685-0636
www.bbonline.com/tn/oldgore

Spring Hill
Sweet Springs Farm
$65
(800) 268-3126

Waverly
Nolan House
$50–$75
(931) 296-2511
www.bbonline.com/tn/nolanhouse

KENTUCKY

Zone 21: Western Kentucky

Auburn
Federal Grove Bed and Breakfast
$65–$75
(207) 542-6106
www.bbonline.com/ky/fedgrove

Bardstown
Arbor Rose Bed and Breakfast
$50–$150
(888) 828-3330
arborrose@bardstown.com
www.bardstown.com/~arborrose/

Bruntwood Inn
$100–$110
(888) 420-9703
www.bbonline.com/ky/bruntwood/

Kenmore Farms Bed and Breakfast
$80–$90
(800) 831-6159
www.bbonline.com/ky/kenmorefarms/

The Mansion Bed and Breakfast
$100–$130
(270) 348-2586 or (800) 349-2586
ddowns@bardstown.com
www.bardstownmansion.com

Talbott Tavern
rates n/a
(800) 4-TAVERN
talbott@bardstown.com
www.talbotts.com

Bellevue
Christopher's Bed and Breakfast
$75–$140
(888) 585-7085
www.bbonline.com/ky/christophers/

Mary's Belle View Inn
$50–$100
(888) 581-8875 www.bbonline.com/ky/belleview/

Weller Haus Bed and Breakfast
$79–$149
(800) 431-4287
www.bbonline.com/ky/weller/

Berea
Berea's Shady Lane Bed and Breakfast
$55–$70
(606) 986-9851
lrwebber@aol.com
www.bbonline.com/ky/shadylane/

Bowling Green
Alpine Lodge
$45–$65
(502) 843-4846
www.bbchannel.com/bbc/p207919.asp

Maple Grove Farm
$60
(270) 843-7433
www.bbchannel.com/bbc/p613728.asp

Burkesville
Cumberland House Bed and Breakfast
$50–$65
(800) 727-5850
www.bbonline.com/ky/cumberland/

Burlington
Burlington's Willis Graves Bed and Breakfast Inn
$75–$125
(888) 226-5096
www.bbonline.com/ky/willisgraves/

Cadiz
Whispering Winds Inn
$90–$175
(317) 293-7853
info@whisperwinds.com
www.whisperwinds.com

Calvert City
Wildflowers Farm Bed and Breakfast
$69–$115
(270) 527-5449 crestes@vci.net
www.bbonline.com/ky/wildflowers/

Carrollton
Gen. Wm. O. Butler Bed and Breakfast
$75–$95
(502) 732-6154
www.bbonline.com/ky/genbutler/

Highland House Bed and Breakfast
$90–$130
(502) 732-5559
rmougey@bellsouth.net
www.bbonline.com/ky/highland/

Danville
A.C. Randolph House
$75–$85
(606) 236-9594
www.bbonline.com/ky/randolph/

Ashhurst Bed and Breakfast
$75
(606) 236-1619
sherronw@searnet.com
www.ashhurst.com

Frankfort
Cedar Rock Farm
$60–$90
(502) 747-8754
www.bbonline.com/ky/cedar/

Graystone Manor
rates n/a
(502) 226-6196; vaughn@dcr.net
www.bbonline.com/ky/graystone/

Ghent
The Ghent House
$50–$110
(502) 347-5807 or (606) 291-0168
www.bbonline.com/ky/ghent/

The Poet's House
$60–$85
(502) 347-0161
BobLonnie@aol.com
www.bbonline.com/ky/poetshouse/

Harrodsburg
Bauer Haus
$60–$75
(877) 734-6289
www.bbonline.com/ky/bauer/

Baxter House
$79–$109
(888) 809-4457
www.bbonline.com/ky/baxterhouse/

Beaumont Inn
$57–$112
(800) 352-3992
cmdedman@searnet.com
www.beaumontinn.com

Canaan Land Farm Bed and Breakfast
$75–$125
(888) 734-3984
www.bbonline.com/ky/cannan/

Louisville
Aleksander House Bed and Breakfast
$85–$129
(502) 637-4985
alekhouse@aol.com
www.bbonline.com/ky/aleksander/

Central Park
$75–$149
(502) 638-1505
centralpar@win.net
www.centralparkbandb.com

Inn at the Park
$79–$149
(800) 700-7275
innatpark@aol.com
www.bbonline.com/ky/innatpark/

Pinecrest Cottage
$125–$155
(502) 454-3800
allanm@prodigy.net
www.bbonline.com/ky/pinecrest/

Rocking Horse Manor
$65–$120
(888) HOR-SEBB
rockinghorsebb@webtv.net
www.bbonline.com/ky/rockinghorse/

Samuel Culbertson Mansion
$99
(502) 634-3100
bandb@culbertsonmansion.com
www.culbertsonmansion.com

Springlee Bed and Breakfast
$125
(502) 485-0113
www.bbonline.com/ky/springlee/

The Columbine Bed and Breakfast
$75–$120
(800) 635-5010
BBColumbin@aol.com
www.bbonline.com/ky/columbine/

Nicholasville
Cedar Haven Farm Bed and Breakfast
$40–$50
(606) 858-3849
www.bbonline.com/ky/cedarhaven/

Sandusky House and Oneal Log Cabin
$85–$120
(606) 223-4730
www.bbchannel.com/bbc/p207846.asp

Owensboro
Helton House
rates n/a
(270) 926-7117
www.bbonline.com/ky/helton

Trail's End
$50–$75
(502) 771-5590
jramey@mindspring.com
www.mindspring.com/~jramey

Weather Berry Bed and Breakfast
rates n/a
(270) 684-US60
members.aol.com/weatherber

Paducah
Farley Place
$65–$85
(270) 442-2488
www.bbonline.com/ky/farley

Fisher Mansion Bed and Breakfast
$79–$145
(270) 443-0716
www.bbonline.com/ky/fisher

Rosewood Inn
$65–$105
(270) 554-6632
rosewood@apex.net
www.bbonline.com/ky/rosewood

Trinity Hills Farm
$70–$130
(800) 488-3998
trinity8@apex.net
www.bbchannel.com/bbc/p600313.asp

Smith's Grove
Cave Spring Farm Bed and Breakfast
$80–$85
(270) 563-6941
www.bbonline.com/ky/cavespring/

Victorian House
$105
(270) 563-9403
www.bbonline.com/ky/victorian/

Somerset
The Osbornes of Cabin Hollow B&B
$60
(606) 382-5495
www.bbchannel.com/bbc/p207945.asp

Versailles
Bed and Breakfast at Sills Inn
$69–$159
(800) 526-9801
SillsInn@aol.com
www.bestinns.net/usa/ky/sillsinn

Inn at Morgan Bed and Breakfast
$119–$139
(800) 972-1026
info@innatmorgan.com
www.innatmorgan.com

Rabbit Creek Bed and Breakfast
$125–$190
(888) 219-5181 or (888) 219-5188
GLENDALEE2@aol.com
www.bbonline.com/ky/rabbitcreek/

Tyrone Pike Bed and Breakfast
$75–$135
(606) 873-2408 or (800) 736-7722
tyronebb@uky.campus.mci.net
www.bbonline.com/ky/tyrone/

Western Fields Guest Cottage
$125
(800) 600-4935
wfield@iglou.com
www.bbonline.com/ky/westernfields/

Winchester
Guerrant Mountain Mission B&B
$100
(606) 745-1284 mountmiss@aol.com
www.bbonline.com/ky/mountmiss

Zone 22: Eastern Kentucky

Augusta
Augusta White House Inn
$69–$89
(606) 756-2004
www.bedandbreakfast.com/bbc/p207891

Blaine
The Gambill Mansion
$100–$150
(800) 485-3362
www.bbonline.com/ky/gambill/

Campton
Torrent Falls Bed and Breakfast
$60–$150
(606) 668-6441
www.bbonline.com/ky/torrentfalls/

The Wayfarer Bed and Breakfast
$65–$95
(270) 773-3366
www.bbonline.com/ky/wayfarer/

Covington
Licking Riverside Historic B&B
$109–$169
(800) 483-7822
freelyn@aol.com
www.bbonline.com/ky/riverside/

Sanford House
$50–$130
(888) 291-9133
DanRRMiles@aol.com
www.bbonline.com/ky/sanford/

Farmers
Brownwood B&B and Cabins
$65–$85
(606) 784-8799
brwnkay@mis.net
www.bbonline.com/ky/brownwood/

Lexington
Blackridge Hall
$89–$179
(800) 768-9308
www.blackridgehall.com

Brand House at Rose Hill
$99–$229
(800) 366-4942
info@brandhouselex.com
www.brandhouselex.com

Cherry Knoll Inn
$75–$95
(800) 804-0617
lfriddle@mis.net
www.virtulcities.com/ons/ky/kyxa5010

Gratz Park Inn
$89–$199
(800) 752-4166
gratzinn@aol.com
www.gratzpark.com

Middlesboro
The RidgeRunner Bed and Breakfast
$55–$65
(606) 248-4299
www.bbchannel.com/bbc/p207889.asp

Maple Hill Manor Bed and Breakfast
$65–$90
(800) 886-7546
www.bbonline.com/ky/maplehill/

Index